MW01171985

THE WESTCOTT STORY

The Enduring Spirit of an American
Family Spanning 400 Years©

CHRISTINE BRODERICK EMMANUEL

Our story. America's story. We're still making history.

Published by Christine Broderick Emmanuel
Pensacola, Florida

Copyright © 2024 by Christine Broderick Emmanuel

All rights reserved.

No part of this book may be reproduced or transmitted in any form or by any means, electronic or mechanical, including photocopying, recording, or by any information storage retrieval system, without the prior written consent of Christine Broderick Emmanuel, except for the inclusion of brief quotations in a review.

Published by Christine Broderick Emmanuel, Pensacola, Florida

Editor: Lorraine C. Lordi

Cover Photograph from Westcott family archives [Westcott descendants, L to R – "GEN 11" siblings Jinks, Yo, and Larry with their mother Joanna Gould Hoke, later becoming "Yolande Westcott Gordon"]

Cover Photograph Enhanced by Ben M. Word
Cover and Interior Design by Damonza

Printed in the United States of America
Emmanuel, Christine Broderick
The Westcott Story: The Enduring Spirit of an American Family Spanning 400 Years

Library of Congress Control Number: TXu 2-447-147
ISBNs:
979-8-9915779-3-9 – hardback
979-8-9915779-4-6 – paperback
979-8-9915779-5-3 – eBook

First Edition
https://www.ChristineBEmmanuel.com

"We're all immortal, as long as our stories are told."

— Elizabeth Hunter, *The Scribe*, 2013

"GEN 10" Hoke siblings L to R - Hampton Westcott (1893-1960), Walter Westcott (1895-1947), Joanna "Yolande" Gould (1897-1956), and Virginia "Nina" Westcott (1899-1973)

The Westcott Story is dedicated to the memory of my mother **Yolande Westcott née Gordon Broderick**, her siblings **Virginia Stone née Gordon Guy** and **Laurance Sterne Gordon, Jr.**, and our American ancestors who descended from 16th century **Guy and Mary née Stukely Westcott** of the village Marwood in Devonshire, on England's southwest shore.

The Westcott Story ignites interest in the human experience
across 400 years and 14 generations in America:

History lends perspective in reference to our past.
Nature keeps us grounded in the present.
People engender hope in our future.

— "GEN 12" Christine Broderick Emmanuel, 2024

Contents - Volume II

ACKNOWLEDGMENTS

What distinguishes *The Westcott Story* from other genealogical accounts is the unbroken thread stemming from the lineage of Guy and Mary Stukely Westcott, parents to my nine-times great ("G9") grandfather Richard and his brothers Stukely and William. As well, this chronicle provides historical context as it traces our family's ancestral bloodline across 14 generations in the span of four centuries in America.

I am indebted to those manifold sources that made possible the development of *The Westcott Story*. From *History and Genealogy of the Ancestors and Some Descendants of Stukely Westcott: One of the Thirteen Original Proprietors of Providence Plantation and the Colony of Rhode Island*, written by Roscoe Leighton Whitman in 1932, I learned a good deal about our English forebears up to and including our "GEN 1" many-times great-uncle "Stukely" who gained fame upon reaching America's eastern shore in 1635. The author Roscoe L. Whitman is a "GEN 10" lineal descendant of Stukely Westcott.

Much of the research cited in Whitman's chronicle came from the late Hon. J. Russell Bullock of Bristol, Rhode Island, an eminent attorney and jurist who in 1886 privately published *Incidents in the Life and Times of Stukely Westcott (of Rhode Island) With Some of His Descendants*.

The Westcott Story also relies upon in-depth research published in *Westcott: The Name Renewed*, by Juneanne Wescoat Glick, Clayton, New Jersey, 1991; and *The Sacketts of America: Their Ancestors and Descendants, 1630–1907*, by Charles H. Weygant, Newburgh, New York, 1907. These genealogical studies capture expansive and richly detailed content on seemingly every member of every branch among the Westcott and Sackett progeny. My story builds upon their work insofar as our lineal ascendants and their nuclear families are referenced.

Remarkable stories about prominent members of the Westcott lineage and their kinsfolk have been documented throughout generations, most recently by my third cousin Richard "Dick" Hampton Neergaard when he set out in the early 1990s to trace our genealogy as a retirement project.

All five family historians produced extraordinary bodies of work for our benefit. Their research is naturally comprehensive and highly informative, which I relied upon as vital to the storytelling found in this chronicle.

Westcott Family Historians / Publication Dates

Hon. J. Russell Bullock / 1886
Charles H. Weygant / 1907
Roscoe L. Whitman / 1932
Juneanne Wescoat Glick / 1991
Richard H. Neergaard in the 1990s

The same can be said of other sources I relied upon to revive this collection of Westcott stories. Citations are not specific to particular sentences or paragraphs drawn from countless Google searches and elsewhere. Rather, in the aggregate, I cite my information sources by generation and within, by family, at https://www.ChristineBEmmanuel. com. I trust this approach without footnoting is acceptable as a means to document our family's and our nation's rich history.

As conveyed in the forthcoming introduction, Dick Neergaard and Susie Newcomb, the wife of my mother's first cousin William Adrian Newcomb, inspired me to give life to our story. I am immensely grateful to them and to my contemporaries among Broderick, Guy, and Gordon relatives whom I relied on to share and verify information. I tapped their knowledge, personal accounts, letters, photos, and family records to great benefit.

I also wish to acknowledge my editor and personal friend, Lorraine C. Lordi (1952-2024). We came together sharing a rich history as classmates at St. Mary's College ('75), Notre Dame, Indiana, and a passion for writing. An accomplished author and *Derry News* columnist with 25 years of experience as a college writing instructor at Rivier College and St. Anselm's College in New Hampshire, Lorraine offered invaluable guidance on writing concisely and in the active voice. With dedication, she also provided me encouragement—every step of the way to the end. Yet she did not live to see the publication of *The Westcott Story*. Diagnosed with terminal cancer in April 2023, my highly spirited friend passed away in Asheville, North Carolina, on October 20, 2024.

Mamie Webb Hixon, an assistant professor of English and director of the Writing Lab at the University of West Florida, led me to apply the fundamentals of English grammar while writing and editing *The Westcott Story*. I continue to benefit from Mamie's technical fluency as facilitator of the weekly "Grammarcize" sessions in which I have participated via the Zoom video platform since mid-2021.

I depended on the knowledge and wisdom of Thomas E. Roberts, Jr. with Raven Cliffs Publishing, LLC as I navigated uncharted "self-publication" territory. A casual introduction to Tom came at just the right time. Drawing from his own experience as an author, Tom skillfully guided me through each phase before reality set in with a published book in hand.

Finally, heartfelt gratitude extends to my husband of 40 years, Patrick G. Emmanuel, Jr., who patiently and lovingly endured the inestimable hours it took me to research, write, edit, and publish my family's story. A fervent reader and student of history, Rick reviewed my completed manuscript cover to cover and offered invaluable critical analysis and editorial suggestions to enhance the quality of this work.

The "Spirited" Lineage of Guy and Mary Stukely Westcott

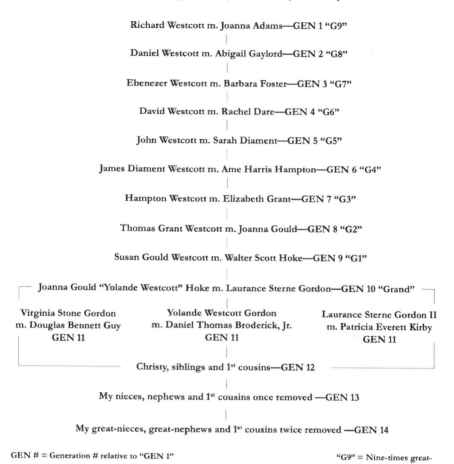

Richard Westcott m. Joanna Adams—GEN 1 "G9"

Daniel Westcott m. Abigail Gaylord—GEN 2 "G8"

Ebenezer Westcott m. Barbara Foster—GEN 3 "G7"

David Westcott m. Rachel Dare—GEN 4 "G6"

John Westcott m. Sarah Diament—GEN 5 "G5"

James Diament Westcott m. Ame Harris Hampton—GEN 6 "G4"

Hampton Westcott m. Elizabeth Grant—GEN 7 "G3"

Thomas Grant Westcott m. Joanna Gould—GEN 8 "G2"

Susan Gould Westcott m. Walter Scott Hoke—GEN 9 "G1"

Joanna Gould "Yolande Westcott" Hoke m. Laurance Sterne Gordon—GEN 10 "Grand"

| Virginia Stone Gordon m. Douglas Bennett Guy GEN 11 | Yolande Westcott Gordon m. Daniel Thomas Broderick, Jr. GEN 11 | Laurance Sterne Gordon II m. Patricia Everett Kirby GEN 11 |

Christy, siblings and 1st cousins—GEN 12

My nieces, nephews and 1st cousins once removed —GEN 13

My great-nieces, great-nephews and 1st cousins twice removed —GEN 14

GEN # = Generation # relative to "GEN 1"
Richard and Joanna Adams Westcott

"G9" = Nine-times great-
grandparents, etc.

INTRODUCTION

THE ENDURING LEGACY OF FAMILY AND NATIONAL HISTORY found in *The Westcott Story* will awaken readers to the real-life experiences of our forebears and the connections that bind us. This 400-year / 14-generation retrospective—Volumes I and II—details the history and genealogy of the Westcott family in America. From immigration to colonization, from armed conflict to industrialization and entertainment, my family's story embodies the spirit and value of cultural icons in every phase of America's history.

The Westcott Story offers a rich, multi-generational narrative that intertwines personal family history with broader American history. The book provides deep insights into the lives, struggles, and triumphs of the Westcott lineage, showcasing their resilience, courage, and determination. The significant contributions and sacrifices made by the family in parallel with our nation's remarkable course make it a compelling read for anyone interested in genealogy, American history, or personal stories of overcoming adversity. The collection of detailed accounts and personal anecdotes emphasizes the importance of family and national heritage and the enduring spirit that connects generations.

Susan "Susie" née Hester Newcomb (1942–present) of Walnut Creek, California, entered my life when she called me out of the blue one day in August 2020. At the time, we were in the throes of the unrelenting coronavirus pandemic known globally as "COVID-19." Susie introduced herself as the wife of **William "Bill" Adrian Newcomb** (1927–1999), a first cousin to my mother, Yolande Westcott Gordon Broderick (1920–1995). Enthralled by her late husband's Westcott ancestry, Susie had set out to find a suitable home for the coveted family archives then in her possession. She hired a private investigator in search of a descendant who would commit to safeguarding the treasure trove of *Westcott* family lore.

With the help of my mother's second cousin, **Richard "Dick" Hampton Neergaard** (1932–2023), the "sleuth" located my brother Dennis—a fellow Cincinnati resident—who put Susie in contact with me. Dick's paternal grandmother **Caroline Sackett née Westcott Neergaard** (1869–1940) is the younger sister of **Susan "Susie" Gould née Westcott Hoke** (1863–1933), my mother and Bill's maternal grandmother—making him a second cousin once removed to my siblings, first cousins, and me.

Tie-in of Newcomb and Neergaard families to the Westcotts

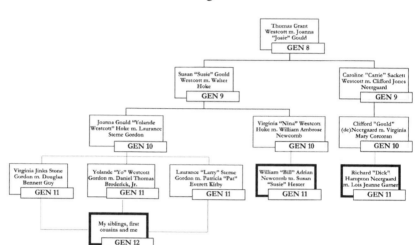

Significantly, in the late 1980s, shortly after the death of his father, **Clifford "Gould" (de)Neergaard** (1896–1988), Dick developed an interest in genealogy:

I came across a most touching letter written by Thomas Grant Westcott to his wife, Joanna 'Josie' Gould [my two-times great "G2" grandparents], eloquently pleading for a reconciliation. It was this letter, the elegance of its prose as much as its content, that piqued my interest. I thought, 'I have got to learn more about this guy!' and started poking. I found two books written about the Westcotts and Sacketts and learned about the Mormons' enormous wealth of family histories and how to access them. A year or so later I retired and, having a sudden vacuum of time and energy to fill, became heavily enmeshed in what appealed to me as an engrossing cross between detective mysteries and crossword puzzles, with the further advantage that the outcome could have value to others and be not just a pastime for me.

Over many years, Susie and Dick worked in earnest to compile documentation tracing Susie's husband Bill and Dick's *Westcott* lineal ascendants to the 1630s in America. Published books by other family historians follow our forebears further back, to 1164, in Devonshire, England. Susie, Dick, and the others accumulated a wealth of fascinating material pertaining to our distinguished and colorful pedigree which I relied upon to develop a picture of my maternal lineage. I did not dive into an independent genealogical study to verify or dispute their findings. Rather, I made assumptions drawing from their collective work to inform and inspire self-reflection.

Dick traveled extensively to peel our ancestral layers with trips to Salt Lake City, Utah; Washington, D.C.; New York City, New York; Trenton, New Jersey; Hickory Run, Pennsylvania; Harrisburg, Pennsylvania; Waynesville, North Carolina; and Bordeaux, France. He poured over national archives and Mormon Church records among countless others to trace our Westcott lineage in hierarchical fashion. His diligent research made possible my own undertaking, which was to revive the Westcotts' stories in the context of America's fascinating history for perspective.

In piecing together our overarching story, I endeavored to connect the myriad names, dates, and associations in a way that informs my living Broderick, Guy, and Gordon relatives—all Westcott descendants—and to engender a sense of intrigue, belonging, and genuine pride. This is us!

In the course of writing though, it dawned on me that our family's story parallels that of our nation and in that sense might have similar appeal to anyone interested in tracing America's history. The universal nature of the trials, triumphs, hopes, and fears experienced by the Westcotts will likewise resonate with readers recalling their own families' stories and history—especially as lived in America.

The Westcott Story captures the wonder of a world far bigger than each of us and our respective families, one that through time ebbs, flows, expands, and contracts as the natural course of life evolves in a cyclical pattern. We meet those moments as inflection points in the history we share.

The Westcott Story weaves our family thread into the fabric of America's history since her European colonization early in the 17th century. The *Westcotts* and the families into which they married emigrated from southern England primarily but also from France and Germany. The story captivates in the sense of what our forebears witnessed in living color, indeed the seminal role many of them played in shaping our nation over the course of nearly four centuries.

Our ancestors lived through the colonization of America, the American Revolution, the signing of the Declaration of Independence, the territorial growth and union of the United States, civil and international wars, Industrial Revolutions, natural disasters, pandemics, Depressions, and many more notable events that define the exceptional history of our relatively young nation.

The venerated Westcotts and familial relations in our line—men, women, and their offspring—endured unimaginable hardship but prevailed with strong Christian faith. On the whole, our forebears defined the determination and resiliency we carry today—not just as a pretty remarkable family but an extraordinary country as well.

There is ample reason to honor the Westcotts—not only for their integrity, perseverance, and many achievements but also for the sacrifices made and their imprint on the greater good of our family, our communities, and our nation. This family-country portrait is a rarity no one else can claim. It belongs to us—as Westcott descendants and as Americans.

The generational approach I adopted to tell our story proved readily conducive to spotlighting notable events that unfold as documented American history. Likewise, joining our forebears generationally as peers enabled me to make connections among and between the interlinked families and people of influence during their day. Those connections transcend the mere union of our lineal ascendants through marriage.

Considering the youngest among us now living, the generational records trace a 14-step lineal descent from Guy and Mary Stukely Westcott, whose three oldest sons—Richard, Stukely, and William—arrive as some of the first European colonists to settle in America. For purposes of documenting my family's story, I reference my foreign-born nine-times great ("G9") grandfather Richard Westcott as a first-generation American ("GEN 1") although technically, this nomenclature belongs to the American-born children of Richard and his wife Joanna. In the storytelling, I associate all kinsfolk down the line—both Westcotts and the families into which they married—in the context of the generation to which they were born relative to Richard and Joanna Adams Westcott.

This chronicle places my siblings, first cousins, and me in line as "GEN 12" behind Guy and Mary Stukely Westcott. The grandchildren of my siblings and first cousins—my great-nieces and great-nephews so far as the Brodericks are concerned—fall at the tail end of this long line as 14th generation ("GEN 14") Westcotts. As of this writing, Oliver Westcott Broderick (b. 2023) is the youngest in our storied lineage to carry the family name.

The first-person point of view used in writing this narrative speaks to *my* relationship to my parents, grandparents, and great-grandparents by degree, and to *our* connection to Westcotts and familial relations as living Brodericks, Guys, and Gordons, collectively.

Richard Westcott is *my* nine-times great ("G9") grandfather as well as the G9 grandfather of my "GEN 12" siblings and first cousins. However, he is not the G9 grandfather of my siblings and first cousins' offspring. Consequently, in this example, I refer to him as *my* and not *our* G9 grandfather. Similarly, because "GEN 12" Brodericks and Guys relate to Laurance Sterne Gordon and Joanna Gould Hoke—later becoming Yolande Westcott Gordon—as their *maternal* grandparents unlike my Gordon first cousins who relate to them as their *paternal* grandparents, for context, I make reference to *my* and not *our* maternal grandparents. Conversely, *our* ancestors and "many-times great-aunts and great-uncles" relate uniformly to all Brodericks, Guys, and Gordons—the collective *we*. Unless the perspective can be uniformly applied as *we* across all three families and all generations of living Westcott descendants, I use the singular *my* as my point of reference.

Much has been written about our country and our family's history, more than I ever could have imagined insofar as our ancestors are concerned. I have captured or paraphrased, reorganized, and edited content from numerous sources, as warranted. In every case, I endeavored to ask questions and seek clarification in an attempt to state the facts as completely and as accurately as possible.

Finally, be mindful of the family diagrams that accompany this narrative. They serve as a useful reference in mapping out who fits where—with and among—the various Westcott family members, virtually all of whom, as depicted, connect us in linear fashion.

Significant publications of our lineal ascendants and their offspring date as far back as 136 years ago. It was abundantly clear to these family historians that there was something about the Westcotts worth documenting. I appreciate the allure. We Westcotts are still making history, still living up to the potential within us. March on and stand proud.

To appreciate the breadth of America's history spanning 400 years, the author strongly recommends reading Volume I: 1588-1940 of *The Westcott Story* before picking up Volume II. Volume I covers the fascinating and eventful history of surnamed "Westcotts" in our lineage and those extended family members brought into the fold through marriage from the period of our nation's colonization through the Civil War and Reconstruction era.

Volume II: 1889–2024

*"Dear to us, every one of them, in the memories
of the past, in the hope of the future."*

— Attributed to members of the
Society of the Cincinnati, 1860

The Progeny of Surnamed "Westcotts"

––––––––––––––––––

WITH A DISPLAY OF INDUSTRIAL MIGHT, my family's timeless American story continues with descendants of surnamed Westcotts and their spouses. Spanning nearly 14 decades to the present, the Westcott progeny actively engage in two world wars, suffer through the Spanish flu and COVID-19 pandemics a century apart, prevail through extreme economic peaks and troughs, pivot from the Industrial Revolution to the digital age, and innovate scientific breakthroughs. All the while, we endure family separation, mental illness, chronic disease, murder, natural disaster, and other harrowing realities.

We begin Volume II with my "GEN 10" maternal grandmother Joanna "Yolande" Gould Hoke (1897–1956) who in 1918 married my grandfather Laurance Sterne Gordon in her hometown of Bordeaux, France, before establishing family roots in Duluth, Minnesota. Throughout five generations to the youngest among us, my family perseveres with dogged determination, playing a hand in our nation's transitory path to become a preeminent military and economic world power and technological leader. Standing on the shoulders of our forebears with a proud legacy and boundless potential, living Westcott descendants carry forward with remarkable drive, extraordinary talent, and trademark resilience.

––––––––––––––––––

Recall from Volume I that **Thomas Grant Westcott** fathered six children, three with his first wife Sara Head—Virginia "Nina," William "Grant," and Elizabeth "Bessie." With **Josie Sackett Gould**, Thomas also fathered my great-grandmother **Susan "Susie" Gould**, Hampton Gould, and Caroline "Carrie" Sackett. Among Thomas's offspring, Nina and her husband William Sweeney did not have children, and Grant, Bessie, and Hampton remained single. Carrie had one small child, Clifford "Gould," before divorcing Clifford Jones Neergaard. Susie and her husband Walter Scott Hoke gave Thomas and Josie four grandchildren before they, too, divorced once the last of their children completed secondary school in Bordeaux, France.

The progeny of Thomas Grant and Joanna "Josie" Gould Westcott through "GEN 10"

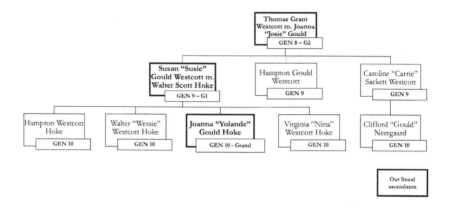

GENERATION 10 – 1889–1973

World War I, the Spanish Flu, and the Great Depression Test the Mettle of the Gordons in Bordeaux, France, and Duluth, Minnesota

---

My Grandparents, Great-aunts, and Great-uncles – 1889–1973

Joanna "Yolande" Gould Hoke & Laurance Sterne Gordon
Hampton Westcott Hoke, Sr. & Charlotte Graves Stark
Walter Westcott "Wessie" Hoke & Dora M. Crawford
Virginia "Nina" Westcott Hoke & William "Bill" Ambrose Newcomb

THIS "GEN 10" SEGMENT features Susie and Walter's four children—Hampton, Wessie, Yolande, and Nina—with a callout to Thomas and Josie's remaining grandchild Clifford "Gould" deNeergaard. [As a young adult, Gould changed his surname from "Neergaard" to "deNeergaard."] As well, attention is given to Henry "Reed" Hoke, the closest first cousin to the Hoke children on their father's side. Both Gould and Reed factored prominently in the Hokes' lives as contemporaries.

In the interest of preserving the conjured images among "GEN 1" through "GEN 9" *surnamed* Westcotts and their kinsfolk, I opted *not* to weave the "in-laws" of forebears from this point down the line into the generational thread found in Volume I. Rather, insights I uncovered regarding the lineage of "spouses" in this last tranche appear parenthetically within the pages that follow. Bloodlines ascending from my maternal grandfather, father, husband, and all others married to descendants of "GEN 9" Walter Scott and Susie Westcott Hoke are traced in this Volume II.

As mentioned in Volume I, Walter and Susie raised their family in Bordeaux, France. The bilingual French and English-speaking Hoke children—Hampton "Hamp" Westcott (1893–1960), Walter Westcott "Wessie" (1895–1947), my maternal grandmother **Joanna "Yolande" Gould** (1897–1956), and Virginia "Nina" Westcott (1899–1973)—trace their ancestry to England and Germany principally, with just a hint of French and Scottish blood.

Joanna "Yolande" Gould Hoke (1897–1956) & Laurance Sterne Gordon (1889–1952)

The birth of my maternal grandmother Yolande in Bordeaux came on January 31, 1897. In 1956, she died two days shy of her 60th birthday in Council Bluffs, Iowa, when I was not yet three years old. I don't believe we ever met, but I recognize myself in a photo of her as a young girl.

My grandmother "Yolande"—born "Joanna"—strikes me as something of an enigma. Did she suffer an identity crisis?

Yolande was the only one of Susie and Walter's four children not to carry "Westcott" as a middle name. The name "Gould" honors her maternal grandmother Josie. Historical records reflect various names for my grandmother. I knew of her as "Yolande Gould Hoke Gordon" for whom my mother "Yolande Westcott Gordon" (Broderick) was named. In fact, my mother strongly disliked her given name, Yolande. The below insight might explain her reasoning.

Some records identify my grandmother as "*Joanna Yolande.*" Ancestry. com mistakenly picked up "*Josephine Yolande.*" Walter identified his daughter in his 1918 passport application as "*Joanne Gould,*" ending her first name with an 'e' rather than 'a.' The name "*Yolande Westcott-Hoke*" appears on my grandparents' wedding invitation. An entry on the birth certificate of her firstborn—my Aunt Virginia "Jinks" Stone Gordon— shows my grandmother's name before marriage as "*Joanna Gould Westcott Hoke*"—including "Westcott" and without reference to "Yolande."

Which name is right? I found the answer in a letter my Uncle Larry wrote to an insurance company following the death of his father in 1952. As Yolande survived her husband, the insurer's claims department required an explanation of her name change which evidently followed her marriage to Laurance in 1918. In his response to the insurer, my Uncle Larry attempts to clarify the matter: "She [Larry's mother Yolande] informs me that after their marriage she took the English way of spelling her first name [from "Joanna"] to 'Yolande' and used the initial 'W' taken from her mother's maiden name 'Westcott.' All of this was decided after her marriage to my father . . . My mother, however, does not believe that there was any legal change on record. They just decided between themselves to make the change. I hope this will clear up the misunderstanding." Curiously, Yolande did not adopt "Yolanda" as a natural translation of "Joanna." I wonder how her father took to Yolande's dropping his surname "Hoke" in favor of "Westcott" as her middle name. Perhaps she withheld that detail from him from afar. In any case, as "Yolande Westcott Gordon," her adopted naming convention suggests that she strongly related to her maternal "Westcott" lineage and to her French connection from birth.

In conversation, my grandmother's sister Nina, and perhaps other family members, reportedly pronounced Yolande as "Yolanda" with an "a" as opposed to the silent "e". Meanwhile, her tombstone reads "Yolande Hoke Gordon." The preponderance of evidence at my disposal points to "Joanna Gould Hoke" at birth, going by "Yolande" and nicknamed "Yoyo" in her childhood years. Incidentally, how would you like to be known as "Yoyo Hoke?"

Based only partly on the variations of her name, Yolande's story is puzzling. Regrettably, my mother "Yo" rarely spoke of her mother, precluding a better understanding of Yolande's childhood, how she and my grandfather grew apart, and her final years in a psychiatric hospital for the mentally ill in Council Bluffs, Iowa.

One can only speculate as to how the "GEN 10"
Hoke family came into the Catholic faith.

The children's aunt "Bessie"—daughter of Thomas Grant Westcott and his first wife—is the first Catholic known to me among our maternal lineal ascendants and their familial relations. As addressed in the Part II "GEN 9" segment in Volume I, Bessie became Sister Mary Beatrice with the Sisters of Mercy in the vicinity of Pittsburgh. Quite possibly, Bessie's mother Sara Head received the sacraments of the Catholic Church herself, and my G2 grandfather Thomas Grant Westcott then converted to Catholicism before marrying his second wife, Susie's mother Josie Sackett Gould.

In 1864, Thomas and Josie baptized Susie in the Catholic faith. Susie's upbringing and the preponderance of Catholics then living in France naturally led Yolande and her siblings to Catholic schools, this in spite of the fact that the "GEN 8" Hokes raised Yolande's father Walter and his six brothers in a family of staunch Protestants.

For a period of four years beginning when the children's first cousin turned 14 years old, **Clifford "Gould" Neergaard** [later changed to deNeergaard] became a member of the Hoke household in Bordeaux. At least for a time while Gould resided with the family, they lived at 207 Boulevard du Président Wilson. Here, Yolande became a talented piano and harp player, and she enhanced her artistic gift with a flair for painting, writing, calligraphy, music composition, and sewing.

The Hokes apparently enjoyed a privileged life in the popular city of Bordeaux as their home and the attire of Walter, Susie, and the children suggests considerable style.

Proximity afforded the Hokes the opportunity to travel across Europe. The expatriates Walter and Susie also had the means to make periodic visits to the States as circumstances warranted.

Yolande's family accounts for the love of animals she acquired early in life. Recall "Pete," the French Bulldog that the American Expeditionary Forces (A.E.F.) located in Bordeaux on her father Walter's behalf in mid-1918. Yolande must have loved that dog. A Pete lookalike appears in family photographs in Duluth where she eventually settled with a family of her own.

Following their education in Bordeaux—the year before France entered World War I in 1914—Yolande's brothers Hampton and Wessie relocated to the States to pursue a postsecondary education in Philadelphia. It appears Walter and Susie accompanied the boys on the cross-Atlantic voyage while the girls remained in France in the care of their aunt Nina Westcott Sweeney awaiting their father's solo return. Susie remained in America for a time to get the boys settled and work through issues that may have undermined her faltering relationship with Walter.

While Hampton and Wessie pursued engineering degrees at the University of Pennsylvania with some financial assistance from their uncle Hampton Cook, Susie reluctantly made the decision to give her marriage one last chance. She saw her daughters finish high school in Bordeaux before folding her tent for good and returning stateside. Yolande and Nina opted to stay behind with their father, at least for a short time. As World War I broke out, Red Cross volunteers mobilized in mass to support the war effort. The sisters responded to the call, engaging as Red Cross nurses in Bordeaux:

> The international Red Cross Society came through as one of the greatest examples of humanitarian aid during WWI. Volunteers emerged alongside American and allied soldiers to provide an invaluable service. In France alone, from July 1917 to February 1919, the American Red Cross established 551 stations, including twenty-four hospitals run jointly with the U.S. Army.

While the State Department decreed that women volunteers could not have a father, son, husband, or brother in the armed services, Red Cross headquarters screened prospects for good temper, discretion, self-reliance, and knowledge of French or Italian. Yolande and Nina met all qualifications and proceeded to nurse wounded soldiers delivered to Bordeaux from the Western Front in Northern France.

Setting aside traditional class and gender roles, these patriots proved tough and determined. All the same, nothing could have prepared my grandmother, my great-aunt Nina, and the other women of the Red Cross for the suffering and death to come from the chosen weapons of warfare topped by the scourge of influenza during this "Great War." Insufficiently protected from exposure to the artillery bombardments and chemical warfare, the soldiers suffered from ghastly wounds, burns, and invisible psychological trauma. As if the horrors of war were not enough, the spread of a most fatal infectious disease caused the death of hundreds of thousands of human beings deep within the trenches and in pockets across the globe.

Like the war itself, the "Spanish flu" epidemic takes its rightful place as a major disaster in world history. Though removed from the front and the shrapnel and chemical release of toxins, lurking danger beset the women of the Red Cross. The waves of infectious influenza did not discriminate. The battle against the dreaded virus proved strenuous and difficult, and many of the women suffered serious illnesses alongside their military brethren. With no vaccine to protect against the infection and no antibiotics to treat secondary bacterial infections, control efforts were limited to non-pharmaceutical interventions. As tonsillitis, bronchial pneumonia, dysentery, and the influenza pandemic swept through the bases, canteens, and hospitals, many of the Red Cross volunteers succumbed themselves:

> Across all bases in Europe, doctors of the A.E.F. hospitalized 340,000 soldiers for influenza and 227,000 soldiers due to battle wounds. In October 1918, as the American Army locked in battle with the Germans in the decisive Meuse-Argonne offensive, 1,451 Americans died from the flu. Incredibly, more 3rd Infantry Division soldiers were evacuated from the front with influenza than from combat wounds. The flu continued to spread and kill for nearly three agonizing years on a scale that had not been seen since the bubonic plague wiped out at least one-third of Europe's population in the late Middle Ages. A fifth of the world's population became infected as this scourge ravaged the earth. The pandemic accounted for 50 million lives lost in total, including some 675,000 Americans—more than the U.S. casualties of all the wars fought in the 20th century combined.

Red Cross volunteers paid a heavy toll in service to the war effort. The heroic women of the Red Cross witnessed gruesome injuries, illnesses, and fatalities. Several lost their lives nursing soldiers injured in combat and infected by the deadly H1N1 influenza. One tally reported 105 deaths by bombing, 246 by disease, and 2,500 with injuries among the Red Cross women. The horrors of the Great War also left many of them with lasting psychological scars—shock, confusion, irritability, anxiety, withdrawal, and hopelessness.

The ordeal may well have put Yolande over the edge, in all likelihood contributing to the ensuing mental breakdown that gripped her in later years. Though not labeled as such during the day, my grandmother likely suffered a post-traumatic stress disorder (PSTD) from the harrowing experience.

If one bright light accompanied the Great War, it was the chance encounter that brought my grandparents together. Yolande was indeed a mystifying beauty. The Red Cross nurse attracted the attention of **Laurance Sterne Gordon** (1889–1952) during his service in Bordeaux with the United States Army Quartermaster Corps as a member of the A.E.F. Perhaps they met at one of the medical supply depots constructed by the Quartermaster Corps and maintained by the Red Cross volunteers. Alternatively, their wartime romance may have been sparked at one of the various social gatherings they attended. As one of the few American host families then living in Bordeaux, the Hokes would have graciously welcomed newly-arrived servicemen to their environs.

My grandfather Laurance came last among the three children born to **John "Gardner" Gordon, Jr.** (1847–1918) and **Frances "Fannie" Maude Sterne Gordon** (1849–1889). He was born in the year of the tenth Exposition Universelle de 1889 in Paris which featured the newly constructed Eiffel Tower—an architectural masterpiece built with 1,710-steps as the then tallest tower in the world. Tragically, Fanny died eight days after giving birth to Laurance on March 2nd.

During the first 20 years of his life, Laurance Sterne Gordon lived in St. Louis where he attended a school for boys, the Manual Training School of Washington University. Founded in 1879, ten years before his birth, the Manual Training School quickly distinguished itself as the largest and most well-attended public high school in St. Louis. A precursor to vocational training programs, the school provided instruction in the use of basic tools common to a variety of jobs alongside general education. The curriculum included science, mathematics, language, literature, history, drawing, and shop work.

Following graduation in 1909, Laurance relocated to Duluth where he worked at Stone-Ordean-Wells Company, then the largest grocery wholesaler in the Northwest. The draw to Duluth rests with two of his father's sisters, Ella and Mary, wives of pioneering men who left an indelible mark on Duluth as early settlers. Notably, Ella's husband, William Reade Stone, founded the company that attracted Laurance as an aspiring businessman. Laurance's highly ambitious uncle William had long served as company president of Stone-Ordean-Wells, and Mary's husband, Joshua Backus Culver, had decades earlier served as Duluth's first mayor (1870–1871). Both men played a formidable role in Duluth's emergence as a Midwest powerhouse. Meanwhile, Duluthians recognized Ella for her significant contributions to Saint Luke's Hospital which St. Paul's Episcopal Church founded as the city's first hospital in 1881. Exceptionally close to her nephew Laurance, Ella developed renown in her own right as a leader in social and charitable endeavors.

The experience of our Gordon branch in Duluth proved emblematic of the spectacular rise and fall of America's storied Second Industrial Revolution, which completely transformed the United States until it grew into the largest economy in the world and the most powerful global superpower.

William Reade Stone was drawn to Duluth by his brother George Calvin Stone (1822–1900). George arrived in 1869 as an agent of the Philadelphia financier Jay Cooke to put infrastructure in place. In that year, Cooke terminated the northern end of his Lake Superior & Mississippi Railroad in Duluth and connected it with his transcontinental Northern Pacific Railroad, making the "Zenith City" that railway's eastern terminus. By this time, business in Duluth was booming. In a Fourth of July speech in 1868, the founder of Duluth's first newspaper coined the expression: "The Zenith City of the Unsalted Seas." The town's population of two hundred grew to over three thousand within 15 months, making a city of Duluth in a flash.

Laurance's uncle William often visited his brother in Duluth from Chicago where he rose in stature as a prominent member of that city's wheat exchange. Spotting opportunity, William moved with his wife Ella to Duluth in 1871 and opened the Pitt Cooke Dock. In 1872, he built warehouses to store flour, feed, salt, lime, ore, and general produce for wholesale trade through the firm "Wm. R. Stone & Co."

With the help of William R. Stone and Jay Cooke's agents from Philadelphia, Joshua Backus Culver and his first wife, Sarah, ventured west, arriving in Duluth in 1855 when he was 25 years old. A native of Tomkins, New York, Joshua enlisted in the 13th Michigan infantry when the Civil War began. He mustered out as colonel in the battles of Shiloh, Chickamauga, Corinth, Perryville, Nashville, Gallatin, Stone River, Chattanooga, Lookout Mountain, and Mission Ridge before returning to Duluth. As a co-founder of the town of 3,100 people, Joshua ran for office as a Democrat, becoming the town's first mayor in 1870. He guided Duluth in its first boom period and invested in William's wholesale company. Joshua married John Gardner Gordon, Jr.'s sister, Mary, upon the death of Sarah, who died days after giving birth to the couple's 10th child in 1873.

Two days before the birth of Joshua and Sarah's daughter, Duluth benefactor Jay Cooke ran out of money. Along with the demise of many others, his failings ushered in the Panic of 1873, triggering an economic depression that spread throughout Europe and North America. The Depression nearly destroyed Duluth as more than half of its population fled. Reduced to village status, the town saw nearly every enterprise grind to a halt. While married to his second wife, Mary Gordon Culver, Joshua stood by the failing city and saw it through a reorganization alongside his brother-in-law William. To fuel economic growth, the brothers-in-law organized the Duluth Lake Transfer Company which operated the steamers *Metropolis* and *Manistee* between Duluth and Buffalo, New York.

As Duluth struggled to survive, the Red River Valley spanning northwestern Minnesota and northeastern North Dakota miraculously sprouted wheat. Shipments of the grain passed east on the Northern Pacific first to Duluth and then further as loads on the Great Lakes merchant vessels. The lumber trade arrived soon after and Duluth boomed once again. William then turned his focus to his wholesale enterprise, incorporating Wm. R. Stone & Company Wholesale Grocers in 1880. The population exploded to 30,000 from just 2,200 people in less than a decade. For a time, Wm. R. Stone & Company fed many mouths as the village's only wholesale grocer.

William's brother-in-law and former business partner Joshua Backus Culver died while in office as a two-time mayor in 1882. One year later, the ambitious Albert Ordean arrived in Duluth. He found a bustling city in the midst of another population boom. The former banker joined forces with William to form Stone-Ordean in tandem with the growth of industrialization across the Northern and Midwestern regions of the country.

In 1893, the partners built a magnificent four-story Romanesque building of brick and brownstone at 203–211 South Fifth Avenue West for $4,800. The building featured a flat corner entrance and arched windows on the top floor. The wholesaler could ship and receive items from railcars along tracks on one side and from ships via a dock in the rear.

A subsequent merger with a Michigan concern followed in 1896, forming Stone-Ordean-Wells. Operating out of three branch offices in North Dakota, four in Montana, and one in Minneapolis, Stone-Ordean-Wells distributed groceries primarily. However, they also sold automobile tires, cigars, and wooden ware. As well, the diversified company manufactured peanut butter, syrup, ground sugar, and coffee. At its peak, the company roasted and ground 3.5 million pounds of coffee annually.

By 1903, Stone-Ordean-Wells had become the largest grocery wholesaler in the Northwest. My grandfather Laurance Sterne Gordon gained employment with the bustling enterprise during its height, in 1909.

Three years following Laurance's arrival in Duluth, his beloved aunt Ella and uncle William retired to Santa Barbara, California, where they had wintered for many years at the Potter Hotel—later known as the Ambassador Hotel. Childless, both William and Ella died in the coastal town, Ella four years after William, in December 1919.

One of the first Duluthians to go to France during World War I, Laurance headed out May 1917 as a single man in the Quartermaster Corps and returned to Stone-Ordean-Wells Company in October 1919 as a major with a wife and child, Yolande and their daughter Virginia "Jinks" Stone Gordon.

The patriot Laurance enlisted in the army in March 1917 and advised his father via telegram in Los Angeles that he had received his commission. At the time, Laurance's father lived in Los Angeles as did his sister

Annette and her husband Maurice Hartman, as well as his brother John "Jack" Gardner Gordon III and Jack's wife Ruth Starr Gordon. On April 6, 1917, John Gardner Gordon, Jr. wrote a handwritten letter to his son acknowledging receipt of the telegram. Laurance's father died nine months later, on January 26, 1918:

> *Dear Laurance,*
>
> *Received your telegram last evening saying, 'Commission received. Expect to be called out soon.' Keep us posted as we will be anxious to know what is going on. Hope everything will work out well for you. Annette is quite worked up, doesn't like the idea of your being called out. Do you know you are the first Gordon to go soldiering since my father was commissioned Brigadier General before I was born, during the Mexican War as far as I know,* [among] *the Sterns, Reinhards, and Harrisons* [Laurance's lineal ascendants].
>
> *We all send you lots of love and wish you lots of success.*
>
> *Your loving father, John G. Gordon*

Backing the fighting elements of the army, the A.E.F. forces required great organization to keep combat units constantly supplied with men and means necessary for operations against the enemy. Under the A.E.F. umbrella, the Quartermaster Corps constructed and operated transportation systems, telephone and telegraph lines, hospitals, depots, docks, mills, repair shops, and factories. In addition to supplying animal transport, fuel for mechanical transport, food, clothing, personal and housekeeping equipment, and pay for the soldiers, the Quartermasters performed services closely related to those supplies, such as laundry and salvage, bathing, and disinfectants. They also took over identification and care of the dead. In little more than a year, the Quartermaster Corps grew from 57 to 4,665 officers and from 1,268 to 96,066 enlisted men by the end of the war, representing roughly 5% of all activated U.S. forces.

The organization in which my grandfather Laurance Sterne Gordon engaged became known successively as the "Line of Communications," the "Service of the Rear," and the "Services of Supply" (S.O.S.). Commissioned as a captain in the U.S. Army Reserve Corps, Laurance received orders to report to duty in May of 1917. In the same month President Woodrow Wilson designated Major General John J. Pershing to command the expedition, the A.E.F. deployed Laurance as Chief Purchasing Officer at the headquarters of Base Section No. 2 in Bordeaux where he remained for the duration of the war. Within two months of Laurance's arrival in May 1917, Massachusetts General Hospital established a base hospital in Talence in the outskirts of Bordeaux, the town and the very facility where my Aunt Jinks was born two years later.

Laurance went to work as a Quartermaster with capabilities he developed at Stone-Ordean-Wells Company. The further logistical skills honed in Bordeaux proved instrumental in the success my grandfather enjoyed when he returned stateside with Yolande and my Aunt Jinks as a babe in arms nearly two and one-half years following his deployment.

As the terminus of one of A.E.F.'s main lines of communication, the Base Section No. 2 operation oversaw dock facilities where the men handled 14,000 tons of cargo each day that passed along some 90 miles of trackage connecting docks, depots, and departure yards within the Section's perimeter. The operation also encompassed rest and embarkation facilities to shelter 20,000 troops; stevedore camps accommodating 13,000 laborers; artillery training camps; and remounts through which more than 50,000 animals passed by 1919. Other installations within the section included a refrigerating plant with a capacity of more than 5,000 tons; a coffee roasting plant with a daily output of about 10 tons; 13 base and nine camp hospitals with bed capacity of nearly 40,000; reception parks operating more than 14,000 vehicles; thirteen sawmills operating in the forests; bakeries; and a salvage plant. The Section handled more than 50,000 troops during its operation and 25% of all cargo (1,749,700 tons) coming into France.

Colonel Charles Gates Dawes (1865–1951), whose father Rufus R. Dawes fought with distinction for President Abraham Lincoln at Antietam, Fredericksburg, and Gettysburg, served as a colonel before his promotion to brigadier general during WWI. In France, he assumed the role of chairman of the General Purchasing Board for the A.E.F. from August 1917 to August 1919. As Chief Purchasing Officer, Laurance ultimately served under Dawes's command.

In Bordeaux on August 1, 1918, in the fog of war and the
unrelenting influenza pandemic, Laurance Sterne Gordon
married Joanna "Yolande" Gould Hoke, eight years his junior.

Laurance and Yolande's wedding announcement came from "Docteur & Madame Walter Westcott-Hoke" and "Monsieur John Gardner Gordon," inviting guests to attend the marriage of "Mademoiselle Yolande Westcott-Hoke" and "Capitaine Laurance Sterne Gordon" on August 1, 1918. Curiously, Yolande and her parents chose to incorporate "Westcott-Hoke" as their joint last name. In fact, the practice of hyphenating last names began in the 15th century, then limited to nobility or couples with great wealth. In Victorian times, the hyphenated surname became more popular and gradually, the practice moved from upper-crust Brits to anyone choosing to adopt the naming convention.

The Army promoted Laurance to major in the month of his marriage to Yolande when he was 29; Yolande was then months shy of 21. The newlyweds lived at 12 rue du Champ de Mars. On the heels of their August wedding, on the 11th hour of the 11th day of the 11th month of 1918, the incessant boom of artillery abruptly fell silent along the Western Front of France. News of the long-awaited armistice quickly spread. After what many considered the worst war in human history, peace negotiations came at last.

In all, 4.7 million men and women served in the regular U.S. forces, national guard units, and draft units with about 2.8 million serving overseas. They strengthened the Allied counterattacks and ultimately helped to defeat Germany earlier than expected. Some 53,402 Americans were killed in action, 63,114 perished from disease and other causes, and 205,000 suffered injuries.

As the war came to an end on November 11, 1918, following the American army's attack into the Meuse-Argonne, much work remained to reverse the great supply engine that Dawes and Pershing had struggled so long to produce. Disposal of World War I surpluses proved to be one of the most difficult and costly tasks undertaken by the government in the immediate postwar years. The value assigned to the surpluses approximated $6 billion, roughly 22% of the net cost of the war to the United States between 1917 and 1921.

The abruptness of peace negotiations that followed the armistice found the United States still in the phase of preparing for war. During the next few months when General Pershing worked to disband the A.E.F. and get the boys back home, Dawes—promoted to brigadier general in October 1918—agreed to serve on the United States Liquidation Board which handled the arduous disposition of surplus A.E.F. property.

In the midst of the post-Armistice stillness and afterward, during the bustle to unravel the machinations of the war effort, Yolande carried the couple's first child. In the month of the birth, Laurance received orders to assist Brigadier General Dawes in Paris with the business of liquidating the massive war surpluses.

Teeming with activity, by May 1, 1919, the Bordeaux headquarters at Base Section No. 2 had become the principal freight port of the A.E.F. The port and neighboring sawmills, warehouses, and hospitals had received 2,197,000 tons of material to supply the war. One could not escape the military presence. This backdrop defined the chaotic life and trying times that my grandparents and great-grandfather lived through during the Great War before guidance came from Brigadier General Dawes to unravel the massive operation and dispose of the enormous war surpluses.

In the month of Jinks's birth, Laurance received orders to proceed to Paris as assistant to Charles G. Dawes (1865–1951), then Brigadier General of the A.E.F. Liquidation Commission of the War Department. Laurance served on the Surplus Sales Board before his official discharge.

A Republican, Charles G. Dawes went on to become the 30th U.S. vice president under Calvin Coolidge (1925–1929) and co-recipient of the Nobel Peace Prize in 1925 for his work on the Dawes Plan. The plan resolved the issue of World War I reparations required of Germany, thus ending a crisis in European diplomacy following the Treaty of Versailles.

At the U.S. Army Base Hospital in the Talence suburb of Bordeaux, Yolande gave birth to Virginia "Jinks" Stone Gordon on May 31, 1919. Her birthdate fell on the last day the hospital flew the stars and stripes. The very next day, the French military took over the facility, so though born in France, Jinks was delivered on American soil.

In Jinks's little girl's baby book, in calligraphy, Yolande captured milestones that defined her firstborn's first year. We learn that she was named after her aunt "Virginia" Westcott Sweeney and also after Laurance's aunt Emma "Stone."

The day after Jinks's birth, the hospital's U.S. Army chaplain baptized her. Yolande's sister Nina was present for the christening as Jinks's godmother; her brother Hampton, then a first lieutenant, came down from Germany to welcome the newborn and stand as godfather by proxy for Wessie who was unable to make the trip from New York. I do not believe Laurance was present for Jinks's birth and baptism, but her grandmother Susie made an appearance and stood by hers and Yolande's side.

Released from the hospital after two weeks, Yolande stayed behind in Bordeaux for another two weeks where the baby "enjoyed the loving caresses of Grandmother and God Mother." On the first day of July, Yolande traveled with Jinks and her French nursemaid Zoé to Paris where they met up with Laurance as he assisted Brigadier General Dawes. Although her A.E.F. identity card places her as a nurse, Yolande did not maintain an active role with the Red Cross following the war's end.

In Jinks's baby book, Yolande recorded their movements:

> *Moved to Paris, Rue des Faux, on July 1, 1919, where Daddy impatiently awaited his little girl. You were taken daily to the 'Trocadéro' gardens, where you slept in your little buggy with Mother by your side, and more than one passerby stopped to admire the pretty little American baby. You visited the various beautiful places in Paris, the 'Tuileries' gardens, the 'Bois de Bologne,' the 'Luxembourg,' the 'Louvre,' the 'Concorde,' the 'Arc de Triomphe,' the 'Bastille,' and the divers wonderful churches. Assisted at the world's Grand Revue* [Grand Victory Parade], *out of one of the windows at the American Military Headquarters on 'Les Champs Elysée.' Went up on the Ferris wheel on August the 28th, 1919. On July 29th, 1919, we decided to visit a part of the devastated country, and went to Rheims* [Reims], *practically in ruins, and took you along with Zoé, Aunt Nina, and a Captain Philips.*

[In Reims] *Visited the wonderful Cathedral, 'Le Fort de la Pompelle,' 'La Cote de 108,' 'Le Plateau de Craonne,' 'Le Chemin des Dames,' and villages after villages where only the names remain. It would be too hard to narrate to you all that your eyes have really witnessed, but unfortunately won't recollect. But remember, little girl, when you are old enough to realise, when hearing people talk about the wide world's war, just remember then, that you were on that soil where the world's destiny was played, where outrages were committed, where thousands of little babies like you, lost their Daddies, homes, and all that they loved and cherished, on that Land now covered with little crosses, where masses of wild red poppies grow.*

On September 9, 1919, one year to the day before the birth of their second child, Laurance, Yolande, her mother Susie, daughter Jinks, and nursemaid Zoé sailed for New York from Brest in western Brittany. They made the voyage on the U.S.S. *Mount Vernon,* before the war known as the *Crown Princess Cecilia,* which during the war was torpedoed by a German U-boat; 36 men aboard then lost their lives.

The U.S.S. *Mount Vernon* crossed the Atlantic in just six days. "Grand Aunt Nina" and "Uncle Westcott" met the entourage in New York. As documented by Yolande in Jinks's baby book: "Spent a delightful month with them at the Normandie, and it was not long before you stole your way in their hearts."

A little more than one month after their arrival in New York, Laurance, Yolande, Jinks, and Zoé traveled by train to California for Laurance's official discharge and to visit Laurance's relatives. "Grand Aunt Nina" Sweeney accompanied them as far as Greenburg, Pennsylvania, her hometown located ten miles west of Latrobe. Yolande's uncle Grant and two relatives on the side of his mother (Sara Head Westcott) greeted them in Greenburg. "Uncle Grant got on the train as far as Pittsburg[h] with us; had dinner there with them, then he took the express back to Latrobe and we proceeded to Chicago." With a two-hour layover, the Gordons and Zoé "then took the train direct to San Francisco where Daddy was to obtain his discharge from the U.S. Army."

Per Spencer Gordon in *Our Gordon Family* published in 1941, Laurance received an honorary citation signed by General John J. Pershing on July 26, 1919, and later, France's "Officer d'Academie Beaux-Arts" decoration on November 20, 1919, a month after his honorable discharge at San Francisco, California, on October 19, 1919.

From San Francisco, the young family proceeded to Los Angeles; Laurance's father died there the year before their arrival. They evenly divided their six-week stay in Los Angeles between Laurance's siblings—first with brother Jack, Ruth, and "Jack Boy"; and then with sister Annette and Maurice Hartman and "baby Gordon." During the month of December, Laurance, Yolande, Jinks, and Zoé continued on to spend what proved a difficult month with Laurance's cherished aunt Ella Stone in Santa Barbara. As recorded by Yolande in the baby book she compiled for Jinks:

> *Your first Christmas was spent in Santa Barbara in sunny California. It was not a very bright Christmas for your Daddy and Mother, as your dear old Grand Aunt Ella Stone, one of the grandest old ladies I ever met and one of Daddy's best friends on earth, was going to her last call. She lived over Christmas and passed away on December 28th, 1919. But the day was bright enough for you, dearie, and you had a lovely assortment of Christmas presents.*

They had planned to stay with Ella at her home but ended up at the Ambassador Hotel when she took ill. Ella's cold developed into bronchial pneumonia and after one week's illness, she died at the age of 83. "The day before she passed, Daddy took you in to see her, and she held your little hands in hers and seemed to be giving you the last blessing. The world lost a beautiful soul when it lost your Grand Aunt Ella Stone."

Ella is known to have authored at least two published books. Released in 1907, *O-So-Ge-To the Hopi Maiden, and Other Stories* is a fictionalized collection of eight children's stories of Native American origin. In 1909, she released *A Cycle of Gleanings – from El Labla Kest One*, a compilation of quotations, one for each day of the year. Curiously, "El Labla Kest One" spells out her name, Ella Blake Stone, with a variation in the spaces between letters to create new words.

On New Year's Day 1920, the Gordons left Santa Barbara for Los Angeles where they spent a couple more days with Jack and Ruth while awaiting reservations for travel to Duluth. Destined for "our own little home," the four-day train ride delivered my grandparents and Aunt Jinks to Duluth in the dead of winter. I did not learn whether Zoé joined them or returned to France. What is certain though, is that baby Jinks ended her seven-month adventure here, showered with love from aunts, uncles, cousins, and great-aunts and great-uncles on both sides of her family.

Leaving behind her father Walter and the only place she knew as home in Bordeaux, Yolande proceeded to make a fresh start in Duluth, Minnesota, with her husband and young child at the start of a new decade in 1920.

Inescapably hardened from the experience of war, Nina joined her mother Susie and brothers Hampton and Wessie in New York, while Laurance and Yolande settled down with baby Jinks in the port city of Duluth, Minnesota, on the northern shore of Lake Superior.

Highly cultured due to her upbringing and arts education in Bordeaux, Yolande likely struggled in her foreign surroundings. She had no choice but to acclimate to the small town feel of Duluth with a population of fewer than 100,000 people, albeit 30% foreign-born. Mostly Europeans, the residents of Duluth worked principally in new jobs with the burgeoning factories, shipyards, and railroads. In contrast, Bordeaux was then nearly three times the size of Duluth, bustling with activity to unravel the remnants of the first world war when the family set off for the United States.

In the far northern reaches of the country's Midwest, the newlyweds faced a frigid winter as well as threatening racial tension that undermined any sense of calm. In the midst of a violent period of widespread racial conflict fueled by the resurgence of the Ku Klux Klan, Yolande and her family arrived in Duluth as a mob of thousands took three African American circus workers from jail. The mob killed Elias Clayton, Elmer Jackson, and Isaac McGhie by lynching on June 15, 1920.

As if these conditions were not difficult enough, Laurance and Yolande found a tired nation and widespread postwar apathy, the result of both lingering physical illness and a general spiritual depression. Almost every family felt the effects of the pandemic as a third major wave of influenza in 1920 claimed another one hundred thousand American lives. A century ago, some 675,000 influenza-related deaths were recorded among 105 million people then residing in the United States.

This post-war period of mass death left the "Lost Generation" survivors disoriented and wandering without direction. However, the pandemic seems to have been little memorialized, partly because of the keen focus on the combat-weary war survivors. As we will learn, the period contrasted sharply with the experience of World War II survivors returning home.

Before continuing with Laurance and Yolande as they raised a family in Duluth, I offer this background on Laurance Sterne Gordon's lineage.

THROUGHOUT FIVE GENERATIONS, the Gordons made a living in business trade, centered primarily on food products covering the spectrum from manufacture to retail sales. By all indications, these ancestors proved themselves as decent, hard-working, and successful people.

I referred to the books, *Our Gordon Family* [privately printed by Spencer Gordon in 1941] and *Gordon Gordon: Ancestry, Family, and Life* [privately printed in 1973 by the sons of "GEN 10" Gordon Gordon—William A. Gordon and Lewis H. Gordon] to round out what I uncovered about our Gordon bloodline. We begin with the "GEN 6" immigrants Alexander and Betsy (or Mary) Boden Gordon. My G4 grandparents **Alexander Gordon** (1719–1794) and **Betsy (or Mary) neé Boden**— the first of the Gordon bloodline to reach America's shores—arrived as newlyweds around 1765. Alexander is presumed to descend from the Galloway or the Lowland region of Scotland, which was populated by devout Presbyterians; the Gordons in the Highlands were staunch Catholics. His parents emigrated from Scotland to Ireland, although Alexander's birthplace—whether Scotland or Ireland—is unknown. We do know that he came to America by way of Ireland, located just across the Northern Channel from Galloway, Scotland.

As mentioned in the two Gordon books referenced above, Alexander Gordon had a wealthy aunt living in Belfast who, according to family legend, disapproved of Alexander's marriage to Betsy. This may have been the impetus for the couple's decision to leave Ireland. Alternatively, speculation suggests that, as a strong Presbyterian, Alexander may have objected to paying tithes to the Church of England!

Like many Scots-Irish at the time, Alexander and his wife Betsy settled in Bucks County, Pennsylvania—home to my G5 grandparents Johannes Conrad Stenger and Anna Catharina Benderin Stenger and their son, our lineal ascendant Conrad Stenger. Alexander and Betsy later moved to Carlisle, Pennsylvania, in Cumberland County.

A granddaughter wrote of Betsy Boden, "a most remarkable woman, high spirited, well educated, and very pious. I often heard Pa say that when she spanked him, she always took him into a private room, prayed over him, and then thrashed away in good style. He venerated his mother." Members of the Secession Church, a branch of Presbyterians, Betsy and Alexander Gordon had five children including my G3 grandfather **John**, William, Mary, Jean "Jane," and Eliza. "All [Alexander] cared for was entertaining clergymen, reading his bible, and praying." Alexander died in Carlisle in 1795 and his wife shortly thereafter. They are buried in Carlisle's Seceder Burying Ground.

Note: the grandson of William Alexander Gordon, "GEN 10" Gordon Gordon (1874–1933) is the subject of the aforementioned book titled *Gordon Gordon*; Gordon changed his surname from "Sowers" when abandoned by his father and embraced by the extended family of his mother, Josephine "Lavinia" née Gordon Sowers.

Laurance Sterne Gordon's paternal and maternal ancestors

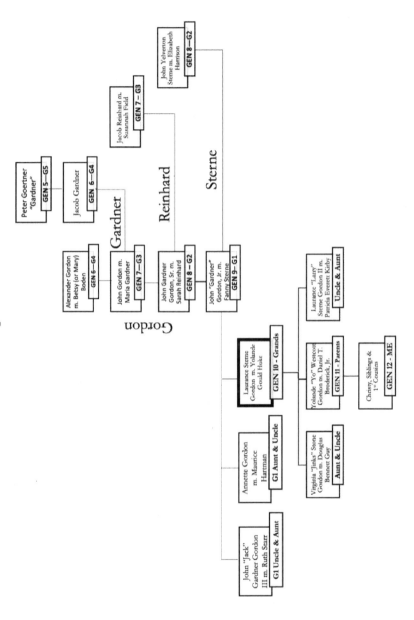

BORN IN BUCKS COUNTY in 1802, my G3 grandfather **John Gordon** married **Maria Gardner** of York, Pennsylvania. York also became the childhood home of my G3 grandmother Sarah Eyster, wife of Henry Ferree Hoke. Perhaps the Gordons and Hokes knew each other. Maria was the daughter of Jacob Gardner and granddaughter of Peter Gardner—originally "Goertner"—who immigrated to this country from the Palatinate near the River Rhine about 1750. [At least for a time, the Palatinate was also home to the Ferree, Rothermel, and Hoke branches of our family.] A wealthy man, Peter Gardner amassed over $100,000. In his capacity as Chief Burgess of the Borough of York, Pennsylvania, he had occasion to meet George Washington as the general's escort. Our lineal ascendant John Gordon, a Jeffersonian Democrat, and Maria's grandfather Peter Gardner, a Whig or Federalist, reportedly never discussed politics for fear of a family feud.

John and Maria became the parents of seven children—William Alexander (b. 1803), Eleanor, Maria Louisa (b. 1809), Alexander (b. 1813), my G2 grandfather **John Gardner** (1812–1877), Lavinia, and Franklin (b. 1817). John established a name for himself as an import-export merchant in Baltimore, leading to extensive business travel.

As an adult, John and Maria's son Alexander wrote an autobiography in which he shared these recollections regarding his parents (my G3 grandparents):

> "At the time of his death [John] was in the mercantile business on Bolys wharf, Baltimore; residence Federal Hill, where he had a rope-walk; was born in Bucks County, Pennsylvania. He had the reputation of being an honorable, upright man. My father had traveled much in foreign lands, had resided in the West Indies, Dutch Guiana and Quito, South America; in the East Indies, at Batavia and in China; in the North of Europe and at Paris and London. His contact with the people of many countries made him quite a polished gentleman. He spoke most of the modern languages. Baltimore being a seaport town, he associated very largely with foreigners, particularly Frenchmen.

"As to his religious belief, I know nothing, except that he was an attendant at Dr. Duncan's church in Baltimore, an independent Presbyterian Church, not connected with the General Assembly.

"Owing to endorsements that he had to pay and his death occurring at a time of unexampled difficulty in the business affairs of our Country growing out of the war of 1812–1815, his estate paid nothing to his heirs, though I have been informed by respectable citizens of Baltimore, that if it [the estate] had been placed in competent hands the result might have been very different; as it was, my mother was left in poverty, with seven children, the oldest 16 years, the youngest one year." [My G2 grandfather John Gardner Gordon, Sr. was six years old when his father died.]

John Gordon died in Baltimore of typhus fever in 1818, prompting Maria to move from Baltimore to Carlisle where her husband's family lived. His untimely death left his wife Maria practically destitute yet determined to raise their family on her own. The widow Maria opened a store and made good progress until the failure of a bank in which her husband's cousin, John Boden, served as cashier. He reportedly forced her out of business.

As her son Alexander recalled in his autobiography, "There was nothing left for my mother but to go to York, Pennsylvania, to my Grandmother Gardner's [Maria's mother] with her [seven] children. My grandmother was living alone in a house large enough to hold us all and was in circumstances which enabled her to keep our family, which she was willing to do, and was unwilling that the family should leave her when the time came that they decided on going west."

Alexander continued, "I would here say that my mother received some assistance from my brother, William A., from the time of his appointment to a clerkship in Washington, but had to sacrifice her jewelry and some of her silver plate spoons in educating her children, which was done cheerfully, as she was very anxious to keep up the respectability of the family by education."

Maria Gardner Gordon later took her family to Canton, Ohio, then to Pittsburgh where two of her deceased husband's sisters, Jean and Mary, resided. Maria survived John Gordon by 29 years and died in Allegheny County, Pennsylvania, in 1847. She rests beside him in Carlisle, Pennsylvania.

Parenthetically, a descendant of John and Maria surmised that, had it not been for the War of 1812 and the low level of imports and exports during the next few years—with no U.S. Navy to protect our merchant ships—and also for gross mismanagement of his estate, the family of John Gordon would have been comparatively well off. Maria would not have had to work to provide her family with the necessities of life.

BORN IN BALTIMORE, Maryland, to John and Maria Gardner Gordon, my G2 grandfather **John Gardner Gordon, Sr.** (1812–1877) apprenticed in the mercantile trade in York, Pennsylvania, before establishing his business in Louisville, Kentucky, where in 1836, he married **Sarah née Reinhard** (1811–1855). Sarah was the 8th of ten children born to the merchant **Jacob Reinhard** (1774–1835) and **Susannah Field** (1780–1866) of Philadelphia. Sarah's parents married there in 1796 before relocating to Louisville in 1818, where Jacob Reinhard died at age 61 in 1835; Susannah lived to age 86.

In Louisville, "GEN 8" John Gardner Gordon, Sr. and his brother Alexander partnered in the shipping and forwarding business on the Ohio River. With their two oldest children, Ella Blake (b. 1837) and Susan Baker (b. 1839), John Gardner, Sr. and Sarah then relocated to Pittsburgh. Alexander soon followed and the brothers operated the business on the banks of the three rivers—the Ohio, Allegheny, and Monongahela.

In Pittsburgh, John Gardner Gordon, Sr. and Sarah found themselves among several extended family members. John Gardner's aunts, Jean Gordon (unmarried) and Mary Gordon Morris, had settled nearby in Washington, Pennsylvania. His mother, Maria, and his siblings Franklin and Lavinia settled closer to the city limits. In time, Alexander's five "GEN 9" children established deep roots in Pittsburgh and neighboring Swissvale (now Edgewood), yet I knew nothing about any of the Gordons' ties to my hometown before researching my genealogy for this story. I wonder—did my mother know of her paternal ancestors' connection to her marital home?

As an aside, I learned that Alexander's son, John Gordon (named after his grandfather), lived for a time in Pittsburgh where he ministered as a pastor before becoming president of the now defunct Tabor College in Tabor, Iowa, and later, president of Howard University in Washington, D.C., from 1903 until 1905. A white man presiding over a Black university, our distant cousin John Gordon became unpopular with the students for attempting to introduce industrial education and manual training into the university's curricula. Facing the ire of both faculty and students who considered his plans an affront to their social positions and cognitive abilities, the university accepted his resignation at year-end in 1905.

During their brief few years in Pittsburgh, John Gardner Gordon, Sr.'s wife Sarah gave birth to their two middle children, Mary Edwards (b. 1841) and Maria Louisa (b. 1843). Meanwhile, the eldest of my G2 grandfather's siblings, William Alexander Gordon (not to be confused with Alexander who remained in Pittsburgh) established himself in Georgetown, Washington, D.C. Here, William Alexander became a clerk in the office of the Quartermaster General of the Army and remained there throughout his career. In later years, he served as Chief Clerk and his sons, William Alexander, Jr. and James "Holdsworth," likewise gained some fame as Georgetown residents; they partnered in the law firm of Gordon and Gordon for more than 50 years.

With a pioneer's spirit, our lineal ascendant John Gardner Gordon, Sr. distanced himself from his extended family in Pittsburgh and Georgetown to follow the westward tide of opportunity. With his wife and four daughters, he settled in Muscatine, Iowa.

In 1844, Laurance's paternal grandfather John Gardner Gordon, Sr. founded J G Gordon & Company in Muscatine, a general store stocked with dry goods, groceries, hardware, and greenware. Reportedly one of the finest and most extensive establishments in the West, the merchant's customer base spanned a radius upward of 140 miles. Laurance's father **John "Gardner," Jr.** (1847–1918) and his aunt Annie (b. 1849) came as the last of John Sr. and Sarah's six children once they relocated to Iowa.

Raised in the time of Thomas Grant and Josie Gould Westcott, "GEN 8" John Gardner Gordon, Sr. was commissioned a brigadier general of the Iowa militia in the year of my great-grandfather Gardner's birth (1847) during the Mexican-American War. Upon Sarah's death eight years after birthing Gardner, John Gardner, Sr. remarried. With Elizabeth Klein Dougherty, he had a son, Glenn, who died in a hunting accident at age 24.

Esteemed as a Mason and member of the Trinity Episcopal Church, John Gardner Gordon, Sr. established a reputation for greeting customers with a hearty salutation, a cheery word, a bright smile, and a cordial handshake. He may well have welcomed author Samuel Clemens (1835–1910)—better known as Mark Twain—who lived in Muscatine in the summer of 1855 while visiting his family when the town's population approached 2,500 people.

Reportedly "prominent and active in business, liberal and zealous in forwarding public enterprises, genial, intelligent, and communicative in society with a rich store of anecdote and reminiscence to entertain friends," Laurance's grandfather "crossed the dark flood, to mingle with the Celestial band on the other shore, in 1877. Surrounded by weeping wife and children, sweetly, peacefully, like a child hushed to gentle slumber, and unconscious of the physical pain too often inflicted by the arrows of Death, he sank to rest, only the still pulse and marble like features indicating the great transition from time to eternity."

> "So fades the summer cloud away,
>
> So sinks the gale when storms ale o'er,
>
> So dies the wave upon the shore."

An unidentified source offered these words in tribute to John Gardner Gordon, Sr.: "Thus passed away one of Muscatine's oldest and most esteemed citizens—one whose form and face and pleasant voice and kind greeting were familiar to the young and old of the city. It will be remembered that the cause of his death was a paralytic affliction."

Without having known my grandfather, Laurance Sterne Gordon, I like to believe he carried some of his grandfather's pleasing traits.

LAURANCE'S FATHER **John "Gardner" Gordon, Jr.** (1847–1918) was the 5th of six children born to John Gardner, Sr. and Sarah Reinhard, in Bloomington, Iowa. His siblings included sisters Ella Blake, Susan Baker, Mary Edwards, Maria Louisa, Annie, and half-brother Glenn. Gardner attended the University of Iowa in Iowa City before relocating. In St. Louis, Missouri, he went into business with his sister Susan's husband, William S. Humphreys, who held membership with the Board of Trade. The brothers-in-law became commission merchants.

In St. Louis in 1883, Gardner Gordon wed Laurance's mother, **Frances "Fannie" Maude née Sterne** (1849–1889), daughter of **John Yelverton Sterne** (1800–1880) and his second of three wives, **Mary Elizabeth née Harrison**. John and Mary Sterne raised Fanny and her sister Laura (future wife of Edwin Harrison) in Monticello, Missouri, along with four girls from John's prior marriage. His first wife died prematurely at age 36.

Gardner's wife Fannie gave birth to three children in St. Louis—John "Jack" Gardner Gordon III (1884–1958), Annette G. Gordon (1886–1967), and my grandfather **Laurance Sterne Gordon** (1889–1952). Given the unique spelling, the family name "Laurance"—assigned to my grandfather, uncle, brother, nephew, and two first cousins—presumably derives from Fannie's older sister and only full-blooded sibling "Laura" Sterne (1847–1921). Only days after giving birth to Laurance, Fannie died in St. Louis at age 39 or 40.

Upon Fanny's passing, Gardner the widower raised the family on his own while earning a living as a furniture store dealer in St. Louis. As adults, all three of the children—Jack, Annette, and Laurance—moved a good distance from their hometown. Upon earning an Engineer of Mines degree from the Colorado School of Mines in Golden, Jack practiced in the mining field in the West and in Mexico. He married Ruth Starr Mauro and the Gordon family name carried on with the birth of Jack and Ruth's son, John Gardner Gordon IV. In 1917, a year before my grandparents Laurance and Yolande wed in Bordeaux, Laurance's sister Annette married Maurice V. Hartman of Mansfield, Ohio, in Los Angeles. As mentioned earlier, Laurance relocated to Duluth upon graduating from the Manual Training School of Washington University, in 1909.

Once retired, my great-grandfather Gardner moved to central Los Angeles, California, living with or near his daughter Annette at 856 Wilton Place [hence the reference to "Californie, Etats Unis" on Laurance and Yolande's wedding invitation, although the couple exchanged marriage vows in Bordeaux]. Eight years after his relocation to Los Angeles and less than a year after Laurance deployed to Bordeaux, Gardner died from a chronic cerebral hemorrhage at age 69. He is buried at Inglewood Park Cemetery in the greater Los Angeles area.

WE NOW RETURN TO LAURANCE and YOLANDE GORDON as newlyweds with a small child making a home in Duluth.

William Reade Stone's resounding success in the wholesale trade business likely captivated Laurance's interest in returning to the burgeoning Stone-Ordean-Wells Company following the war, although his uncle was deceased by this time. Perhaps no other local establishment stood to benefit more from the experience Laurance gained in purchasing and logistics as a Quartermaster and Chief Purchasing Officer at the headquarters of Base Section No. 2 in Bordeaux. The well-connected and highly influential surviving business partner, Albert Ordean, would have been thrilled to bring Laurance back into the fold upon his return from military service in World War I.

As mentioned earlier, upon marrying Joshua Backus Culver, Laurance's aunt Mary became stepmother to his ten children, many of whom remained in Duluth as adults. Yolande likely welcomed those extended family connections in this foreign land.

For 50 years beginning in 1880, Minneapolis became known as the "Flour Milling Capital of the World." The mills received grain via rail lines stretching across the grain belt in the Northern Plains into the Dakotas and Canada. Trains then carried the milled flour to Duluth and to eastern U.S. destinations for export and domestic distribution. Sometime in the 1920s, Laurance split off from Stone-Ordean-Wells Company, entering into a partnership to establish a flour brokerage known as Draper, Gordon Company. Somehow, his brokerage business managed to survive the structural headwinds that gave rise to the Great Depression. However, the enterprise founded by his uncle William Reade Stone in 1872 did not survive the tumult.

The stock market crash of 1929 gave way to the worst
economic disaster in American history and the downslide
of Laurance's former employer, Stone-Ordean-Wells.

Stone-Ordean-Wells Company continued operations after the passing of partners William R. Stone in 1915 and Albert Ordean in 1928. However, the firm ceased operations within a decade of the stock market's crash. Having operated for 65 years, the Fifth Avenue West facilities of Stone-Ordean-Wells closed in 1937. Following occupancy by three subsequent unrelated businesses, demolition of the buildings made way for the expansion of Interstate 35 in 1966.

> The stock market crashed on "Black Thursday," October 24, 1929, triggering a prolonged worldwide "Great Depression." By the time of Franklin Delano Roosevelt's inauguration as our 32nd president in 1933, the banking system had collapsed, nearly 25% of the labor force was unemployed, and prices and productivity had fallen to one-third of their 1929 levels. Reduced prices and output resulted in lower wages, rents, dividends, and profits throughout the economy. Factories shut down, farms and homes caved to foreclosure, owners abandoned mills and mines, and people went hungry. The resulting lower incomes challenged people to spend or to save their way out of the crisis, thus perpetuating the economic slowdown in a seemingly never-ending cycle.

The Depression hung on until 1941, when America's involvement in the Second World War triggered the drafting of young men into military service and the creation of millions of jobs in the defense and war industries. Americans weathered the prolonged slump and as a nation, we emerged stronger than ever, prepared to take on the new challenges of another world war.

Laurance prevailed in business during the period of his former employer's downward spiral. In 1930, he operated the flour brokerage while simultaneously forming the Duluth Nut Company with wholesale and retail operations located at 404 West Superior Street and 203 West Superior Street. At that same time, he served as chairman of the Rotary

Boys' Work Committee, one of the most active committees of the Rotary Club which he joined in 1928.

The flour brokerage Draper, Gordon Company eventually morphed to became food brokers by the name of Draper, Gordon & Walker. As reflected on stationary in a letter Laurance penned in 1948, Draper, Gordon & Walker was located at 405 East Superior Street. Just two years before his death in 1952, Laurance retired to Phoenix, Arizona.

Coinciding with Laurance's success in establishing roots and building his business, Yolande composed music and like her mother Susie, she continued to paint and write. She took up poetry as a pastime in the early years before leaving Bordeaux for a new life in Duluth. On April 8, 1920, she penned a most touching poem in calligraphy to her 10-month-old daughter Jinks:

To My little Daughter!
Eyes, which in deep darkness would shine,
Eyes, which so searchingly seek mine,
Lips made for the Angels to kiss,
A smile from them, a world of bliss.

Brow which knows no danger no fear,
Confident heart to me so dear.
Cherished head nestled to my breast,
Finding all comfort, untold rest.

Dimpled arms clasped around my neck,
Still would cling through triumph and wreck.

Little feet toddling by my side,
Unconscious, following their guide.

White lillies, heavenly grace,
Purity sealed on a small face.

At the bottom of the poem, she identified herself as "Yolande Westcott Gordon," the name she unofficially claimed on arrival to the United States from France, and the official name chosen for her second-born child.

Fifteen months younger than Jinks, on September 9, 1920, Yolande gave birth to my mother, **Yolande "Yo" Westcott Gordon**. My Uncle Larry—**Laurance Sterne Gordon, Jr.**—came nearly two years later, on July 15, 1922.

Perhaps the best news to greet Yolande on arrival from Bordeaux was the ratification of the "Susan B. Anthony" 19th Amendment to the U.S Constitution guaranteeing women the right to vote in 1920.

Women's suffrage certainly sparked celebration in Duluth and elsewhere, offering a promising future for Yolande's daughters Jinks and Yo and the white majority among America's 50 million women and girls. [The U.S. Census of 1920 tallied 106,021,537 residents nationwide— less than one-third the 2020 count.] Despite the passage of the 19th Amendment and the perennial contributions of women of color, poll taxes, local laws, and other restrictions continued to block this segment of the population from voting. It would take more than 40 years for *all* women to achieve voting equality, although contentious voting laws prevail to this day. Meanwhile, the proposed Equal Rights Amendment to the U.S. Constitution has yet to pass in this country.

I do not get the sense that my French-speaking grandmother was a feminist, let alone a political activist. Rather, I believe her refined upbringing in Bordeaux influenced her many creative pursuits. A Renaissance woman at heart, Yolande was endowed with an artistic streak that spanned languages, sewing, writing, poetry, calligraphy, hand-painted photography, and music—perhaps additional outlets as well.

As her children grew, Yolande continued to write, and thanks to her talent as a pianist and harp player, she composed music as well. She started "the French Club," a French class for Jinks, Yo, and Larry along with twelve to fifteen neighborhood children. In one of her classes, she wrote and composed a play—in French. Yolande used all of her artistic talents in the production. Madame Gordon even sewed the children's costumes. Her students proudly performed at a local playhouse for the enjoyment of the entire neighborhood. Among her other talents, Yolande is credited with hand-coloring numerous vintage family photographs in my possession. The technique heightened the realism of those images before the invention of color photography.

Two years before Walter's death in 1940—once my mother completed high school—Yolande brought Jinks, Yo, and Larry to Bordeaux to visit their grand-père at which time the Gordons lived at 2424 East 2nd Street in Duluth. By all appearances, Yolande had aged beyond her years. This trip afforded my grandmother the last opportunity to see her beloved father.

I presume Laurance got to know his father-in-law, Walter, while stationed in Bordeaux during World War I. Perhaps he recalled their time together when in 1942, two years after Walter's death and while in the throes of another world war, Laurance pursued a return to the Quartermasters Department of the United States Army. A Duluth doctor, J.R. Manley, M.D., authored a letter to U.S. Senator Joseph H. Ball in Washington, D.C. on June 10, 1942, requesting support of Laurance's effort to obtain a commission. I assume Dr. Manley penned this letter on behalf of my grandfather and not my uncle by the same name. Laurance was then 53 years of age and evidently very patriotic:

> "Mr. Gordon has been a friend and patient of mine for twenty years. He has the following physical defects: (1) insufficient natural teeth but with serviceable replacements, (2) right inguinal hernia incomplete, indirect, with no symptoms, (3) old primary childhood pulmonary tuberculosis, healed, non-symptomatic, (4) simple Tachycardia. These defects have been noted by the medical examiners of the army.

> "Mr. Gordon carries on an active business and does considerable physical work in caring for his garden and lawn. He has done so for many years.

> "In my opinion Mr. Gordon is fully capable of assuming arduous duties of a supervisory nature in the Quartermasters Department."

I did not ascertain the result of Dr. Manley's appeal but assume Laurance did not carry through with his desire to support the WWII effort. Meanwhile, his namesake, my Uncle Larry, entered the war as a master sergeant and joined Laurance in his food brokerage business at Draper, Gordon & Walker following his discharge.

As to family life in Duluth, Larry Jr. as an adult reflecting on his childhood once said, "My sisters and I grew up in a very ideal life. I never heard a sharp word between my folks, and I have a vivid memory that Dad never left the house to go to work at his office failing to kiss my mother goodbye. The many family fishing and camping trips, picnics, etc.—I never doubted then, nor do I now, that our family relationship was a little different from our friends. We were lucky."

Upon his return to Duluth from his four-year deployment with the U.S. Army Air Corps in 1946, my Uncle Larry observed a material change in his mother's demeanor, thinking her separation from her children had profoundly affected her outlook on life somehow. By that time, she was just shy of 50. In later years, Larry said, "As I look back, I can recognize that a change was taking place in Mom. She still played her piano, wrote, and painted, but her mind was someplace else." Even her stable relationship with Laurance was off-balance. According to Larry, the doctors pointed to "the great change in her environment, the stress of two wars, and the physical changes that take place in women of her age" as taking a toll. My grandmother's trip to her beloved France in 1938 may have triggered a spiraling state of depression as the visit—her last to see her father—was cut short by the imminent threat of another world war. Yolande's declining mental health began to strain the couple's relationship and Laurance's physical health as well.

In a heartfelt letter to Jinks and her husband, Doug, penned in 1948, Laurance addresses his health and conveys his hopes for his family.

Four years before his passing, on May 26, 1948, Laurance wrote a handwritten letter on Draper, Gordon & Walker letterhead addressed to "Virginia" and her husband Doug. In a pensive mood, Laurance starts his letter by addressing the subject of "favorites." He then expresses pride in his family and his desire that his children always stick together before sharing news of a concerning heart condition that ails him:

Received your nice letter Virginia also the note from "my son" Doug. Thanks a lot for all the nice things you said Virginia—it means a lot to me—more than you will ever know. I have always been accused of your being my favorite. That I can't truthfully say today or have I ever allowed myself to pick one of you above the other. You were our first—you had [the pick] *of first choices all your life. When it was a case of getting only one of something, you got it first and the "pass on" went to the others. It wasn't always easy to see the question in one of the others' eyes. We always tried to buy exact duplicates where we could and the old pocket book would afford it.*

That's what makes it so tough sometimes in later life for the oldest daughter to realize that she no longer gets the "First" all the time. The other brothers and sisters marry and have success too, sometimes far more than one of the others. Take our own family. Uncle Jack has far more than I have but I love him dearly—there is no envy—never has been. My sister has done well. I finally have probably passed her. Take Nina, she had everything she wanted, for a while there with Bill [presumably referring to Nina's former husband Bill Newcomb]. *Would I trade places with any of them, no, a thousand times no. I wouldn't give up my family for any family in the world (sound natural?). To me they are tops. Faults-lots of them but thank God, they have lived clean, honest God-fearing lives. Do you think I am afraid to meet my maker when I leave such a heritage behind? Not for a minute. My one hope and prayer is that you three children, come hell or high water, knit your families closer and closer together and if ever one needs help, the Gordon clan sticks together.*

How did I get started on all of this? I started out to put you up-to-date on the so called invalid. Don't know what the family told you so I will make a quick review.

It all started, I guess, two weeks ago last Saturday. Had a long trying meeting at the office and Larry and I didn't get home until about two-thirty pm. We had a big late lunch and I went right out in the garden to rake and burn leaves. Worked all afternoon not too hard and came in for dinner. Got dizzy at the table, said I was going to bed. Had quite a pain across my chest. It finally went away. Got up the next morning and felt fine. Put in a really hard day of work Sunday and a very busy full day of work all the next week.

A week ago Saturday we had another meeting at the offices but broke up early. Larry and I got home about 1pm. Like a nut I ate a big lunch and went right out in the garden to work. In about ten minutes I felt dizzy, went in to lay down on the couch. The pain started again across my chest and got lots worse. I called Mother to call Dr. [presumably Willliam D.] *Rudie. He arrived shortly, gave me a shot of morphine, called Dr.* [Raymond E.] *Wheeler, the heart specialist that took care of me* [before], *to meet me at the hospital, called the ambulance and home in the am. They have been pumping oxygen in me for the first three days, now I feel like a million dollars, look like a . . . in bed. I get quite a kick out of having the nurses give me a bath and waiting on me hand and foot. They say I will be laid up for six weeks—time will tell.*

It's tough to be laid up right now—the weather is beautiful—the trees are just budding. Mother and Pat [Larry's wife] brought me a bouquet of lilies of the valley and forget-me-nots from the garden, just now.

Glad to hear David's finger is better. Give my . . . love to Dianne – tell her I hope to get together with her this summer.

Don't worry. Lots of love, Dad

Sometime after Laurance's health scare, my grandparents parted ways though they did not divorce. With little advance notice, Laurance moved from Duluth to Phoenix, Arizona, perhaps needing to create distance from Yolande for his own wellbeing. Alternatively, he may have been drawn to the warm, dry climate Phoenix offered in benefit to his compromised health. No other family members are known to have resided in the Southwest outside of California.

Larry was left to shoulder the weight of his mother's failing mental health. He did not take well to the news that his father was relocating and criticized him for his abandonment. Initially, Larry and his wife, Pat, moved Yolande out of her house into supervised residential quarters not far from their home. Occasionally, they received calls from the facility informing them that Larry's mother had left the premises. Yolande would be found wondering the streets at night in downtown Duluth, sometimes in her nightgown. Her deteriorating condition placed my Uncle Larry in the difficult position of having to find his mother suitable treatment.

My grandfather died in Arizona on January 15, 1952, presumably of a heart-related cause. Laurance Sterne Gordon and his father John Gardner Gordon, Jr. are both buried at the Inglewood Park Cemetery in Los Angeles.

On "Mrs. M.V. Hartman" letterhead with an address of 15750 Foothill Boulevard, San Fernando, California, Annette wrote her niece Virginia "Jinks" a letter six weeks after Laurance's passing. Though my grandfather had executed a Will, Annette wanted to weigh in on the subject of Laurance's house and what should become of it:

Dear Virginia,

Your letter arrived and I was indeed interested in every word. I do truly believe the house should be yours. I do think your dad wanted you and Doug to have it. I wrote to Uncle Jack to see if he could straighten it out. He said he knew you were always closest and dearest to your dad and that also you could use it to better advantage as Larry has a wonderful opportunity to make around $15,000 or more a year, and Danny [my father] likewise had things made easy for him. Your dad when he was here said he was changing his will and leaving a portion to Larry on account of his children. After all they were his grandchildren and if anything did happen to Larry, "how were they to be taken care of," as Pat's family could do nothing. It was entirely on account of the young ones that he included Larry. I also know he set up certain parts for your mother, so the house would not affect that. I do wish I could help you in this matter. I know your dad said the house was not to be part of the estate. Am only sorry Uncle Jack doesn't seem to be definite. Virginia, don't give up, write and tell the administration just exactly how you feel and what you know.

Love to all, Aunt Annette

With a letter dated April 15, 1952, directed to my uncle, "L.S Gordon, Jr." at Draper, Gordon & Walker in Duluth, Robert Kersting enclosed "the April check" from my grandfather's estate for the benefit of "Mrs. Gordon." He copied Virginia Gordon Guy and Yolande Gordon Broderick. Evidently, the house did not pass to Jinks:

"I yesterday received from Paul Louis ll the verified partnership accounting and your consent to your father's will on behalf of Mrs. Gordon. We are at present working on the state and federal inheritance taxes and should complete the same within the next ten days. The house here should sell within the next week or so for an amount in the vicinity of $9,500.00 [equivalent of $113,000 in 2024 dollars].

"I will, of course, advise you, Paul [the accountant], and the other heirs when these matters have been concluded. Shortly thereafter, we should be able to obtain final distribution in Arizona and transfer the funds of the estate to the Duluth bank."

Yolande Hoke Gordon lived in Duluth at least
through 1948 and likely a few years longer. Toward
the end of her life, she became institutionalized at
a psychiatric facility in Council Bluffs, Iowa.

As mentioned, Laurance and Yolande's relationship fell apart some-time after Jinks, Yo, and Larry left the nest. The same can be said of Yolande's parents, Walter and Susie, who parted ways after Hampton and Wessie left home and around the time Yolande and Nina joined the Red Cross in Bordeaux. Yolande's failing mental health may have precipitated the breakup. Conversely, perhaps the separation from Laurance aggravated her mental illness. The toll may have been exacerbated by memories of her parents' divorce those many years earlier. Her service in WWI and the protracted Depression that devastated her generation beginning in 1929 certainly could have contributed to her suffering as well.

As further speculation, social isolation or loneliness may have affected Yolande's mental health. Her birth and upbringing in France by expatriates led to raising a family apart from her own in a foreign country when she moved to Duluth. Here, she became physically distant not only from her father who stayed behind in Bordeaux but also from her mother and three siblings who found comfort in close proximity to each other in New York. Unquestionably, Yolande carried a heavy weight on her shoulders.

If my grandmother's mental state proved hereditary, the gene could have passed from her mother's lineage. Recall the affliction of Yolande's uncle Hampton Gould Westcott, triggered when he testified at the Standard Oil anti-trust trial. He was institutionalized for a brief period before release to his aunt Caroline Gould Keller in Waynesville, North Carolina, who with his sister, Carrie, cared for him for the remaining days of his life. Caution in drawing a connection to heredity is warranted in this case, however, as the mercurial treatment Hampton received for syphilis before the introduction of penicillin could have induced his psychotic state. As we'll learn, though not as acute, Yolande's brother Wessie suffered mental lapses as well.

> The question I've been unable to answer definitively
> about Yolande's institutionalization—why Council
> Bluffs, Iowa? I believe the answer rest squarely
> with the charitable Sisters of Mercy.

As noted, Yolande and her siblings and cousin Gould attended Catholic school in Bordeaux. Yolande's mother Susie's half-sister, Elizabeth "Bessie" Grant Westcott, professed her vows of poverty, chastity, and obedience to the Sisters of Mercy in Pittsburgh as Sister Mary Beatrice. Though "Bessie" died 35 years before Yolande, the Westcott family evidently remained loyal to the Sisters. Bessie's sister Nina Westcott Sweeney, with whom Yolande enjoyed a close relationship, gave considerable sums to a convent in Latrobe, Pennsylvania, presumably in devotion to "Sister Mary Beatrice" and the Sisters of Mercy congregation.

Putting pieces of the puzzle together, I learned that, in 1831, two Sisters of Mercy from Minneapolis began nursing the sick in Council Bluffs, Iowa. Their small hospital emerged as the forerunner to St. Bernard's Hospital where Yolande spent her last years. St. Bernard's Hospital admitted patients from six Midwestern states including Minnesota.

Living in close proximity to Yolande in Duluth, Larry and his wife, Pat, played an instrumental role in deeming St. Bernard's the most suitable quarters for her:

> By their 100th anniversary in 1931, the Catholic facility in Council Bluffs had evolved to include a motherhouse, chapel, auditorium, kitchens, a cafeteria, private dining rooms, and a general hospital with a 275-bed capacity used exclusively for psychiatric nursing of mental and nervous patients. The services that supported in-patients included the following: hydrotherapy and massage; electric treatments; and occupational therapy centered on weaving, basketry, leather work, needle work, and manual training. In the belief that the souls of the patients need more care than their disease and ailing bodies, the Sisters of Mercy ministered with spiritual services as well.
>
> With a building complex aptly featuring a mansard roof of the French persuasion, oriented to furnish sunshine and light to all the

rooms, the grounds of St. Bernard's Hospital on 15-acres included a beautifully landscape lawn, stately trees, graceful shrubs, and bright flower beds.

My Uncle Larry alone accompanied his beloved mother on the train ride to Council Bluffs from Duluth. It would have been terribly heartbreaking to say goodbye and leave her behind. He stayed in regular contact with the hospital, learning that, among other therapies, her medical treatment included electrotherapy. Distance from family notwithstanding, Yolande's loved ones could not have envisioned a more desirable setting or better care than what the compassionate Sisters of Mercy provided.

Tragic as her circumstances played out, I believe my grandmother's good fortune placed her in the most attractive private hospital available, ministered by the merciful nuns. At another time, her ill-equipped family would have shouldered the greater burden of her illness. Yolande died in Council Bluffs on January 29, 1956, four years after Laurance. She is buried at Calvary Cemetery in Duluth, Minnesota, along with her son Larry and daughter-in-law Pat.

A decade after Yolande Hoke Gordon's passing, St. Bernard's Hospital merged with a "general" hospital run by the Sisters of Mercy in Council Bluffs. The administration subsequently made the decision to raze the outdated St. Bernard's Hospital complex.

For whatever reason, my mother rarely if ever spoke of her mother, her mental condition, or her institutionalization. The stigma attached to mental illness, particularly during that time, could explain her silence and why we know so little about my grandmother's circumstances. I wonder about their relationship, though. Was my mother riddled with guilt given the nearly 1,000 miles that separated her in Pittsburgh from her frail mother in Council Bluffs? Did she detach from her mother to protect herself from emotional strain triggered by Yolande's mental state? The same goes for Jinks in Palo Alto, California. At least Larry had occasion to visit his mother from Duluth. I naturally regret not having asked the big questions when my mother, aunt, and uncle lived.

THIS "GEN 10" SEGMENT WRAPS UP with details gathered on Yolande's brothers, sister, and cousin Clifford "Gould" deNeergaard who spent his teenage years living with the Hokes in Bordeaux. I also call out Henry "Reed" Hoke—a first cousin to Hampton, Wessie, Yolande, and Nina on their father's side. Though one of many paternal first cousins, Reed enjoyed an especially close relationship with my grandmother and her siblings. As we'll learn, Reed put his stamp on our nation's then burgeoning "direct mail" industry, getting his start in my hometown of Pittsburgh.

The four Hoke siblings shared a closeness that stayed with them throughout their adulthood in America.

Hampton Westcott Hoke, Sr. (1893–1960) & Charlotte Graves Stark (1914–2004)

Jinks, Yo, and Larry's uncle **Hampton "Hamp" Westcott Hoke** studied engineering at the University of Pennsylvania in Philadelphia sometime after moving stateside from Bordeaux. In 1916, at age 23 years, he resided with Wessie at 3415 Walnut Street while they completed their post-secondary studies. Upon graduation, Hamp worked as an engineer for Bell Telephone Company in New York City, in close proximity to his brother.

Hampton enlisted with the U.S. Army during World War I, becoming a first lieutenant while serving as an interpreter.

In a 1925 "Enumeration of the Inhabitants of the 7th Assembly District of New York," Hampton and Wessie are listed as engineers, aged 32 and 30; their mother "Susan Hoke" is registered as a housewife and 60 years of age. The 1930 Census lists Hampton as a "guest" of the head of household (possibly living with Wessie) and as a salesman with a public utility in New York City. A list of citizens compiled five years later shows Hampton living at 36 Harvest Street, Forest Hills, Long Island.

In 1939, at the age of 46, a Catholic priest officiated at the wedding of Hampton and **Charlotte Graves Starke** (1914–2004) in New York City. Originally from the Bronx, Charlotte was then nearly half his age at just 24. When they married, Hampton worked for Consolidated Edison, which was located by Union Square at 4 Irving Place. At the time of their marriage, while living at 455 W. 23rd Street in the Chelsea neighborhood, nearby Queens played host to the 1939 New York World's Fair. Hampton and Charlotte's only child, Hampton Westcott Hoke, Jr. (1941–2012), came along two years later.

Hampton, Sr. survived his brother Wessie by 13 years. He died in 1960 at age 66, reportedly struck by a car as a pedestrian in New York City, though I was unable to confirm this cause as fact. At the time of his passing, Hampton's son, Hampton, Jr., was 19 years old.

Hampton Jr. (1941–2012) later married Mary Patricia Warder (1946–1979) with whom he raised their two sons in the Bronx—John Patrick (b. 1969) and Brian Michael (b. 1972). My second cousin Hampton Westcott Hoke, Jr. died in Floral Park, New York, and he is buried in Calverton, New York.

Hampton Westcott Hoke, Sr. is buried at the Long Island National Cemetery in Farmingdale, New York. In a 1960 record of Interment, he is identified as Catholic. His wife Charlotte then lived at 450 W. 24th Street in New York City.

Harriet "Hattie" aka "Tattie" Stenger Hoke—daughter of Walter's oldest brother Edward and the artist of an oil painting in my possession—became especially close to her first cousin Nina. On May 17, 1960, Hattie wrote an endearing typewritten letter with condolences to Nina on the passing of Nina's brother Hampton. Hattie addressed the letter to Nina at 635 East 14th Street, New York City, with a return address reflecting Hattie's Chambersburg home at 3 North Second Street. [Hattie, the oldest of Henry Elias and Harriet Stenger Hoke's 24 grandchildren, died in Chambersburg in 1968 at age 94.]

> *Dear Nina,*
>
> *Last night I intended calling you, but by the time I had worked out how to reach you by the new direct dialing it was rather late and it also occurred to me that your telephone number might have changed. The one I have for you is ORE 3-0733.* [Phone numbers from the 1930s to 1960s started with letters instead of digits. Deriving the first three letters from actual names, ours was *FI-1-5842*—pronounced "Filbrick"-#-####, which translated as 341-5842.]

At any rate it might not be so satisfactory, but I want you to know I think of you even though words seem inadequate to express the love and interest one feels for those who are dear to us.

As you may know, Dora [Wessie's widow] *wrote me a lovely letter which I appreciate very much. Please thank her for it. She spoke so beautifully of you and told me much about Hampton's passing that I wanted to know.*

Then I had a long letter from Reed [son of Walter's brother Charlie] *yesterday and he was able to give some other information, but I do wish Chambersburg could be reached more easily so that you and I might have frequent visits.*

Some people seem to feel family ties more deeply than others and I realize what Hampton meant to you so you can be grateful for the years of close relations from childhood and that he was able to help you through some sorrowful experiences in the past, and it is well to remember the many happy joyous occasions of a brother-sister relationship.

Lillian [wife of Walter's youngest brother John Wesley Hoke] *came to see me Saturday evening the 6th, but I have not seen or heard from her since. In my other letter I told you that she talked to me Saturday morning. I seldom call her because she is so busy and I believe it may not always be convenient for her to reach the telephone. I think she has a special hearing attachment on the one in her room.*

I am expecting someone who will mail this for me so will not write more at this time.

My love always, Tattie

Walter Westcott Hoke (1895–1947) & Dora M. Crawford (b. 1908)

Walter Westcott "Wessie" Hoke followed Hampton as the second oldest among Walter and Susie's four children. Wessie attended private school, graduating from Bordeaux's Sainte-Marie Gran Lebrum in 1911 at age 16. His siblings and cousin Gould may have attended Sainte-Marie Gran Lebrum as well. Wessie then received a Bachelor of Arts in sciences and languages from the University of Bordeaux in 1913, at which time he chose to further his education with his brother in the States.

In 1917, Wessie earned a Bachelor of Science in electrical engineering from the University of Pennsylvania where he became a member of the French Club, the Chess Club, and the Honorary Electrical Engineering

Fraternity known as Eta Kappa Nu. His student registration card characterizes Wessie as "small framed, 5'8", medium build, with brown eyes and black hair." He listed his address at 306 W. 80th Street in New York City.

Based on a photograph in my possession, the brothers Wessie and Hampton evidently played classical music and may have performed in a symphony or orchestra. A family with musical talent, the brothers' sister Yolande played the piano and harp, and their mother, Susie, played the banjo and perhaps other instruments as well.

Wessie advanced from his first job with Philadelphia Electric Company when he moved to Bell Telephone Laboratories (later "Bell Labs"). With an inventive nature borrowed from his father Walter who had designed various dental gadgets, Wessie developed a new method of calibrating power-factor indicators at the company, that is, the relative phase of the power line voltage and the power line current. He then assisted physicist Gustav Elmen at Bell Labs with the development of permalloy, a nickel-iron magnetic alloy notable for its magnetic permeability that proved useful as a magnetic core material in electrical and electronic equipment.

In 1922, Bell Telephone sent Wessie to London in connection with the manufacture of the first transatlantic permalloy cable. That same year, he made application for a passport from New York for business travel with the intention of visiting England, France, Belgium, Spain, and Italy. In 1924, Wessie is listed among U.S. citizens as a passenger sailing on the French steamship *La Savoie*. This same vessel, scrapped at Dunkirk in 1927, carried Walter on his return voyage to France after accompanying his sons Hampton and Wessie stateside in 1913 from Le Havre to New York City.

Beginning in 1926, Wessie became wholly engaged in patent work. He associated with a former Bell Telephone Laboratories colleague initially, then through a merger, with the law firm of Williams, Rich & Morse. The U.S. Patent Office admitted my great-uncle Wessie as a patent attorney in 1934 without him having attended law school to my knowledge. He specialized in chemical and electrical inventions—notably the chemically-induced flotation of ores—and later became chief patent attorney for General Foods at their headquarters in Hoboken, New Jersey.

Wessie married **Dora M. Crawford** (b. 1908) whose father was a successful produce merchant on the Ohio River in East Liverpool, Ohio. Dora supervised accounts receivable at Young & Rubicam, a marketing and advertising firm in New York when it ranked second largest among advertising companies worldwide. [In 1951, the ad agency reached the $100 million mark in total billings, becoming the largest advertising firm in the world. By 1973, annual billings grew to $3.2 billion; $21.4 billion in 2023.]

At the time of their aunt Virginia "Nina" Westcott Sweeney's death in 1943, Yolande's sister Nina with her 16-year-old son, Bill, lived with her brother Wessie and his wife Dora in Garden City, New York. Without children, Wessie had the luxury of time to experiment on the electro-magnetic treatment and casting of metals in a home laboratory located on Long Island at 7 Huntington Road in Garden City. He secured two patents from this curious yet ambitious pastime. Wessie also made time to complete an application for membership in the Sons of the Revolution in the State of New York, having established eligibility through his G3 grandfather, Captain John Westcott.

Nina shared memories of Wessie as a kind, sweet man. Sadly, Nina's son Bill recalled mental lapses in his uncle when in Wessie's last years, Bill found him talking with himself and to the devil.

Bill was 20 years old when his uncle Wessie passed away in 1947. Survived by his three siblings, at just 52 years of age, Walter Westcott Hoke died of a heart attack at his New York City home at 52 Irving Place by Gramercy Park. Following funeral services at St. Ann's Catholic Church in Manhattan's East Village neighborhood, Wessie was laid to rest at the Riverview Cemetery in Dora's hometown of East Liverpool, Ohio.

Upon Wessie's passing, his cousin Gould deNeergaard, who as a teen-ager lived with the Hokes in Bordeaux, introduced the widow Dora to Denis Sibson, the father of between eight and ten children. The couple married and Denis died a few short months after Gould, in 1988.

Virginia Westcott Hoke (1899–1973) & William Ambrose Newcomb (1889–1941)

The baby of the family, **Virginia Westcott Hoke**—Jinks, Yo, and Larry's aunt Nina—left Bordeaux after her service in the Red Cross around the same time her sister Yolande and her new family moved to Duluth. Nina stayed in Bordeaux long enough to witness the birth of her niece, my Aunt Jinks, on May 31, 1919. Their mother Susie traveled to Bordeaux from New York to lend support upon meeting her first grandchild.

In 1919, a list of U.S. citizens aboard the *Lorraine* sailing from Le Havre to the port of New York includes Susan Westcott Hoke at age 53 and her daughter Virginia Westcott Hoke at age 20. Another document lists their residence at the Marie Antoinette Hotel at Broadway and West 66th Street in New York City on January 18, 1920. Months later, Nina's sister gave birth to my mother in Duluth, on September 9, 1920.

As you will recall, Nina's father referred to her in letters from Bordeaux as "Tiny" when her sister Yolande went by "Yoyo." While visiting Yolande and family in Duluth, likely for the birth of my mother, Yolande Westcott Gordon, Nina met her future husband **William "Bill" Ambrose Newcomb** (1889–1941).

Born in Kansas City, Missouri, Bill moved with his family to Macon, Georgia, as a teen. He then studied at Fordham University in New York City before pursuing a career in hotel management. With properties owned by his father and a partner throughout the Midwest, Bill spent eight years managing two hotels in Duluth where he is listed as a resident as early as 1917.

As proprietors, Newcomb Hotel & Co. managed The Spalding (built in 1889), then Duluth's largest hotel. A week before my mother's birth in September 1920, the Newcomb Hotel Co. closed on the purchase of the Holland House Hotel at 501 W. Superior Street in Duluth where Nina had booked a room. Bill operated both the Holland House and the Spalding as manager.

One day before the closing of the Holland Hotel for roughly $500,000, Bill's father, John A. Newcomb, arrived in Duluth from Pensacola, Florida, where a week earlier, Newcomb Hotel Co. purchased the luxurious seven-story San Carlos hotel, also for $500,000. The acquisition of the Holland expanded to seven the collection of hotels owned or operated by Newcomb Hotel Co.

The lovely and personable Nina Hoke married William Ambrose Newcomb in New York City in 1923. The wedding took place at the Church of the Holy Trinity at 213 West 82nd Street, followed by a wedding breakfast at the Hotel Belleclaire Central Park. The couple then lived in New York for three years before relocating to the West Coast.

In 1927, as part-owner, Bill staged an elaborate opening and managed the Hotel Sainte Claire in San Jose, California. The couple lived at the hotel, then considered "the most prominent institution of that city." Here in San Jose, Nina gave birth to **William Adrian Newcomb** (1927–1999).

One year later, Bill's father with his partner, Leon W. Huckins, developed the Sir Francis Drake Hotel in San Francisco. The hotel developers set out to make the Sir Francis Drake a hotel to impress. With amenities like an indoor golf course, the extravagant interiors made the hotel famous. In 1928, Huckins-Newcomb Hotel Company honored young Bill with the vice-presidency. The company also played a role in development of the distinctive Hotel Sainte Claire which Bill occupied with his young family as resident manager.

Within five years of the birth of their only child, William Adrian Newcomb, Nina divorced Bill Ambrose Newcomb upon learning of his infidelity. He reportedly fell in love with his secretary or a staff member, possibly an employee at one of the hotels he had managed in Duluth. Young Bill conjured the only memory of his father at age 11 when they met for the one and only time following the couple's separation.

Humiliated, Nina remained bitter toward her husband. As a Catholic, she had difficulty acknowledging her status as a divorcee. To save face, she gave the impression of widowhood.

By some accounts, Nina's ex-husband died by suicide in his early 50's. A priest witnessed him entering the Pacific Ocean in Santa Cruz, California, where he drowned. Without knowing definitively, the priest raised doubts that he took his own life.

Reportedly without savings, alimony, or child support from her ex-husband when they separated, Nina and young Bill went to live with Wessie and Dora in Garden City, New York. Wessie and Dora eagerly helped to raise Bill since they could not have children of their own. Wessie became an important male role model in Bill's formative years, inspiring him to become a physicist. Meanwhile, Nina worked for 19 years as an office supervisor with the Doubleday Publishing Company in New York.

Nina simply radiated sharpness, according to Dick Neergaard, her first cousin once removed. Dick recalled that Nina ran a highly successful bridge club and a few minutes into any encounter with her, you were left with no doubt that she had a very keen mind. Attractive in looks and personality, Nina was also a lot of fun and dated often. Sometime along the way, according to her daughter-in-law Susie Newcomb, Nina and her first cousin Reed Hoke engaged in a romance, but she never remarried. Reed—the oldest son of Nina's uncle Charles Elias Hoke—lived in Garden City near Wessie, Dora, and Nina at the time of their brief fling.

Yolande's sister talked a lot about her family and saved everything, much of which ended up in my hands, thanks to Susie Newcomb. A caring soul, Nina became the connector as well as the collector of family memorabilia. She cared deeply for her sister and stood by Yolande's side before her institutionalization. Recalling the mental breakdown of their uncle Hampton Gould Westcott coinciding with the Standard Oil antitrust affair and brother Wessie's lapses in his later years, Nina must have been heartbroken to witness her sister's mental state as she declined, perhaps also wondering if she herself was susceptible.

Shortly after young Bill Newcomb's marriage to Susie née Hester in 1964, Nina retired from Doubleday. Nearly destitute, she came to live with the newlyweds in Walnut Creek in the East Bay region of San Francisco. Bill expressed reluctance, but Susie regarded her mother-in-law with great affection and insisted it was the right thing to do. Because Nina did not have means of her own, Bill and Susie supported her financially. Nina died shortly after moving in with them, at age 73 in 1977. My Aunt Jinks had invited her aunt Nina to several Guy family gatherings in Palo Alto and consoled Bill and Susie at Walnut Creek upon Nina's death.

Nina had always talked about wanting to be buried next to her mother. A college friend of Susie's worked as a mortician in Napa and succeeded in his quest to locate the burial ground of Nina's mother. A month after her passing, Bill and Susie arranged Nina's burial at Mercer Cemetery in Trenton, New Jersey, next to her mother, Susie Westcott Hoke, alongside Nina's maternal grandparents Thomas Grant and Josie Gould Westcott and her maternal great-grandparents Isaac and Susan Smith Sackett Gould.

Learning that his grandmother Susie Westcott Hoke had been buried in 1933 without a marker, Bill and his wife Susie Newcomb at once purchased tombstones for both Nina and her mother. Acknowledging that the grounds as situated in a high-crime area were no longer safe, the cemetery closed its doors immediately following Nina's burial in 1977.

Clifford "Gould" deNeergaard (1896–1988) & Virginia Mary Corcoran (1900–1988)

William Adrian Newcomb's second cousin and a close first cousin of Hampton, Wessie, Yolande, and Nina Hoke on their mother's side, **Clifford "Gould" deNeergaard** (1896–1987) was the only child of Carrie Gould Westcott and Clifford Jones Neergaard. As a toddler, Gould moved with his mother from New York City following his parents' divorce. Later, they relocated to Waynesville, North Carolina, where Carrie's aunt Caroline and her husband Simon Keller brought them into their home. A doctor by training and without children of her own, Caroline played a significant caregiver role in Gould's formative years. At age 14, Gould went to live with his mother's sister Susie Hoke and her family in Bordeaux, France. Upon returning stateside four years later, he briefly lived with his mother in Waynesville before heading off to college.

In Atlanta, Georgia, Gould competed on the gymnastics team at the Georgia Institute of Technology where he earned a Bachelor of Science in architecture. He went on to earn a Master's degree in the same field from Columbia University in New York City, later working as an architect in Chicago before relocating to Philadelphia.

In 1932, Gould's wife, **Virginia Corcoran**, gave birth to their only child, Richard "Dick" Hampton Neergaard in New York City. According to Dick, "When the Depression curtailed architectural activity, he [his father Gould] took up a parallel career as an associate professor of Descriptive Geometry at the City College of New York (now CUNY). Despite the arcane nature of the subject, his class became extremely popular due to his irreverent sense of humor and his unique Continental-cum-Huck-Finn charm. While in New York, he moved from Manhattan to City Island, then to Pelham Manor. After retirement, he and his wife moved to Fort Lauderdale." Once Proctor & Gamble reassigned Dick from Europe to its company headquarters, Gould and Virginia made their way to Cincinnati where they enjoyed close proximity to their son and his family.

Although he didn't read music, Gould's musical talent was formidable. His son Dick shared that "he played a joyfully raucous honky-tonk piano and within minutes of picking up any instrument could have it singing. He sometimes composed impromptu second and third-part harmonies to the melody as he went. When Gould and Virginia, a noted concert pianist and educator, did four-hand improvisations on the piano, she with her classical style and he with his ragtime, the music inevitably brought the house down."

Gould's paternal ancestors came from Denmark. According to Dick, "a branch of the Neergaards in Denmark had been ennobled in the mid-nineteenth century, resulting in a 'de' being placed before their name. Gould, persuaded as a young man that he was a descendant of this branch, adopted the 'de' and for the rest of his life gave his surname as 'deNeergaard.' Research since his death has shown that this belief was incorrect; the 'de' does not attach to his branch of the family."

Gould served as a member of the Larchmont Shore Club; City Island Yacht Club; Sons of the Revolution; Sons of the American Revolution; St. Nicholas Society; Society of Colonial Wars; and Elks (Fort Lauderdale). Registered as an architect in Pennsylvania, New Jersey, and New York, he became a member of the Society of American Registered Architects and the Architectural League in New York.

Clifford Gould deNeergaard died at the age of 91 in Cincinnati. At Green Hill Cemetery in Waynesville, North Carolina, Gould is buried alongside his wife Virginia Mary Corcoran deNeergaard; his mother Caroline "Carrie" Sackett Westcott Neergaard; great-aunt Caroline Gould Keller; his uncle Hampton Gould Westcott; and son Richard Gould Neergaard who died in 2023.

Henry "Reed" Hoke (1894–1970) & Lucille "Lucy" Hearn (1898–1991)

In addition to Gould, the Hokes enjoyed a close personal relationship with their first cousin **Henry "Reed" Hoke** on their father's side. Though not a direct descendant in our lineage, Reed established early roots in my hometown of Pittsburgh and developed an interesting and rather colorful business in the emerging field of direct mail. This "GEN 10" segment closes with a profile of Reed.

Reed's father Charles "Charlie" Elias fell in line as the 7th of Henry Elias and Harriet Stenger Hoke's eight sons, following my great-grand-father Walter by two years. As you'll recall, Charlie became a widower when his wife died giving birth to their third child [much like my great-grandfather John Gardner Gordon, Jr. when his wife Fanny died after giving birth to their third child, my grandfather Laurance Gordon]. The eldest of the three children born to Charles and Sara Reed Hoke in Baltimore, Reed grew up in Chambersburg, Pennsylvania, where his siblings John Lindsay and Sara "Sally" Reed were born. Their mother died when Reed—the oldest—was just nine years old.

Initially pursuing the ministry, Reed attended Washington & Jefferson College in Washington, Pennsylvania. From there he earned a Bachelor of Science in economics from the Wharton School at the University of Pennsylvania in Philadelphia. In his early years, Reed worked in a number of manufacturing plants, but he started his life's real work in advertising during the early 1920s in Pittsburgh. Reed and Lucille "Lucy" Hearn married in 1920 and had their first of three sons that same year, Henry Reed "Pete" Hoke, Jr. (1920–1998). Their sons Charles Hearn "Hearnie" (1922–2011) and John "Jack" Ray (1924–2009) were also born in Pittsburgh.

Widely known for simple but successful selling campaigns by mail, in 1929, Reed moved to Queens, New York, to become the business manager of a prominent advertising trade publication. Later, he became the executive manager of the Direct Mail Advertising Association. After 27 years of marriage, Reed and Lucy divorced in 1947. A year later, he married Kathleen "Kitty" Creaglo.

While living in New York, Reed regularly socialized with his cousins Hampton, Nina, and Wessie, and Wessie's wife Dora. He also enjoyed a close relationship with his uncle Walter whom he visited more than once in Bordeaux. Somewhere along the line, Reed developed a short-lived romance with his cousin Nina in New York after her divorce from William Ambrose Newcomb.

In 1938, Reed founded his own magazine and counseling service. He wrote, lectured, and taught for many years on the subject of good, clean advertising, going so far as to launch crusades against fraudulent advertisers. When late in 1939 he stumbled accidentally into some disturbing facts about the use of U.S. mail by the Nazis, Reed went off on a chase which led him to describe his experiences and conclusions in a book titled *Black Mail.*

Active in the emerging "Direct Mail" market, Reed seemed to be a complicated person. In the words of a colleague, he was "loved, hated, admired, feared, respected, misunderstood, criticized, pitied, envied, ridiculed—sometimes in the same year by those closest to him." Insights into the famed author and trade editor are found in an undated issue of the direct mail magazine that Henry Hoke created—*The Reporter of Direct Mail Advertising:*

> "He *loved* direct mail . . . Like a cat protecting her kittens, he'd fend off anyone who dared to hurt, misuse, attack, ridicule the medium he devoted more than 53 years of his life to. Such dedication was not solely in self-interest to protect his worldly assets. He loved people. Direct mail in its simplest form was (is) the communications tool of people, the individual. Letters. Good grief, he was nearly a fanatic on letters, letter writing . . . on how to project warmth, friendliness, sincerity. 'Direct mail is the people's medium, the medium the little guy can afford,' he used to say.

"Thus, during his extraordinary lifetime, Henry ["Reed"] Hoke was chief defender, merciless critic, champion, teacher, and the reporter of direct mail advertising, the name of his game especially after 1938 when he founded the very magazine you are reading.

"It all started, according to one of the thousands of stories Henry Hoke could tell so well, with writing love letters for guys who were too lazy to write their ones-and-only. This, while a junior and senior at the Wharton School of the University of Pennsylvania in 1916–1917. He learned to put himself in the other guy's shoes. He learned how powerful, useful, resultful letters could be.

"After school, he got a job at E.I. DuPont's wartime, shell-loading plant at Penniman, Virginia, near Williamsburg. With the war concluded, he moved to Pittsburgh and took a job with the Homestead Steel Works in their water purification department. But a life in industry wasn't for Henry Hoke. He hated it. So when a chemical supplier offered "HH" an office managership at Sterling Equipment Supply Company, he grabbed it. And manage he did, as well as listen to the woes of Sterling salesmen about business. It occurred to the budding executive that what worked in communication affection might work in acquiring leads. So, he wrote some letters and mailed them with reply cards. They worked. And he wrote some more.

"One day a Multigraph salesman came along and made the absurd suggestion that Sterling needed their own letter duplicating capability. One was bought, then more equipment, more supplies, and more people, until Henry Hoke had quite a thing going to the dismay of Harry Baer, the owner. What words were exchanged we'll never know, but it resulted in the transformation of this early in-plant facility to an outside, commercial affair called Sterling Sales Service, Inc., creators and producers of direct mail advertising (220 Stanwix Street in Pittsburgh). About 1922. This I gather as I look over a four-page letter/broadside dated October 29, 1924, and signed H.R. Hoke, president. The letter introduced a display of glowing testimonial letters from pleased clients about successful direct mail campaigns executed by Sterling's Henry Hoke.

"In 1928, the Direct Mail Advertising Association's [DMAA] annual convention was held in Philadelphia. Pittsburgh's leading creative producer made a speech which delighted John Howie Wright, publisher of *Postage And The Mailbag*, the direct mail magazine of that day. Such enthusiasm ought *not* to be stuck away in the steel city.

"So Henry Hoke was offered greener pastures in New York as business manager of *P/M* starting January 1, 1929. Then the Crash. It wasn't kind to DMAA, either. Membership dwindled. Sometime in 1933, the board asked John Howie if they couldn't borrow Henry Hoke for a year or so to put the association back on its feet. The sabbatical was granted. Henry Hoke dug-in to put direct mail on the map alongside newspapers, magazines, and radio. An education road show was developed which, each year, started out at the annual conference. Each year a new theme, surrounded by commercial exhibits. Tens of thousands in major cities were exposed to the 49 Ways to Use Direct Mail, The Trails to Sales, etc.

"By 1938, DMAA was better known than ever before. And *Postage in the Mailbag* had folded. In May, urged by former P/M'ers Mae Strutzenberg and Fannie Stern [no relation to my G1 grandmother Fannie Sterne Gordon], Henry Hoke started *The Reporter of Direct Mail Advertising* and left DMAA. As a trade paper, it was different, personal, crusading, hell-raising. In 1938, war clouds were over the horizon. The new publisher became concerned with the rising tide of Nazi propaganda appearing in schools, churches, businesses, homes.

"Nazi Germany was pouring tons of subversive "direct mail" into the United States to divide and conquer segments of the marketplace. The personal crusade resulted in two books. *Black Mail* (a best seller) and *It's a Secret*, a sequel. Henry Hoke's exposé led the Dies Un-American Activities Committee of Congress to close up the German Railroads office in New York and other German propaganda outlets in the U.S. This led to an invitation to head the Graphic Arts Victory Committee during World War II, a coordinated effort on the part of paper mills, envelope companies, printers, and lettershops to help government communicate war programs to the people. The effort was an extraordinary direct mail campaign.

"The years following the war were devoted to defending direct mail against the vicious attacks of the newspapers and the massive 2nd class lobby to keep 2nd Class Mail rates low. He continually chided his good friends in publishing—that massive cut-rate, short-term subscription offers through the mails were a joke; that publishers ought to pay their fair share of postage, easily financed by an additional half a buck to a dollar on the subscription price. The publishing community winced at his pictures of glaring inequities in first, second, and third class mail, but the Post Office Department quietly applauded his good sense, undivided loyalty, and affection for the postal system.

"Shortly after starting this magazine, Henry Hoke sponsored the first direct mail school of sorts in the splendid oak halls of the old Stillman home atop the National City Bank Building at 17 E. 42nd Street in New York, which had become the magazine's offices . . . Thus, it was with a deep sense of pride when Ed Mayer phoned *this reporter* yesterday (November 23rd) that the Senior Institute of DMAA's Educational Foundation has been renamed the *Henry Hoke Collegiate Institute*, an assurance that young minds in their senior and graduate years in college will continue to learn the power and place of direct mail each fall of the year. Henry Hoke will be pleased with that idea."

Upon Reed's death at age 76, his family arranged his burial at Loudon Park Cemetery in Baltimore.

Besides Carrie Westcott Neergaard's son, Gould, all of my grandmother Yolande's first cousins came from her father Walter's side. Twenty Hoke cousins in total, they included Edward's three children—Harriet "Hattie" or "Tattie," Arthur, and Harry; Harry's six—Clarence, Ethel, Eric, Ralph, Walter, and Margaret; George's six—Robert, Norman, George, Christine, Helen, and Mary; Howard's son Russell; Charlie's three—Henry "Reed," John, and Sara; and John's daughter Harriet.

This wraps up "GEN 10" covering my maternal grandparents along with Yolande's siblings and first cousins Gould and Reed. The lifetime of our relatives in this generation spans nearly a century, from 1889–1988, although the last among the children of Susan Gould Westcott and Walter Scott Hoke, Nina Hoke Newcomb, died in 1973.

We now turn to the children of Yolande Hoke and Laurance Sterne Gordon—my mother Yolande "Yo" Westcott Gordon and her siblings Virginia "Jinks" Stone Gordon and Laurance Sterne Gordon, Jr.—and spouses Dan Broderick (Yo), Doug Guy (Jinks), and Pat Kirby (Larry). The following "GEN 11" segment also features Jinks, Yo, and Larry's first cousin William "Bill" Adrian Newcomb and their second cousin Richard "Dick" Hampton Neergaard who share lineage as direct descendants of "GEN 1" Richard and Joanna Adams Westcott.

GENERATION 11 – 1919–2018

The Greatest Generation Reaps the Benefit of an
Expansionary Period on the Heels of World War II

My Parents, Aunts, and Uncles

Yolande Westcott Gordon & Daniel Thomas Broderick, Jr.
Virginia "Jinks" Stone Gordon & Douglas Bennett Guy
Laurance Sterne Gordon, Jr. & Patricia Everett Kirby

MUCH LIKE OUR FOREBEARS, my parents, aunts, and uncles distinguished themselves as survivors. With a heavy dose of courage, perseverance, and sorrow, "GEN 11" Westcotts toiled through the Great Depression and World War II, though I learned nothing of their protracted struggles in the aftermath of the infamous market crash of 1929. It would have been up to their parents to navigate a way out of the proverbial abyss, but together they somehow mustered through the worst economic downturn in the history of the industrialized world. It lasted a full decade.

Our parents—among the "Greatest Generation"—carried the scars of the economic war as they entered a period of military bloodshed. As we are about to learn, however, "GEN 11" Westcott descendants lived through an era of unprecedented prosperity as well. In their case, the worst of times preceded the best of times. As we all know too well, nothing lasts forever.

At the end of this narrative on the Gordon siblings and their spouses, I bring into focus their two closest contemporaries on the side of their mother, Yolande—first cousin William "Bill" Adrian Newcomb (wife Susan "Susie" Hester) and second cousin Richard "Dick" Hampton Neergaard (wife Lois Gardner). This book would not have come to fruition if not for the invaluable family archives provided by Susie Newcomb and Dick Neergaard. Their enthusiastic embrace of our family's legacy helped me piece together the complicated puzzle that put *The Westcott Story* in motion.

In lieu of addressing each of our "GEN 11" relatives in age order, I opted to begin with my mother—the middle child—and then branch out to my extended family. The Brodericks, Guys, and Gordons are profiled in this sequence in the remaining generational segments that follow.

Yolande "Yo" Westcott Gordon (1920–1995) & Daniel Thomas Broderick, Jr. (1919–2010)

In Duluth, Minnesota, on September 9, 1920, Yolande Hoke Gordon gave birth to my mother, **Yolande Westcott Gordon**, on the northern banks of Lake Superior—the largest of the five Great Lakes in North America. Recall that **Yolande Westcott Gordon** is the name my grandmother unofficially claimed for herself upon arriving from France a year earlier.

Just months after Yo's birth, the first commercially licensed radio station—Pittsburgh's KDKA—began broadcasting with America's first full-time announcer Harold W. Arlin. Airing live results of the presidential election in which Republican Warren G. Harding of Ohio won a landslide victory over Democratic Ohio Governor James M. Cox, word quickly spread of this unprecedented medium for transmitting breaking news. By the time Yo's brother Larry came along two years later, radios began to proliferate across the country. By 1926—nearly a century ago—the radio signals broadcast from more than 700 commercial stations gave birth to America's mass media.

Yo and her siblings **Virginia "Jinks" Stone (Guy)** (1919–2002) and **Laurance "Larry" Sterne Gordon, Jr.** (1922–1998) enjoyed a comfortable upbringing in Duluth despite the setbacks associated with the Great Depression. They were raised in a loving family home with French furnishings transported from their mother's beloved homeland, and the radio proved a welcome source of entertainment.

The Gordon children maintained a healthy relationship although Yo became particularly close to Larry as they grew older with families of their own. In Larry's own words referring to "Yolie" shortly before her passing in 1995: "Through the years we have been closer than most brothers and sisters and have had some very good times together." It certainly seemed that way from my perspective. Uncle Larry also became keenly interested in maintaining close ties with his Broderick and Guy nieces and nephews throughout our adult years before his death in 1998.

Although my maternal grandfather was brought up in the Presbyterian Church whose doctrine has roots in the Protestant Reformation led by Martin Luther, Laurance and Yolande raised their children in the Catholic faith. In Duluth, the youngsters attended Holy Rosary, later becoming Sacred Heart School, which was affiliated with the Benedictines' Holy Rosary Cathedral. Yo and Jinks then continued with the Benedictine Sisters at the all-girls St. Scholastica High School.

The nuns established the high school in Stanbrook Hall which sits on the Villa St. Scholastica campus on a ridge overlooking Lake Superior. It is situated next to the original St. Scholastica monastery, an academy for elementary students, and the College of St. Scholastica. Larry attended Duluth Cathedral High School—then all-boys and now co-educational and known as Marshall School.

From my mother's diary, which she dutifully maintained in tiny print from 1936 to 1939, I learned much about her teenage years. She refers to her parents as "Mother" and "Dad." The Gordons evidently employed a helper. "The maid was out so I cooked dinner." Yo hung out some with Jinks and her boyfriend and future husband, Cy Liscomb, as she mentioned "going to the Liscombs for dinner." The family kept dogs. "We got a month-old pup, 'Chum'," named after their old dog. Activities, mostly routine, included the following: attending daily mass, typically at 9am, and occasionally missing prayer breakfast; walking to church to say Confession [now known as the Sacrament of Penance and Reconciliation]; helping her mother with dinner and the dishes; taking classes—in French, Latin, History, Religion, Social Science, Geometry, English, and English Literature; walking or getting to and from school either riding with her dad or a family friend or neighbor, or taking a bus, streetcar, or taxi; doing homework, studying, and going to the library;

reading; listening to the radio; knitting sweaters as early as 15 years of age; "putsing" or "monkeying" around the house or fooling around with friends; joining friends after dinner; dating—often; hitching a ride downtown to go shopping; going to the movies—a lot; playing monopoly, cards, bridge, and Chinese checkers; ice skating, roller skating, and gliding down the toboggan slide; eating ice cream, candy, burgers, chili, baked beans and rolls, bread, and donuts; making French fries and candy; and talking on the telephone—incessantly. As to the latter, "Dad bawled me out for talking so long on the telephone . . . Then [so and so] called. Was Dad ever mad!"

From the diary entries, I also learned just how brutal the Duluth winters could be. "The radio said 30 degrees below zero. Mom didn't want us to go to school." "I did not need to go to school because it was 25 degrees below zero." "Temperature 32 below zero so no school." In 1937, my mother entered in her diary that she had been quarantined due to the flu and missed school for longer than one week. To my knowledge, she was healthy otherwise.

In 1938, accompanied by their mother and brother,
Yo and Jinks boarded the storied SS *Île de France*
destined to study at La Sorbonne in Paris, France.

For years, Laurance and Yolande intended for the girls to study at La Sorbonne after Jinks and Yo both finished high school. Yolande had insisted they become proficient in her native language. Upon her graduation in 1937, Jinks studied for one year at St. Mary's College, the sister school neighboring the University of Notre Dame in Indiana, where my sister Kathleen and I attended a generation later. During this time, Yo completed her senior year of high school in Duluth.

A caption beside Yo's senior year photo in the Stanbrook Hall yearbook reads, "And surely she had a fair personality." The yearbook also makes note of her "famous French translations." In addition, she is remembered for her youthfulness.

Once Yo graduated in the spring of 1938, Laurance and Yolande followed through on their long-contemplated game plan. Yolande accompanied Jinks, Yo, and Larry on a voyage that led them to Paris with a subsequent stop at Yolande's birthplace in Bordeaux to visit her father, Walter Scott Hoke. The idea called for Yolande to return to Duluth with Larry after dropping the girls off on their return to Paris. On the back end following one year of studies at La Sorbonne, their father Laurance would meet the girls in Paris to accompany them home.

Yolande and her children traveled by sea on the exquisite French ocean liner SS *Île de France*, likely in third class as the family lived a relatively modest lifestyle. Crossing the Atlantic on the *Île* would have been especially thrilling given the publicity and fascinating history of this vessel:

> Built in 1926 at a cost of $10 million for the Compagnie Générale Transatlantique (CTG) with a capacity of 1,786 passengers, the *Île* set sail as the first major liner erected after WWI. The Paris Exposition des Arts Decoratifs et Industriels Modernes of 1925 gave birth to the term "Art Deco," which greatly inspired the SS *Île de France's* décor. Considered the most beautiful vessel built by the CTG, an indirect lighting system illuminated all rooms of the 791-foot ocean liner, which featured kitchens reputed to serve the best cuisine on the Atlantic; trend-setting interiors; a chapel executed in the Gothic style with fourteen pillars and a seating capacity of 100; a shooting gallery; a 60-car garage; an indoor swimming pool; a bowling alley; a children's merry-go-round; a 350-seat film theater; and a state-of-the-art gymnasium.

Upon disembarking from the SS *Île de France* at Le Havre port in 1938, Yolande, Jinks, Yo, and Larry visited Paris where they met up with Laurance's brother, Jack, who happened to be traveling abroad on business. Meanwhile, the children took the opportunity to apply the fluency they developed speaking French at home and studying in school, rather than relying on their mother to negotiate their way. They had the time of their lives practicing their French while visiting the cathedrals, the Eiffel Tower, Montmartre, Versailles, and of course, the famed patisseries.

From Paris, the Gordons traveled to Arcachon, a seaside resort town in close proximity to Yolande's birthplace in the southwest of France. They then visited their grand-père Walter Hoke in Bordeaux and found him "a delightful person to get to know" as my Uncle Larry later recalled.

At the time, my great-grandfather would have been a 78-year-old retiree and a resident of the port city for some 54 years. Here, they met some of Yolande's childhood friends and their families. Based on Larry's comment about "getting to know" Walter, I get the sense that Jinks, Yo, and Larry had not previously met or traveled abroad to visit their maternal grandfather. Despite the distance, Yolande did manage to maintain a close relationship with her father from Duluth.

In an instant, rumblings of another world war
shattered the Gordons' ambitious plans.

As Jinks and Yo prepared to enter La Sorbonne in Paris, Nazi Germans threatened to invade Czechoslovakia. Having lived through WWI as a Red Cross nurse in Bordeaux, Yolande grew justifiably fearful of the real possibility of another world war. Consequently, and in abrupt fashion, our family aborted their ill-fated plan for the girls and instead scrambled to find safe passage back to the United States. In Bordeaux, the Gordons found themselves perilously close to military moves that ultimately led to France and the United Kingdom declaring war on Germany:

> After the first world war, the re-drawn map of Europe captured the formation of several new countries. Three million Germans found themselves living in Sudetenland, the part of Czechoslovakia that had been stripped from Austria by the Treaty of Saint-Germain at the end of World War I. When Chancellor Adolf Hitler came to power in 1933, he set out to unite all Germans into one nation, including those living in the Sudetenland. In 1936, he sent German troops into the Rhineland and in March 1938, he took Austria, joining it with Germany. Czechoslovakia became the logical next step for his aggression. Führer Hitler directed the German Nazis in the Sudetenland to stir up the trouble, which led to the ensuing crisis and the Gordons' troubles abroad.

As news of French mobilization broke in response to Nazi Germany aggression, Yolande clamored to exit the country with vivid memories of her experience in Bordeaux during WWI. Bidding a terribly sad and final adieu to her father, Yolande and the children faced difficulty getting back to Paris in the presence of heightened activity gearing up in preparation for possible war. On arrival, Yolande contacted an executive with the Cunard Lines whom she knew, perhaps associated with the family's recent inbound voyage on board the SS *Île de France*. She learned from him that German ships provided the only option to get back to America directly from France. They contemplated the possibility that the ships would become interred if the factions declared war. Alternatively, the cruise line executive suggested an indirect route that took them first to Scotland where they found space on the U.S. luxury liner SS *Washington* destined for New York. The ship was predictably overcrowded due to the mass exodus prompted by the threat of war.

The anxious SS *Washington* passengers could not
have imagined a threat greater than the one they
escaped in Europe as they powered through billowing
clouds and gathering swells in the open seas.

A few light moments came when the Gordons encountered Fats Waller among those aboard the ship. At age 16, my Uncle Larry joined the acclaimed American musician and composer in entertaining passengers who naturally felt ill at ease. But an emerging natural disaster cut short their playful diversionary tactics.

As if the circumstances were not already dire, the SS *Washington* got caught in the crosshairs of a tropical cyclone while making the transatlantic crossing toward New York. Thick, overhead clouds almost close enough to touch gave way to squalls and intensifying gale force winds. As the ocean liner rolled furiously in mountainous seas, sickened passengers literally strapped themselves to their beds, hanging on for dear life. They rode out the terrifying ordeal hungry, barely able to stand, surrounded by rivers of their own vomit. The "Great New England Hurricane" of 1938 became one of the most destructive tropical cyclones in recorded history to strike the region of Long Island and southern New England:

Without warning, the officially unnamed Category 3 storm developed near the Cape Verde Islands in the eastern Atlantic the day after my mother's 18th birthday, on September 10, 1938. While expected to make landfall in south Florida, the storm suddenly changed course, instead threatening the Northeast corridor. With Europe on the brink of war over the worsening Sudetenland crisis, the media gave little attention to the powerful hurricane at sea where my grandmother, mother, aunt, and uncle found themselves sitting ducks on a passenger steamship in the middle of the Atlantic Ocean.

Advanced meteorological technology such as radar, radio buoys, and satellite imagery had not yet been developed to warn of the hurricane's impending approach. By the time the U.S. Weather Bureau learned of the CAT 3 storm's collision course with Long Island on September 21st, it was too late to alert those in its direct path. The back page warning about the approaching hurricane in the *New York Times* hardly received notice as readers devoured page after page of unnerving reports and commentary about Hitler's aggressive stance toward Czechoslovakia. The last tropical cyclone that had come close to Long Island and New England struck 35 years earlier, in 1903, and it had proved inconsequential.

Surges of ocean water and waves 40 feet tall swallowed coastal homes along the south shore of Long Island, New York. In New London, Connecticut, a short circuit in a flooded building started a fire fanned by 100 mph winds, consuming much of the business district. Winds in excess of 120 mph caused a storm surge of 12 to 15 feet in Narragansett Bay, Rhode Island, destroying coastal homes and entire fleets of boats at yacht clubs and marinas. Bay waters submerged the downtown area of Providence, Rhode Island, under more than 13 feet of water. An observatory south of Boston recorded astounding 185 mph wind gusts. "Old Ironside"—the historic ship U.S.S. *Constitution*—ripped from its mooring in Boston Navy Yard. All told, the devastating tropical cyclone took 600 lives.

As calm followed the ferocious storm, passengers on the SS *Washington* regained their footing and finally received permission to move about. Yolande, Jinks, Yo, and Larry arrived on deck just as the Statue of Liberty came into view on approach to New York City. An overwhelming feeling came over our family and the others as the weary passengers absorbed the reality of having survived this nightmare. A universal symbol of enduring freedom and democracy dedicated in 1886 by the people of France to the people of the United States to commemorate the countries' alliance during the American Revolution, the "crowned lady" holding the lit torch made a lasting impression on anxious passengers who were more than ready to disembark on American soil. They emerged as survivors of the deadly natural disaster and safely distant from the man-made one then brewing on the other side of the Atlantic Ocean.

My grandfather Laurance traveled from Duluth to meet his distraught wife and children in New York. As New York residents, Yolande's siblings Hampton, Wessie, and Nina undoubtedly comforted the Gordons with their presence as well.

Jinks and Yo likely suffered grave disappointment knowing how narrowly they missed the opportunity to spend a year in Paris fulfilling their mother's long-held desire for them. Instead, their father drove the family from New York and dropped the girls off at St. Mary's College where Yo entered as a freshman and Jinks returned as a sophomore. The quietude of the small Midwestern liberal arts Catholic women's college contrasting with the vibrancy promised in the "City of Light" brings to mind the adjustment required of Yolande when she moved to Duluth from Bordeaux 18 years earlier.

At Notre Dame, Yo met the partner who would
give her a future in Pittsburgh, Pennsylvania, and
set the course for the next 56 years of her life.

As providence would have it, Yolande Westcott Gordon found the pearl in her oyster, not at the Cathédrale Notre-Dame de Paris but at the University of Notre Dame across the road from St. Mary's. The stars aligned with the blind date that brought my parents together during Yo's one and only year as a St. Mary's student. In the fall of 1938, Yo Gordon met her future husband, **Daniel "Danny" Thomas Broderick, Jr.** (1919–2010), then a sophomore enrolled at the University of Notre Dame.

A native of Pittsburgh, my father was the oldest of four boys born to **Daniel "Danny" Thomas Broderick, Sr.** (1893–1988) and **Charlotte Olive née Phillips** (1900–1977). Dan and Charlotte raised their sons in the township of Dormont at 1812 Montpelier Avenue in Pittsburgh's South Hills. Danny attended the neighboring pre-K to 8th grade Brookline School and later, Dormont High School followed by Duquesne Prep School. Danny's father "DTB Sr." had realized much success in the wholesale lumber trade in spite of his own limited formal education. As a result, he and Charlotte had the financial means to put their children through college.

At my grandfather's urging, DTB Jr. enrolled in the engineering program at Notre Dame. Quickly learning that he did not have a mind for sciences, he changed his major to journalism instead. As extracurricular activities, he contributed articles to the student newspaper and "woke up the echoes" cheering the *Fighting Irish* to victory as a cheerleader and avid fan of the famed football program. Thus began my parents' lifelong obsession with everything "Notre Dame."

> The legendary Knute Rockne had led three national championships during his 13-year run as head coach of the Fighting Irish from 1918 to 1930. Football standout Frank Leahy continued the winning streak with four more national championships during his coaching tenure in the span of 11 seasons, from 1941–1943 and 1946–1953. These "wins" followed Irish championships in 1929 and 1930 when Leahy played tackle at Notre Dame for coach Knute Rockne.

As revealed in her diary, Yo spent time in South Bend at The Moderne—a restaurant, soda fountain, and candy store at 110 W. Washington Street (1929–1967); The Philadelphia, a confectionary, restaurant, soda fountain, and bakery at 116 N. Michigan Street (1901–1972); the Oliver Theatre (1909–1953) at 126 N. Main Street; and Rosie's Sunny Italy Café (1926–present)—still a staple patronized by the Brodericks when at Notre Dame for home football weekends. She also references LaSalle Grill, German Village, and the Progress Club at 601 W. Colfax (1895-present), a women's organization dedicated to community improvement through volunteerism. Yo is known to have crossed over U.S. Route 31 to Notre Dame for mass and breakfast. She also spent some time at St. Edward's Hall; attended Notre Dame football and basketball games; and dressed for a prom—"Got an orchid. Henry Busse Orchestra. Wonderful."

Despite the allure of Notre Dame's fighting Irish and the romance that grounded her to the campus, Yo spent just one year at St. Mary's College.

News of Adolf Hitler's audacious and swift attacks grew tensions and strategic maneuvering abroad and at home.

I do not know why my mother left St. Mary's, but presume the declaration of war on Germany on September 3, 1939—at the start of what would have been her sophomore year—may have been a contributor if not *the* deciding factor:

> When Hitler occupied what remained of Czechoslovakia in March 1939, it appeared too late for successful diplomatic or military resistance by U.S. allies, yet a failure to resist risked German domination of the continent. On September 3, with the decision by the Soviet Union to sign a pact with Hitler, and two days after Nazi Germany invaded Poland, the French and British governments reluctantly declared war on Germany.

As tensions rose on both sides of the Atlantic, Jinks and Yo returned home from St. Mary's and continued their studies on familiar grounds at the all-women's College of Scholastica in Duluth as "day-hoppers."

The College of St. Scholastica closely parallels St. Mary's rich history, Catholic affiliation, liberal arts orientation, architectural style, and expansive natural surroundings. St. Scholastica dates to 1892 with the founding of a mother house and an academy for elementary students by the Order of St. Benedict. The high school came along three years later, which the Benedictines situated in Stanbrook Hall before adding the four-year college in 1924. The Sisters of the Holy Cross founded St. Mary's College even earlier, in 1844.

Both during high school and when they attended the neighboring college at Villa St. Scholastica, Jinks and Yo would have been dropped off at the base of the steep entryway for the long climb to reach their classrooms if they took the streetcar or bus as was often the case.

In 1940, the Gordon sisters served together on the college's "Date Committee," Jinks as a junior and Yolande as a sophomore. The "Bio-Scriptions" column in the May 8, 1940, issue of St. Scholastica's *Scriptorium* had this to say about my mother: "A perpetual fixture in the Alpha Chi [a club for non-residents], she's pigeon-toed in a cute way—vivacious and always has an answer for every remark—she's French and oh la la—qui qui bonjour *Yolande Gordon*."

According to school records, Yo left the College of St. Scholastica after her sophomore year, but I could not ascertain whether Jinks pulled out at the same time without graduating. Shortly after leaving St. Scholastica, Yo's name came up in the November 27, 1940, issue of the *Scriptorium*. In the column, "Kathy Tells Who's Doing What, Where, When and With Whom," Kathy writes, "And here I still am with my echo and shadow . . . life is 'ard! Do you remember *Yolande Gordon*, who was here last year? She has just had a unique and right enviable trip to Notre Dame U., which had several climaxes . . . notably, the Sophomore Cotillion dance, and the Iowa-N. D. game." Yo's beau "Danny" would have been enrolled as a Notre Dame senior at the time, so the reference to the "Sophomore" Cotillion is inexplicable. [Incidentally, the erratic 1940 football season left the Irish with seven wins and two losses in consecutive shutouts to Iowa and Northwestern.]

Dan Broderick remained at Notre Dame to complete his journalism studies while maintaining a long-distance romance with Yo Gordon who then lived in Duluth. They exchanged letters often. In the autumn of his senior year in 1940—a full year before the Japanese attack on Pearl Harbor—the first peacetime draft instituted in U.S. history required all men between the ages of 21 and 45 to register.

Midway through the football season while living in Room 104 at Sorin Hall next to Notre Dame's landmark "Golden Dome," Dan Broderick completed his registration on October 16, 1940. Then aged 21 years, his draft card (Order # 920) reflects these features: "white race; blue eyes; brown hair; light brown complexion; 5'10" tall; 155 lbs." The card did not capture "handsome" as one of his distinguishing physical marks.

Up to this point, U.S. ambivalence about the war grew out of the isolationist sentiment that had pervaded the American political landscape since World War I. Democrat Franklin Delano Roosevelt (1882–1945), who won a record four presidential elections, chose to assist the Allies but remain out of WWII. "FDR" increased America's presence in the North Atlantic with the congressionally approved Lend-Lease bill in March 1941. He then mobilized the Atlantic Fleet, making clear our country's intention to protect lend-lease supplies going to our allies while sealing my father's fate in support of those plans.

Dan Broderick answered the call of duty by enlisting with the U.S. Navy upon his graduation from Notre Dame in the spring of 1941. For 16 weeks, he attended the United States Naval Reserve Midshipmen's School at Northwestern University in Chicago, Illinois, before finding himself drawn into the fray as a commissioned junior officer:

> Northwestern University, Columbia University, and the University of Notre Dame entered a contract with the federal government to support a Midshipmen's School to train and produce naval officers. Most candidates graduated from officer training by completing a three-month course focused on navigation, seamanship, and ordnance. In Chicago, around the same time Dan Broderick trained, a young John F. Kennedy attended a two-month accelerated program for commissioned officers before receiving PT boat training in Melville, Rhode Island. Eventually, my father was to follow a similar course in Melville.

Studies, drills, exercises, and inspections endeavored to trade the men's civilian habits for those of the U.S. Navy. While Dan Broderick received 16 weeks of instruction, the Midshipmen's School also produced "90-day wonders" upon completion of the accelerated training program. By the time the war ended in 1945, nearly 25,000 men from around the country received training on Northwestern's Chicago campus where they quickly became accustomed to the midshipmen's life.

Appointed "midshipman" on October 16, 1941, Daniel
T. Broderick, Jr. spent a brief period on the home
front preparing for deployment before the catastrophic
December 7, 1941, attack on Pearl Harbor unleashed all
forces with America's declaration of war. DTB Jr. received
his commission as "Ensign" on January 16, 1942.

In the early stages of the war, as the United States engaged its navy
to support her allies in Europe, Japan strongly allied with Germany. At
the same time, Japan removed itself militarily as the island nation instead
focused on waging a war of conquest in Southeast Asia. The progression
of U.S. preparation for entry into WWII culminated with the Japanese
attack against U.S. naval and military bases at Pearl Harbor on December
7, 1941. Japan's devastating surprise attack on U.S. soil destroyed 188
aircraft and two battleships—the USS *Arizona* and USS *Oklahoma*—
and sank or damaged three cruisers, three destroyers, and an anti-aircraft
training ship and minelayer. In a stunning offensive move, the military
strike by the Imperial Japanese Navy Air Service killed 2,403 Americans
and wounded 1,178 others.

America's true colors came to light with the declaration of war following the horrific Pearl Harbor attack. One day later, Congress declared
war on Imperial Japan with only a single dissenting vote. Japan's allies,
Germany and Italy, responded by declaring war against the United States.
German Unterseebooten "U-boat" submarines sunk ships almost as fast
as the U.S. and our allies could build them. The Maritime Commission
established 18 new shipyards along America's West, East, and Gulf coasts,
producing 5,500 vessels in assembly-line fashion. Among them, 2,751
mass-produced Liberty ships supported the war effort.

As reprisal following the Pearl Harbor blitz, Americans rallied in
enthusiastic support of the war effort. Putting isolationism aside, our
patriotic nation pooled resources from all corners with everyone contributing in some capacity. United in resolve to defeat the Axis powers,
America emerged as a formidable world power in her own right.

A call to action cascaded from President Franklin D. Roosevelt
to patriotic communities across the country, among them
my father's alma mater, the University of Notre Dame.

Emblematic of the patriotism that followed America's declaration of war, Notre Dame President Rev. Hugh O'Donnell, C.S.C. addressed the university's faculty and students with this urgent appeal:

> "The hour has come. Our Chief Executive and Congress have spoken. We are at war with its accompanying death, bloodshed, and suffering. Our armed forces will respond to the call as will all true Americans. Today, Notre Dame is One. She has known the grim horrors of past wars. The fact is that the peaks of her history are shrouded in the mists of war. In accordance with her strong tradition of patriotism, the University pledges unswerving loyalty and devotion to the Commander-in-Chief of our country and places her facilities at his disposal. We stand united behind him and pray hourly to God to strengthen his arm during the perilous days that lie ahead. We also bespeak Divine Guidance for Congress and all military and civil authorities in execution of their trust so that in due time our country may be victorious and peace may be restored to the people of the world who love and cherish it.

> "There is no reason why students should become unduly alarmed at this time, notwithstanding the swiftness with which war has come. Do not be carried away by violent emotion, which leads to confused thinking and acting. Go about your normal ways until such time as our country calls. This is what Notre Dame expects of you; this is what your parents desire of you. This is the best way to serve our country.

> "As our beloved President so well expressed it yesterday in his message to the Congress: 'With confidence in our armed forces—with the unbounded determination of our people—we will gain the inevitable triumph—so help us God.'"

The University of Notre Dame faced a dilemma shared by many of the nation's colleges as WWII heated up. The draft and volunteers recruited for the war effort placed a severe strain on student enrollment. Pressed to find a solution, University President Rev. Hugh O'Donnell, C.S.C. allowed the Navy to establish training programs on campus. The Navy responded with an influx of cash and some 12,000 trainees over the course of the war. The action literally saved Notre Dame from closing its doors.

When my father started his senior year in the fall of 1940, Notre Dame enrolled a total of 3,252 students. He is counted as one of 5,639 former students who entered the armed forces of World War II as of mid-November in 1944. Overall, as the world plunged into global conflict 21 years after WWI ended, 16 million men and women answered the call to serve during WWII, representing 11% of America's population of 140 million in 1945.

Dan Broderick activated overseas on three separate occasions:

March 20 to October 1, 1942
March 1 to December 18, 1943
April 29 to November 15, 1944

In 1950, the Commonwealth of Pennsylvania credited my father for 24 months of active domestic service and 23 months of active foreign service, authorizing $500 in total compensation in the form of a "bonus."

Beginning little more than three months following Japan's attack of U.S. naval and military bases at Pearl Harbor, Ensign Dan Broderick entered the fray as a gunnery officer on merchant vessels supplying goods and war material to our allies around the world.

The vital role of the naval auxiliary Merchant Marine gave rise to the "Liberty" fleet and Dan Broderick's engagement during both his first and second foreign deployments:

> The Merchant Marine served to support the U.S. Navy by delivering military personnel and a lifeline of supplies to Allied—and eventually American—fighting forces overseas. Men at the fronts depended

on these mariners for explosives, fuel, guns, ammunition, army tanks, planes, food, medicine, and sundry other materials needed for warfare.

The U.S. acknowledged that if Great Britain fell to Germany, we would have no allies in Western Europe. Under the Lend-Lease program which enabled the President to transfer arms and equipment to any nation deemed vital to our defense, the U.S. agreed to build commercial ships for Great Britain according to the Royal Navy's design specifications.

The U.S. government controlled the cargo and the destinations, contracted with private companies to operate the ships, and put guns and naval personnel on board—my father among them. The government trained civilian merchant sailors to operate the "Liberty" ships and assisted them in manning the guns through the U.S. Maritime Service. Each Liberty ship carried a crew of between 38 and 62 mariners and another 21 to 40 naval personnel who operated the defensive guns and communications equipment. Introduced in late 1943 and early 1944—around the time Dan Broderick moved from the Merchant Marine to a PT squadron in the Central Mediterranean—the larger, faster "Victory" joined the Liberty fleet carrying a typical crew of 62 private seamen and 28 naval personnel.

Considered ugly ducklings, the cargo vessels lacked speed and maneuverability, but they were easy to build quickly because of the simple design. The Liberty ships reached a top speed of just 11 knots; the Victory carried a cruising speed of 15–17 knots.

Unable to secure the complete military records of Daniel Thomas Broderick, Jr., I did not learn which convoys he joined with the Merchant Marine, only the dated increments of his foreign service. I do know that his training took him along several unknown routes with allied merchantmen during his first foreign deployment, from March 20 to October 1, 1942.

During his first break from active service as a gunner under unrelenting enemy attack, my father returned stateside from October 2, 1942 to March 1, 1943. Within a week of his return, he married his long-distance sweetheart in Minnesota.

Ensign Broderick married Yo Gordon at Our Lady of the Rosary Cathedral in her hometown of Duluth on October 8, 1942. The wedding announcement appeared days later in the *Pittsburgh Sun-Telegraph*. Dan Jr.'s brother Bill and Yo's sister Jinks (then married to her first husband Charles "Cy" C. Liscomb) served as best man and matron of honor. The wedding party included four attendants, four ushers, and Dan's youngest brother, Bob—16 years his junior—serving as page boy. The Broderick family traveled to Duluth from Pittsburgh via train for the celebratory occasion.

The newlyweds later left Duluth on a trip to Pennsylvania and New York with a stopover in South Bend where they stayed at the LaSalle Hotel. As detailed later, Jinks's husband Cy died tragically during a bomber pilot training exercise in Lubbock, Texas, a mere 21 days after Danny and Yo's wedding.

Though unconfirmed, I'm guessing that Danny and Yo spent some of their honeymoon in Pittsburgh enjoying the sites in the "Steel City." Preparing for his second foreign deployment, while my father spent four weeks in "Armed Guard" training at Little Creek, Virginia, his bride remained in Pittsburgh with his parents Dan and Charlotte Broderick. Yo also stayed with them during his second rotation in Europe, which lasted from March 1 to December 18, 1943.

As a naval officer returning for his second tour of duty, Ensign Broderick joined seamen attached to the Merchant Marine amid Arctic convoys destined for the Soviet Union on the Murmansk Run. Among all the convoy routes of World War II, the Arctic channel proved the most treacherous.

The dangers lurking in the open seas were especially acute where my father was shipped out to command a gunnery crew on the Murmansk Run aboard a cargo ship with the Merchant Marine's Liberty Fleet. As we'll learn, the perils along this route are well documented in historical military records from World War II.

Early in the war, Germany invaded and occupied many neighboring countries in mainland Europe. Germany and the Soviet Union had secretly signed a non-aggression pact agreeing that they would not attack each other, but Germany invaded the vast country in June 1941 and soon pushed deep into Soviet territory. With this turn of events, the Soviets joined the Allied powers. With justification, the western Allies quickly reached agreement to send supplies in order to assist the Soviets in their fight against the invaders. They reasoned that if the Soviet Union fell, Germany could then turn its full military might to the west.

Axis domination of the Mediterranean left open only two Allied supply routes to the Soviet Union. One, through Iran, required a sea journey of more than 13,000 miles. The second, more practical yet perilous northern route of under 2,500 miles crossed the unforgiving Arctic seas around the North Pole. This Arctic Ocean route became known as the "Murmansk Run."

Led by the British Royal Navy with the active support of her Canadian and American allies, the "Arctic Convoys" typically sailed from the United Kingdom and Iceland to northern ports in the Soviet Union, primarily Arkhangelsk (Archangel) and Murmansk, both in modern-day Russia.

German U-boats, floating mines, surface raiders, and aircraft lined up, ready to blow apart the ships and disrupt the flow of supplies destined for our Allied forces on the Russian front. Given the lurking danger, strict orders precluded merchant ships from stopping for any reason, even to assist companion ships with repairs or to rescue sailors found overboard. Eyewitnesses aboard ship recounted the terrifying moments when fellow seafarers were blown into a flaming sea of burning oil and left to die of wounds, burns, or hypothermia.

Winter brought nearly four months of unbroken darkness which helped conceal the convoys from the enemy but made navigation especially challenging. Polar ice that pushed down from the north forced all ships to make the voyage closer to German-held Norway. By one account, the subzero winds howling off the polar cap could reach hurricane velocity and whip waves as high as 70 feet. At such temperatures, sea spray froze immediately and created a top-heavy covering on anything exposed to it. The seamen had to chip away the ice to prevent the Allied ships from capsizing. While binoculars, guns, and torpedoes iced up, mirror-smooth frozen decks made it nearly impossible for the crewmen to navigate aboard ship.

Visibility also presented a problem when warmer waters of the Gulf Stream blended with the frigid Arctic waters, often creating thick fog and occasional blinding snow. The risk of collision to ships escorting or intercepting the convoys made the mission extremely dangerous. Each delivery became an epic achievement against all odds.

A call by the British Admiralty ordering commanders to scatter on July 4, 1942, culminated in an unfathomable disaster for the PQ-17 convoy, the largest and most valuable in the history of the Murmansk Run.

By the time Ensign Broderick received orders as a gunner to accompany the Merchant Marine with deliveries destined for Russia on his second tour of duty, several convoys had already run the Murmansk course carrying planes, tanks, and other war material needed by the Soviets. Knowledge of the harrowing crossing by convoy PQ-17 would have chilled him and every seaman to his core:

Undeterred by the losses of former convoys routed to the Soviet Union, PQ-17 set sail for Murmansk and Archangel in June 1942 with a cargo worth a staggering $700 million. Nearly 300 aircraft, 600 tanks, more than 4,000 trucks and trailers, and a general cargo exceeding 150,000 tons found space in the bulging holds. Leaving Reykjavik, Iceland, six destroyers and 15 other armed vessels escorted the 35 cargo ships—22 American, eight British, two Russian, two Panamanian, and one Dutch.

The ships took up their appointed positions in nine columns and plodded ahead at only 7 or 8 knots. Trailing PQ-17 by roughly 200 miles, the British Home Fleet provided distant cover. The reinforcements included the battleship "Her Majesty's Ship" HMS *Duke of York*, two cruisers, and 14 destroyers backed by the battleship USS *Washington* and the carrier HMS *Victorious*. A cruiser force consisting of HMS *London* and *Norfolk*, USS *Tuscaloosa* and *Wichita*, and three U.S. destroyers engaged 40 miles north of the convoy to provide closer cover. Unknown to the men of PQ-17, German intelligence already held in hand details of the convoy's size and importance. The patrolling submarine *U-456* spotted the convoy as soon as it reached open water.

Acknowleding the imminent danger, the British Admiralty stripped PQ-17 of all protection and abandoned with orders to scatter. The admiral of the fleet, Sir Dudley Pound, opted to save the warships and let the merchantmen fend for themselves. He reasoned individual ships stood a better chance of survival against superior surface forces than vessels crowded together with the restrictions of a convoy.

Upon receiving confirmation of the orders, PQ-17's protection turned at high speed to join the cruiser force some 40 miles away. Before the last of the escorts disappeared over the western horizon on July 4, 1942, the ships of the convoy began breaking up their well-disciplined lines in all directions. The order to scatter resulted in a predictable German slaughter. The attacks continued for four days without respite beginning on July 5. Frantic distress signals from stricken ships reached the Arctic airwaves to no avail. Today, twenty-three of the merchant ships—14 of them American—and their cargoes lie sprawled on the ocean floor of the Arctic Circle, the wreckage resting on the Barents seabed. More than 120 seamen were killed, countless others crippled and maimed. With the loss of 210 combat planes, 430 Sherman tanks, 3,350 vehicles, and nearly 100,000 tons of other cargo, the financial loss exceeded half a billion dollars.

For the Royal Navy, the massacre of PQ-17 and the abandonment of the convoy became one of the most shameful episodes of the war at sea. Sir Winston Churchill called it "one of the most melancholy naval episodes in the whole war."

Following the launch of Russian deliveries by the subsequent PQ-18 convoy, in November 1942, the Royal Navy halted Murmansk runs temporarily as the military urgently needed ships to support *Operation Torch*, the Allied invasion of North Africa. The stoppage came the month following the nuptials of Dan and Yo Gordon Broderick in Duluth and lasted nearly three months. The treacherous Murmansk sea campaign resumed during the latter part of my father's five-month domestic service as he prepared for his second foreign tour with the allied seamen.

Ensign Dan Broderick would have been keenly aware of the PQ-17 fiasco when he set out for the North Arctic with the Merchant Marine. He reported for assignment on this route as a gunnery officer beginning on March 1, 1943. However, after running one convoy each in January and February, the Royal Navy suspended shipments to Russia through the Barents Sea to allow for the pivotal Battle of the North Atlantic. In what both the Allies and her foe considered "the greatest convoy battle of all time," the Germans fired 90 torpedoes and sank 22 merchantmen totaling 141,000 tons in the span of five days and nights, from March 12th to 17th. In the three weeks since my father began his second foreign deployment, the Allies suffered the cumulative loss of 97 merchant ships and escorts and 500,000 tons of supplies. The devastating blow caused the British Admiralty to suspend the Murmansk Run until September.

Anecdotally, I learned that the convoy to which my father and his fellow naval officers and the merchant mariners reported on March 1st became stranded and seemingly forgotten at Archangel at the edge of the frigid Arctic circle, more than 4,000 miles from America's shores. Here, upon making a vital delivery of cargo, the seafarers were informed of the suspended action which effectively delayed their exit by several months— far longer than the men imagined possible. While my father was waylaid in Archangel, the U.S. Naval Gun Crew of the USS *Francis Scott Key* presented him with a shell casing. Decades later, in an early version of his Will, he called out my brother, Terry, to receive his prized possession.

Awaiting favorable weather conditions to embark at the Archangel port with the "Lost Convoy," Ensign Dan Broderick received orders to move into the Mediterranean Theatre of operations with patrol torpedo (PT) boat Squadron Fifteen. He returned stateside for training following his second tour that ended on December 18, 1943.

The heroics of the seamen on the Murmansk Run during and after my father's naval service with the merchantmen are indelibly marked in military history:

> The Battle of the Atlantic stands as the longest continuous military campaign in World War II, lasting from September 3, 1939 to May 8, 1945. With the exception of several months at the peak of the protracted battle, the Merchant Marine convoys traversing the perilous

Arctic supply route to the Soviet Union ran from 1941 until the war's end. By one estimate, a total of 41 convoys made the Murmansk Run carrying an estimated $18 billion in cargo from the United States, Great Britain, and Canada during this period. The millions of tons of supplies included 12,206 aircraft, 12,755 tanks, 51,503 jeeps, 300,000 trucks, 1,181 locomotives, 11,155 flatcars, 135,638 rifles and machine guns, 473 million shells, 2.67 tons of fuel, and 15 million pairs of boots.

Nearly 100 ships succumbed to enemy action and the abysmal weather. Allied losses in the Arctic eventually exceeded those in the sea lanes of the North Atlantic. Before the war ended, the Arctic route accounted for nearly 37% of all Allied surface ships sunk in all theatres of the war. President Roosevelt paid homage to the unflagging efforts of the Merchant mariners when he said, "[Mariners] have delivered the goods when and where needed in every theater of operations and across every ocean in the biggest, the most difficult and dangerous job ever undertaken." A total of 243,000 civilians served with the Merchant Marine in the war; 9,521 perished while in service, and yet, unlike my father and his fellow navy seamen, the merchant mariners did not receive benefits afforded WWII veterans as members of the armed services.

Upon receiving orders to join a PT squadron in the Central Mediterranean, Ensign Dan Broderick prepared for his third and final tour in the spring of 1944.

Returning to the U.S. for four months before Dan Broderick's third and final tour, my brother Danny was conceived. Sometime during this same timeframe, between December 19, 1943, and April 28, 1944, my father received eight weeks of training at the Motor Torpedo Boat Squadron Training Center (MTBSTC) on the outskirts of Portsmouth in Melville, Rhode Island. Nearly all of the 14,000 PT boat officers and enlisted men trained at the small Navy base on Narragansett Bay— Lieutenant John Fitzgerald Kennedy among them. Here, Dan Broderick got his first taste of high-speed drills specialized in patrol torpedo "PT" boat operations.

During training on vessels powered with a designed speed of 41 knots, the men lived in Quonset huts on the base. These metal huts each housed roughly two dozen sailors, their gear, cots, and a stove heater in the center of the room. Despite the inclement New England winter weather, the men mustered through snow and ice to complete their training on shore and at sea. Just in time for the spring thaw, Dan Broderick prepared to ship out. From April 29, 1944, to November 15, 1944, my father resumed active foreign duty aboard one of 42 PT boats in the Mediterranean attached to one of 41 PT squadrons commissioned by the U.S. Navy during World War II.

On the home front, workers built more than 500 PT boats in American yards during the war, including Higgins Industries' PT fleet in New Orleans, Louisiana:

> PT boats offered accommodation for three officers and 14 enlisted men for a total crew of 17. Each PT squadron carried 12 boats during WWII. Armed with torpedoes, rockets, mortars, and machine guns, the PTs intercepted ships of larger classes with firepower.

> Primarily designed for high-speed torpedo attacks against much larger adversaries, PT boats fulfilled a host of vital roles in the Pacific, English Channel, and Mediterranean during World War II. Their sleek hulls and engine power provided the Allies with a ready shallow-draft gun platform that proved fast, seaworthy, and highly maneuverable. The PT boats penetrated minefields, harbor defenses, and harassing enemy coastal traffic, shore installations, and small craft. As the war progressed, the PT boat became strictly a gunboat, distinguishing herself as a highly versatile combat vessel.

> In the Mediterranean Sea, PT boats patrolled the coasts of southern France and northern Italy. The squadrons focused on disrupting and destroying enemy supply ships, particularly German vessels supplying troops in North Africa. The Higgins PT boats ruled this theatre, primarily using the torpedo as the weapon of choice because of the types of ships they encountered.

The Navy promoted my father to lieutenant and commander of *PT-201*, one of the 42 PT boats that served in the Mediterranean. Higgins Industries placed the 78-foot *PT-201* in service from New Orleans,

Louisiana, in January 1943. However, Lieutenant Broderick did not take command of the vessel before April 1944 when he returned for his third tour of duty. With the exception of 36 PT boats loaned to Britain and the Soviet Union under the Lend-Lease program, the fleet served for varying lengths of time under U.S. colors:

> In addition to the 42 PTs that served in the Mediterranean, roughly 350 PTs deployed in the Pacific theater and 33 in the English Channel. By war's end, the American fleet had fired 354 torpedoes and reportedly sank 38 vessels totaling 23,700 tons. The Americans lost four PTs with five officers and 19 men killed in action. All told, a total of 1,554 American and foreign flag ships sank due to war conditions, while hundreds of others incurred damage caused by torpedoes, shelling, bombs, kamikazes, and mines.
>
> President John F. Kennedy, who in 1943 commanded the ill-fated *PT-109* in the Solomon Islands as a scrawny 25-year-old lieutenant, said "PT boats were an embodiment of Field's words: 'I wish to have no connection with any ship that does not sail fast, for I intend to go in harm's way.' PT boats served an important role in the shallow waters, complementing the achievements of greater ships in greater seas."

For his service with the United States Navy, Lieutenant Daniel T. Broderick, Jr. received a commendation from Acting Secretary of the Navy Artemus L. Gates with the following citation:

> "For outstanding performance of duty as Captain of a PT Boat, operating with Motor Torpedo Boat Squadron FIFTEEN during offensive action against the enemy in the Central Mediterranean from June to October 1944. A fearless and resourceful leader, Lieutenant Broderick skillfully conducted numerous extremely hazardous patrols in hostile waters and carried out many vital intelligence and raiding missions despite severe opposition prior to and during tactical operations which culminated in the successful advance of our armies on the Italian Mainland and the invasion of Southern France. By his expert ship-handling and cool courage throughout this important period of bitter hostilities, Lieutenant Broderick contributed materially to the expeditious attainment of major objectives by the Allied forces and upheld the highest traditions of the United States Naval Service."

While my father and his PT crew fulfilled a vital role in the Mediterranean theatre, his pregnant wife rode out the anxious months in Duluth, by this time living with her parents. Just one week following my father's return from his last foreign deployment, on November 22, 1944, Yo gave birth in Duluth to my oldest sibling, Daniel Thomas Broderick III.

In the months following Danny's birth, a series of monumental historical events unfolded in rapid succession, becoming indelibly etched in the minds of war-weary 20th-century Americans.

On April 12, 1945, the revered President Franklin D. Roosevelt died of a cerebral hemorrhage early in this fourth term in office. Vice President Harry S. Truman scarcely saw President Roosevelt and had received no briefing on the development of the atomic bomb. Upon assuming the presidency, he learned details of the "Manhattan Project," a secret U.S. government research project that endeavored to create the first atomic bomb. "I felt like the moon, the stars, and all the planets had fallen on me." Along with this development, a host of emerging wartime problems of a sudden became Truman's to solve.

Nearly six months after Danny's birth and one week following Adolf Hitler's suicide, on May 8, 1945, the Allies accepted the unconditional surrender of the Axis powers. As news of Germany's surrender broke, elated crowds gathered in the streets at home to celebrate the declared "Victory in Europe" (V-E) Day. Their reception contrasted sharply with WWI's aftermath when the dispirited "Lost Generation" returned home to the debilitating Spanish flu. This time, though over 400,000 Americans made the ultimate sacrifice, "the Greatest Generation" that came of age during the Great Depression carried the torch with a resounding victory facing a jubilant throng.

The Allies' exuberance carried on V-E Day proved short-lived, however. On the heels of the declared victory in Europe, Lieutenant Broderick received orders to deploy with *Operation Downfall* for the invasion of Japan. The orders followed the carnage that befell our military during the island-hopping battles and suicidal kamikaze attacks into enemy targets at Leyte Gulf, Saipan, Iwo Jima, and Okinawa.

Set to begin in November 1945, responsibility for proposing an Allied plan for the invasion of the Japanese home islands fell to U.S. commanders of all armed forces who offered differing viewpoints on the course forward. A key meeting occurred in the White House Oval Office on June 18, 1945, with President Truman and his chief military advisors. Truman then signed orders to shift the necessary additional troops from the European theater to the Pacific. The intent of the highly ambitious and complicated plan would have all forces invade, occupy, and bring about the unconditional surrender of Japan within 18 months of the defeat of Germany, requiring the mobilization of an astounding 1,700,000 U.S. troops.

With massive naval forces arrayed for the first phase of *Operation Downfall,* code-named *Operation Olympic,* the likelihood of victory favored the U.S. and her allies but with a horrific price to be paid. The U.S. Navy projected the sinking of no fewer than 95 U.S. ships, damage to 995 ships, and death to between 5,000 and 12,000 U.S. seamen in *Operation Olympic* alone. If executed, it would become one of the costliest battles in U.S. naval history.

In preparation for the invasion of southern Japan, the U.S. Navy temporarily stationed my father near Tacoma, presumably at Navy Yard Puget Sound in Bremerton, Washington. During this time, my mother Yo and infant Danny III joined him on the west coast and rented an apartment in Tacoma. They could not have known the gravity of what lay ahead if *Operation Downfall* had been executed as planned:

Once the atomic bomb became available, Army General George Marshall envisioned using it to support the Japanese invasion if the U.S. could produce sufficient numbers in time. The administration put in motion two planned assaults—*Operation Olympic* and *Operation Coronet.* As part of the overarching plan, the U.S. Navy's role in *Operation Olympic* called for virtually every navy unit in the

Pacific, in addition to several gathered from the European theatre. Once an amphibious landing proved successful, airbases would then set up to support *Operation Coronet*.

On President Truman's authorization, the United States detonated two nuclear weapons over the Japanese cities of Hiroshima and Nagasaki on August 6 and August 9, 1945, respectively.

Leveling extensive destruction of civilian installations, great fires raged in each city and utter confusion immediately followed the explosions. As many as 115,000 lives—perhaps many more—perished with no fewer than 95,000 injuries to soldiers and civilians in Hiroshima and Nagasaki.

The United States canceled the planned naval assault following the unconditional surrender of Japan on August 15, 1945. At long last, the weary servicemen prepared to head home. Daniel T. Broderick, Jr. separated from active service in Seattle with an honorable discharge on September 26, 1945; on June 1, 1946, the Navy retroactively promoted him to the rank of Lieutenant Commander.

A sense of normalcy returned to the home of the brave on the heels of World War II. As an acknowledged power on the world stage, America then entered an expansionary period marked by boundless opportunities.

Like our forebears, "GEN 11" in this Westcott saga developed great resilience by virtue of overcoming unprecedented adversity. In my parents' era, the harsh reality of the Great Depression pushed men, women, and children to a higher standard of personal responsibility and sacrifice. World War II went further to distinguish this generation because they united in bringing victory and restoring peace to all people at great peril.

Seemingly every man, woman, and child contributed to the successful conclusion of the war. While the warriors fought, Americans at home mobilized to equip them with the essentials for war. As well, they willingly rationed consumption on everything from rubber, gasoline, and fuel oil to sugar, coffee, meat, butter, milk, and soap.

In their own way, my parents epitomized this generation of humble, frugal, hard-working, ambitious, God-fearing Americans. Through their sacrifices and with integrity, they instilled the values that my contemporaries hold dear in their honor. With the hard-fought war finally won, the time came to put it behind them and seize the opportunities that our democratic ideals made possible:

> On the home front, the massive mobilization effort during WWII put Americans back to work. Unemployment, which had reached 25% during the Great Depression and hovered at 14.6% at the start of the war, dropped to 1.2% by 1944.
>
> By 1945, Americans saved at abnormal levels, averaging 21% of their personal disposable income compared to just 3% in the 1920s. Eager to spend their money, consume they did. The U.S. experienced a period of phenomenal economic growth and middle-class expansion, fueled largely by automobile sales and a housing boom for returning servicemen. Home ownership provided the single greatest opportunity for wealth accumulation.
>
> The G.I. Bill, formally known as the Servicemen's Readjustment Act of 1944, afforded a range of benefits to returning service members, including training, secondary and higher education, and housing assistance through the Veterans Administration (VA). Many service members qualified for housing assistance through the VA, but not all homes were considered insurable by the Federal Housing Administration (FHA). The FHA placed policy limitations and restrictive covenants on homes found in many impoverished urban neighborhoods; in its underwriting manual, the FHA advised that "the presence of inharmonious racial or nationality groups made a neighborhood's housing undesirable for insurance." As a consequence, many minority veterans, and especially Black Americans who also fought gallantly in the war, faced a difficult transition with fewer opportunities to secure mortgages and thereby build wealth through home ownership.

When the war ended, my father returned to Pittsburgh with his bride and infant son. According to his father, Daniel Thomas Broderick, Sr., Dan Jr. returned from WWII a changed man. Evidently, though not surprisingly, the war hardened him. But it did not stop him from riding the expansionary wave in the wholesale lumber trade while growing a family in his hometown where his parents, brothers—William "Bill" Phillips, John "Jack" Martin, and Robert "Bob" Edward—and many of his aunts and uncles also lived. For a time, Dan Sr. employed all four sons in his wholesale lumber business, D.T. Broderick Lumber Company. Eventually, only Bob left Pittsburgh; he pursued master's and law degrees from the University of Michigan before establishing a real estate law practice in Rutland, Vermont, where he and his first wife, Anne, raised their two sons. Among this generation of Brodericks, only Bob still lives. He resides with his second wife, Sue, in Hendersonville, North Carolina.

The Brodericks' proud heritage in Pittsburgh stemmed from my great-grandparents, the Irish immigrant John J. Broderick and his wife Mary Jane Dillon.

MY GRANDFATHER'S PATERNAL LINE descends from the southwestern Irish countryside of Ballylongford, a "town land" located outside of Listowel in County Kerry. My paternal great-grandfather **John J. Broder** (1860–1949) was born to **Patrick** and **Honora Broder** in the year of my maternal great-grandfather Walter Scott Hoke's birth in 1860. Coinciding with a move into the town of Listowel from Ballylongford, my family anglicized the "Broder" surname to "Broderick." As a means of assimilating and gaining acceptance by the British whose parliament then governed the Emerald Isle, many Irish families adopted an anglicized version of their surname upon moving from "town lands" into the town centers.

John J. Broder(ick) arrived in America around 1879, during the time of Ireland's second potato famine:

> Known in Ireland as "The Great Hunger," the first "Irish Potato Famine" marked a period of mass death from starvation and disease between 1845 and 1852. Dispossessed of their ancestral land following centuries of British colonial rule, most of the native Irish, Catholic population lived in extreme poverty and depended on the potato as their main food source for survival. Part of the United

Kingdom at this time, Ireland lived in the shadow of Britain's boom years in the throes of the industrial revolution. As Britain exported critical food sources from Ireland for their own benefit, the island's masses fell victim to starvation, diseases that preyed on people weakened by food loss, and eviction with no relief from the exorbitant rents imposed by unscrupulous landlords. The Great Hunger devastated Ireland with more than one million deaths and another 1.5 million forced to flee the country.

The 1879 famine, which mostly affected the west of Ireland, leveled a new round of raging hunger to the struggling people. Just three decades following the Great Hunger, a potato crop ravaged by blight and the fear of starvation and eviction returned to Ireland's door. Driven by panic and desperation, another wave of emigrants left the Emerald Isle, many destined for the United States.

On arrival to America from County Kerry as a young man, John went directly to Pittsburgh where he joined an Irish contingent on the north side of the Allegheny and Ohio rivers, in close proximity to present day Heinz Field. Settling in the North Side Irish ghetto that neighbored a ghetto of German immigrants, my great-grandfather gained employment with Jones and Laughlin Steel Corporation. Originally producing only iron, the enterprise began the production of steel in 1886. Over the ensuing 60 years, J&L expanded its facilities and operations along both sides of the Monongahela River along the city's southern border. An immigrant himself, partner James Laughlin retained a large number of Irish in his employ. John Broderick reportedly worked at J&L for fifty years.

In the "Three Rivers" city, John Broderick married an Irish lass, my paternal great-grandmother **Mary Jane née Dillon** (1867–1952). The couple raised my grandfather and his nine siblings on the "North Side" before their relocation six miles south to the township of Dormont in Pittsburgh's South Hills.

The second of ten children, **Daniel Thomas, Sr.** (1893–1988) grew up with siblings John V., Elizabeth (Ligday), Matthew "Matt", Mary (Zimmerman), Catherine "Kay," Nora, Margaret "Marg," Robert "Bob" J., and Dorothy "Dode." Except for Matt who raised a family in Philadelphia, the others remained in the Pittsburgh vicinity. Among my paternal great-aunts and great-uncles, John, Kay, Nora, Marg, and Dode remained single and lived together throughout their adult lives in their family home at 1464 McFarlane Road in Dormont where we visited every Easter throughout my childhood. The youngest of the clan, Dode outlived the others and died there in 2007 at age 95.

As reflected in his obituary, when my great-grandfather John J. Broderick died at age 89 in 1949, he left behind his wife along with all ten of their children, 14 grandchildren, and six great-grandchildren. Great-grandmother Mary Jane survived John by three years when at age 85 she passed away in 1952—the same year my maternal grandfather Laurance Sterne Gordon died.

The Broderick lineage

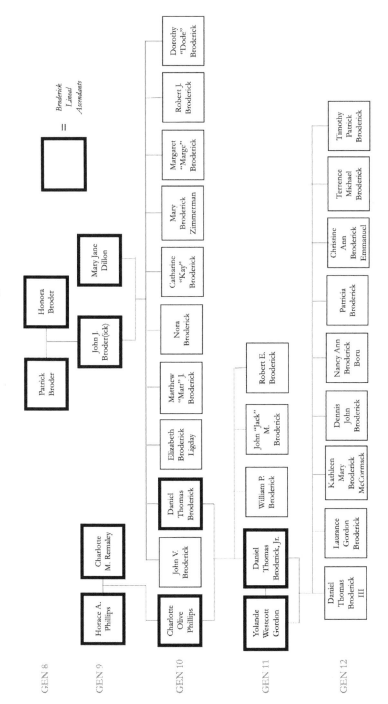

The Brodericks epitomized the *Baby Boom* generation
with eight of us born in 11 years during some of the
most prosperous times in American history.

As a youngster, my oldest brother Danny III coined the nickname
"Ooh Ooh" for my grandmother, **Charlotte Olive née Phillips Broderick**
(1900–1977). When my mother came calling on her in-laws a block away
from our summer home in Madison-on-the-Lake ("Madison"), Ohio, Yo
would holler, "Yoo-hoo, anyone home?" Danny III translated "Yoo hoo"
as "Ooh Ooh" and it stuck among her many grandchildren throughout
the decades.

Charlotte and her sister Helen Margaret Phillips Ellis (1898–1974)
were born to **Horace A. Phillips** (1854–1916) and **Charlotte M. neé
Remaley Phillips** (1872–1962) and raised in Pittsburgh; they are buried
at Chartiers Cemetery in the borough of Carnegie. Upon marrying,
Helen and her husband, Frederick Curtis Ellis, moved to Madison, Ohio,
where they raised two children and presumably enticed Charlotte and
Dan Broderick to establish a second home. As a pharmacist, Fred owned
and operated a drug store in the town's center.

My grandpa Daniel Thomas Broderick, Sr. and I enjoyed a special
bond. As a timid child—the seventh of nine and the only one among
the first seven with blonde hair—I delighted him somehow. I felt quite
safe with and mutually loved by him before he died in 1988 at age 94
when I was 35 years old. My grandparents had raised their four boys with
tough Catholic love. But I found Grandpa's soft spot without even trying.
He touched me deeply, even more so when he singled me out to receive
two pieces of fine jewelry that had belonged to Ooh Ooh—his "Rock of
Gibraltar"—once she had passed. Moreover, he willed to me his and Ooh
Ooh's 11-piece mahogany dining room set which I cheerfully accepted
upon his passing.

Without ever meeting my maternal grandparents or knowing much
of anything about their heritage, I rationalized my sense of belonging
based largely on what I knew of my father's parentage. We are *Brodericks*,
after all. Everything about my Pittsburgh upbringing possessed patriarchal

elements associated with a profound sense of our Irish heritage, reinforced by our close ties to the Notre Dame *Fighting Irish*. I knew the Gordons hailed from Scotland but nothing more. The *Hokes* and *Westcotts* struck me as removed familial relations, left solely to my imagination with little knowledge gained about them and my English, German, and French bloodlines—until now.

Grandpa Broderick navigated a scrappy existence in his formative years in "blue collar" Pittsburgh. Advancing only so far as a third grade education, he sold newspapers early on to help support his family. Among others, he sold papers with his friend and fellow North Side neighbor Arthur "Art" Joseph Rooney, Sr. (1901–1988), who later became the founding owner of the Pittsburgh Steelers, from 1933 until his death—also in 1988.

As a lad entering his teenage years, Daniel Thomas Broderick, Sr. went to work as an office boy with Forest Lumber owned by the Diebolds. An enterprising young fellow, he proved himself an asset to the company. The Diebolds promoted him to general manager when he was about 40 years of age. He stayed on with the company for a few more years before striking out on his own. Around the time his eldest sons returned from World War II, he launched D.T. Broderick Lumber Company and put the boys to work in his wholesale business. With great success, he afforded three of his four sons a livelihood to support their families.

As a resident of Dormont in Pittsburgh's South Hills, my grandfather regularly took the trolley downtown. Having experienced a car accident in his adulthood, he vowed never to drive a car again. His siblings looked up to their brother Dan for "making it" in business. His success appeared evident as Ooh Ooh drove him in luxury to every appointment, always in a sparkling Cadillac. Invariably, Grandpa exited the most dignified vehicle sporting a three-piece suit, pocket watch, and fedora looking like a million bucks. [My father, too, drove a Cadillac over the decades, but without my mother as his chauffeur!]

With traits I internalized as defining my father and our family, our Grandpa Broderick exuded pride, discipline, a strong work ethic, and Christian faith above all else. An active parishioner, he sat on the finance committee at St. Bernard's Church, and he donated one of the enormous bells the size of a car which still rings from the belfry.

Daniel Thomas Broderick, Sr. never seemed to age. His snowy white hair stands out as far back as I can remember—certainly as far back as Dan and Yo's wedding day in 1942. "Dapper Dan" had his wits about him along with a sense of humor. My grandfather outlived his "Rock of Gibraltar" Charlotte by 11 years. At age 94, he died peacefully in his sleep, leaving behind his four sons, 16 grandchildren, and 15 great-grand-children—among the latter, his namesake Daniel Thomas Broderick IV. The four "DTB's" lived simultaneously for 12 years before Gramps's passing in 1988. Daniel and Charlotte are buried next to his parents John J. and Mary Jane Broderick at Calvary Cemetery in Pittsburgh.

WHILE HER FAMILY AND FRIENDS throughout her life referred to my mother as "Yo" or "Yolie," my father alone called her "Yolande," never deviating. "Danny," as my mother called him, made a living for his family in the wholesale lumber industry, getting his start in his father's business, D.T. Broderick Lumber Company.

Seemingly by design, the mass-production machine of the post-war era churned out a flurry of babies which in symbiotic fashion created needs. In quick succession, my parents had eight children in 11 years, fol-lowed by an unplanned surprise birth five years later when Timmy came along. Manufacturing hummed throughout the nation with residential communities to house growing families, automobiles to transport them, and televisions to entertain and communicate with them. "Baby boomer" aptly describes this brisk output spanning the period from post-WWII to the time of my youngest sibling's birth in 1960.

With the arrival in 1946 of their second child, Laurance "Larry" Gordon—my maternal grandfather Laurance Gordon's namesake—my parents bought their first house on Apache Road in Brookside Farms in Pittsburgh's South Hills. Here, they had four more children—Kathleen "Kathy" Mary (b. 1947), Dennis John (b. 1948), Nancy Ann (b. 1950), and Patricia "Patty" (b. 1951).

Five years after the purchase of their Apache house, in 1951, Dan and Yo Broderick bought property and built a compact summer vacation home on approximately two acres in Madison, Ohio. My father modeled the house after the tight quarters of a naval ship with a small galley for a kitchen to optimize the limited space. A distance of three hours from their primary residence in Pittsburgh, the property sat a block from Dan's parents' second home fronting Lake Erie. As mentioned, Charlotte's sister Helen's relocation to Madison likely influenced my grandparents' decision to establish their summer home in the same township. My grandparents built their lakeside home at 7745 Lakeside Boulevard in 1947 and sold it in 1973. Over many years, my family spent entire summers in close proximity to Ooh Ooh and Grandpa in Madison. Now nearly three-quarters of a century standing, Dan and Yo's Madison home remains in the Broderick family.

Business continued to do well at D.T. Broderick Lumber Company into the 1950s. By 1952, shortly after completing the buildout of their vacation house, Dan and Yo had outgrown their Apache Road home. To accommodate their still growing family, they relocated to a beautiful property at 30 Vernon Drive in the affluent Mt. Lebanon township, also in Pittsburgh's South Hills and some six miles from downtown.

Our Vernon Drive home was previously owned by an executive with Isaly's Dairy Companies headquartered in Pittsburgh, which gained fame for its farm-fresh dairy products—notably Klondike Bars—and chipped chopped ham. The game room featured a soda fountain counter with stools similar to what you would find housed in the local drugstores of the 1950s. A mural lined the four walls depicting an authentic Wild West town with cowboys, horses, cattle, a saloon, and an Isley's store among other details. With our friends, as kids we had a ball playing cowboys and Indians while enjoying ice cream sodas. The young families who occupied the flourishing Vernon Drive neighborhood provided a quintessential upper-middle class childhood experience for the Brodericks.

The last three of the couple's nine children came during the family's residency on Vernon Drive—(me) Christine "Christy" Ann (b. 1953), Terrence "Terry" Michael (b. 1955), and finally, Timothy "Timmy" Patrick, who arrived as a February 29th leap year baby in 1960.

In 1957, my father broke from his family's business and started his own wholesale lumber company, Western Spruce Sales, Inc., which he developed into a highly profitable enterprise.

Residing in the Vernon Drive home for just 12 years, Dan Broderick, Jr. made his most ambitious move in 1964. He relocated the family of 11 three miles further south to a spectacular mansion built in 1935 on a 28-acre parcel in toney Trotwood Acres in the township of Upper St. Clair.

While Dan Broderick put bread on the table, Yo kept the large household going. She prepared meals for the 11 of us, every meal—every single day before the girls reached an age to lend a hand with table set-up and clean-up and with the other household chores as well. Dinner preparation fell to our mother, always. Although she loved her sweets—bridge nuts, peanut brittle, and peanut M&Ms among other favorites—Yo retained her petite figure, even after giving birth to nine children over 16 years.

Before long, my father expanded the 241 Orr Road property with the purchase of four additional acres. Elevated on grounds with majestic oaks lined down either side of a magnificent drive to the main house and a four-car garage apartment, the property dominated the surrounding lush green, wooded rolling hills. The Broderick home also featured a two-bedroom apartment atop a four-door garage, a vegetable garden, a detached stone structure that served as our tool shed, and a stately three-story, three-stall barn at the base of the hill where we kept a couple of horses year-round. What a fabulous home to entertain guests and get in trouble with my middle and high school friends!

While our dad enjoyed his cigars—nearly smoking us out on the long summer drive to and from Madison with the windows to his Cadillac rolled up—Mom preferred Winston cigarettes. Sometime after I left the nest for college, I heard about the fire she caused in our parents' bedroom. Reportedly lighting up while dressing in her "boudoir" on Orr Road, Yo went downstairs after leaving a still burning butt in the wastebasket. I can only imagine the trouble she occasioned by that high drama.

Among her many interests, large family gatherings topped the list of what my mother most enjoyed, especially those held in Madison. Easily entertained, she had a lot of fun with us, carried a sense of humor, and played along with the antics that colored our time together—always a good sport. Perhaps sunbathing ranked second among Yo's favorite pastimes. A sun worshipper to the core, she sported a glowing golden tan by summer's end each and every year.

The Brodericks inherited the creative gene from my mother, which she undoubtedly picked up from her mother, Yolande. Yo mastered many art forms—decoupage, wood engravings, oil painting, crewel embroidery, knitting, beaded flowers, mosaic tile designs, liquid plastic pourings, even candle dripping. The latter started with a tapered candle placed atop a chianti bottle and then another on top of another candle dripping to create an ever-larger mass that eventually became one giant glob measuring three feet tall and probably 100 pounds. She obsessed until she became bored and picked up the next hobby. In the meantime, she enjoyed golf, bridge, card games, Yahtzee, gardening, and football, notably the Fighting Irish but also professional football. Of course, we all rooted for the Pittsburgh Steelers. In her last active years, seashell gathering at Marco Island, Florida, became her passion. With a flashlight in hand, she canvassed the beach each morning long before dawn for the day's choice selections. Returning to Pittsburgh from the Marco condo unit they rented in southwest Florida each winter in retirement, Yo fashioned exquisite floral arrangements from her abundant collection of seashells. Though compulsive, she distinguished herself with remarkable creative talent and justifiable pride.

As college football came to pass each season, Yo prepared the home for Christmas—her absolute favorite holiday. Beautiful decorations and a mountain of wrapped gifts augmenting what Santa had in store made this season a joyous one for all of us, perhaps with the exception of my father who financed her elaborate creations and generous gift-giving. As crazy as it sounds, he did not partake in the raucous gift opening on Christmas mornings. Utterly consumed with excitement, we hardly noticed his absence as he typically slept through it all.

A time-honored tradition, we decorated the tree each year on Christmas eve in the company of a large gathering of family and friends. At the crack of dawn on Christmas morning, the kids assembled at the top of the steps until our mother could account for everyone. Then, on the count of three, we stampeded down the stairs and into the living room where all bedlam let loose. Upon locating the stocking that displayed our embroidered name placed atop a pile of presents, the wrapping paper went flying. It is difficult to imagine the time, effort, and expense that went into staging the spectacle.

Dan Broderick baffled his children as a highly complicated man, the definition of a conundrum. A devout Catholic, he nonetheless demonstrated an inability to forgive the transgressions of others. His incapacity to exhibit emotions unnerved me and the whole lot of us. Although our dad had limited capacity to reveal warmth, he nonetheless demonstrated extreme generosity in providing for our family. A tough, no-nonsense man, DTB Jr. at the same time developed a reputation among friends as fun-loving, gregarious, humorous, always generous, and above all, charismatic.

From our mother, the Brodericks inherited the creative gene; from our father, a strong work-ethic, the value of proper English, and a cutting sense of humor. As a couple, they modeled the meaning of an active social life.

Like his father, DTB Jr. stood proud and set the example of hard work in the lumber business and in the immaculate grounds he maintained at our family homes in Pittsburgh and Madison. With the help of the boys, he kept the lawns looking immaculate. Drawing from his study of journalism at Notre Dame, our father demanded the use of correct grammar at all times. He called out anyone who didn't speak up, speak clearly, or enunciate, and he had no tolerance for slang such as 'yep' and 'nope.'

Meanwhile, Dan Broderick fully embraced his own warped sense of humor. The more shocking or humiliating, the better. Among us, our mother took the brunt of his jokes. In a letter to me once I left the nest, he referred to her as "the toad who continues to grow fatter daily." She wasn't fat at all. In another, "Mother has an appointment at the fat ladies' department of Kmart for a fitting of her dress for your wedding." In response to hearing that my Yugoslavian friends Mia and Peca would be joining me in Pittsburgh during a Christmas break while in graduate school, he wrote: "We shall be happy to greet your Czech friends, but will they feel at home here? I understand Eastern Europeans are accustomed to bunking with farmyard animals in winter months. I could fix up the hayloft in the barn and borrow a few sheep and pigs from the Gilfillans [local farmers], if you think it should be appropriate. Let me know."

As distasteful as his sense of humor came across, we encouraged our dad by laughing in kind for these were the rare moments when we would catch him in a good mood. More often than not, he appeared abrupt and to the point. "Speak up!" "Speak right!" "Stand straight." "Behave!" "Eat!" We were often ill at ease in his company, but relieved on those rare occasions when we saw him loosen up.

As a couple, Dan and Yo enjoyed an active social life with a large circle of close friends. Bowling, golf, and dinner parties filled much of their time together outside the home. They went out every Friday or Saturday evening in ritual fashion. The kids considered it a treat to see them decked out for their special night out and a bonus when they hosted a party at our house. We were allowed to come downstairs to say hello to their guests, but otherwise, we had to stay upstairs where we would take turns sneaking peeks through the stair railing to observe the revelry. With the Wohlebers, Cotters, Dattilos, Gottschalks, Frankenberrys, Tetlows, Otises, Cannons, Downeys, and others, our parents knew how to have a good time.

With all of the kids, our mom spent the entire summer each year in Madison from Memorial Day to Labor Day. Dad made the weekend commute from Pittsburgh virtually every weekend. Not infrequently, a couple of their friends would visit for a weekend from Pittsburgh with their kids who tracked closely in age with the Broderick children. It was a lot of fun for everyone.

During the winter months in Pittsburgh, my father found relaxation in ice skating. His forward strides with hands clasped behind his back still conjure in my mind iconic images of Dutch ice skater and storyteller Hans Christian Andersen (1805-1875). In the summertime at Madison, he found entertainment in horseback riding (until we had a place to corral the horses on the Orr Road property), golf, softball, and keeping wood fires going indoors at the Norton Drive house where the family savored s'mores on many a cool summer weekend evening.

In 1961, as the good times rolled, Democrat John Fitzgerald Kennedy emerged as our 35th and first Catholic president. In his words,

"Those who dare to fail miserably can achieve greatly." Dan Broderick embraced that thinking and achieved mightily. The administration, too, put action behind those words with President Kennedy's desire to put a man on the moon before the end of the decade. Throughout the 1960s, Dan Broderick realized success in his business while the National Space Aeronautics Administration (NASA) made headway on the administration's daunting challenge.

In the meantime, though, a terrible tragedy jolted the nation with news of President Kennedy's assassination in his third year in office. The murder of our beloved Catholic president at the hands of Lee Harvey Oswald on my brother Danny's 19th birthday, November 22, 1963, left the country roiling in a state of vulnerability. The events that unfolded in the aftermath of the assassination defined one of the most tumultuous and divisive decades in our nation's history—certainly in my lifetime. In the 1970s, Americans simultaneously dealt with the civil rights movement, the Vietnam War and antiwar protests, the political assassinations of Reverend Martin Luther King and President Kennedy's younger brother Robert F. Kennedy, and the emerging "generation gap" that brought divergent opinions regarding politics, beliefs, and values into sharp focus.

A sign of hope peeked through this devastation for both our country and my family. In 1969, the nation took "one giant leap for mankind." With NASA's bold decision to send Apollo 8 all the way to the moon on the first manned flight of the massive Saturn V rocket, astronauts Neil Armstrong, Buzz Aldridge, and Michael Collins made history. When the struts of the Apollo 11 Lunar Module met the powdery surface of the moon on July 20, 1969, Commander Neil Armstrong marked the arrival with an eight-word message back home. "Houston," Armstrong said. "Tranquility base here. The Eagle has landed!"

That same year marked the best in Dan Broderick's business career. At age 50, he oversaw a bustling wholesale lumber operation that included ownership of six sawmills in British Columbia. A formidable player in western Canada, Daniel T. Broderick, Jr. entered the space at an opportune time. Western Spruce Sales, Inc. achieved significant success, much like my mother's G2 maternal grandfather Isaac Gould and his brother Stephen as lumbermen in central Pennsylvania little more than one century earlier.

With financial stability, my parents placed a high priority on giving their children a quality education in private schools. At the height of his career in 1969, DTB Jr. supported four children in elementary and high school, four in college, and one in medical school. His wherewithal enabled all nine children to graduate from Catholic colleges—all five boys from the University of Notre Dame, Kathleen and me from St. Mary's College, Nancy from Duquesne University, and Patty from the University of Dayton.

The Brodericks experienced the best of times through the 1960s and into the early 1970s. My parents enjoyed great success simultaneously supporting nine children, presiding over a growing business, and maintaining an active social life. They managed it all by exerting great effort and a "can do" attitude.

"A woman's work is never done," especially facing a World Series that the Pittsburgh Pirates had not taken since 1960 when they won the title in 1971.

The 1971 World Series played out as the fourth won by the Pirates—they prevailed over the Detroit Tigers in 1909; the Washington Senators in 1925; and the New York Yankees in 1960. The 1971 series marked the second of two won by legendary Hall of Famer Roberto Clemente (1934–1972) during his iconic 18-year career with the team before his untimely death in a plane crash. The Pittsburgh Pirates beat the Baltimore Orioles for the series title, and they went on to knock out the Orioles a second time, in 1979—on both occasions going all the way to Game 7. They have not taken the title since then. Roberto's protégé, Willie Stargell, scored the winning run in Game 7 while leading the National League in home runs in 1971; he received "Most Valuable Player" recognition for the Series in 1979.

Yo worked around the clock to host Dan's out-of-town business clients and then prepare for a dinner party following the 7th game of the World Series in 1971. In a letter I received that fall, shortly after taking off for St. Mary's College as a freshman, she described the pace of their activity and her domestic work schedule. Giving a hint of the balancing act required of her to raise nine kids spread 16 years apart—each and every day without a break—my mother's description of what was involved to pull off this "World Series" feat is enough to make anyone's head spin:

> *I intended to write you all week but you won't believe what it's been like around here this week. Absolutely, positively the most hectic week I can ever remember.*
>
> *As you know, this has been World Series week to begin with and also it was on Saturday that Dad had planned to have a dinner party at our house for some of his business friends and some of our [personal] friends. The party in itself was enough to have kept me busy with cooking, cleaning, polishing silver, washing crystal and china, etc. etc. on top of making beds, shopping, washing clothes, cooking, washing dishes, etc. (a woman's work is never done).*
>
> *But there was the Series after we beat San Francisco in the playoffs the week before. So Dad started getting calls from all over the place requesting tickets for the game. On Monday night they [the guests] arrived. Three from Canada, one from Georgia, and one from Boston . . . We put up three here.*
>
> *So Monday I was up to my ears in changing beds, cleaning bathrooms, dusting and sweeping the whole house. Tuesday morning, I cooked breakfast for them and then we all left to go to the game at 11:30. Dad took them all out to dinner then brought them home. After they (the two who were staying at the Sheraton) left, the ones here went to bed at 3:30.*
>
> *Wed morning everyone had those things you get after a big night of celebrating the night before (Pirates won their first game here after losing 2 in Baltimore). I really felt awful. But I got them their breakfast and wondered how I would be able to get at my party work feeling the way I did when they left for the office. That's when Dad said, why don't I go out and get a ham or something and plan to have a buffet dinner for them, all before the game on Wednesday night—I nearly died. But being the dutiful little wife, I again had to forget the party for Saturday night and plan for the dinner that night. Beds, clean up the dead soldiers, store, cook, etc. etc. Dinner at 6:00 and without even starting to clean up the mess, we all left for the game. Again we won, but we went right to bed when we got home. Celebrations were in order but no one was up to it.*
>
> *Thursday morning—breakfast, beds, tidy up, bath—meet Dad at office at 11:00 for game. We won again!! He had to go to a business meeting with some of the men after the game—Larry too. So he asked me to drive one of them out to the airport on my way home. Being a dutiful wife, I did. Home at 6:00. Terry had left for N.D. so I took Timmy out to dinner—came home and Dad was back again with his friends. I went to bed and died.*

Friday morning. One day before the party and I hadn't even planned what I was going to serve much less all the other things I had to do. Dad left with the men at 7:30. They went back to Canada, and then I got going on party arrangements. I ran around all day Friday, Friday night, at 6:00 Saturday morning, and an hour before party time I was all set. We had 14 . . . Party was a success, I hope. Most left at 1:30—Wohlebers at 3:30. Today it's clean-up day, but no pressure, so no sweat. And that's why I didn't get a letter written to you (before now).

Nary a complaint from my mother facing the household demands and brisk schedule, they were the best of times, alright. But as we learned from the periods of rapid industrial growth in Duluth, the economy cycles through peaks and valleys. In the second half of the 19th century and into the 20th century, our Gordon relatives witnessed first-hand the pattern of recession that often follows expansionary times. The latter decades of the 20th century thereby traced a predicable course.

The nation's post-war economic engine ground to an abrupt halt early in the new decade of the 1970s. Leading up to that time, through regulation, the U.S. mortgage market relied heavily upon savings and loans to lend money to home owners at competitive rates. The favorable interest rates they offered to working- and middle-class workers on savings accounts enabled the thrifts to loan the accumulated reserves as relatively low-cost mortgages. As inflation rose from under 2% to over 6% however, surging interest rates rendered thrifts less competitive, leading to a disintermediation crisis and a doubling of the cost of a new home. In turn, price and wage controls coupled with an oil embargo imposed by members of the Organization of Petroleum Exporting Companies (OPEC) during the 1973 Arab-Israel War triggered a crisis in steel demand and a plummeting stock market. The combination of these macroeconomic factors led the nation into a severe recession.

Market conditions severely tested the resilience of the interest-sensitive U.S. housing market on which Dan Broderick's livelihood depended. The downturn foreshadowed major setbacks to which my parents ultimately surrendered.

Naturally, the crash trickled down to material suppliers. Canadian lumber mills failed and then fell into bankruptcy, necessitating the sale of Western Spruce's sawmill holdings at auction for pennies on the dollar. The worsening market forces then compelled my father to lose control of his company. He sold Western Spruce Sales to a couple of penny-stock brokers in Pittsburgh's North Hills who provided the working capital while Dan Broderick continued to run the company for Winchester Corporation. The new owners evidently knew little about running a business, however. As the recession loomed in 1974–1975, Winchester failed and brought down Western Spruce Sales with it.

Dan then formed Trotwood Spruce and Log Sales and operated a relatively small-scale wholesale lumber business out of his and Yo's adjoining garage apartment on Orr Road. Whereas in one month alone he had sold 500 carloads of lumber during Western Spruce's peak in 1969, at Trotwood he sold but 5-6 cars per month in 1974-75. Meanwhile, by 1978, his earnings had put eight kids through college and the oldest through medical school; our parents still had one to go.

In 1980, sometime after Timmy had left the nest for college, Yo returned to her roots in Duluth for the first time in 15 years. With her brother, Larry, she saw a lot of people she had grown up with, including a close high school friend and her husband, both of whom had attended my parents' wedding as a bridesmaid and groomsman. The two couples had double-dated when Dan came to Duluth during their courtship. Walking down memory lane, Yo also saw friends she hadn't seen since grade school. In a letter, she told me how much fun she had:

> *I went to mass where I always went, where I went to school, and where Dad and I were married. I saw a lot more people there that I had known, then we took a nostalgic drive past our old house, past the house where* [her brother] *Larry was born, then past the one where I was born, and the hospital where* [my brother] *Danny was born. It was so good to be back there again. So many memories and almost all good ones. Then to the country club where we used to go to dances and parties in high school and college . . . When we were all together the reminiscing was rampant. We laughed our heads off at some of the things we used to do or at some of the stories they'd tell. Anyhow all good things must end . . . on Monday morning I flew home.*
>
> *Believe me though, I was still glad to be home. Dad met me at the airport and he looked mighty good to me.*

I wonder if that last comment was to suggest that my mom's childhood friends hadn't aged as gracefully as Dan Broderick. In fact, both of my parents retained youthful looks and slim figures throughout their years despite the wear of raising so many kids.

Sometime after Timmy graduated from Notre Dame in 1982, my brothers Danny III and Larry bought the Orr Road property from my parents which enabled them to remain in their beloved home. However, the going became even tougher with the passage of time.

In the years that followed, Dan and Yo experienced one serious, personal hardship after another on the heels of the failed business: the murder of their firstborn, Danny III, and his new bride Linda; Yo's deteriorating health; the loss of their coveted Orr Road home; and seven divorces among their nine children (two by their middle child).

To be expected, my parents never recovered from the tragedy of Danny III's and Linda's murders in 1989. For my mother, the devastating news immediately triggered tremors that led to a diagnosis of Parkinson's Disease, of a sudden denying her the use of hands she relied upon for artistic expression. The following year, my brother Larry's own wholesale lumber business failed in Colorado. The liquidation of Rivendell Forest Products came as a huge disappointment to our father. He had lived vicariously through Larry and our youngest brother Tim whom Larry employed at Rivendell. Their business had kept DTB Jr. connected to the industry and all of his old friends and contacts in the lumber trade. Also in 1990, Larry and his wife, Kathy, divorced. My parents had been particularly close to Kathy. Financial circumstances then forced Larry to sell the Orr Road property as he could not carry it on his own. The sale became the final crushing blow for Dan and Yo Broderick, especially when the new owners opted to level the magnificent home in favor of a newly constructed replacement on the original footprint in 1994. Our parents reluctantly elected to move year-round to our summer home in sleepy Madison, Ohio. For Yo especially, the dislocation brought a monumental change in lifestyle and severe depression.

Yet another layer of turmoil came with not one, but two criminal trials a year apart, ultimately leading to only a second-degree murder conviction in the killing of Danny and Linda. Not first-degree murder? We received news of the verdict with outrage. In 1991, the mother of four of my parents' grandchildren received a 32-years-to-life sentence. [As of this writing, she remains incarcerated in a California prison.]

As my mother's health rapidly deteriorated—her voice nearly gone; her strength, mobility, and coordination slipping badly; and her weight dropping steadily to 86 pounds—she visibly mourned the indescribable loss of her firstborn until her own horrible death at age 74. Bedridden for 2-1/2 years at the Inn-Madison nursing care facility—the best Madison had to offer—the spirited Yolande Westcott Gordon Broderick succumbed to her illness on February 20, 1995. Although she had severe advanced Parkinson's disease, she died from acute pneumonia—diagnosed within 24-hours of her passing. None of her family was informed of the downturn and consequently, the news of her death came without forewarning.

Earlier on that fateful day—Loretta Dake and her friend arrived at Inn-Madison to bring Communion to some of the residents as they were accustomed to doing most mornings. Uncle Larry relayed these details in a letter to a family member sent days later:

> *Yolie was a favorite of theirs so they stopped off at her room first. She was in such a deep sleep that they decided to come back later. Just as they turned to leave, one of them noticed a small bird fly by, turn and land on the outside window sill. There is an old superstition about this and as they left, one said to her friend, 'Someone is going to die today.' They later returned and Yolie received Communion as she usually did.*

> *Mrs. Dake was correct. Late that afternoon, Yolie was having a little discomfort with breathing and the nurse decided that oxygen would give her some relief and from then on, she looked in on her every 15 minutes or so. A little later she found that Yolie had very quietly left us.*

Crushing heartache for each of us came from the fact that our mother died alone despite having raised nine children. Alone, not even with our father by her side although he lived only miles away. Tormented, he had the stamina to see her at the nursing home only briefly each day, invariably departing in mourning. While she left behind her husband of 52 years, eight children, and 20 grandchildren, only my father, Uncle Larry, my siblings and I attended her funeral at my father's behest. The meager gathering left us disconsolate knowing she deserved so much more.

Uncle Larry's letter continued with further details:

Arriving in Cleveland late in the afternoon, I rented a car and went directly to Behm Funeral Home. The family had left for a meeting with the priest and I had the opportunity to spend some time, alone, with Yolie. She looked like the Yolie that I knew five to ten years ago and, fittingly, in the coffin with her was a stuffed teddy bear (I found out later that Kathleen named him P Bear), a [crinkly] *multi-colored caterpillar that Chris*[ty] *had given her for Christmas* [owing to its tactile features], *and a picture of Tim, Ann and the boys. I met the clan for dinner at the Old Tavern, an evening of toasts, tears and laughs.*

There is another old adage that says, 'Happy the bridge that the sun shines on and the deceased that experiences the soft rain.' Thursday was one of those days of intermittent light rain. We took Yolie to the church at ten that morning and after Mass we escorted her down the aisle to the sound of the soloist singing 'Danny Boy.' At the cemetery the priest said the final prayers and then Dennis gave a short eulogy on his affection for his mother and ended it with a taped [Bing Crosby] *recording of 'Tura Lura Lura.' A very tearful climax but a touch of class.*

Our final dinner together was that night at the Geneva Inn that was located right across the road from the Howard Johnson where I was staying. The mood was considerably lighter with a few more refreshments than we might have needed. After dinner, Tim asked for the floor so that he might give a toast to his mother. I think that you are aware that he, of all the kids, was closest to his mother. At that time the supper crowd had thinned out somewhat. Tim was sitting at one end of the table and his dad at the other and, in order for Big Dan to hear, Tim was speaking louder than usual. As he went on, I noticed that the conversation at a table of four across from me had grown silent and when he finished all four of them were drying their eyes. They were not alone.

My childhood friend Joe sent a touching condolence note that read, "I have only fond memories for your mother. I know she was always the steady influence in your remarkable family, and she always greeted life with a sense of humor." True enough. "No one ever spent more time with you, worried more about you, or cared anymore for you than your mother." Joe's last statement paid homage to every mother. As to mine, she not infrequently had made the point that she tried the best she could. No doubt our mother sacrificed much to provide for her large family.

Curiously, the scales tipped momentarily yet decisively in favor of the Broderick girls on the occasion of our mother's passing. She willed her considerable fine jewelry collection to her four daughters alone. At our

Madison home following her funeral service, our father read her wishes—
that we girls draw numbers and take turns in round-robin fashion until
we claimed all of her jewelry. Dad spread out the jewelry on the bed in the
master bedroom while the boys stood surrounding us. It felt so strange.
Nancy drew #1—Patty # 4. Kathleen alone had first right to the coveted
diamond-studded ring that had belonged to our G2 grandmother Josie
Gould Westcott, should Kathleen choose it in the first round. She did.
A seeming inequity presented itself in execution of the plan, however.
It quickly dawned on us that Nancy had first pick on every "round"—
meaning Patty picked last each time her turn came around. The better
idea would have been to sequence the "picks" as 1—2—3—4—4—3—
2—1—1—2—3—4—4—3—2—1. Lesson learned. All the same, my
mother gifted each of us several beautiful treasures we still cherish with
genuine gratitude. In the eyes of this beholder, the greatest gift in the collection was Josie's diamond ring followed by Mom's signature diamond
pendant, which Nancy naturally claimed as her first choice.

Returning to our father, in a dramatic reversal of life's fortunes, everything headed south during the last four decades of his life following the
peak of his business at the age of 50 in 1969. In his later years, he became
a more difficult man, preferring to be left alone. Bitter, ornery, stub-
born, and negative, he became reclusive. While he grumbled about his
physical ailments (vertigo, diverticulitis, colitis, arthritis, a nagging issue
with his esophagus) and Notre Dame football—the Irish did not win a
national championship in the last 22 years of his life—our father never
complained about any of the rest of it. And like most military veterans,
he rarely talked about his experience in World War II.

Shortly after the death of his partner "Yolande," Dan moved to San
Diego where he lived with his favored son, Terry, and his wife, Jennifer,
for a short time, until they broke the news that they were expecting their
first child. In 1999, he moved to Notre Dame, Indiana. For the last 10
years of his life, our father resided independently at Holy Cross Village-
Notre Dame, a continuing care retirement community on the campus
of Holy Cross College beside St. Mary's College and across the street
from his beloved University of Notre Dame. While he remained reclusive,
DTB Jr. found respite living in close proximity to *Our Lady* and his

coveted Fighting Irish. At Holy Cross, his health gradually deteriorated, four of his children divorced, and all but one of his friends passed away. The last among them whose pleasant disposition endeared her to all of us, Mary Wohleber died in 2022 at age 102.

In the final year of his life once he reached 90, my father transferred from independent living to the assisted living facility at Holy Cross Village. Immediately after his heart attack and shortly before his passing, Terry came from San Diego and spent five days with our dad. Terry met one of the nurses who shared how much she got a kick out of Dan Broderick. Sometimes, when she went into his unit, Dan told her to "Get the hell out of here." With a smile, she would respond with, "I pray for you." Each time, he reportedly replied, "Thank you."

Unaware, on his last night at Holy Cross Village, Terry spent our father's last supper with him. Later that evening, Terry alerted the nurse of our dad's chest pains. The following morning before leaving for his flight home, Terry made a final visit. Before departing, he saw Dad's rosary beads and handed them to him. He put his hands on our father's shoulders, leaned over close to his ear, and clearly enunciated, "I love you, Dad." Dad looked at Terry and said, "Thank you."

Later that day, on "8-9-10"—two weeks shy of his 91st birthday—Daniel Thomas Broderick, Jr. died of a heart attack. The cause recorded on his death certificate lists acute myocardial infarction, atherosclerosis, and hyperlipidemia. He outlived "Yolande" by 15 years. His surviving progeny at death included eight of his nine children, all 23 grandchildren, and eight of his now 26 great-grandchildren.

From the funeral mass held for my father at Immaculate Conception Catholic Church, a bagpiper accompanied our family across the street to the North Madison Cemetery. There, four members from the Notre Dame Glee Club awaited our arrival. The choral ensemble sang "Anchors Away;" "The Notre Dame Victory March;" "The Notre Dame Alma Mater;" and "Danny Boy". The 24 mournful "Taps" on bugle then followed a 21-gun salute. Orchestrated by our brother Dennis, the grand sendoff ended with the bagpiper's rendition of "Amazing Grace."

A fine sendoff for a man who endured, sacrificed, and accomplished so very much in his lifetime, the memorial touched us deeply.

Peace came at last for Daniel Thomas Broderick, Jr. He is buried at North Madison Cemetery alongside his wife of 52 years, my mother Yolande Westcott Gordon Broderick.

WE NOW MOVE TO YOLIE'S SIBLINGS Jinks and Larry who shared the sorrow of her premature passing.

Virginia "Jinks" Stone Gordon (1919–2002) & Douglas Bennett Guy (1919–2007)

As photos attest, Yo and her older sister looked close enough alike to be twins. A year apart, Jinks and Yo grew out of their adorable early years to become attractive women with composure and a sense of humor. Thanks to their mother, the girls also acquired an affinity for the French language.

Named after her aunt *Virginia* "Nina" Hoke Newcomb and her father's aunt Emma Gordon *Stone*, my aunt **Virginia "Jinks" Stone Gordon** followed closely in her mother Yolande's footsteps. Both were born in Bordeaux and both served in the Red Cross during world wars when they met their life partners.

Jinks was born on May 31, 1919, at the U.S. Army Base Hospital in Talence, in the outskirts of Bordeaux. As reflected on her birth certificate, her father "Laurance Sterne Gordon" and mother "Joanna Gould Westcott Hoke" then lived at 12 Rue du Champ de Mars in Bordeaux.

With her parents, Virginia relocated to Duluth as an infant immediately following the war. The neighborhood boys referred to her as a "jinx" sometime during her childhood. The nickname somehow stuck with the revised spelling of "Jinks."

Beginning sometime in high school, Jinks began dating **Charles "Cy" Cleland Liscomb** (1920–1942). A year younger than Jinks, Cy attended Duluth's Central High School where he developed athleticism. The school recognized him as a "cooperative, trustworthy student well-liked by teachers and fellow students."

Perhaps Cy's attraction to Jinks stemmed in part from one of his two favorite subjects—French and history—as picked up on his college application to Carleton College. An Episcopalian, Cy was an active reader. He worked for a short time as a chauffeur at $2.00 a day and at the shipyards in a boiler shop in Duluth at $4.00 a day. His father, Charles F. Liscomb, owned a fire, casualty, and surety insurance company and served as president of the Duluth Chamber of Commerce.

While continuing to date Cy, Jinks completed two years at St. Mary's College in the spring of 1939. However, she pulled out at the same time as her sister "Yolie." The fun-loving sisters together transferred to the College of St. Scholastica in Duluth where Yolie studied for just one year, and possibly Jinks as well. Recall that their high school was situated on the overarching "Villa" campus. As picked up in the October 8, 1939, issue of St. Scholastica's *Scriptorium*, "Two of the latest additions to our midst have already started upon their quest for fun. Betty Clark and *Virginia Gordon*, popularly known as 'Jinks,' drove to Minneapolis last weekend and from there they traveled on to Carleton." At that time and given their age, it would have been considered a big deal for the girls to drive the distance from Duluth, particularly since the trains provided a reliable means of transportation.

With his older sister, Barbara, Cy attended Carleton College in Northfield, Minnesota, south of the Twin Cities. Two months into his freshman year, his parents wrote the school requesting permission for Cy to miss his Saturday morning classes. They advised of their intention to take their two children to Minneapolis to attend the Minnesota-Notre Dame football game. At Carleton, Cy played with both the football and intramural baseball teams, but he found the school too small with too many rules and restrictions. Following his freshman year (1937–38), he transferred to the University of Minnesota in Minneapolis.

In September 1941, Jinks and Cy married. Yolande made her daughter's satin wedding dress with a hint of handmade tatted French lace sewn around the collar.

According to his father, Cy enlisted in the Army Air Corps on December 8, 1941—the day the U.S. declared war on Germany, within 24 hours of the Pearl Harbor attack. He took his boot camp training at Kelly Field in Texas. Jinks then joined Cy in Lubbock, Texas, where he was stationed as a Flying Cadet with the U.S. Army Airforce at Reese Air Force Base. The City of Lubbock had offered 2,000 acres to the War Department to build the airfield.

Five months after breaking ground on construction of the military installation, the Lubbock Army Air Corps Advance Flying School officially opened in January 1942. Later that same year—13 months after his marriage to Jinks—Cadet Charles Cleland Liscomb lost his life in an accident while training as a bomber pilot. Although Cy completed his night training unharmed, the fatal accident occurred when he honored his friend's request to co-pilot his final night training flight. Cy became the first World War II casualty from Duluth. The *Duluth Herald* reported his death on October 29, 1942:

"Cadet Liscomb, 22 years of age and the son of Mr. and Mrs. Charles F. Liscomb of 2532 East Fourth Street, died as a result of injuries suffered in a midnight parachute jump from a United States army air force plane in Texas.

"Cadet Liscomb was stationed at Lubbock, Tex. He was to have received his wings as a lieutenant in the air force Nov. 10. His father, prominent in state and national insurance circles and former president of the Duluth Chamber of Commerce, said that his son had died when he bailed out of a bomber plane. Liscomb had been on a routine training flight when one of the plane's engines failed. The bomber was losing altitude and he received radio orders from his instructor on the ground to bail out. With him was a co-pilot.

"When the order came through to abandon the ship, the two were at an altitude of approximately 1,000 feet. They bailed out. The co-pilot landed safely but Liscomb's parachute opened too late. He died of the injuries he received in landing.

"His wife, the former Virginia Gordon of Duluth, who has been residing with him in Texas, is returning to Duluth. A sister, Barbara, is now the wife of Capt. John M. Allen of the U.S. army, stationed at Camp Forrest, Tenn."

Cy died three short weeks following the marriage of Dan and Yo Broderick. I do not know if he joined Jinks in Duluth for their nuptials. Cy was just days away from receiving his commission as a pilot and the War Department's wings when he perished. Jinks would have become a member of the "Gold Star Family" as a result of her husband's death during military service. Shortly afterward, she answered the call of duty herself by joining the Red Cross. She trained in Washington, D.C. and then served in Walla Walla, Washington:

The involvement of the American Red Cross in World War II preceded the entrance of the United States into the conflict. When hostilities began in Europe in 1939, the Red Cross became the chief provider of relief supplies for the civilian victims of conflict distributed by the Geneva-based International Red Cross Committee.

In February 1941, the Red Cross responded to a request by the U.S. government to begin a Blood Donor Service to produce lifesaving plasma for the armed forces in anticipation of America's entry into the war. After the attack on Pearl Harbor on December 7, 1941, the Red Cross quickly mobilized a volunteer and staff force to fulfill the mandates of its 1905 congressional charter requiring that the organization "furnish volunteer aid to the sick and wounded of armies in time of war" and to "act in matters of voluntary relief and in accord with the military and naval authorities as a medium of communication between the people of the United States of America and their Army and Navy."

Many of the new hospitals opened on March 5, 1943, including those in Washington state at Vancouver Barracks, Spokane, and Walla Walla. McCaw General Hospital, a 1,502-bed general hospital, operated at Fort Walla Walla.

Assigned to McGaw General Hospital, Jinks met **Douglas Bennett Guy** (1919–2007) at the same hospital where he served with the Army Medical Administrative Corps in Walla Walla. Founded in 1920, the Medical Administrative Corps grew rapidly during WWII, from fewer than 100 officers in 1939 to over 22,000 by 1945. As relayed by their daughter Dianne, Doug took notice when Jinks walked into the dining hall at the hospital. She was attractive, but he also observed her "terrible posture" and teased her about it in later years.

My Uncle Doug came from Moose Jaw, Saskatchewan, Canada. At age five, his family moved from Canada to Santa Monica, California, eventually settling in San Francisco and then San Mateo. Doug entered San Mateo High School as a freshman where he became active in school politics and journalism with an interest in writing sports articles. His father suffered heart issues and died young, when Doug was in high school. His mother then joined the workforce as a dental assistant.

As a junior, Doug became a high school sports correspondent for the *San Francisco Chronicle* and other Peninsula newspapers. While he earned an income as a journalist, the fathers of some of his friends encouraged him to pursue a college degree. To pave the way, he kept this job writing while enrolled one year at a community college and after, when he transferred to Stanford University. Like my father at Notre Dame, Doug graduated in the class of 1941 with a degree from the School of Journalism. He maintained his athleticism as a member of the swimming team at Stanford, which later greatly influenced his children's interest in aquatic sports.

Doug became an American citizen while serving in the U.S. Army. In 1944, the couple married in Walla Walla where one year later, Jinks gave birth to their first born, Dianne. Following the war, the newlyweds and their infant child moved to Menlo Park in the San Francisco Bay Area where Doug worked for a short time in advertising before opening his own advertising and marketing agency in Palo Alto. He enjoyed great success with many significant local and regional accounts. Ever creative and always innovative, he also developed a variety of mail order products and ideas. Meanwhile, he loved art. He painted, drew, and maintained a lifelong interest in marrying words with images, often as a cartoonist to the delight of his family and friends as recipients of his many creations— myself included.

In Palo Alto, Doug and Jinks raised six children—**Dianne Gordon** (Hoge) (b. 1945), **David James** (b. 1947), **Laurance Bennett** (b. 1948), **Joanne Hoke** (McNamara) (b. 1951), and fraternal twins **Denise Sterne** (Incerpi) and **Theresa "Terrie" Ann** (Bugay) (b. 1958).

Around 1960, the couple bought a vacation home for the family in Aptos, some 50 miles south of Palo Alto and due east of Santa Cruz by 11 miles. They had purchased a parcel of land directly on the waterfront intending to build. However, when it came to their attention that they could not get flood insurance, they traded the lot for the Aptos house perched on a cliff with a view of the bay. My first cousin David bought the home from his parents in 1986 and resides there to this day. Meanwhile, Doug and Jinks moved their primary residence from Palo Alto to Los Altos where they remained for the rest of their lives.

With tremendous pride, Doug and Jinks passionately supported their six children through college and doted on their twelve grandchildren.

Together, the couple enjoyed golf and Stanford football. Jinks had a great sense of adventure and thought nothing of dropping everything to take road trips with the kids, whether cross-country or to Mexico. She once met up with the twins as college students while they traveled in Europe, when Dianne and her family lived briefly in Covington, England. From Great Britain, the trio took off for the mainland where Denise and Terrie observed first hand their mother's command of the French language as it quickly came back following many years of dormancy.

My Aunt Jinks and her family were a lot of fun to be around, although we Brodericks didn't see them nearly often enough. Aunt Jinks volunteered at her children's schools and remained active in gardening, golf, bridge, church activities, and various clubs. In her later years after Doug retired, she worked for a time as a real estate agent and at a wedding shop in Palo Alto.

Known as "Mimi" to her grandchildren, Jinks endured a lengthy struggle with Alzheimer's. Her granddaughter Kim recalls with fascination how the disease activated her long-term memory. All of a sudden, in her compromised state, "Mimi" began speaking fluent French and playing an eloquent rendition of the "Notre Dame Victory March" on the piano. Both talents came back to her momentarily as if in a dream.

Virginia Stone Gordon Guy died on December 6, 2002, at age 83 after 58 years of marriage and a fulfilled life with her beloved family.

An avid golfer and tennis player until the last years of his life, Doug— known as "DoDo" by his grandchildren—spent many happy days at Sharon Heights Country Club in Menlo Park. With distinct memories of Doug's writing, paintings, and caricature drawings, his family fondly recalls his creativity, wit, charm, humor, gentle spirit, and caring manner. "With his broad infectious smile, a self-deprecating shrug of his shoulders, and that twinkle in his eyes, he could soften any moment and light up any room." He spent his sunset years in an assisted living facility at Pilgrim Haven in Los Altos.

Surrounded by family, Douglas Bennett Guy died peacefully in Los Altos on October 24, 2007, at age 88.

Laurance Sterne Gordon, Jr. (1922--1998) &
Patricia Everett Kirby (1927–2018)

The youngest of the three Gordon children, **Laurance "Larry" Sterne Gordon, Jr.**, was born on July 15, 1922. Following his schooling at Holy Rosary and Cathedral High School in Duluth, Larry attended junior college for a year but did not graduate. He stayed close to the Gordon homestead in Duluth, Minnesota.

Outside of school, for many years Larry worked with his father and his partners at Draper, Gordon, & Walker in the food brokerage business in Duluth. The one interruption in business came with the outbreak of World War II.

During the war, Larry served as a master sergeant in the China-Burma-India (CBI) Theatre although he was not on the front lines in combat. As a non-commissioned officer in the U.S. Army, he readied the soldiers as a radio communications operator and became particularly fascinated with the Indian culture during his deployment.

> Once the United States entered the war, American strategy called for building up China as a source of manpower, as a base for bombers, and the eventual invasion of Japan. Given the "Germany First" strategy, however, the CBI Theatre lay far down the Allies' list of priorities. As it played out, despite the best efforts of numerous Americans, notably those with engineering and logistics feats, CBI contributed little to Japan's defeat, except perhaps to keep China in the war and thereby tie up sizable Japanese resources on the Asian mainland.

In 1947, Larry married **Patricia "Pat" Everett Kirby** (1927–2018). Her parents, Tressie née Everett and John Kirby, Jr., raised Pat and her older sister Barb in Biwabik, Minnesota, 60 miles north of Duluth. Pat's father worked on the iron ore range in Minnesota; her mother, at a women's downtown clothing store (Shapiro's) in Virginia, Minnesota. In later years, Larry referred to his bride as "Maude," the television character played by Bea Arthur in whom he and others observed a strong resemblance.

Larry and Pat had four children—**Patricia Kirby** (League) (1948–2013), **Laurance Sterne III** (b. 1950), **Jeanne Starr** (Dietz) (b. 1952), and **Elizabeth Armella** (Ramstad) (b. 1955)—all born in Duluth.

Larry stayed on with Draper, Gordon & Walker when he returned from the war and for several years after his father relocated to Phoenix. In the intervening years, father and son had an unexplained falling out. My Uncle Larry eventually bought out the interest of his partner Doug Walker, long after Draper had passed. On his own, Larry formed L.S. Gordon & Associates. The food brokerage business gave him and Pat occasion to travel a fair amount, and they got the bug. For several years beginning in the mid-1950s, the family of six drove south and vacationed in southeast Florida for a couple of weeks each summer.

In 1955, Larry commenced the building of a second home in Twig some 15 miles northwest of Duluth, also in Saint Louis County. He loved to build things. He began with a rather rudimentary cabin comprised of a living room, kitchen, and wood-burning fireplace. He situated two twin beds on either side of the fireplace before building a bunkhouse for the girls, and then a bunkhouse for his son, Larry, with a sauna in the rear. Next, he added a deck in front of the house followed by a breezeway. A decade later, Larry wrapped up his protracted home construction project with the addition of a barn.

Situated on Grand Lake, the affectionately named "Red Barn Inn" gave the Gordons the opportunity to enjoy life's simple pleasures each summer. The family savored the great outdoors with neighbors from sunrise to sundown—biking, fishing, rowing, canoeing, pontoon boat riding, horseback riding, and more. My Uncle Larry sustained a long-standing tradition by hosting a grand 4th of July celebration each year with many friends coming up from Duluth. The vacation home with its natural habitat also provided respite for Larry and Pat throughout their retirement years.

In 1960, Larry relocated the family to Minnetonka where he opened up a second L.S. Gordon & Associates office while retaining a business presence in Duluth for another eight to 10 years. He further expanded by placing sales people in North and South Dakota although he did not open offices there. For some time, Pat worked as a physical education teacher at Immaculate Heart of Mary where the children attended elementary school.

From Minnetonka, the family summered in Twig with Larry joining them on weekends, much like my father joined us in Madison, Ohio, on weekends each summer. Otherwise, Larry and Pat traveled extensively with business associates as the years passed.

Once the children left the nest, Larry and Pat turned their sights to the warm climate in Florida. For years, they motored their luxury Airstream to winter in the Florida Keys. Later, they established a permanent pad at the canal-fronted River Ranch RV Resort on the west bank of the Kissimmee River in central Florida. Here, they rolled their motor home in each winter and established lifelong friendships. When it became too much for them, they left the RV permanently stationed at River Ranch where they continued to winter while maintaining their homes in Minnetonka and Twig. Each spring for many years, my aunt and uncle also made the trek to the New Orleans Jazz Festival to enjoy a week of music with friends.

Pat became an avid cross-stitcher, cook, and Gopher Hockey fan while Larry maintained close contact with the Brodericks and Guys. He truly loved his extended family, and he did his best to visit and stay in close contact with us. He amused us with his fun-loving spirit, mischievous nature, and colorful storytelling.

In his retirement years, around the time when Dick Neergaard delved into his ancestral history, Uncle Larry undertook a similar endeavor. Larry had not yet completed his genealogical research when he slipped away in his sleep at Twig on September 11, 1998, at age 76. Regrettably, I was unable to obtain any documentation stemming from his extensive research about the Gordon and Westcott families.

Surviving Larry by 20 years, Pat passed away in her sleep at age 90 in 2018 after her third battle with cancer. Larry and Pat are buried at the Calvary Cemetery in Duluth. Their eldest child, Patricia Kirby Gordon (League) predeceased her mother by five years, having succumbed to cancer herself, in Colorado Springs on February 24, 2013, at age 64.

ALONG WITH THEIR SPOUSES, this "GEN 11" segment wraps up with background on the Gordons' maternal first cousin William Adrian Newcomb and second cousin Richard "Dick" Hampton Neergaard. We begin with the renowned scientist Bill Newcomb and his wife, Susie, who knows no greater treasure than what is found in these pages about our family's enviable heritage.

William "Bill" Adrian Newcomb (1927–1999) & Susan "Susie" Jane Hester (1942–present)

William "Bill" Adrian Newcomb was five years old when his parents, William Ambrose and Nina Hoke Newcomb, divorced. Always strong and upbeat, Nina left her husband behind as resident manager of the Hotel Sainte Claire in San Jose, California, to raise Bill on her own. In the throes of the Great Depression, she drove cross-country with young Bill and their pet monkey, "Pedro," who misbehaved and ended up in a zoo. Without child support from her ex-husband, Nina and her son lived in Forest Hills, New York, before moving in with Wessie and Dora Hoke in nearby Garden City. His uncle Wessie greatly influenced Bill's interest in science during his formative years and as a student at Garden City High School. Bill completed his secondary studies in three years, graduating in 1944, three years before Wessie's fatal heart attack.

Young Bill studied diligently in hopes of receiving financial aid. New York recognized his academic achievement by granting him a full scholarship to attend any college in the state. Bill elected to attend Cornell University in Ithaca, New York.

Nina's son broke from his academic pursuit long enough to serve his country as the military prepared for emerging geopolitical tensions in the wake of World War II. During this time, President Harry S. Truman grappled with both the signs of a Cold War with the Soviet Union and the role of the United States as an emerging superpower. At the dawn of the atomic age, our nation found itself leading the "free world" with potential enemies on multiple fronts while postured with a peacetime training focus.

One year into his post-secondary education, in the Spring of 1946, Bill enlisted in the Army infantry. He headed off to Officer Candidate School at Fort Dix, New Jersey, before landing in the Air Corps at Buckley Field, Colorado, where he received radio operations and mechanics training. Within four months of his enlistment, which included a brief stint at Scott Air Force Base, Illinois, Bill took off for Japan and then Korea during the earliest stage of the Cold War. He taught calculus and mathematics to the officers and, oddly enough, a course on venereal diseases to the enlisted men as well. The Army released each recruit with a requisite supply of condoms upon completing Bill's class and passing a test on sexually-transmitted diseases. In later years, Bill got a kick out of talking about the experience and his vital contribution to military preparedness as an Army Air Force sergeant.

> Around the time Bill completed his deployment, the National Security Act of 1947 brought significant changes to the armed forces, separating the Air Force from the Army and establishing the unit as an independent branch of the newly-created National Defense Establishment. The Act also created the Joint Chiefs of Staff and the National Security Council.

Bill returned to Cornell University in the fall of 1947, just in time to celebrate his 20th birthday. One year later, he earned a Bachelor of Arts & Sciences in mathematics, physics, and general studies with distinction, and he graduated as valedictorian of his class. Immediately thereafter, Bill entered the University's graduate school on a financial scholarship and went on to earn a doctoral degree in physics. For three years, he held a teaching assistantship in Cornell's Physics Department. In his fourth and final year of the Ph.D. program, Bill received a fellowship to teach mathematics.

Privileged to study at Cornell under the tutelage of world-renowned American theoretical physicist Richard Phillips Feynman (1918–1988), in 1952, Bill wrote his Ph.D. dissertation on the obscure subject of "Mass Corrections to Hyperfine Structure in Hydrogen and Deuterium." Years later, in 1965, for his contributions to the development of quantum electrodynamics, Bill's mentor Feynman received the Nobel Prize in Physics with Julian Schwinger and Shin'ichirō Tomonaga.

Although Bill once considered getting into the practice of medicine, he ultimately became a theorist in the field of plasma physics. His fascination came from discovering the behavior of matter when atomic particles are so highly energized, they lose their distinctiveness and structure. Bill developed this interest during his brief tenure as a faculty member at Princeton University in New Jersey. The Manhattan Project had piqued his curiosity early on, but Bill determined he would rather work on the peaceful use of atomic energy than nuclear weaponry. He then took his training to the flourishing Lawrence Livermore Laboratory, a federal research facility in Livermore founded in 1952 by the University of California, Berkeley. Here, he became a theoretical physicist and professor of theoretical plasma physics in the graduate program at the University of California, Davis, Department of Applied Science, located in Livermore.

At Lawrence Livermore Laboratory, Bill became a leading world expert in plasma physics. To his wife, Susie, Bill described plasma as the gas surrounding the sun. "It's as hot as the hydrogen bomb; we want to be able to use this energy for peaceful means." The nuclear reaction that comes from smashing hydrogen atoms together—a process known as nuclear fusion—preoccupied Bill's thinking during his illustrious career.

> Bill would have been ecstatic to learn of the landmark achievement of "fusion ignition" at the Lawrence Livermore Laboratory in December 2022. Decades in the making, the nuclear fusion breakthrough produced more energy from fusion than the laser energy used to drive it, bringing us closer to advances in national defense and the future of clean power. Building on the contributions of generations of Livermore scientists including the legendary Bill Newcomb, this astonishing scientific advance puts us on the precipice of a future no longer reliant on fossil fuel.

Bill wrote several papers with Gregory Benford (1941–present), a well-known American science fiction author and astrophysicist who with Bill studied the stability of plasma in magnetically-confined fusion devices at Lawrence Radiation Laboratory early in their careers. In one of his books, Benford pondered whether he could forage Bill Newcomb's papers on plasma stability for story material. Gregory claimed "The man's a gold mine."

Bill's measure involved far more than plasma physics. Never getting stuck in a single field, he discovered a mathematical method of calculating stability conditions but did not publish his finding. Bill then became world-renowned for a puzzle he devised. The idea occurred to him in

1960 and he discussed it with some Princeton philosophers. Their vexation with the problem kept it alive in such circles without any formal publication:

> "Newcomb's Paradox" refers to a problem in decision theory in which the seemingly rational decision ends up with a worse outcome than the seemingly irrational one. The paradox revolves around a particular example, where an agent will give you rewards depending on how it predicts you will act. Intricately tied to problems in prediction, causality, decisions, and free will, Newcomb's Paradox remains as perplexing as when first conceived more than half a century ago. The thought experiment involving a game between two players, one of whom is able to predict the future, continues to be discussed in the literature to this day. Published by the Cambridge University Press as recently as 2018, *Newcomb's Problem* by Arif Ahmed attests to the staying power of the paradox attributed to Bill Newcomb. [You can see a visual of "Newcomb's Paradox" on YouTube.]

Early during his 35-year tenure at the Lawrence Livermore Laboratory, Bill met **Susan "Susie" Hester**, then a student majoring in French and history at the University of California, Berkeley. First crossing paths in the pool area of her apartment complex near campus, they quickly sparked a romance despite a 15-year age difference. The adage—opposites attract—proved spot on. Susie observed that with a quiet disposition, Bill did not fraternize with his professional colleagues. In contrast, she was quite talkative and social. Yet his intellectual curiosity and sense of humor drew her in. According to Susie, Bill had one of the most brilliant minds of the century, "but he couldn't operate a shovel, a remote control, or a microwave oven."

On July 4, 1963, in front of a judge and two witnesses at Mill's College in Oakland, Susie married Bill right out of college at age 21. Bill loved good food, and so after the nuptials, the newlyweds proceeded directly to the Cliff House in San Francisco where they hoped to enjoy Chateaubriand for lunch. Susie had to provide proof of her age before the waiter would serve her wine, and the beef presented to them was burnt. Overcoming the disappointment, they capped their wedding day with a live performance of *Kiss Me, Kate*. On their 4th of July anniversary each year, they made a tradition of taking a ferry ride to San Francisco for the dual celebration of their wedding and our nationhood with adoption of the Declaration of Independence.

The age difference between the couple did not bother Susie's parents. In fact, they were crazy about Bill and relieved that he offered their daughter financial security. Bill was stunned by the generosity of the wedding present they gifted him—a calculator valued at $1,000. How apropos! Shortly after their wedding, Bill bought a lovely age-in-place home on a three-quarter-acre parcel in Walnut Creek where Susie lives to this day. He partially financed the $34,000 investment with the $4,000 savings he inherited from his father's aunt.

In Walnut Creek, located in the eastern region of the San Francisco Bay area, Bill and Susie raised **Geoffrey** (b. 1965) and **Silvia** (b. 1969). In 1973, while the children were still youngsters and soon after *Scientific America* published an article on his paradox, Bill accepted an invitation to teach at New York University for six months. The notable mathematics and science scholar Martin Gardner paid the Newcombs a visit at their New York City apartment to share an enormous box containing letters from people fascinated by Bill's paradox. The volume of letters attested to the fame he had gained, although Bill never liked drawing attention to himself.

Susie's mother had studied at New York University and often talked about Madison Square Garden, which prompted Susie's interest in checking it out. One day Susie took Silvia to the coliseum, which by chance featured a horse show for their entertainment. Four-year-old Silvia became enthralled and could not stop talking about the spectacle until her mother put her on a horse when they returned to Walnut Creek. Given her young age, Silvia rode a Shetland pony and trained to enter a horse show of her own, in turn spurring her mother's interest in raising purebred Lipizzan horses. Susie put a lot of time into finding suitable stables and training the equines for sale—eight or nine in total before health ailments slowed her down. She sold her first mare, a superstar, for $24,000, and later sold the other Lipizzans when the suckling fouls reached four-months-old. Taking in $6,000 to $10,000 for each sale, Susie earned just enough from the enterprise to qualify for Social Security before calling it quits.

While Susie raised the prized horses in the Bay Area, Bill continued his plasma physics research in earnest. His scholarly work and expertise in magnetism at the Lawrence Livermore Laboratory drew the attention of Russian scientists in the mid-1970s. During the term of Leonid Ilyich Brezhnev (1906–1982) as General Secretary of the Communist Party of the Soviet Union (1964–1982), Russia became keenly interested in figuring out how to contain plasma gas. They experimented with an oversized donut-shaped magnetic device they call a tokamak, and they wanted to tap into Bill's knowledge in their quest to solve the containment puzzle. Having achieved nuclear parity with the United States by the early-1970s, the Soviet Union invited Bill to bring his young family over and work at the Moscow Energy Institute. Only one other American scientist had done so previously.

As a couple with two young children, Bill and Susie endeavored to make the proposition a reality in the belief that they would live in an apartment complex in Moscow with other Russians. In preparation, the Lawrence Livermore Laboratory fronted $4,000 for the family to study Russian at the Berlitz in Oakland. Resolute in her desire to learn the language to ensure the best possible outcome for her family as they planned to navigate their way behind the sealed off "Iron Curtain," Susie went full-bore and succeeded in becoming fluent in Russian as her third language behind English and French. Susie and Silvia even attended the local Russian church on Sundays in preparation. Before grasping English, young Silvia quickly learned to read and write Russian as every word is spelled phonetically. While speaking the language conversationally, Susie gained insights from the Russians she met stateside who shared riveting stories of their precarious efforts to escape the autocratic Communist regime.

The thrill of discovery came to the Newcombs when the family returned from New York to Walnut Creek where they immersed themselves in the Russian language and raising Lipizzans. The parents of students at the elementary school Geoff attended in New York City had raised funds to purchase a simple computer to help their children learn programming. Finding inspiration in the parents' endeavor, Susie learned of a notable program for young students to get an education in computer science closer to home. The Lawrence Hall of Science, affiliated with the

University of California, Berkeley, hosted a computer with interactive programming to inspire children's interest in science and math.

As a result of her ingenuity, Susie and a friend discovered a way to tap into a port at "The Lawrence" which enabled the students at Walnut Acres Elementary School to access the science center's mainframe and sophisticated interactive programming remotely. The endeavor simply required the placement of a teletype terminal at the school and a telephone hookup that cost about $100 per month. The lab motivated the students to learn by thinking logically and working with the metric system of measurement. It also provided an outlet to engage the parents in their children's learning with access to the teletype and a class offered to them by the Lawrence Hall of Science.

Through fundraising, Susie leaned on friends and other parents to underwrite the cost while Bill taught a class in programming for the school's fourth and fifth graders. Remote access to a mainframe computer in benefit to the education community was unprecedented in the mid-1970s. Walnut Acres Elementary School was then located in the nation's 10th largest school district, yet no middle or high school had access to a computer. Secondary school teachers clamored for an opportunity similar to what Susie and Bill made possible for their children and Geoff and Silvia's classmates.

Meanwhile, the Newcombs made final preparations for the move to Moscow in 1975 when Bill suffered a major heart attack caused by blockage of his left anterior descending artery. He lost the vessel completely. At age 48, he became one of the first patients in the U.S. to receive a defibrillator implant which delivered electric shocks when needed to restore his regular heart rhythm. While the device prolonged his life by 24 years, the experience altered his life's course. Instead of Bill joining the scientists at the Moscow Energy Institute, the Russians instead traveled to California to tap into Bill's expansive knowledge. Bill became convinced that they would not figure out how to effectively contain plasma gas, at least not in his lifetime. His hunch evidently proved accurate, as the quest continues to this day according to Susie.

Bill smoked heavily and rarely exercised before his heart attack. But it was a wakeup call, so he made up his mind that he would take better care of himself. With but two vessels pumping his heart, in his late 40s, Bill took up running marathons and ultra-marathons with the "Hash-House Harriers," one of an international group of non-competitive running social clubs based in San Francisco. He ran no fewer than 200 races and often ran 50 milers including one race from Sacramento to Auburn, California—this one in 107-degree heat that took him 11 hours to complete. Although he plodded along slowly, Bill earned his "Ultraman" nickname as a regular and consistent runner until the last days of his life.

Bill retired from the Lawrence Livermore Lab in 1991, but he continued to teach graduate students at the Department of Applied Sciences in Livermore. Shortly after his retirement and before his death in 1999, he stepped in to serve as an adjunct professor at the University of California, Davis. Within a year of wrapping up teaching, his heart finally gave out. Despite pleas by Susie and their son Geoffrey, Bill could not obtain insurance to cover the exorbitant cost of a heart transplant due to his senior status. He died at age 72.

Uniquely gifted, Bill is remembered by colleagues for his rigor in analyzing problems in benefit to the Lab and for his ability to teach advanced technical courses and to mentor Ph.D. candidates on behalf of the University. The Hash-House Harriers recall the "Ultraman" with his wry smile as kind, soft-spoken, fun, and tough as nails.

With tremendous stamina, Bill was tough but one of the kindest people Susie knew. Although his mother Nina raised him Catholic, Bill gave up on organized religion during college. An agnostic, he once told Susie, "I believe in the gods." He loved P.G. Wodehouse, a British author and one of the most widely read humorists of the 20th century. Susie recalls that Bill liked Wodehouse's dirty limericks, especially the Catholic ones. A voracious reader, he enjoyed the classics, notably William Shakespeare's *Macbeth*, and he developed in-depth knowledge on a wide variety of subjects, especially those dealing with nature including dendrology and astronomy. Susie marveled at the varied book titles Bill had strewn in virtually every room of the house when he died. He was the definition of a renaissance man.

Susie described her husband as fair, absolutely honest, and above all else, a consummate intellectual. He was also funny. He always laughed. He read to their son every night as a child, and later, when Geoff stopped by the house as an adult, Bill continued to read out loud to him. They laughed their hearts out with Geoff sometimes falling to the floor in hysterics. Theirs was an endearing relationship.

Lawrence Livermore Laboratory and running club colleagues held separate memorial services to honor Bill for his extraordinary life. He was proper and wished nothing to be done with his ashes that would be considered ghoulish or illegal. With his family, Bill's running club observed his wishes and reportedly scattered his ashes in a most dignified manner.

Now aged 82 and still living in the Walnut Creek home Bill bought shortly after their marriage, Susie is the source of the treasure trove on family lore shared with my brother Dennis and me. My newfound soul sister still marvels at what she came to learn of Bill's extraordinary pedigree.

Born in Chicago, Susie comes from a pioneering family line herself, dating at least to the American Revolution. Around 1770, her paternal ancestor Simon Kenton came as an explorer from Virginia to the new territory of "cane" land which the Indians referred to as "Kain-tuck-ee." Simon is known to have saved the life of fellow American frontiersman Daniel Boone in their fight against the raiding warriors. Referring to salt licks, the "Blue Licks" Battlefield State Resort Park in northeastern Kentucky, site of the last battle of the Revolutionary War in Kentucky, features a memorial to Simon Kenton. To this day, two log cabins built prior to 1790 stand on the original site of Simon's property 20 miles northeast of the park in Washington, Kentucky, and many townspeople and streets still carry Susie's maiden name—"Hester."

Shortly after her birth in Chicago, Susie relocated with her family to California and then Seattle, Washington, before moving to Idaho Falls, Idaho. Here, Susie attended elementary and intermediate schools and learned to snow ski before continuing her studies in Lausanne, Switzerland. For two years, Susie studied at the French-speaking Brilliantmont International School as a boarder. A skiing accident at a chalet resort in Villar, Switzerland, set her back, but Susie's parents let her stay an extra year with summer and winter vacation time spent in Davos in the Swiss Alps.

As a young adult while working as a camp counselor in Montecito, California, Susie found herself in the company of Julie (Eisenhower) and Tricia (Cox), daughters of President Richard and Pat Nixon. Susie participated with the campers in horseback riding and water skiing after which time Tricia Nixon Cox became a good friend of Susie's sister.

Early on, Susie developed a passion for cooking, entertaining, and gardening. She often entered baked good contests in county fairs in her hometown of Idaho Falls and acquired a taste for fine food in Switzerland. The "foodie" gained a reputation for preparing flavorful dishes while entertaining guests. Her coveted garden still flourishes with flowers, herbs, and vegetables.

Perhaps Susie's proudest endeavor came from her research and lobbying efforts on behalf of the critically endangered California condor. With a wingspan of 9.5 feet and weighing up to 25 pounds, it is the largest land bird in North America. She personally appeared before then Governor Arnold Schwarzenegger appealing for removal of lead from the condor range. In 2007, he signed the Ridley-Tree Condor Preservation Act, creating a non-lead zone for hunters within the range of the California condor. In 2013, the governor signed legislation requiring the use of nonlead ammunition statewide for the taking of all wildlife. As a consequence of the actions of Susie and others, the wild condor population—once numbered under 22—has steadily increased, reaching 561 in 2023 according to the U.S. Fish and Wildlife Service.

Just months after Bill's death in 1999, Silvia gave birth to "GEN 13" **Michaela Carbaat** and three years later, to **Miles Carbaat**. Recently completing her studies at the University of San Francisco School of Law while pursuing an interest in "The Innocent Project," Michaela has been immensely helpful to Susie in pulling together family records documenting the Westcotts' rich history. Her brother, Miles, is enrolled in the criminal justice program at California State University, Sacramento. Susie's children and grandchildren all live in the San Francisco Bay area.

Two and one-half years following the introductory phone call I received from Susie that set *The Westcott Story* in motion, I had the good fortune to meet her in person at her home in Walnut Creek in March 2023. During our visit, I also met her daughter, Silvia, and granddaughter,

Michaela. In San Francisco, I introduced Susie to three of my Guy cousins, Dianne, Joanna, and Denise. She welcomed the occasion to meet her husband Bill's extended family, and we were delighted to meet Bill's extraordinarily gifted widow, Susie Hester Newcomb.

Richard "Dick" Hampton Neergaard (1932– 2023) & Lois Gardner (1934–2023)

The son of Clifford "Gould" and Virginia Corcoran deNeergaard, **Richard 'Dick' Hampton Neergaard**—second cousin to Jinks, Yo and Larry—retired from an illustrious career with Proctor & Gamble in Cincinnati. As mentioned, with Susie Hester Newcomb, he is the source of much of the family history gathered for this story, including our Westcott pedigree chart. Recall his fascination with a letter written by "GEN 8" Thomas Grant Westcott to his wife Josie which launched Dick's own genealogical research undertaken as a post-retirement project.

Gould and Virginia raised their only child in uptown Manhattan near Columbia University. Sometime after transferring from one grammar school to another, Dick's records were cleansed along with his birth surname. He had already been told that "Neergaard" did not warrant the "de," so at that point, Dick simply dropped it without taking any official action. He went by "Neergaard" thereafter.

In New York City, Dick graduated from Regis High School where physician-scientist, immunologist, and former National Institute of Allergy and Infectious Diseases director Anthony Fauci attended a generation later.

Dick entered Cambridge-based Massachusetts Institute of Technology (MIT) in the 1954 class with his close fraternity brethren. After one year, he headed for West Point where, in Dick's words, he became "spiritually and physically" toughened. After returning to MIT for two more years, Dick volunteered for the draft, thereby securing GI support for his final year at MIT. Following two years with the U.S. Army, in 1957, Dick earned a degree in business and engineering administration. Upon graduating, he found himself in an environment that sought out "techies." He told interviewers of his interest in international opportunities because "I would know things they wouldn't, and vice versa—we could learn from each other." He admired the ethos of Proctor & Gamble from whom he received the best employment package, and off he went.

Dick met his life partner, **Lois Jeanne Gardner**, while studying at MIT. Also raised in New York before her family relocated to Lenox, Massachusetts, Lois embarked on a child and teen modeling career and later graduated with a Bachelor's degree in interior architectural design from the Rhode Island School of Design in Providence. As described in an email to me in 2021, "I crashed a party, saw a delicate beauty in the center of the room surrounded by admirers, and . . . WOW! *Coup de foudre.* She had in fact been the cover girl on several *American Girl* magazines. When a youth's hormones are fired up, judgment doesn't stand a chance. Waving away warnings of neuroses, I put my head down and charged. We're still married." Dick passed away a month and a half after Lois, on December 1, 2023. His parents likewise died in the same year, in 1988.

In the week following his college graduation, Dick and Lois married, honeymooned in Canada, and moved to New Jersey to launch Dick's 30-year career with Proctor & Gamble. True to its promise, the conglomerate placed him in its international division—eight years each in Belgium and Germany.

Dick started work at P&G's Staten Island factory as foreman in the detergent-making department. The around-the-clock shifts changed every week. Four and one-half years and two children later, after he advanced to "day work" as a department manager, P&G posted the family in Europe.

Placed in P&G's plant in Malines north of Brussels, Dick found the atmosphere "as sweet as the New York plant factory had been tough." Eighteen months later, P&G transferred Dick to assist with start-up operations in the Rhineland-Palatinate city of Worms, Germany, a rural port town situated on the west bank of the Upper Rhine River. Famed for both the Edict of Worms in which Martin Luther was declared a heretic and for the semi-sweet German wine Liebfraumilch, Worms separated Dick from the Cincinnati, Ohio-based corporate headquarters by a great distance both physically and culturally. When the startup proved successful, P&G gave him responsibility for the plant's entire production operation—packing, warehousing, and shipping with a staff of 500.

Dick took in the panoramic views on approach to his family's quarters on the east bank of the Rhine driving home from the Worms factory.

"The sun, setting behind me, would illuminate the dark underbelly of the cloud that usually hung over the Rhine at that time of day, turning it black and orange, and bathing the hill and castle on the far side in gold." The Neergaard family enjoyed a most charmed life in western Germany near the Pyrenees and the foothills in both northern Spain and southwestern France.

The business grew, demanding more bureaucracy, and in 1967, Dick moved out of the warm camaraderie of plant operations to the company's more formal quarters near Frankfurt, as manufacturing liaison. He oversaw marketing, research and development, purchasing, finance, and manufacturing in other P&G subsidiaries while also coordinating German production scheduling and administering manufacturing capacity and capital planning. In 1970, Dick transferred to P&G's European headquarters in Brussels to perform these same functions for the entire European continent.

Finally, Dick transferred to corporate headquarters in Cincinnati, Ohio, in 1978, again to do manufacturing liaison work and coordination, this time for paper products—primarily Pampers and Luvs disposable diapers—for the company's international businesses. The logistics of moving massive amounts of such light, bulky goods around the globe proved formidable. At one time, on both the Atlantic and Pacific oceans, P&G emerged as the biggest single shipper of sea-vans, a type of shipping container. The company then moved rapidly to build on-the-ground capacity in each individual market, eventually obviating the need for an international manufacturing liaison and for Dick personally.

In 1983, P&G gathered Dick with half a dozen similar "white elephants," people whose then current functions had evaporated but who were too senior to fire and, in Dick's words "too mavericky to be inserted atop an innocently by-standing part of the business." The "mavericks" followed orders to go off and "invent the factory of the future!" They pondered and mulled and finally worked out a plan of attack as the first order of business. They attempted to uncover details behind the business strategies of the individual categories of products to be manufactured and quickly discovered that, not only did they not know the strategies, neither did anyone else in the company.

Forgetting factory design, they took off on what proved to be the most intense learning period of Dick's life and the most exciting segment of his career. As Dick explained it, the group set out to find out what exactly a "strategy" means, then worked out how to help business teams construct one. Moreover, the mavericks learned how to help the work groups understand the systems in which they had immersed themselves, and, finally, how to master them. The profound experience opened Dick's window to discover how the world works—not just its machines. He learned about human behavior and relationships, and in the process, something more about himself. "It was a sort of organizational psychiatry and profoundly satisfying, but I must admit that it was coincident with my retirement in 1989 that P&G stock took off."

Dick rode out a 30-year career in manufacture management with P&G, retiring one year after the passing of his parents, Gould and Virginia. For the ride, Dick and Lois gave their four children the European experience his father Gould enjoyed for four years with the Hokes in Bordeaux in his formative teenage years.

Dick hesitated to talk about his and Lois's sojourn abroad. Other expat friends who had previously returned to the U.S. warned that, should Dick and Lois go swooning on about the thrills of Alpine skiing and the marvels of restaurants in Provence, they would simply invite resentment. When they returned stateside, they tested those waters once or twice and found the warning to be spot on. "It seemed so unfair—we weren't trying to show off, just share with friends fascinating moments that had delighted us."

Dick and Lois's offspring include a daughter, Susan "Sue" Westcott (b. 1958), and three sons—Arthur Hampton (b. 1960), Richard Corcoran (b. 1963), and John "Peter" (b. 1964). According to Dick, having lived sixteen years in Europe, "We discovered it is a very good deal indeed to possess the cultural ease that comes of being an American, while at the same time enjoying the many elegances of Europe, elegances which are achieved by folks there having been brought up constrained to do things only the 'right way.'" Of great importance to Dick and Lois, moving about in Europe allowed their children to make the liberating discovery early in their lives that there can be more than one "right way" of doing things.

To my knowledge, Susan "Sue" Westcott Neergaard, great-grand-daughter of Caroline "Carrie" Sackett Westcott Neergaard, is the *only* "GEN 12" descendant of "GEN 8" Thomas Grant and Josie Gould Westcott given the name "Westcott" as a middle name at birth. The name passed to one or more descendants of Carrie's sister Susan Westcott Hoke in every generation down the line through "GEN 14" —except "GEN 12."

After graduating from the University of Cincinnati, Dick and Lois's daughter, Sue, eventually made her way into the Human Resources department of General Electric's plastics plant in the Netherlands where she met and in 1995 married Jan Willem van der Werff, who runs operations for Deceuninck, a global Belgian firm that manufactures PVC window systems and building products. They have two boys, Willem and Nick, and are building a home on 32 acres in Cincinnati's western exurbs.

Arthur graduated from MIT as a mechanical engineer and followed his father's footsteps at Proctor & Gamble. Based in Cincinnati, he typically operates in other parts of the world, currently a resident of London while commuting between an equipment fabricator in Switzerland and a P&G factory in China.

Following his graduation from Tufts, Richard also worked with P&G, eventually becoming marketing manager of the company's subsidiary in Egypt, where in 1994 he met and married Ishraq. Richard later left P&G and became General Manager of the Israeli subsidiary of Benckiser—a German consumer-goods company—in Tel Aviv. As an artist, he is developing "Car Art" in conjunction with Formula One teams that provide him with pieces to make his collages while experimenting with poured resins. Richard and Ishraq have two children, Samer and Lila.

Peter became enamored of computers in his mid-teens. After graduating from Carnegie Mellon in applied math, he continued for some years to work in the University's computer department, then in networking for a private software company in Pittsburgh where he lives with his wife Cathy. They have two sons, Steven and Alex.

With a sudden vacuum of time and energy to fill in retirement, while wading through family memorabilia, Dick immersed himself in the subject of his rich heritage. He traced ancestral roots stemming not only from his paternal Westcott line, but from his maternal Corcoran line and his wife's Garner line as well. His Corcoran ancestors immigrated to Cincinnati in the 1850s from Germany and Ireland. Following his maternal line, Dick's uxorial investigation took him to Basel, Switzerland; Leesburg, Virginia; New York City; and Lenox, Massachusetts. Armed with what he already knew about each ancestral family, mostly from the Family Services division of the Church of Jesus Christ of Latter-day Saints, he searched newspapers and visited the cities' halls of records, churches, local libraries, and cemeteries. In the process, he succeeded in unfolding many layers of fascinating ancestral history.

Dick and Lois made their final resting place in Cincinnati where Mark Twain reportedly wanted to be when the world ends because "everything here happens ten years later." They sometimes yearned for the liveliness of favorite places such as "crisp New England, charming Brussels, and sumptuous southern France," but they built a pleasant life in Cincinnati during Dick's final working years and chose to remain after his retirement. At first, he did a bit of consulting, but then as he wound down from a career-oriented life, it dawned on him that he didn't have to put up with this aggravation. Until health issues impaired their mobility, Dick and Lois spent their time travelling, visiting their far-flung children, and doing inconsequential but enjoyable domestic projects like gardening, playing tennis, and for Dick anyway, indulging his interest in genealogy. Dick was also drawn to classical dance and music, notably as a true symphonic and opera aficionado.

Highly creative and technically proficient, Dick became skilled using Photoshop, allowing him to customize digital greeting cards for his family and friends as a favorite pastime. His drill, after coming up with a theme, was to search the Internet for an appropriate scene, download it, then using Adobe Photoshop, insert a photo of the head of his subject—the card recipient. Like a scientist, he stripped out unwanted background and matched not just sizes and angles, but tended to the saturation of colors and the intensities of light. He then used the free download Mozilla Composer from SeaMonkey® to make up a web page where he dropped the image for viewing. To bring the object to life, he sometimes added sound, requiring yet another process step. Impressive technical skills for a gentleman into his ninth decade!

Although we never met in person and did not speak on the phone before his 90th birthday in April 2022, Dick and I exchanged countless emails following our introduction in December 2020. His colorful tales would have made for a far more engaging story about the Westcotts than what I have managed in my own telling. Consider what Dick relayed to me, his pen pal, about the stories his father Gould shared with him as a youngster and his own memory of exploits with his dad:

His [Gould's] *stories of Bordeaux were from the point of view of Huck Finn on the loose in France . . . of how he'd regale his Jesuit teachers with tales of Indians running around Manhattan scalping people, and with weird and wonderful stories of Buffalo Bill and Davy Crockett. He spoke also of adventures involving slingshots, spitballs, and reaching around from behind gentlemen in trams to goose ladies standing in front of them. Tales of Waynesville* [NC] *were no different: cow-tipping, dunking braids into inkwells, spiking watermelons on the vine with gin then taking a girlfriend out on a moonlight raid. I didn't believe half of it. But when I was about 20, we drove together to Waynesville and I met some of the folks he grew up with. They'd slap their thighs and croon 'Goooo* [Gould] *. . . do y'all ruhmembuh . . .' It turned out the exaggerations were actually the other way; he hadn't told me the half of it.*

He wanted me to have a taste of white lightning. He found a classmate (the sheriff) to ask where he could get some. 'Down the highway to that big ol' gnarley pine, turn up a dirt road to a clearing with a stump. When the dogs get tired of yammering, put a ten-dollar bill on the stump, back off, return in about a half hour, keep goin' on up to the end of the road.' We did that, arriving at a ramshackle log cabin. A rawboned woman in gunnysack emerged carrying a gallon jug and three 8-ounce glasses and asked if we'd like a drink. 'Why sure.' She filled the glasses. Chug-a-lug. My eyes teared up, my nose ran, for the rest of the day my esophagus felt as if it was being pleasantly warmed by a blowtorch.

On that highly entertaining note, I offer one last anecdote on Dick Neergaard. We met virtually based on genealogical records he developed post-retirement that Susie Newcomb shared with me in 2020. Now in my post-retirement years—also following a lifelong corporate career—I am struck by the quality of the relationship I developed with my colorful second cousin once removed. Except for one phone conversation, we regularly conversed solely via email for nearly three years.

As I came to know him, Dick struck me as a real-life renaissance man with intellectual curiosity who stoked a passionate heart tapping into the arts and humanities for sustenance. He not infrequently shared gems with me such as a Fred Astaire vocals / instrumental; an Eleanor Powell and Fred Astaire tap dancing routine; a clip of the Masquerade Suite Waltz from *War and Peace*; a video of Mikhail Lobukhin et Anna Nikulina performing in Spartacus's Ballet du Bolshoi; and a Moscow Nights operatic performance by Anna Netrebko and Dmitri Hvorostovsky—all extraordinary performances. I found Dick's taste in classical entertainment captivating and delightful.

Dick's beloved wife of 66 years died peacefully at age 89 on October 20, 2023. Richard "Dick" Hampton Neergaard followed Lois into the hereafter at age 91 on December 1, 2023. I will sorely miss him and will forever credit my second cousin once removed for breathing life into *The Westcott Story*.

At Green Hill Cemetery in Waynesville, North Carolina, Dick's family made plans to bury him with his parents Gould and Virginia deNeergaard, alongside his paternal grandmother "GEN 9" Caroline "Carrie" Sackett Westcott Neergaard, Carrie's brother Hampton Gould Westcott, and Carrie's aunt Dr. Caroline Gould Keller.

We now proceed with coverage of the "GEN 12" Brodericks, Guys, and Gordons—my siblings, first cousins, and me. The introduction leading into this next generation narrative applies equally to my first cousins, the Guys and the Gordons. The story continues with my memoir about my siblings and me, and "GEN 12" ends with snapshots of each of my first cousins.

GENERATION 12 – 1944–2024

Baby Boomers Break Loose by Challenging the Status Quo

My Siblings, First Cousins, and Me

Brodericks
Guys
Gordons

AS THE WESTCOTT STORY EVOLVES, we arrive at the present, well into the 21st century and approaching four centuries in America. In the blink of an eye, my siblings, first cousins, and I emerge as the "senior" generation, best positioned to leave a lasting imprint on our children and theirs. We carry forth what we inherited from our ancestors, both witnessed and unseen, known and heretofore unknown. Traces of Westcotts illuminate the characters who define this 12th generation. Fortitude transcends trials and heartache to reveal prodigious achievements.

I cannot help but bring personal perspective and, by default, emotional bias into my family's present story. To my brothers and sisters especially, I intend no offense by sharing some of our blemishes as this chronicle spanning 14 generations unfolds as history. Transcending the bumps along our lineal path, I still marvel at our rare qualities—more so now knowing of the source that derives from our rich Westcott ancestry.

Before delving into our story since 1944, allow me to set the stage on reflection of the revolutionary changes—what we call "paradigm shifts" in present parlance—that bring us to our current place in American history. Among the many hallmarks that define our generation, the birth of rock and roll stands out as one of the most enduring. Growing up in the counterculture era, we challenged the status quo at every turn, even in our choice of music. With self-reliance and a deep sense of independence, we forged a path that took America's trademark "experimentation" to a new level.

The story of "GEN 12" Westcotts of necessity brings to the forefront the dramatic societal changes we have experienced in our lifetimes. More than any other advance, the ubiquitous microchip has revolutionized our present-day norms.

Since the 1960s, the technological advancement of society across virtually every discipline has transformed our way of living, working, playing, traveling, communicating, investing—even how we secure our national interests. I wonder how our ancestors would regard this new normal, whether with fascination, anticipation, dismay, or utter outrage.

Given their inventive nature, my great-grandfather Walter Scott Hoke and his son Walter Westcott "Wessie" Hoke—Yolande's brother—would have likely been awestruck by the dramatic technological and scientific advances of our day. Conversely, the American author, educator, and media theorist Neil Postman eschewed present-day technology as creating "a culture without a moral foundation and undermining social relations between humans." This latter viewpoint brings to mind the unintended consequences of progress witnessed in my lifetime.

Every aspect of early 21st-century living has undergone radical trans-formation thanks to the proliferation of seemingly intelligent devices incorporating miniaturized electronic circuitry and flexible embedded software that orchestrate functionality—highly "technical" terms but our present-day reality. It is almost surreal to recall how society functioned little more than a quarter of a century ago before the advent of the smart phone and capabilities in messaging, navigation, email, Internet brows-ing, remote commerce, bill-payment, data hosting, cloud computing, and a host of other breakthrough applications in the guise of the microchip through integrated circuitry—even photography! Yolande Hoke Gordon comes to mind, considering the laborious hand-painted technique she employed to add color to photographs in her day. Hers was a comparatively primitive yet beautiful form of artistic expression.

Few of us as "GEN 12" Americans can forget the boom of the late 1990s that coincided with massive growth in Internet adoption, a proliferation of available venture capital, and the rapid growth of valuations in new dot.com startups. No sooner did technology stocks soar to exuberant yet unsustainable levels, the freefall that came with the new millennium marked the painful dot.com bust. But resilience ultimately prevailed, as it has time and again.

Contrasting life before and since the chip spurred this technological revolution, I wonder how—not if—future generations will experience so dramatic a lifestyle shift with any new invention or development. The seismic waves of change coursing through America's history—notably during the American Revolution, the Industrial Revolution, and now this digital age of enlightenment—underscore the inventive genius that continues to propel us forward in the name of progress.

I am reminded of a recent article featuring Dr. Stephen Hoge, M.D. in a publication of the University of California San Francisco (UCSF), the medical school from which he graduated in 2003. In an interview with Moderna Therapeutics' president, son of my first cousin Dianne Guy Hoge and her husband Ron—and a "GEN 13" Westcott descendant—Stephen spoke of the role of prior research on present-day capabilities. In the context of basic mRNA research, Stephen offered this viewpoint: "Science is a collective effort with different groups playing different roles at different times."

Supporting his statement, Stephen recalled the genesis of the Moderna vaccine: "It all came together on January 13, 2020, but it was not accomplished in that hour. It was accomplished over the two to three decades of work leading up to that moment, not only at Moderna but across the scientific community. You want to be circumspect as a scientist or clinician and recognize that you're just running your leg of the race." In the *UCSF Magazine*, contributor Katherine Conrad noted that "the speed with which Moderna whipped up the vaccine belies the decades of experimentation and painstaking research that led to that moment." On a broader scale, the same can be said of the progression of each of America's "revolutionary" technical and scientific breakthroughs that led us to the current digital leg in this seeming race against time.

We can credit our forebears for the successive advances they made possible with ingenuity and a degree of independence not seen in many other parts of our world. The microchip at the root of this digital age has opened the floodgates as we imagine the possibilities. Americans edge closer to the next frontier buoyed by artificial intelligence and augmented reality applications scarcely comprehensible to the common folks among us in my age group—now gray-haired "seniors."

> I consider myself and my "GEN 12" peers distinctly privileged to relish the days of yore when nature inspired a way of living simply; when tradition motivated our actions; when as a people we coveted our American heritage above all else. Our "GEN 11" parents instilled these values in us.

As we straddle across the realm from our innocent youth to old age in this highspeed "Information Age," I recall the extraordinary life our parents made possible for us on their own account when technology did not rule the day.

Coursing through time, this 12th generation benefited from the subtle yet notable shift in current as a feeling of exuberance breathed life into the post-World War II expansionary era. Cautiously optimistic with the Depression in their rear view and underpinnings of frugality grounding them, our "GEN 11" parents tiptoed into a period of wealth accumulation that had not come so freely to their more immediate ancestors—notably our "GEN 9" great-grandparents whose lifespans traversed the American Civil War and both world wars. My great-grandfather Walter Scott Hoke endured the visceral experience of all three before his death at age 80.

The capitalistic pursuit that came from revving all engines to propel the economy in the post-WWII era created opportunities like never before and rewarded investors for their ability to create wealth. Our parents—the "Greatest Generation" with common-sense values—spurred vitality that rippled through America's economy, financially benefitting my generation in the process. As reflected in the following anecdotes, our rich inheritance afforded us distinct privileges we especially enjoyed as youngsters.

That breakout sense of liberation permeated every aspect
of living in our parents' time post-World War II—
challenging even the norms in naming their children.

Breaking with their past, "GEN 11" Brodericks, Guys, and Gordons cracked a centuries-long tradition by foregoing "Westcott" to name any of their children. The audacity!

"GEN 12" Westcott Descendants and Spouses
(descending order of marriages)

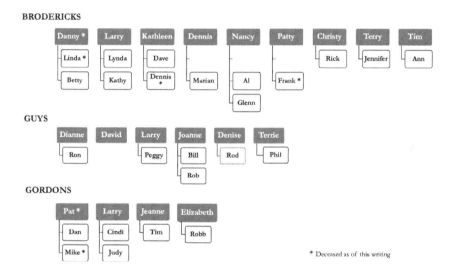

"Westcott" (or a derivative spelling) passed down the line to one or more people in every single generation heretofore traced to our family's lineage as a surname or middle name. Yet not one of my "GEN 12" siblings, first cousins, or I claim "Westcott" as ours. As we'll learn, the name rebounded to its rightful prominent spot among select 13th- and 14th-generation descendants. *Surely* the "Westcott" name will pass to our great-grandchildren and the generations that follow "GEN 14" without a further gap. In honor of the rich inheritance stemming from our Westcott forebears, it seems only right.

Brodericks (1944–present)

BOOM boom . . . boom . . . boom . . . boom boom boom . . . boom BOOM!

Except Daniel "Danny" Thomas Broderick III and Laurance "Larry" Gordon Broderick whom Dan and Yo named in turn after their fathers, my parents assigned names arbitrarily to their remaining seven children. Without any association to any of their ancestors to my knowledge, they simply went with names they liked: Kathleen Mary, Dennis John, Nancy Ann, Patricia "Patty," Christine "Christy" Ann, Terrence "Terry" Michael, and Timothy "Timmy" Patrick. Dennis's middle name may have derived from our father's grandfather "John," but I found no connection otherwise. Patty justifiably felt shortchanged as the only one among us not given a middle name. Legend tells us that Terry and Timmy were named after collies our family once enjoyed as pets. In fact, canines and a variety of other animals—notably horses, ponies, a donkey, birds (canaries "Tweetie" and "Sweetie" and an exquisite long-tailed finch), Easter chicks and bunnies, and lambs "Regis" and "Michael"—gave life to our family throughout a rather colorful childhood.

Anyone looking in would likely acknowledge something curious about the Broderick family.

For as long as I can remember, I've been told by many people who know me well, "You could write a book." I believe their reasoning came from my background in Pittsburgh as one of nine kids raised in the Irish Catholic tradition. But there was something more. Our patriarchal family yielded to a combative nature, cutting humor, and a lack of emotional support to my way of thinking. The characteristic Broderick quirks and pervasive family drama aside, each of us has persevered, collectively with some remarkable achievements.

Except for Timmy who broke the mold with a public high school education beginning in 1974—when the nation's economy found itself in a world of hurt—the rest of us attended parochial schools through high school. The top eight attended St. Bernard's Catholic School—grades 1 through 8—before the family's move from Vernon Drive to Orr Road in 1964.

Around 1962, shortly before the move, the U.S. prepared for the possibility of a nuclear war with the Soviet Union. As an uninformed nine-year-old, I somehow escaped the chaos and fear surrounding the Cuban missile crisis, yet I recall how as school children we rehearsed the imminent threat by hiding under our desks at the sound of a bellowing siren. Protected in the veil of secrecy about the meaning and nuclear implications of this "duck-and-cover" drill, we simply did as we were told in response to the nuns' stern warnings. Meanwhile, the threat of a missile attack sent panic waves across a weary nation and much of the world:

> As mentioned, the United States detonated two atomic bombs over the Japanese cities of Hiroshima and Nagasaki that ended WWII in 1945. In the wake of the unprecedented devastation wrought by the bombings, with their respective allies, the U.S. and the Soviet Union led by Nikita Khrushchev (1894–1971) engaged in ongoing political and economic clashes known as the Cold War (1945–1991). Four years following the explosions, on August 29, 1949, the Soviet Union detonated its first nuclear device at a remote site in Kazakhstan, signaling a new and terrifying phase in the Cold War.

> By the early 1950s, schools across the United States were training students to dive under their desks and cover their heads. The now infamous "duck-and-cover" drills simulated what should be done in case of an atomic attack, thus channeling growing panic over an escalating arms race. As part of President Harry S. Truman's Federal Civil Defense Administration program (now the Office of Defense Mobilization), the school drills aimed to educate the public about what ordinary people could do to protect themselves.

> The Cuban leftist revolutionary leader Fidel Castro (1926–2016) aligned with the Soviet Union—then led by Premier Nikita Sergeyevich Khrushchev (1894–1971)—once the latter seized power of the island. During the Cuban Missile Crisis in 1962, the opposing sides in the U.S.-Soviet arms race engaged in a tense, 13-day standoff over the installation of nuclear-armed Soviet missiles on Cuba, just 90 miles from U.S. shores. The administration of President John F.

Kennedy (1917–1963) had already launched an attack on the island in 1961—the failed "Bay of Pigs" invasion. Castro and Khrushchev saw the missiles as a means of deterring further U.S. aggression. Acknowledging the presence of Soviet missiles in Cuba, President Kennedy enacted a naval blockade around the Caribbean nation, preparing to use military force if necessary to neutralize this perceived threat to national security. An attempt by the Soviets to breach the blockade would likely have sparked a sobering confrontation that could have escalated to a nuclear exchange.

Both Premier Khrushchev and President Kennedy recognized the devastating possibility of a nuclear war. The conclusion of our "duck-and-cover" drills at St. Bernard's came with the superpowers publicly agreeing to a deal in which the Soviets would dismantle the weapon sites in exchange for a pledge from the United States not to invade Cuba.

Although the truce averted the nuclear threat, the "Cuban Missile Crisis" convinced the Soviets to increase their investment in an arsenal of intercontinental ballistic missiles capable of reaching the U.S. from Soviet territory. The Soviet Union (1922–1991) dissolved by internal processes as the communist bloc teetered on the brink of collapse in 1991, resulting in the fall of the Berlin Wall and the end of USSR's existence as a sovereign state.

For a brief time, the piercing sound of those alarms reverberated like an echo chamber inside the walls of our grade school. But everlasting is that sense of pride the Brodericks carry in association with St. Bernard's. Here, our father became the parish's first baptized baby in 1919 when the original church counted 180 families as parishioners. Construction of the church on its current site began in 1942.

Inspired by a 12th-century Romanesque landmark, the builders of the Gothic Revival Roman Catholic church created a magnificent structure on the high spine of the old Washington Pike. Considered one of the most architecturally significant buildings in Western Pennsylvania, St. Bernard's Church sits perched atop the highest of Pittsburgh's "South Hills" with a splendid view of the area's mogul-like terrain and lush green vegetation. In the year of Kathleen's birth in 1947, on Palm Sunday, the congregation celebrated its first Mass in the upper level. Here where

Patty married Frank Cappelli (1979), I married Rick Emmanuel (1984), and Patty's daughter Caroline married her first husband, Scott Crimone (2008), the building features rough-faced gray, tan and red stone, medieval diaphragm arches, a ribbed dome covering the sanctuary, a rare "Apocalypse" mural depicting the complete Book of Revelation, and brilliant stained glass.

In my time as a parishioner, St. Bernard's featured both an upper and lower church. With its large congregation, two floors provided a choice between High Mass said in Latin and the more contemporary Low Mass. We typically attended the last of as many as 10 liturgical services conducted between the two levels each Sunday while also observing Holy Days of Obligation.

Among the parishioners, the church records among the earliest donors our grandfather Daniel Thomas Broderick, Sr. who gifted one of the three massive bells from the towering belfry that stands 1,428 feet above sea level. The joyful ring lays witness to our family's prominent place in the annuls of this fine institution with a congregation which now numbers ten thousand people—more than 3,500 families.

The eldest among the Broderick children, my brother Daniel Thomas Broderick III also left an indelible mark on St. Bernard's. In 1951, a photographer with the *Pittsburgh Press* desired to capture the morning light cast against the arched breezeway at the school. Granting his request, the principal recruited Sister Edwin to pose for the photo. According to my father, Danny had missed the early bus and arrived late to school that day. He happened upon Sister Edwin as the photographer prepared to stage his shot. It profiles Danny as a second grader on opening day with the shadow of his future stretched before him. Standing respectfully with book bag in hand, he is looking up at Sister Edwin in her characteristic St. Joseph habit, their shadows long in the morning light. The award-winning black-and-white photograph adorns an interior school wall to this day. My siblings and I honored our family's legacy with pride when we passed that framed photograph each day as elementary students. As Danny looked up to Sister Edwin, we looked up to our oldest sibling as our guiding light.

When Danny and Larry attended St. Bernard's, the school enrolled roughly 2,000 students, with 50 students each assigned to five classrooms per grade. The size and guidelines changed by the time I entered seven years after Larry. The Sisters of St. Joseph then designated just four classrooms for each grade which they distinguished by academic achievement as A, B, C, and D. While the arrangement may have incentivized some to pursue a higher rank, it surely humiliated those of us who fell behind the others.

At St. Bernard's, Larry recalls a visit by Dr. Jonas Salk in 1955. From his lab at the University of Pittsburgh, Dr. Salk successfully applied a vaccine to prevent polio following seven years of experimentation and testing. Polio had affected more than half a million Americans in the preceding 40 years, among them President Franklin Delano Roosevelt (1882-1945) who was diagnosed with the crippling infantile paralysis at age 39 in 1921. Starting in April 1955, thousands of Pittsburgh children were vaccinated in local schools. St. Bernard's pastor, Fr. Joseph Lonergan, gave Dr. Salk the greenlight to personally administer shots to St. Bernard's school children before his team gave shots at the neighboring schools. Later, around 1961, Patty remembers our mother bringing all but Timmy to Mt. Lebanon High School where hundreds of school-aged kids waited in line with their parents for a dose of the reformulated pink sugar cube polio vaccine—much preferred to the harrowing experience of being poked with a needle.

My vivid memory at St. Bernard's came on the afternoon of November 22, 1963, when the principal interrupted classes to announce the assassination of President John Fitzgerald Kennedy (1917-1963) in Dallas, Texas. With the early dismissal of classes, we found ourselves glued to the television while mourning the death of our beloved president—America's 35th and first Catholic. The chilling news coverage of the two shots fired by Lee Harvey Oswald in the open convertible brought each of us to our knees as we watched replays of the blood-covered president slumped over toward his wife, Jacqueline Lee Bouvier Kennedy (1929-1994). Jackie was left a widow at age 34 on Danny's 19th birthday.

As the Catholic Church has evolved, St. Bernard's has changed dramatically since we were students:

Although the Catholic Church remains larger than any other single religious institution in the United States with over 17,000 parishes, declining membership in recent years has curtailed school enrollment. With just over 250 students, St. Bernard's merged in 2020 with St. Thomas Moore, St. Anne, and Our Lady of Grace in Pittsburgh's South Hills. Consolidating into two campuses, the elementary school is now known as "Ave Maria Academy." Absent the Sisters of St. Joseph, the school is now run totally by lay personnel with the former St. Bernard's convent repurposed to house parish offices. Meanwhile, St. Bernard's lower church holds masses only for overflow on Christmas and Easter.

Following elementary school, the four older boys attended the all-boys' South Hills Catholic High School—now Seton LaSalle Catholic High School—with the Christian Brothers, including Brother Regis and Brother Michael for whom our two baby lambs were named. The four girls went to Fontbonne Academy where we continued on with the Sisters of St. Joseph, much as our mother and Aunt Jinks remained with the Benedictines over the course of their first twelve years of Catholic education in Duluth.

At home, the male gene predetermined our course as Brodericks, meaning our father and brothers dominated in all things. Self-anointed male superiority is what I knew growing up as a Broderick. Harmless sibling rivalries, ribbing, and laughter filled each day in our household before Larry emerged as the stronger, more assertive of our two oldest brothers. The younger kids yielded to the dominance he gained as he took rough-housing to a new level. Larry set the tone for the entire family by rallying the boys and leading the girls into a permanent state of rebellion.

As our mother called upon the girls to wait on the boys, we were relegated to servitude in a sense, though I'm sure our brothers would take issue with that characterization. In our formative years, the older boys cast the girls aside as "yuks," which they were quick to define as "too low to kick and too wet to step on." The girls heard the term often, connoting our subservient place in the family as female-gendered. Ha ha ha. Hysterical to the boys. Stinging to the girls.

Larry's regard for the opposite sex is illustrated in a memory I heard him recall of his elementary school years at St. Bernard's. He and Danny typically walked the mile home from school together. During the winter months, they would team up and throw snowballs at girls all the way home. What Larry remembered most vividly was that he never once even considered throwing a snowball at another boy. He said "this is what guys did—the fun of it came from targeting the girls."

I never understood why our mother tolerated the boys' disparaging treatment of their sisters. Perhaps she justified their actions as acknowledgement—indeed acceptance—of her subordinate role to our father as his wife and the mother of his nine children.

Something else struck me as highly curious about the family dynamic in our formative years. The boys emerged as a force overwhelming the girls without question. They were so strong! What is interesting though, is that the girls never teamed up to resist the stronghold the boys had on us. The boys would get into arguments, fight, or horse around with each other all the time. But when the girls were involved—watch out. While the boys went after us, the girls went after each other!

The target for the girls became the one closest in age who was younger, smaller, weaker. Nancy in particular had a lot of pent-up anger inside her. The middle child, she was a bit of a tomboy and highly spirited. She typically went after Patty. Like dominoes, Patty would pounce on me as the next youngest, and I badgered Terry in turn. Unfortunately for me, Terry was feisty and clearly stronger. He was also our dad's favorite. In fact, Dad spoiled him rotten. None of us much cared for that, least of all me as the one closest in age and the youngest girl in the family. Our father commissioned an oil portrait of Terry at age four or five with our beloved collie "Lassie." It hung prominently in our home as a visible reminder to all of us that Terry was the object of our father's singular affection so far as he was able to express it.

Competition underscored every aspect of living
as a Broderick, which meant keeping score.

Who would call "shot gun" first, granting access to the coveted front passenger seat on trips to the penny candy store or somewhere else? The first utterance won.

Who goes first? Virtually everything was decided by "shink." First calling out even or odd and with fingers then randomly splayed simultaneously from two hands, the sum determined the winner. Best of three, "1, 2, 3, shink . . . 1, 2, 3, shink." If one's call, even or odd, didn't strike twice—best of three—"1, 2, 3, shink."

Who could blurt out the sibling names in sequential order quickest?
Danny Larry Kathy Dennis Nancy Patty Christy Terry Timmy
Danny Larry Kathy Dennis Nancy Patty Christy Terry Timmy
Danny Larry Kathy Dennis Nancy Patty Christy Terry Timmy
Danylarykathydenisnancpatychristerrytim
Danlarkathdennancpatychristerytim

Who could gather the most candy on Halloween or locate their basket of treats hidden by the Easter Bunny before anyone else?

Who could conduct the most "mischief" on Devil's Night . . . without getting caught?

Who could accumulate the most property in Monopoly, or strategically conquer the world in the game of Risk?

Perhaps the most significant score revolved around gender count. A power struggle ensued with each new addition to the family which was ultimately decided when our youngest sibling came along to break the tie.

With my birth in 1953, girls outnumbered boys for the first time and only briefly before Terry came two years later yielding a second tie. The final count arrived in 1960, a leap year. The battle of the sexes was ultimately decided with Timmy's birth on February 29th.

	BOYS	GIRLS
Danny	1	
Larry	2	
Kathleen	2	1
Dennis	3	1
Nancy	3	2
Patty	3	3
Christy	3	4
Terry	4	4
Timmy	5	4

At the time Timmy came along, six of us attended St. Bernard's elementary school. We found ourselves in the playground during the lunch break, anxiously awaiting word of the birth and the newborn's sex. Knowing that Mom had gone into labor, at lunchtime, Larry—then in 8th grade—got a dime and dialed McGee Hospital from a pay phone. After telling him to wait, the nurse returned a few minutes later with the news that she had delivered a boy. Larry proceeded to the playground where he told Dennis and then found Kathleen. Mom had her baby. It's a . . . BOY, it's a BOY, a BOY, BOY!!!

The news quickly spread. The excitement of our classmates and teachers filled the air, but they did not grasp the meaning of the spoken word for the scales permanently tipped in favor of the boys. All the same, we united in adoration of our baby brother. The girls doted over him as a living, pliable baby doll who you could not help but love with all your heart.

Even before the males ultimately prevailed as the majority, the girls waited on our brothers as if they were royalty, and they treated us much like their personal servants—or so it felt to us. While shopping and cooking fell to our mother as her sole domain, the girls made the boys' beds and changed their dirty sheets and bath towels. We set their place at the long dinner table, served their dinner and dessert, refilled their water glasses, and cleared and cleaned their dirty dishes. If they asked us to bring them another serving or more water, we of course would squawk before our mother stepped in and usually said, "Just do it, Christy!" or

"Nancy!" or "Patty!" [Kathleen typically complied without a fuss as the dutiful eldest daughter.] Don't ruffle feathers. Don't screech when they make "play" while inflicting pain. The worst was their condescending attitude. From my brothers especially, I learned that life is not meant to be fair.

While the cat's away the mice will play. None of us would dare get out of hand or raise our voices in the presence of our father. Given his unpredictable nature, we never knew what kind of mood we'd find him in—best to remain invisible. But he worked long hours and traveled a fair amount, meaning that, when he was on the road, the strongest among us had free reign to dominate throughout much of each day after school and into the evenings. It baffled me that our mother tolerated the shenanigans in our father's absence to the detriment of the smaller and weaker of the kids—notably the girls. Larry himself recalled lying in bed with Danny and Dennis as young boys until late at night, discussing and dreaming about their plans for tormenting the girls the following day. The ritual did not break before they went off to college.

Television became a welcome outlet in our
formative years in the 1950s and 1960s.

Taking a break from the brewing chaos that kept the weakest among us on guard, we united when given the opportunity to watch TV. With technological advances leading to approval of the first color television standard by the Federal Communications Commission (FCC) in 1950, we together enjoyed a flurry of captivating TV programs produced in short order.

Popular Broderick TV series

1948	The Ed Sullivan Show	1955	Lawrence Welk
1949	The Lone Ranger	1955	Fury
1950	The Jack Benny Program	1957	Perry Mason
1951	I Love Lucy	1957	Leave It to Beaver
1951	The Roy Rogers Show	1958	Shirley Temple
1952	American Bandstand	1958	The Rifleman
1952	Ozzie and Harriet	1959	Bonanza
1952	Dragnet	1959	The Twilight Zone
1952	Superman	1960	Andy Griffith Show
1954	Father Knows Best	1960	My Three Sons
1954	Rin Tin Tin	1961	Mr. Ed
1954	Lassie	1962	McHale's Navy
1955	Alfred Hitchcock	1964	Bewitched
1955	Gunsmoke	1965	The Big Valley
1955	Honeymooners	1966	Tarzan

We watched a lot of TV! These titles bring back happy images of family time gathered together in relative harmony. Each of us had our own favorite shows and choice characters whom we got such a kick out of. *Shirley Temple* and Wally on *Leave It to Beaver* stand out to me, and Hoss Cartwright on *Bonanza*, Barney Fife on the *Andy Griffith Show*, Ricky Nelson on *Ozzie and Harriet*, *Tarzan*, the horse named *Mr. Ed*, and of course, Timmy and his beloved *Lassie*.

I remember Nancy's partiality for the Lennon Sisters on *Lawrence Welk* while Danny gravitated to Dick Clark's *American Grandstand*. The younger ones among us were drawn to the groundbreaking *All in the Family*, which debuted in 1971. Creator Norman Lear claimed that his own father was a bit of an Archie Bunker played by Carrol O'Connor. We, too, could relate to Archie as the irascible, obstinate, insolent character who personified our father's inclination.

Early on, Danny and Larry engaged in wrestling matches over whether they would watch Danny's favorite, *American Bandstand,* or a "guy" TV show like *Yancy Derringer*, which Larry preferred. Larry and Nancy would argue over whether to watch *The Sound of Music* given Larry's infatuation with Julie Andrews or a special featuring Nancy's idol

Barbra Streisand. With time, the matches and competitions of every form picked up steam. Someone gaining the upper hand became a constant source of angst up and down the line among us . . . as long as any two or more remained in the household.

Television and infighting aside, fun and games filled our days with the seasonal changes in Pittsburgh and throughout the carefree days of summer in Madison, Ohio.

Besides year-round card and board games, in Pittsburgh the kids enjoyed kickball, tag football, and football game watches in the autumn; sledding, ice skating, snowman-making, and snowball-throwing at each other in the winter; and coming out for skateboarding and whatever else was in store in the spring. A shock of color then painted the drab Pittsburgh landscape green with splashes of pink, red, and yellow as the brilliant flowers came into bloom.

Throughout most of our childhood, the Brodericks spent entire summers from Memorial Day to Labor Day in Madison with our father joining us from Pittsburgh on weekends. Although our parents adopted a disciplinary approach in raising us, we grew up with freedom at play in the great outdoors. A block from our Madison home, our grandparents' property on Lake Erie afforded us opportunities for swimming, sailing, motorboating, waterskiing, rafting, and sun worshipping. Danny in particular became quite adept at waterskiing and Larry at sailing his catamaran. It was a charmed existence for which we all are eternally grateful.

In Madison, we found many ways to entertain ourselves in the great outdoors. Badminton, volleyball, and softball games became coveted summer weekend rituals, the latter drawing players of every age group from throughout the neighborhood to our back yard. My paternal grandfather, father, and a passel of kids played ball while the others across generations—myself included—participated as loyal spectators. What a leisurely way to spend a Saturday afternoon!

With freedom to roam, Danny and Larry rode their horses for hours on end during the summer days of the mid- to late 1950s. Those of us brave enough to negotiate "wild" horses saddled up the equines our parents rented for a time before buying them outright. Many a horseback riding accident injured family members at different times—it wasn't for me! Nancy with her keen memory and love of riding helped me recall perhaps all of our horses and ponies over the years—Rex, Billy, Daisy, Skyrocket, Blackie, Lady, Chautauqua, twins Jet and Prince, Champion, Buster, Pat, Spook, Comanche, our beloved Dancer whom Danny dutifully nurtured as his own, and one of Lady's foals named Dancer who came subsequently. With a black coat and a white star on her forehead, Danny's Dancer reminded us of *Fury*, the lead in one of our favorite Saturday morning TV shows. One of the saddest days ever in Madison came when we had to put down injured Dancer and then witnessed her burial in the corralled area of our back field.

Bordered by weeping willows, the acreage in Madison accommodated both the baseball field and fenced-in corral with a little barn for the horses and ponies until our parents boarded them in Pittsburgh sometime after the family's move to Orr Road in 1964. In Madison, a large ship's bell posted in the yard with a distinctive ringtone could be heard from a great distance. When the dinner bell rang, we gathered at the table as a family every day without exception. The evenings concluded with more outdoor games like tag-and-release or hide-and-seek which drew kids from the neighborhood like a magnet. When our father arrived on weekends, we together enjoyed a wood-burning fire he kept going for hours in our cozy living room. Activities continued from sun-up to bedtime without interruption each and every summer night.

A long-standing tradition, celebrated Christian
holidays brought the Brodericks together
across generations in Pittsburgh.

Back in Pittsburgh, a vivid childhood memory for all of us came from visits to see Ooh Ooh and Grandpa every Christmas and Easter. Our paternal great-aunts, great-uncles, aunts, uncles, and first cousins joined us at our grandparents' house for a celebratory reunion following our custom of opening gifts at home each Christmas morning. As part of the Easter ritual, we obliged our great-aunts and great-uncles with a brief visit to the nearby home where some of them lived—where their parents, our great-grandparents, John and Mary Jane Broderick, had also lived. Befitting the occasion, we arrived adorned in our finest ensembles—matching outfits, hats, and neckties.

I rather dreaded the visits to see our "greats" because I could not tell them apart and the house felt cramped with so many of them scattered amongst the eleven of us in relatively small, dark quarters. We would approach their home with our eyes on the clock, figuring how soon we'd be able to leave before we even entered the house. "No more than half an hour, okay?" We would single file in, exchange mushy kisses, pile our coats on one of their beds upstairs, pull dining room chairs into the living room, place our Coca-Cola order, enjoy the chocolate candies and Bolan's chocolate-sandwiched cinnamon wafers, and then sit down and pretend to be interested in the small talk. "Oh, let me look at you! Oh my, you've gotten so big, Christy. And look at that pretty long hair!" Cackle, cackle. They were so nice, but they were also "so old!"

The aunts in particular had distinct personalities, but that didn't prevent me from getting them confused. It became much easier as I got older. Kay was hard of hearing. "What did you say, Nance? Speak up, will you?" Dode, whom we nicknamed "Lucky" because she often won at Bingo, didn't say much. Marg was the bossy one: "Dode, go in the kitchen and bring out the ashtray, will you?" Of course, Kay didn't like Marg and Dode smoking in the house one bit, and she made it perfectly known. John as the oldest was, well, really old. The others among the visiting "greats" seemed to fade in the crowd.

None of our great-aunts and great-uncles had Grampa's charisma although they seemed to be a fun enough bunch. I think they were as amused by us as we were by them. We could not imagine growing up and choosing to live with siblings our entire lives and in the same house no less, as the bachelor John and spinsters Kay, Nora, Marg, and Dode had done at 1464 McFarlane Drive in Dormont for what seemed an eternity. Never having families of their own, they seemed genuinely entertained by us and by the kidding that went on between us in their company.

We'd each do our level best to keep a straight face and pretend to be interested in the conversation, but it was no easy feat with one of the kids in the background making faces trying to break you up and embarrass you in the process. Before long—though never soon enough—the time came to reverse the order of our arrival. Eying the clock, someone would say, "Oh darn, we really have to be going." "Oh, do you have to?" "When are you going to come back and see us?" "Are you sure you don't want another cinnamon wafer?" Chuckle, chuckle.

We would return our Coca-Cola glasses to the kitchen, put our chairs back where we found them in the dining room, grab our coats from upstairs, go from one great-aunt to the next then the great-uncles and repeat the mushy kissing scene one last time. Out the door, we would laugh and make fun in two cars the whole ride home. What an ungracious bunch!

The "senior" Broderick clan was a hearty bunch, all but one of the siblings a lifelong Pittsburgher. As many as five of the ten siblings lived into their nineties including Gramps and his sisters Elizabeth, Kay, Mary, and Dorothy "Dode"; John, Nora, Marg, and Bob died in their seventies or eighties; Matthew predeceased all of his siblings when he died in his adopted home of Philadelphia at age 62. Upon widowhood, Mary moved in and died at the family home at age 101 in 2006, one year before Dode, the youngest, who survived them all when she passed at age 95.

Now with 26 great-nieces and great-nephews of my own on the Broderick side—the offspring of my 23 nieces and nephews—I wonder what image they will create of their soon-to-be gray-haired *old* Aunt Christy and the rest as the years roll by. They will undoubtedly come up with many colorful stories about their "greats," some of which follow below.

MY BROTHER **DANIEL "Danny"** Thomas Broderick III (1944–1989) holds distinction as the eldest among Guy and Mary Stukely Westcott's "GEN 12" lineal descendants. In the mold of our ancestors, he set a high bar for his siblings in academic prowess and professional success and made our parents and each of us exceptionally proud.

Danny was born in Duluth one week following our father's return from commanding a PT boat in the Mediterranean Theatre as his last tour of duty during World War II. He is the only one among us born with sparkling *brown* eyes which he inherited from our mother; the rest of us share our father's blue eyes. At an early age, our big brother revealed a beautiful smile, a zest for life, a sense of humor, and remarkable self-discipline. Competitive sports aside, he excelled at just about everything he undertook, from horseback riding and water skiing to academics and the practice of law.

Upon learning about our Westcott lineage, I discovered that my G3 grandfather Hampton Westcott carried a frame of just 5 feet 3-¾ inches—if not an error on a note his brother wrote in cursive to authorities requesting an expedited passport on Hampton's behalf. My great-grandfather Walter Scott Hoke and his son Walter Westcott "Wessie" Hoke were also short men at a height of 5 feet 8 inches as conveyed on Walter's passport and Wessie's college student registration card. It may well explain the slight frame of my brothers who were known to sit on a telephone book in order to see over the wheel while driving. In high school, Danny's childhood friend, Jim Hampsey, recalled him getting stopped by the township police for looking too young to drive.

At age 16, Danny was the first of the siblings to get his driver's license, a fact which he lorded over us unmercifully. During television commercial breaks in Madison, with calculated forethought he might yell "Candy run!" and bolt out the door to the car. Anyone without money on them or not in the room at the time would lose out while the others stampeded out in close pursuit. Danny loved the trepidation that came over any of us tempted to leave the room for a moment in search of a snack or to go to the bathroom and in so doing, miss an opportunity. Returning from the penny candy store before the next TV program started, he would pop candies into his mouth, loudly smacking his lips as close as possible to those of us who had the misfortune of missing out.

One of Danny's favorite pastimes came when he spotted a rotten apple to throw at one of us when we weren't looking. He got an absolute charge when he found his target, cackling as loudly as he possibly could when the softened fruit splattered on his prey.

"Broderick humor" probes to see where the defenses are weakest before jabbing with a proverbial needle at precisely the right time. Danny excelled at this and at quickly turning oncoming attacks to his advantage.

With that sparkle in his eye, he would smile when a friend in later years ascribed this type of humor to some "rogue gene" in the Broderick family.

With nearly the rest of us, Danny shared a love of Notre Dame, and in 1962, he entered his freshman year with the Fighting Irish. He developed a fascination with words and an uncanny vocabulary. He must have studied *Webster's Dictionary* cover-to-cover without the modern convenience of the Internet and its search engines. He embraced certain words like prized possessions and used them to challenge the kids during his visits home. Pronouncing a word no one knew the meaning of made him feel especially triumphant. As I recall, he especially got a kick out of exaggerating his enunciation of the word "succulent." Danny's credibility was questioned just once when he returned from college during one holiday arguing that, much like geese is the plural of goose, meese is the plural of moose. So convincing, he almost had our mom believing him! It was a pleasure when Danny came home for visits. He seemed to get such a sweet kick out of everything and everyone.

Though confident and charismatic, Danny was not cocky or arrogant. He surrounded himself with people he cherished, and he loved nothing more than to laugh with us and his wide circle of friends. Though not typically the center of attention in social situations, he was nonetheless in on all the fun. In each of us—even the next generation of Brodericks— Danny engendered a love of "oldies" music, but stood unparalleled doing the twist, jitterbug, and every other form of dance moves. Neat, fastidious, and very handsome, he was an impeccable dresser. Like his namesake, our grandfather Daniel T. Broderick, Sr., he always looked like a million bucks. Suffice it to say, Danny was our idol. Though far from perfect, we loved nearly everything about him.

In his first year at Notre Dame, Danny grew by inches. The others among the boys followed suit as late bloomers. During those four years in college, Danny consistently made the Dean's list and developed a standard of personal excellence that would guide him throughout his life. He set a sterling example for his eight siblings. From Notre Dame with a Bachelor of Science in pre-med, Danny went on to Cornell University's medical school in New York City where he earned a Doctor of Medicine. While most people would view securing a medical degree as a lifetime achievement, Daniel T. Broderick III wanted more. In 1970, he entered Harvard Law School in Cambridge, Massachusetts, to pursue his chosen profession. He discovered he would rather become a lawyer than a doctor because he didn't foresee the day-to-day routine in medicine being as interesting as the practice of law.

Danny became one of some 200 people in the country with dual medical-law degrees when he graduated from Harvard University in 1973. With his wife **Elizabeth "Betty" née Bisceglia** (b. 1947) and two daughters **Kimberly Curtin** (b. 1970) and **Lee Gordon** (b. 1971), he moved to sunny California where his skills as a lawyer become quickly apparent to the legal community. He clerked with a law firm in Los Angeles before signing on with Gray, Cary, Ames & Frye in San Diego. Though reticent to leave the comfort of a large firm, he struck out on his own five years later to become a solo practitioner with a focus on personal injury and bad-faith insurance cases.

"Dan," as Danny became known professionally, pursued a specialty in medical malpractice as a plaintiff's lawyer. He quickly developed a reputation as a brilliant mind, a magnificent and eloquent speaker, and a man of unquestioned integrity. His medical training provided him a valuable dimension, making him a particularly tough legal adversary in medical cases. Author Craig K. Collins quoted our brother in a San Diego article featured in the *Metropolitan*'s "Downtown Law" section in 1988. "I always thought once I established in this work I would be treated as a pariah and would be ostracized by doctors. But I've always been treated very nicely." Collins said of Dan, "Friends admire him, colleagues respect him, and foes view him with a sense of awe." Collins went on to say, "This man casts a long shadow across courtrooms in San Diego, and the respect he has won seems almost too universal to be true." Though his chosen profession required Dan to cope with human tragedy facing clients whose bodies had been maimed and whose lives had been irrevocably damaged, he found it satisfying to be able to do something for these people. He really liked what he did and couldn't imagine being anything besides a lawyer.

In La Jolla, as Dan built a flourishing solo practice, he and Betty had two more children—his namesake **Daniel "Danny" Thomas IV** (b. 1976) and **Rhett Terrence** (b. 1979)—and the family of six enjoyed a privileged life. Cracks in the marriage revealed themselves early on, however, causing Dan to file for a divorce around 1985. Increasingly tumultuous years led to protracted divorce proceedings and Betty's escalating retaliation at the expense of the children. During and after the divorce proceedings, all hell broke loose, but Danny remained devoted to his children. As best as he could, he persevered with them and for them under unimaginable circumstances.

Danny wanted and deserved nothing more than to restore his family and move on with his life. He hoped to do so when he met and then married **Linda Bernadette née Kolkena** (1961–1989) on April 22, 1989. Sixteen years younger than Danny and a flight attendant before they met, Linda became Dan's legal assistant. She was a beautiful, vivacious, smart, fun-loving young woman with a bubbling personality. Her parents Arnoldus "Arnold" Johannes Kolkena (1929–2003) and Everdina "Diny" Bernadette Smit (1933–1973) emigrated to America from the Netherlands in 1953. Diny arrived with her family before she and Arnold married in 1955 and established themselves in Murray, Utah. The youngest of their four children, Linda had a wonderful sense of humor and a sweet disposition that matched Danny's perfectly.

We were pleased and so grateful to see our oldest brother, the linchpin of our family, develop a healthy relationship with Linda whom he absolutely adored. Danny was a true blessing to us and we wanted only the best for him.

Cast in a Golden Dome-like hue, my seven siblings and I still place Danny on a pedestal. There was absolutely no denying every single exemplary quality he had going for him. The superlatives speak to his many redeeming traits—a handsome, personable, fun, smart, driven, honorable character who just so happened to be our brother—an extraordinary human being.

Linda offered Dan a new lease on life, a second chance. She gave him the optimism to marry again and entertain the notion of a second family. Together they delighted family and friends with their broad smiles, rich laughter, and sweet terms of endearment. Linda added to Danny's other riches with her beauty, wit, and arresting personality. We reveled in their company during the exhilarating matchup between the Fighting Irish and Miami Hurricanes on October 15, 1988—the last time I saw them before their wedding:

> The two teams met at Notre Dame undefeated—Miami ranked #1 with a 36-game regular season winning streak and the Irish ranked #4. Before the pivotal game, some Notre Dame students created the "Catholics vs Convicts" slogan to promote t-shirt sales. The colloquial moniker has come to define the closely contested game in which the Irish prevailed victorious. On a glorious autumn day in front of the landmark "Touchdown Jesus" and 59,075 thrilled spectators, with 45 captivating seconds remaining in the fourth quarter to quash Notre Dame's one point lead, Miami head coach Jimmy Johnson opted to go for the win with a two point-conversion. Failing to convert, Notre Dame snapped the Hurricanes' winning streak. In a 2005 poll conducted by the University of Notre Dame, the 31-30 win over Miami was voted the "greatest victory in Notre Dame stadium history." The Irish went on to beat contestants in each of the remaining five games of the season. Coached by Lou Holtz, the Irish beat the West Virginia Mountaineers 34–21 in the January 1989 Fiesta Bowl, claiming their 11th and last national championship in college football as of 2024.

Dan and Linda wed six months following the celebratory Irish victory. Linda exuded striking radiance on their wedding day in San Diego. On April 22, 1989, Dan added the Dutch flag to the American and Irish flags flying in front of their home to salute his new bride as the guests arrived to witness their nuptials.

That same day, at the Guadalajara Grill following the reception with family and friends in tow, Linda wore her wedding gown sporting white sunglasses; Dan came adorned in his tux wearing black Ray-Ban's. His friend David Monahan serenaded them with some ridiculous song while Dan did his best impression of a very sad man as he wiped a tear from the corner of his eye in play. With that sweet smile, it seemed there was not a happier guy in all the world than our dashing brother appeared on the night of his and Linda's wedding.

An inconceivable tragedy took place little more than six months later when Dan's vindictive former wife snuck into Dan and Linda's home with stolen house keys while they slept in the early hours on November 5, 1989. She crept up the stairs and at point-blank range aimed her Smith & Wesson revolver, shooting them both dead. Danny tragically left us at age 44; Linda at just 26 years of age. Dan's children were then 19, 18, 13, and 10 years old.

Among the accolades that poured in following Dan and Linda's appalling deaths, we heard much about Dan's stature in the legal community of San Diego. Justice William B. Enright, U.S. District Court with the Southern District of California in San Diego, said "Dan Broderick was all that we could hope for in a lawyer. His word was his bond, his reputation his most prized possession. Possessed of great compassion for his fellow man, the qualities tumble out: courage—tenacity in his cause—there was no quit in Dan Broderick . . . Dan never lost the high idealism of his youth. A dynamic, leading force within his profession; a noble and worthy adversary in every sense of the word; but above all else, Dan Broderick was a good and thoroughly decent human being."

In his eulogy, my brother Dennis recalled a memorable early image of Danny when Dennis was 7 or 8 years old; Danny then 11 or 12:

One night during a school week, the kids were scattered around the house, most of us doing our homework—either in our bedrooms, or in a study in our home which had a few desks where a number of us could study at the same time. In the middle of this quiet study time, the electrical power in the house went out, the house went dark, the studying stopped, and all hell broke loose among the kids. Older and stronger siblings preyed on younger and weaker brothers and sisters, and wails and screams filled the house. All joined the fray, except Danny. In the midst of the uproar and chaos, Dan lit a candle, put it on his desk, resumed his schoolwork, and finished his assignments.

What I witnessed in Dan that night from this small scene, and what his siblings witnessed in Dan throughout his life in much more significant endeavors, was a single-mindedness, a sense of purpose, a steadfast resolve that allowed him to achieve one accomplishment after another in his life amidst obstacles and distractions that would have derailed most people. Dan's record at Notre Dame, his medical degree from Cornell, his law degree from Harvard, his law practice in San Diego, all speak to focused determination, which has served as a shining example for his brothers and sisters.

Dan's single-mindedness was matched by the honor, dignity, and integrity with which he lived his life, even in the most adverse conditions. He handled his achievements and his disappointments, good times and bad times, with equal dignity, grace, and humor. His life reminded each of his siblings that honor, integrity, and dignity are cherished attributes never to be compromised whatever the circumstances, whatever the objective, whatever the outcome.

As the oldest sibling, Dan set a sterling standard of excellence for us in school, in work, in character, in whatever he did. His high standards were particularly exemplified through his wife Linda, his children, the quality of his work, and the quantity and devotion of his friends.

Dan brought endless credit to his brothers and sisters. He was a badge of honor that each of us wore openly and proudly. To this day, his memory burns brightly within us as he continues to light our way.

Though certainly not perfect, I believe Dan possessed the qualities of true greatness. Few would doubt that his and Linda's most significant achievements were yet to come. For one, he would have eventually written a novel, a captivating bestseller with the benefit of more time. That is one thing he said he would like to do. "It would be wonderful to make a lasting contribution that you'd always be remembered for." To the last man standing, his boundless contributions hold a prominent place in our minds and hearts as warm and wonderful stories continue to be told about this remarkable human being. "Oh Danny Boy, we loved you so . . ."

Oh, Danny boy, the pipes, the pipes are calling, from glen to glen, and down the mountain side. The summer's gone and all the roses falling, it's you, it's you must go and I must bide. But come ye back when summer's in the meadow, or when the valley's hushed and white with snow, it's I'll be here in sunshine or in shadow, oh Danny boy, oh Danny boy, I loved you so.

Besides his children whom Dan nurtured the best he could, an important and essential part of his life was his Irish heritage. From his Irish Catholic roots in Pittsburgh to the University of Notre Dame, to the west of Ireland where our paternal ancestors hailed, to San Diego where Dan was among the city's most prominent Irish leaders—notably a past-president and loyal patron of the Friendly Sons of St. Patrick—Ireland, o' Ireland, was the cornerstone of the man we remember. [Like the rest of us, I believe he knew little about our mother's ancestral bloodline traced to England.]

Dan was instrumental in forming and a regular donor to the San Diego chapter of the American Ireland Fund which sponsors social and cultural projects in Ireland. In 1990, the American Ireland Fund in San

Diego held a benefit dinner in his honor that raised $40,000. Knowing of his Irish roots in Listowel's nearby village of Ballylongford in county Kerry on the south bank of the River Shannon, Dan's loyal friends and admirers designated the collection for the Listowel restoration at St. John's Square. The program distributed at the black-tie affair captured the essence of our cherished brother:

> "In the west of Ireland there were ever a few lochs, and a few pubs, and many a leprechaun, and a man's smile is enough to open a door or heart. One man's smile was his signature—a poem, a song, bright, and real. Easily offered, never forced, it came accompanied by laughter, transporting anyone in its presence across a cargo of pain. The smile stood the man, a pied piper with a glint to his eye, a fellow to gather them of all ages and walks to the hollow of his heart.

> "It mattered not where you found him—rather where he found you—amidst his family in Pittsburgh, under touchdown Jesus at Notre Dame, a friendly gathering of the Sons of St. Patrick in San Diego, anywhere. Being with him was owning a permanent passport to joy and love. He was a lawyer, doctor, father, brother, and friend. He was a storyteller with the uncommon gift of listening, hearing what others had to say. He was the definition of a winner, a marvelous soft spring rain of a man who walked with sunshine always peeking over his shoulder. A man of charity and compassion, he was ever a stranger to cynicism and bigotry.

> "On this night, he would not want you to mourn; he was never one to be maudlin. But he would want you to allow him to be the generous host to your memory; for just a second, reflect on who he was, and the causes for which he stood. He would want you to have fun! Remember Daniel T. Broderick III as he would have wished . . . WITH A SMILE."

In 1991, the townsfolk formally dedicated the restored Balcony of St. John's Listowel Square—the North Kerry town's Arts and Heritage Centre—known henceforth as "The Broderick Balcony." The Balcony houses the rich literary archives of North Kerry and West Limerick. An announcement stated that "the dedication in Dan's name will be remembered in Ireland and in Listowel for as long as the sunlight of life shines on this fair and gentle land." Built with the money raised in San Diego, the memorial, in what had been the disused St. John's Protestant Church, is part of a center devoted to the art and heritage of southwestern Ireland. The portion of the center dedicated to our brother is devoted to writers from the area, among them Maurice Walsh (1879–1964). The famous novelist wrote a short story that appeared in a 1933 edition of *Saturday Evening Post,* later published in a book titled *The Green Rushes.* The book was adapted for director John Ford's famous 1952 movie *The Quiet Man* featuring John Wayne—an absolute favorite of Dan's and his Irish-American brethren.

The Irish bar and restaurant "Reidy O'Neil's" in which Dan became a financial partner with friends Michael *Reidy*, Leo Sullivan, and Mike *Neil*, opened its doors in downtown San Diego just one month after our brother and Linda were slain. When it opened, a fabulous oversized bronze sculpture of John Wayne stood outside Reidy O'Neil's front door; *The Quiet Man* ran continuously on television monitors; and excerpts of Walsh's story were printed in the restaurant's menus. The partners—all American Ireland Fund patrons—had no knowledge that the funds dedicated in Dan's memory would support a room featuring the writings of Marice Walsh himself. Divine providence brought Daniel T. Broderick III and the celebrated author together as a living tribute to two legendary Irishmen. Sixteen of Dan's family and closest San Diego friends attended the dedication in Listowel, including his daughter Kim and my surviving brothers Larry, Dennis, Terry, and Tim.

In Linda's honor, her friends commissioned a statue of Our Lady of Bernadette after whom she was named. Once the statue was carved in Germany, it was placed in her home parish at St. Vincent Church in Holladay, Utah, a kind gesture that warmed the hearts of Linda's father Arnold, stepmother Elise, and siblings Margaret "Maggie," Raymond, and Roger Kolkena (1960–2018).

Linda's gravestone reads:

> *She who kisses the joy as it flies*
> *Lives in eternity's sunrise.*

Such a beautiful sentiment for a lovely Dutch girl with so much promise.

Unyielding, the shameless press exhausted the reserves of Dan's and Linda's grieving families who clamored to keep our joyful memories alive. Launched as a cable television channel in 1991, *CourtTV* aired sensational courtroom coverage of the murderess's trial immediately following the network's inaugural program, which featured the rape trial of William Kennedy Smith, nephew of former President John F. Fitzgerald. As Smith took the stand in his own defense, a six-member jury acquitted him on all charges—play-by-play for the public's viewing pleasure. Like Smith, our brother and Linda became subjects of intense public scrutiny. Unlike Smith, however, neither Danny nor Linda could testify in their own defense from the grave—a terrible injustice to my way of thinking. Both trials turned into a media circus, watched by millions of viewers nationally as a televised spectacle.

The homicides deeply affected Dan's and Linda's family members. The shocking news triggered nearly instantaneous tremors in my mother that led to an advanced Parkinson's disease diagnosis. Her own death came prematurely, little more than five years later at age 74. My father's mournful existence in the last 21 years of his life came in large part as a result of the murders of his firstborn and Dan's second wife of just six months. Worst of all, Dan's four children became orphans.

> *But when ye come and all the flowers are dying, if I am dead, as dead I well may be, you'll come and find the place where I am lying, and kneel and say an Ave there for me. And I shall hear, though soft you tread above me, and all my grave will warmer, sweeter be, for you will bend and tell me that you love me, and I shall sleep in peace until you come to me.*

"Danny Boy" softly echoed at the funeral of our grandfather Daniel Thomas Broderick, Sr. in 1988 and again at the service for Danny and Linda one and one-half years later. A week or so after burying Dan and Linda, I remember the jolt that nearly knocked me off my feet as reality set in. In no time, our family lost not one, but *two* "Daniel Thomas's." The very essence of being a Broderick had somehow been shattered.

Dan's and Linda's short lives gave meaning to the "sands of time." On November 9, 1989—just four days after they were slain—as the

Soviet-led communist bloc teetered on the brink of collapse, the Berlin Wall dividing communist East Germany from West Germany came down. The anti-communism sentiment that followed the reunification quickly spread in Eastern Europe with free elections and economic reforms. In a blink of the eye, Dan and Linda had no knowledge of the historic event that reshaped the modern world by solidifying the West's democratic ideals against the threat of Communist rule. The mark of this milestone on the world stage slipped by them, bringing me in closer touch with my own mortality at age 36.

AS PROMINENT AS THE NAME "DANNY" BECAME in the extended Broderick family, "Larry" took center stage on our mother's side. Yo's brother Laurance Sterne Gordon, Jr. was named after their father. When they had kids of their own, Mom, Uncle Larry, and Aunt Jinks all named a son after their father. Then my brother, Larry, carried on the tradition by naming his son Laurance Gordon Broderick II. That left us with a grandfather Larry, Uncle Larry, cousin Larry Gordon III, cousin Larry Guy, brother Larry, and nephew Larry II. Whew! The only other Larry I knew growing up was one of the raucous *Three Stooges* (with Moe and Curly) which aired regularly in our home before our mother banned us from watching. Featuring violent anarchic slapstick and comedy routines, Nancy recalls hating the TV show "because I thought it gave the boys ideas on stuff to do to us [girls]."

At the funeral of my uncle in Duluth in 1998, I met a man named Larry who reportedly lived in the same house as Uncle Larry and cousin Larry Gordon III for a time several years prior. Can you imagine three "Larry's" in the same household? The priest who officiated at the Mass for Uncle Larry, an Irishman from Listowel—the seat of the Broderick lineage of all places—was named . . . you guessed it, "Father Larry!"

Throughout his life, **Laurance "Larry" Gordon Broderick** (b. 1946) seemed to overshadow the rest of us with his assertive personality. Always plotting with his eye intently fixed on the prize, he invariably overcomes adversity and prevails victorious.

I recall the 16-year-old with his coveted driver's license. Hungry to earn a buck, Larry secured a route delivering the Sunday edition of the *New York Times*. Requiring a vehicle to deliver the hefty papers the considerable distance between homes in our suburban neighborhood, he also needed a lackey to run the paper up or down Pittsburgh's steep driveways to each subscriber's front door. He astutely minimized his financial outlay by opening bidding among his younger dim-witted siblings. The willing sucker coming in with the *lowest* bid amount won out, earning yours truly $.50 to Larry's $11.50 take on each Sunday route. For the privilege, I routinely came down with carsickness, and I developed the reputation of an imbecile!

A master of strategy, Larry developed shrewd business acumen at a very young age. In spite of his relatively small frame, he also built physical strength—as a wrestler, boxer, and cheerleader. At just 80 pounds, Larry reigned as the lightweight wrestling champion for the Diocese of Pittsburgh as a high school junior in 1963. Four years later, weighing 130 pounds, he became a lightweight boxing champion with the Notre Dame Bengal Bouts, an annual tournament that raises funds in support of the Bengal Missions in India. For three consecutive years through his senior year with the Fighting Irish, Larry also succeeded in his tryouts with the cheerleading squad. Physically fit, I recall the tough guy's ultimatums, our frequent "uncle" cries in surrender, and my cowering when he so much as threatened to pin me down to pinch a muscle above the kneecap. Those so called "horse bites" exacted excruciating pain and sent a powerful reminder of my fragility in his presence.

Larry entered Marquette University in 1964 and then transferred to the University of Notre Dame as an incoming sophomore. He graduated from Notre Dame with a B.A. in business administration/finance in 1968. During his tenure, the all-male student body heard rumblings of the university's planned conversion to a coeducational institution. Somewhat ironically, many students voiced opposition to the acceptance of women on the sacred grounds of "Our Lady." In his senior year, Notre Dame football team captain James R. Lynch (ND '67) organized resistance with the rallying cry, "Better dead than coed." As an interim step, the administration contemplated the addition of women as cheerleaders to the squad.

Larry shared that, in the Spring of 1968, the dean of students, Rev. Charles I. McCarragher, summoned him for a meeting in his office. At that time, Larry stood out as a Notre Dame cheerleader, Bengal Bouts champion, and "stay senator"—a student senator representing his Howard Hall residence and one of six senators elected to "stay" on for the following year to lead the Senate through the annual transition. Father McCarragher informed Larry that both Father Theodore Hesburgh and Father Edmund "Ned" Joyce, university president and executive vice president, respectively, believed that inviting St. Mary's students to serve as Notre Dame cheerleaders would be a logical first step in their pursuit of making Notre Dame a coeducational institution of learning. Father McCarragher asked Larry to introduce a motion to the governing student senate calling for St. Mary's girls to serve as Notre Dame cheerleaders the following football season.

For the record, Larry conveyed to me that he was already in favor of Notre Dame going coed. "All-male colleges were not normal life, anachronistic for 1968, and with a ratio of six boys to every girl [at St. Mary's]—absurd! So, I said I would do it but it would not be popular."

The student news magazine *Scholastic* published an article titled "The Sacred Gridiron" which I found reprinted in *Thanking Father Ted: Thirty-Five Years of Notre Dame Coeducation* released in 2007. In his capacity as a student senator, Larry reportedly made a motion stipulating the conditions under which women could join the cheerleading squad. On a 17–14 vote, passage of his motion by the student senators provoked emotional outbursts from the constituency. As reported by *Scholastic*, "Broderick, a cheerleader, explained that under his plan the girl cheerleaders would not receive Notre Dame monograms, would appear only in home games, [and] would be carefully selected for appearance and agility by the ND cheerleaders themselves." A petition for reconsideration gathered 2,000 student signatures with a referendum that effectively delayed passage.

On the last day of his final exams as a graduating senior in 1968, Larry reintroduced the motion in support of St. Mary's cheerleaders at Notre Dame. "I convinced a very slim minority to vote their consciences and not with the referendum. It passed by a couple of votes. St. Mary's girls were on the field the next autumn."

In 1969, nine male members judged 13 "Belles" chosen from a field of 30 St. Mary's contestants. According to squad head Uel Pitts, the men made their selections on the basis of "appearance, personality, energy, potential for adapting to whatever new cheerleading moves we may want to try, and leadership." On September 20, 1969, Missy McCrary, Ann Stringer, Molly Tiernan, and Terry Buck—arguably the most photogenic cheerleader in Notre Dame history—made their debut in the new coed cheerleading squad at the victorious ND-Northwestern home game coached by famed Ara Parseghian and led on the field by junior quarterback Joe Theismann. Although I did not learn whether they received monograms in their inaugural year, the debutantes *did* join the team when they traveled to away games. The squad led the cheering crowd in witness to an 8–1–1 season record, although the Irish lost to the top-ranked Texas Longhorns in the Cotton Bowl in Dallas—one of just ten college football bowls at the time.

Breaking from campus life, in the summers of 1964 and 1965, Larry gained valuable business experience, first working at our father's lumber mills in Canada and after, full-time at his Pittsburgh-based wholesale lumber company, Western Spruce Sales. Traveling extensively to supplier mills and to Western Spruce's customer and competitor sites, Larry observed first-hand the extent of Dan T. Broderick, Jr.'s activities at the height of our father's success in the lumber trade.

In the year following his 1968 college graduation during a period of heightened unrest over the Vietnam War, Larry was drafted:

> At the height of the war effort in 1968, President Lyndon Baines Johnson approved an increase in the maximum number of U.S. troops in Vietnam, at 549,500. The year also became the most expensive in the Vietnam War with Americans expending $77 billion ($696 billion in 2024 dollars) for the effort, this in spite of the huge hit in public support following the Tet Offensive in which the North Vietnamese staged attacks against five major South Vietnamese cities, dozens of miliary installations, and scores of towns and villages throughout South Vietnam.

> The decade of the 1960s is well chronicled as a turbulent time with fomenting civil rights and peace movements converging at once to shape revolutionary changes. Alongside Reverend Martin Luther King's resolve to dismantle racial segregation, a counterculture emerged with war protests, draft resistance, "hippies," free love, pot smoking, acid, and rock and roll. College campuses around the country staged growing clashes as the new culture war and radical

ideologies took form. Disillusionment then spread to greater segments of the taxpaying public as some 40,000 young men were drafted into miliary service each month.

With this backdrop, the first draft lottery since 1942 commenced in late 1969. Before then, there was no system in place to determine order of call besides the fact that men between the ages of 18 and 26 faced vulnerability to be drafted. While many soldiers supported the Vietnam war, at least initially, to others the draft seemed like a death sentence as they prepared to fight for a cause they did not believe in.

The sheer number of "Baby Boomers" allowed for a steep increase in exemptions and deferments, especially for college and graduate students. Many young men found creative ways to evade the draft without a legitimate exemption, whether by failing to register with the Selective Service System, faking a medical condition, fleeing to Canada, joining the Peace Corps, or entering officer candidate school as possible options. According to Canadian immigration statistics, as many as 30,000 draft dodgers may have left the United States for Canada during the Vietnam War. Draft evasion carried steep fines and the possibility of jail time, however. Nearly 210,000 men were charged with draft evasion, including boxing great Muhammad Ali, whose conviction was later overturned by the U.S. Supreme Court.

Most eligible men submitted to conscription. The Selective Service System drafted more than 228,000 men in 1967, likely more in 1968. Before the draft ended in 1973, roughly 1.8 million young men had been mobilized.

In February 1969, with 85+ other men, Larry was inducted into the United States Armed Forces at the William S. Moorhead Federal Building in downtown Pittsburgh. During processing, the inductees learned that six among them would be taken into the U.S. Marines. No one responded to the call for volunteers. Following internal deliberations, a staff sergeant entered the room an hour later and read out the names of the six men whom the Marines had selected. "Laurance Gordon Broderick" was the first name called.

Larry immediately shipped off to the Marine Corps Recruit Depot Parris Island, a sprawling base south of Beaufort, South Carolina, where slouchy teenagers and college graduates are chiseled into straight-backed military men. Stepping off the bus at Parris Island, Larry would have stood on yellow footprints painted on the pavement outside the recruit receiving barracks. Amidst screaming drill instructors, the footprints give the men their first taste of military life, marking where and how to stand in formation and at proper attention. Here, a recruit once recalled what a drill instructor conveyed as the two possible ways the men would leave the island—either in a pine box or as a Marine.

Larry trained with Company 238, one of four recruit companies, each comprised of 80+ recruits commanded by three drill instructors. He characteristically stood up to the brute challenge with uncanny mental toughness and physical readiness. First came a few days of processing: the haircut, several shots in the arm, clothing issue, and aptitude tests. Then it was off to basic training with an unrelenting regiment to turn the boys into men. The typical 12-week program was cut short for a time, given the mounting pressure to quickly deploy soldiers to the front lines in Vietnam.

Common boot camp exercises included sit-ups, push-ups, bends and thrusts, and a 300-yard shuttle run. Recruits also engaged in team building exercises such as the obstacle and confidence courses, log drills, rope climbing, body carrying, and tug of war. They then received instruction in hand-to-hand combat techniques with bayonets and pugil sticks. At the rifle range a month or more into boot camp, Larry attempted to qualify with the M-14 rifle, requiring a minimum 190 score out of a possible 250. On the first day of pre-qualification shooting for score, he shot 205 when the range record of a recruit was 138, ranking him third highest in his platoon.

Larry persevered in the hostile and highly competitive environment as only he could, earning special recognition and his family's utmost respect when we witnessed his graduation with the four recruit companies on May 10, 1969. My first foray outside Pittsburgh and Madison at age 16, I was awestruck by the beauty of the stately moss-draped oak trees of Beaufort and the ceremonial honors bestowed on these men who had earned the esteemed title of United States Marine.

At the end of the 10-week training regimen and just before graduation, the drill instructors from each company selected one recruit as the "Outstanding Marine." Larry's selection by Company 238 qualified him to receive "dress blues" and an automatic promotion to the rank of private first class. He immediately proceeded to nearby Camp Lejeune where he entered 12 weeks of advanced infantry training. He was ultimately assigned a military occupational specialty (MOS) of 3441 (auditor) and sent to Quantico, Virginia, for the duration of his tour of duty.

Following his honorable discharge from the Marines in early 1971, Larry volunteered and served with the Federal Sky Marshal Program for one year. Deployed to counter airplane hijackers, as a sky marshal Larry flew all over the world out of John F. Kennedy International Airport in Queens, New York, with Pan American World Airways (Pan Am). He then joined our father in his wholesale lumber business for a brief period before venturing out on his own, self-assured with his entrepreneurial mindset.

In 1974, Larry married Patty's classmate and childhood friend **Kathryn "Kathy" Alexia née Schmitt** (b. 1951), one of nine children who tracked in age with the Brodericks at our elementary and high schools. Soon after, the couple moved to Montrose, Colorado, where Larry formed "Lothlorien Lumber & Logging Company." Named after the idyllic forest featured in his all-time favorite *The Lord of the Rings* trilogy by J.R.R. Tolkien, in Montrose, "Lothlorien" repurposed sawdust, planer shavings, and sawmill waste wood from neighboring lumber mills to manufacture fireplace logs by compression from heat—no wax. He packaged and shipped logs on van trailers to retail outlets in the East— notably 84 Lumber Company and a couple of supermarket chains in Minnesota—and to one or more ski resorts principally in Colorado. Making use of scraps, he bundled the broken fragments and marketed to the region's ski resorts as fireplace starter wood.

Distinctly generous, Larry has afforded job opportunities for family and friends in need of work over many years. At Lothlorien, he employed me right out of college as an office clerk in 1975. He put Nancy's first husband Glenn to work to fill pressing needs as a clerk, yard loader, and mill hand. He also hired Patty's then boyfriend Rob to manage account-ing and bookkeeping.

Unbeknownst to me as a lowly office clerk, Lothlorien encountered some unplanned bumps during its brief history as a highly seasonable business. Although retailers placed product orders in the short timeframe of autumn and early winter, the company produced logs year-round for the sake of efficiency. A local Montrose bank advanced a revolving line of credit that carried Lothlorien through its off-season. After some eight months of making and building inventory, however, the bank became unnerved by the size of the inventory and pulled the line—overnight. Without cash reserves, Larry shut down the mill and started liquidating assets. It took from the summer of 1975 to the spring of 1976 to liquidate everything and bring Lothlorien to an end, but not before paying in full what the company owed to the bank and all suppliers. Larry also paid off the $40,000 principal with accumulated interest that our father had loaned him to start the business.

Not long after the birth of Larry and Kathy's first child, **Casey O'Meara** (b. 1975), in Montrose, the trio moved to Ohio where Larry became a commodities broker. He cleared trades for his customers first through Merrill Lynch and shortly thereafter through Clayton Brokerage. Working out of Clayton's Cleveland office enabled the family to spend their time in Madison. Of course, this delighted "Grinny" (Yo) who doted over her adorable granddaughter. Larry subsequently worked out of Clayton's headquarters in St. Louis before again relocating his family, this time to Denver where he worked out of Clayton's local office. In Denver, Kathy gave birth to the couple's second child, **Laurance "Brodie" Gordon II** (b. 1978).

Shortly after Brodie's birth, Larry bought our grandparents' second home located at 7745 Lakeshore Drive in Madison. He purchased the lakefront property from the couple who had bought it from Gramps and Ooh Ooh in 1973. Situated on Lake Erie just a block from our parents' second home, the residence provided water access which naturally pleased those of us who visited during the summer months.

By 1979, Larry set up a remote office at the lake house where the growing family spent the summers away from Denver. Rather high tech for the times, he established connectivity with two phones and a quotation machine that kept him live on commodity market changes in real- or near real-time. As our mother observed, the phone rang all day and more often than not, he was on both phones at the same time.

Larry was affiliated with Clayton Brokerage out of Denver when he formed Rivendell Forest Products, Ltd. in a 50/50 partnership with Conrad Pinette in early 1980. Denver-based Rivendell purchased and transported lumber from Canadian mills to the distribution facilities it leased where product was staged for sale. Larry named the start-up after a forest in J.R.R. Tolkien's fictional world of Middle-earth which represented both a place of sanctuary and a magical Elvish otherworld. Six or seven years later, Larry bought out Conrad's 50% interest.

Throughout the 11-year life of Rivendell, Larry continued as a broker with his brokerage partner, Jim Paul, changing clearing houses two or three times along the way for better commission splits. Interestingly, Larry made more money as a broker in each and every one of those years than he ever did at Rivendell.

Larry employed our siblings Patty, Terry, and Tim at Rivendell Forest Products, Ltd, as well as Patty's husband, Frank Cappelli. Though Patty, Frank, and Terry were relative short-timers, Tim came in right after graduating from Notre Dame in 1982 and remained with Larry in Denver throughout his working career. [In more recent years, Larry has employed his two daughters and three of Tim's four sons at his current company, Acme Manufacturing.]

The youngest of Larry and Kathy's children, **Colleen Dillon** (b. 1986) was born and raised with her siblings in Denver. During the ten years Larry and Kathy owned Grandpa and Ooh Ooh's former lake house, Larry's family and our mother spent entire summers in Madison with irregular visits from the rest of us as our work schedules permitted from afar. "Grinny" became particularly close to Kathy and the kids due to their proximity. She occasionally drove cross-country with them between Madison and Denver before Larry and Kathy sold the lakefront house in 1989.

Rivendell established precedent in the computer software space when in 1993 the company filed a lawsuit against the Georgia-Pacific Corporation with the U.S. District Court for the District of Colorado [*Rivendell Forest Products, Ltd. v. Georgia-Pacific Corp.*, 824 F.Supp. 961 (D.Colo. 1993)]. Rivendell had developed a proprietary "live" computer software program—the *Quote Screen* System—for quoting delivered lumber pricing to its customers. Considered state-of-the-art at the time, a former employee allegedly stole a copy of the code and provided it to his new employer, Georgia Pacific Corp. In 1994, the United States Court of Appeals for the Tenth Circuit reversed the decision of the U.S. District Court for the District of Colorado, holding that Rivendell had demonstrated that its software was protectable as a trade secret [28 F.3d

1042 (10th Cir. 1994)]. With the ruling, the court awarded Rivendell a seven-figure payment.

Rivendell flourished during the decade of the 1980s, much as our father's Western Spruce Sales had done in the decade of the 1960s. Larry's company steadily increased annual revenue from $1 million to $130 million when the market crashed in 1987. Rivendell failed at the height of the 1990–1991 recession as interest rates spiked and construction therefore cratered. The failure pained him deeply.

Early in his business career, Larry qualified for, and was invited to join the Young Presidents Organization (YPO). YPO is comprised of presidents of companies of a certain minimum size, who were at the time of admission to YPO, under 40 years of age. Through YPO, Larry gained access to a worldwide network of young presidents.

Larry faced a difficult period following the murders of Dan and Linda in 1989, by which time he had separated from Kathy. While working through divorce proceedings, his several real estate investments with our oldest brother came apart as a result of Dan's death. As executor of Dan's estate, Larry was awarded custody of Dan's minor children at this same time. Moreover, as he managed a voluntary liquidation of Rivendell, Larry became a party to 18 different lawsuits—more than one stemming from the murders of Dan and Linda.

Despite the many setbacks, Larry was determined not to give up. In 1992, with a fellow member of the YPO, he bought Steelworks Corporation, an underperforming distributor of metal shapes, along with its sole supplier, a manufacturer. Together these two companies manufactured and distributed metal shapes for the do-it-yourself (DIY) trade. Much as lumber is provided as the raw material for woodworking projects, Steelworks provided the hardware industry with the raw material of metalworking projects. Larry paid $400,000 to acquire the Steelworks Corp, half of which came from the investment of his financial partner.

Larry endeavored to make it as easy as possible for retail hardware companies to buy product from Steelworks. He set out to deliver quality product, fair pricing, and far and away the best turnaround times and fill rates in the industry. Already one of the best at this in the trade with nine-day turnarounds and 93% fill rates, he proceeded with a simple formula, that is, do what you say you are going to do and carry a LOT of inventory.

Within a couple of years, Steelworks ran at 2.4-day turnaround times and 99.9% fill rates.

In 2000, Forbes Magazine published a flattering article about Larry's business genius, titled "The Man of Steel." The two companies acquired in 1992 had produced full-year sales of less than $1,000,000 and never generated a profit. Now known as Acme Manufacturing, Inc., the company has grown more than 100-fold since the acquisition. Diversifying its product line, the collection of seven different divisions supplies various metal products to hardware stores, manufacturers, distributors, and original equipment manufacturers (OEMs) across the country.

Celebrating thirty years in 2022, Denver-based Acme Manufacturing has thrived under Larry's and Tim's capable leadership through acquisitions, spinoffs, organic growth, and masterful strategic planning and execution. In mid-2023, our brother Tim as president and chief operating officer retired from the company; Larry continues to preside as chief executive officer and chairman of Acme's board of directors.

In 2002, Larry met **Lynda née Chergui** (b. 1973), a Frenchwoman of Moroccan descent who was born and raised in Paris where the couple married in 2005. Twenty-seven years Larry's junior, Lynda attended the Institute des Beaux Arts and studied fashion design at *École supérieure des arts et techniques de la mode (ESMOD)* in Paris. She keeps Larry young with extensive international travels. A charmed life, they also enjoy regular getaways to their retreats in Grand Lake, Colorado; Vail, Colorado; and Paris, France.

THE THIRD IN LINE, **Kathleen Mary Broderick McCormack** (b. 1947) is the oldest among the four Broderick girls. She naturally offered great support to our mother, readily helping her tend to the six younger children. Dutiful, nurturing, lady-like, and whimsical, Kathleen stepped right into the maternal role. As the closest to our mother among the girls, she followed orders, rarely making waves like the rest. But she found herself subordinated to patriarchal domination which in time proved increasingly challenging, perhaps made worse as the youngsters protested her thinking she could tell us what to do.

Despite her request to be called "Kathleen" instead of "Kathy" in her late teenage years, a contingent among the siblings still addresses her as

"Kathy." Mindful of appearances, Kathleen "the pretty one" followed our mother's lead, retaining a slim figure, polished nails, a stylish hairdo, and a playful personality.

Kathleen dated often, both in high school and when she headed off to St. Mary's College in 1965. The ratio of Notre Dame men to St. Mary's women then hovered at 6 to 1. During those years, increasing numbers of girls attended college, but custom still encouraged young women to get married and have children before—or perhaps instead of—pursuing a career. As they faced a cultural shift that drew increasing numbers of women into the workplace, the young ladies faced a crossroads inasmuch as their mothers as role models were substantially all homemakers.

Kathleen graduated from St. Mary's in 1969 with a B.A. in psychology, possibly motivated by her desire to understand our complex family dynamic. One year later, *The Mary Tyler Moore Show* became one of the first popular television programs to feature an independent woman, let alone one in a leading role. The show would have been inspiring to any young woman ready to strike out on her own in the workforce.

Given her maternal instinct, Kathleen could have easily followed our mother's path to marriage and raising a family right out of school. She fell madly in love with a Notre Dame student, but he broke her heart by calling off their romance during her graduation weekend. He loved her enough to know that marriage to an aspiring actor would not bring the life she deserved. So, like many of her peers, Kathleen found herself in uncharted territory, navigating an unfamiliar world while attempting to find her place as a working woman. Over the decades, she took on several jobs to make ends meet but did not establish an enduring profession per se.

Out of college, Kathleen earned a Montessori certificate from Fairleigh Dickinson University in New Jersey before establishing roots in Cleveland, Ohio, where she worked as a Montessori teacher. Disenchanted, she moved to the Office of Aging with the County of Cuyahoga, from 1975–1978. On the heels of the 1973–1975 recession that put an end to the post-World War II economic expansion, stagflation—high inflation and unemployment coupled with sluggish growth—placed a financial and psychological strain on those of us in the market for work. Like myself as a 1975 college graduate, Kathleen struggled knowing that no one wanted what she had to offer. Perhaps fueled by an inferiority complex, insecurity set in for both of us as we came to believe we didn't even have that much to offer. The job searching experience was demoralizing, yet Kathleen found work in the county's senior safety and security program, endeavoring to reduce the victimization of the elderly. A far cry from a career, she plodded through in misery.

By this time, Kathleen was smitten. While living in an apartment on a floor immediately below our brother Dennis, she dated Cleveland native **Dennis Patrick McCormack** (1941–2023), a hospital equipment sales representative. Following an eight-year courtship, they *finally* married in 1979. By 1985 when Kathleen was 36, they had two children named after hers and our mother's maiden names, **Kelly Broderick** (b. 1983) and **Casey Gordon** (b. 1985). A preemie, Casey weighed just 3 pounds-15 ounces at birth, but with time he gained weight and fortunately did not experience lingering health issues. Although she did not start a family as soon as she would have liked nor as early as most women at the time, Kathleen naturally fell into the groove. She loved her role as a mother.

Ready for a change of scenery, the family of four moved from their Rocky River home in Cleveland to Seattle, Washington, in 1987. Though far from home, Kathleen welcomed some distance from family. Dennis McCormack's sales territory then covered all of Canada, leaving Kathleen alone with the children when he traveled on business. Meanwhile, the beauty of the great Northwest captivated the couple. The vast ocean, lakes, forests, mountains, and desert afforded many novel experiences for the young family.

Kathleen started a small business in Seattle to earn supplemental income while raising the kids with Dennis. She launched "Welcome Home" in Bellevue in 1989, targeting real estate agents with custom gifts tailored to new home buyers. The business was short-lived, however, as the family moved back to Cleveland in 1991. Triggered by the deaths of Danny and Linda in 1989, Kathleen became concerned for our parents' welfare. Along with her husband, Dennis, she also began to feel homesick for the change of seasons they had left behind with the move to the Pacific Northwest. They put their house on the market just as the Persian Gulf War broke out. The war disrupted the real estate market and delayed their move by several months:

Before the start of the Persian Gulf War in 1990, economists had high hopes for the real estate market. Although the economy had entered a recession, projections pointed to a drop in interest rates and a rise in home sales. Instead, Iraq's military action in the Middle East fueled a spike in oil prices while U.S. interest rates shot up to fend off inflation. Of a sudden, optimism about the housing market got lost in the shuffle as Iraqi leader Saddam Hussein ordered the invasion of neighboring Kuwait, accusing the nation of siphoning crude oil from oil fields along their common border.

As U.S. Air Force fighter planes aligned with Saudi Arabia as part of a military buildup dubbed "Operation Desert Shield," troops sent by NATO allies and several Arab nations captivated the world's attention as we glued ourselves to TV coverage from the security of our homes. Awestruck, we watched as CNN's journalists and cameramen captured the screaming air raid sirens, the thunder of explosions, an unearthly lightshow from exploding ordnance, and the Iraqis lighting up the sky with anti-aircraft fire. As the only global 24-hour satellite news network at the time, CNN broadcast the war live, giving the world an astounding blow-by-blow account of the opening night of the war. That night made television history and catapulted CNN into permanent news prominence. From that moment on, live news coverage is what audiences demanded and news organizations still strive to deliver—even in the face of war.

The U.S. real estate market rebounded once the Iraq-Kuwait conflict was put to rest. In Cleveland, Kathleen obtained a license to sell residential real estate while Dennis continued his work in sales. However, after their first, then second long winter along the southern shore of Lake Erie, they realized the mistake they had made leaving a part of the country they had come to love. So, in 1994, the family returned to Seattle. Kathleen completed the requisite coursework to sell real estate in Washington state while Dennis resumed his occupation in hospital equipment sales.

Throughout the years, Kathleen remained especially close to our mother. They were similarly endowed with a whimsy that compelled them to decorate to the nines in commemoration of each holiday. They developed a passion to bring "festive" to the seasons honoring St. Patrick, the Easter Bunny, witches and goblins, and Santa Claus in secular fashion.

Mom took Christmas to the top while Kathleen still favors Halloween. With refined taste, they shared that talent to beautify, deck out, embellish, garnish, ornament what comes to them naturally. With her big heart, Kathleen brings out the make-believe and fun-making with gusto in everything she plans, ensuring that her target delights in the holidays and special occasions with marvel and joy.

When Kathleen and her family returned to Cleveland in 1991, our parents lived 50 miles away in Madison. As Yo's health rapidly deteriorated from Parkinson's disease, Kathleen stepped in at exactly the right time to offer support and navigate her healthcare options. Patty resided 2-1/2 hours away in Pittsburgh, our brother Dennis a further distance in Cincinnati, while the rest of us were scattered further across the country. Boots on the ground, Kathleen kept us informed by letter, orchestrated the rotation of our phone calls and scheduled visits, and regularly looked after our mom once she entered the Inn-Madison nursing home. Kathleen brought her sweets and placed stuffed animals and an oversized concrete goose in Yo's room. Having supplied a changing wardrobe, I'm sure Kathleen gave the inanimate goose a name. With each visit, she adorned that goose with a new wardrobe and made quite a fuss over it to endear our mother with smiles. At the expense of her own family, Kathleen did everything she possibly could to make Mom comfortable and to lift hers and our father's spirits.

To her eternal regret, Kathleen pulled stakes and returned to Seattle just six months before Yo's passing. Though ill-timed as her departure no doubt proved heartbreaking for our mother, we remain tremendously grateful for the sacrifices Kathleen and her family made during their three years back in Cleveland. No one else had the devotion nor wherewithal to step up as Kathleen did, yet she needed to make her way with priority for her own family.

Within seven years of their return to Seattle, in 2001, Dennis and Kathleen divorced as their eldest prepared to head off to college. Abandoning real estate sales, Kathleen remarried in 2005. Originally from Spokane, Washington, **David Martin Canning** (b. 1944) and Kathleen moved to Pullman, Washington, soon after they wed. They planned to fulfill Kathleen's dream of owning and operating a bed and breakfast with the charm that emanates from the inns dotting the countryside in picturesque New England. Pullman seemed a suitable spot as home to Washington State University and affordable by Seattle standards, so the couple bought land with designs to make Kathleen's dream a reality. Before completing construction of the new quarters, however, Kathleen realized the grave error in her thinking—the small-town feel of Pullman with its agricultural roots in the remote southeast region of the state did not measure up to her expectations. She could not muster enthusiasm for the foreign surroundings, so the newlyweds abandoned their plans, sold the property, and moved to the state capital of Olympia. Here, Kathleen secured employment with the state of Washington in 2008 before transferring to a similar role in Tacoma where the couple established a permanent home two years later.

A retired residential real estate broker, Dave focused his practice on land acquisitions and new construction. At age 70, Kathleen retired from the state position in which she monitored welfare recipients and helped them to secure gainful employment. Since then, she landed a part-time job with an upscale assisted and senior living facility as activities coordinator, bringing her full-circle to her earliest employment days at the Broadfield Manor nursing home where she worked during two summers with Nancy in Madison, and later, to the Office of Aging with the County of Cuyahoga in Cleveland. Delighting the seniors at Weatherly Inn Tacoma suits her perfectly. Kathleen enthusiastically decorates their common quarters, suits up in costume during the holidays, and brings endless smiles to the appreciative elders much as she did for our mom as a resident of the Inn-Madison nursing home before her passing in 1995.

As an adult, our oldest sister has developed a propensity to dramatize, to pull pranks, and to embarrass those of us who happen to witness her improvisational moves. I can't say I know a single person on earth who does that sort of thing with complete strangers. Imagine this scenario: You are seated with her at a lounge, engaged in conversation when she becomes distracted by a delicious looking mound of mashed potatoes on the plate in front of a man across the bar. She says "Excuse me," grabs a fork, walks over to the guy's plate, takes a bite of his potatoes, chuckles flirtatiously, and walks back to pick back up where she left off. Who does that?!?

A few short years back, we four sisters and their daughters met in Pittsburgh for a mini-reunion. Following lunch one day, we browsed while taking a stroll downtown. Stopped at an intersection, we spotted two guys in a convertible, top down, waiting for the light to turn green. Kathleen approached the vehicle and then proceeded to grab the door handle and step in. In her inimitable way, she teasingly giggled while instructing the driver to get going. A block down the road, she stepped out and continued on her merry way, meeting back up with her sisters, daughter, and nieces without missing a beat.

In celebration of her 60th birthday in 2007, Kathleen and Nancy flew to Pensacola, staying with my husband, Rick, and me. Kathleen texted to tell me her plane had landed. I drove to the airport to pick her up outside baggage claim; but she didn't come out. I reluctantly left my car at curbside—subject to getting a ticket—and went in search of her. Becoming increasingly frustrated knowing her plane had landed, I spotted a strange looking elderly woman sporting glasses, pinned up grey hair, and a frumpy hat. Hunched over, she wore a long housedress with Birkenstock sandals and nearly calf-high socks. She glanced my way as I passed by her. Finding Kathleen nowhere in sight in the baggage claim area, I walked the concourse continuing my search when the old lady drew my attention once more. It was Kathleen! She had put on a wig and changed into her "make believe" at a layover on route to Pensacola looking the part for the entirety of her second leg journey from Seattle. She then proceeded to trick Nancy as she stood next to her at the turnstile awaiting her baggage minutes later.

Nancy recalls a time when Kathleen went grocery shopping. Just for the fun of it, she dropped to the floor and yelled out, "Customer down on aisle 4!" With that peculiar sense of humor, she succeeds in garnering a reaction alright.

At a Broderick family reunion in Madison in 2021, as a softball game was underway with some 60+ of us gathered as players or spectators, Kathleen emerged, masked in disguise and hunched over. She walked along the perimeter of the property on approach toward the activity, gradually drawing curiosity that then rose to a feeling of unease. Who IS he—this masked man? Take a guess.

Kathleen seeks out attention-getting ways to make people laugh—or frown. Gotcha! She's very good at it. And she's quite fond of gathering the youngsters at each family reunion with fun and games and candy and toys to win their favor over all others. God knows she tries!

Upon settling in Tacoma, Washington, in 2008, Kathleen and Dave put countless hours into improving their home and grounds. I would not have pegged Kathleen as a manual laborer, but the two nearly single-handedly completed a major renovation to beautify and expand their homestead with a second story. They designed the overhaul to accommodate short-term rentals on one of the two stories as a way to supplement their income. Among other grueling tasks with lasting wear-and-tear consequences, with a chisel and hammer, Kathleen painstakingly broke apart the mortar and removed perhaps 7,000 exterior bricks. She now sports aches and pain to show for it. An avid gardener, Dave germinates flowers from seeds and delights in the abundant flowers he plants that attract onlookers as do the over-the-top Halloween decorations Kathleen puts her heart into creating each year as a showpiece.

IN THE SHADOW of Danny, Larry, and Kathleen, **Dennis John Broderick** (b. 1948) inherited that same rogue gene defined as sharp-witted Broderick humor. I assume it came from our father's side, as I found little trace of it in my research on the Westcotts. On the other hand, the talent, drive, and resilience of my three oldest brothers correlates strongly with our maternal line. Much like Danny and Larry, Dennis's quick wit and intellectual curiosity similarly bode him well. He went on to achieve great success in his professional career as an in-house corporate lawyer.

Like the rest of the clan, Dennis has always enjoyed having and making fun. From an early age, he teased often and developed an endearing personality. In his early years and as a young adult, he liked to dress up, and he built an impressive hat collection that probably numbered 200 before his interest began to wane. Among others, he took great pride in his "Quick Shooter" hat made famous by "King of the Cowboys" Roy Rogers. He claimed no one messed with him when he wore it in grade school and high school!

In a showing of the 1976 remake of *King Kong*, Dennis arrived early sporting a gorilla costume. At an opportune time, he stood up among the theatre crowd pounding his chest with a mighty roar that startled the audience before they belted out riotous laughter. Such was Dennis's proclivity before lawyering at least marginally settled him down. Always scheming with tricks up his sleeve, that episode is etched in our memories as one of his best. But another, far more grandiose ploy got the best of our family when he returned early from his deployment to the Western Pacific during the Vietnam War in 1972. I will come back to the series of surprises he executed shortly.

As the protracted Vietnam War continued unabated into Dennis's senior year at Notre Dame, the U.S. Selective Service initiated the first military draft lottery since World War II for men born between 1944 and 1950. The order in which their birthdays were drawn from the bin determined the order in which the men would be drafted; the first chosen were the first to serve. Born on the seven-year anniversary of the Pearl Harbor attack, Dennis drew number 16.

Upon graduating from the University of Notre Dame with a B.A. in political science in 1970, Dennis enlisted in the U.S. Navy Reserve whose mission is to provide strategic depth and deliver operational capabilities to the U.S. Navy and Marine Corps.

During Dennis's deployment aboard the USS *Alamo* (LSD-33), the amphibious warfare ship circumnavigated the Gulf of Tonkin with a well dock to transport and launch landing craft and amphibious vehicles. The sailors took their posts in one of five departments—Engineering, Deck, Supply, Navigation, and Operations. For 21 grueling months, Dennis served as Petty Officer Storekeeper Third Class ordering supplies for the landing ship docking (LSD) vessel during the time I attended St. Mary's College as a freshman and first-semester sophomore.

Writing from the port at Long Beach, California, or at sea while aboard the USS *Alamo*, I heard from Dennis as well as his Commanding Officer who sent periodic updates to the seafarers' family members. From these communications, I gained some insight into his service and with the rest of the family, I found a semblance of peace knowing he was not among the countless active combat units on the firing line pitting communist North Vietnam and its Viet Cong allies against the South Vietnam government and the United States:

In all, the war dead included as many as 2 million civilians on both sides, roughly 1.1 million North Vietnamese and Viet Cong fighters and more than 200,000 South Vietnamese soldiers. The hideous, protracted war that lasted from 1961 to 1975 claimed 58,200 members of the U.S. armed forces who died or went missing.

To lighten spirits for the long voyage to the Far East, prior to her departure, the crew aboard the USS *Alamo* (LSD-33) adopted an Irish Setter puppy as the ship's mascot. The sailors named her "Lady". Leaving Long Beach with Lady on March 31, 1972, the *Alamo* participated with a group of eight Navy ships simulating a merchant ship convoy to Hawaii. The exercise trained and tested the inactive Navy Reserve personnel who were carried on board for two weeks. Should the need arise, they would become part of the organization our country would depend on to get convoys successfully to their destination.

On April 6, after six days of something less than a smooth transit, *Alamo* entered Pearl Harbor in Oahu, Hawaii. Dennis wrote during the brief two-day weekend stop on route to Guam. He noted that "Guam is 3,500 miles from Hawaii, which is 1,900 miles from California." During off-duty hours, the crew investigated the wide variety of entertainment available in Honolulu and around the island of Oahu. Dennis had no work aboard the *Alamo* on Saturday afternoons or Sundays. In Oahu, he and a few others rented a jeep to tour the island. He observed that Honolulu beaches were teeming with lovely young natives.

The 8th of April found *Alamo* taking leave from Hawaii and starting the second long leg of her journey to the "WestPac"—next stop Guam. "It is rumored that we might be in Nam before we see May." During the transit, the crew continued training in order to achieve a high state of readiness. However, they did manage to intersperse some play into their work schedule.

Two times a day for 5–10 minutes, Dennis and another sailor hosted a sports show over Radio SMILE, the *Alamo's* entertainment system broadcast throughout the ship to decrease the feeling of loneliness during the long periods at sea. As a sports announcer, "I can editorialize at will, and it gets pretty funny at times." With Dennis at the microphone, one can just imagine.

April 17th saw *Alamo* arrive and depart Guam, but not before she offloaded much needed supplies along with a Cessna Skyhawk aircraft for the Guam Flying Club and three private automobiles for Navy men stationed there. *Alamo* lived up to her unofficial motto: "You call, we haul." Following completion of offloading, refueling, and resupplying, *Alamo* set off on that same day for Subic Bay in the Republic of the Philippines.

Arriving at Subic Bay, the crew was only to remain overnight. After onloading desks, chairs, beds, and other materials that U.S. bases and civilian organizations had contributed to the Republic of Vietnam through "Project Handclasp," the *Alamo* set sail for Vung Tau, Vietnam. Here, the crew offloaded these materials and other goods. From Vung Tau they set sail for Da Nang, Vietnam, on April 25, onloading equipment destined for "home" as part of a Vietnam withdrawal program and took it back to Subic Bay. Nearly a month after leaving Long Beach, the *Alamo* had traveled at sea more than 8,000 miles.

In late September, Dennis wrote, "After 26 miserable, dark, dreary, dank days in Subic Bay, we departed the flood-ravaged Philippine Islands on August 22 and arrived in the equally miserable Gulf of Tonkin [the northwestern portion of the South China Sea] with plans to remain in the Gulf until October 7th or 8th, at which time we will offload the embarked Marines in Okinawa and begin our 10,000-mile trek back to the States. We've been in the Gulf of Tonkin for 32 straight days."

Dennis conveyed in his October 2, 1972, letter that the command had granted his early-release request, cutting short his deployment by three months. "My parole board has commuted my sentence, from 24 months to 21 months . . . instead of 6 months to serve, I now have but three . . . I've been as dispirited over the past year and a half as I've never been before . . . To date we have spent 40 straight days in the Gulf . . . By the time we alight in our next port, we will have spent an incredible 50 days at sea." On October 14, 1972, Dennis wrote, "We expect to arrive in Long Beach on November 4 . . . I won't grouse anymore about Navy life—you know how I feel; suffice it to say I am elated—ecstatic even—that the cruise and my service are almost over." Upon arrival on November 8, the ship's public address system broadcast the "Lone Ranger" theme song to the delight of loved ones awaiting *Alamo*'s return to the West Coast.

The Navy released Dennis from active duty several weeks after he disembarked at the Long Beach Naval Station. Rather than notify the family of his intention to arrive home in time for Christmas—we were expecting him days later—he decided to have a little fun by making his early arrival a surprise. Renting a car and driving cross-country, he pulled the wool over my eyes first, as I was the furthest west on his route eastward toward Pittsburgh. Living on campus in the first semester of my sophomore year at St. Mary's, I observed a gentleman leaning his back against a tree with a hat pulled below his brow as I walked the quad toward the dining hall for supper. Just as I was about to pass him, the lone gentleman directed a suggestive comment to me before revealing his identity. Naturally, I went nuts, first with shock then unbridled exhilaration as I welcomed Dennis home.

Dennis then continued east with a stopover in Dayton, Ohio, where Patty and her Pittsburgh friend—Larry's future wife Kathy Schmitt—studied at the University of Dayton as seniors. While they worked as cocktail waitresses in the casual, cozy ranch-style setting at Cork 'N Cleaver restaurant and bar, Dennis walked in with make-up impersonating a very old Black man. He kept the pretense going for two solid hours before the "reveal." While she waited on this apparent stranger, Patty obliged his request to buy him cigarettes from the dispenser. At his urging, she lit one from his quivering lips as Dennis's hands trembled in disguise. He pulled off the scheme to Patty's and Kathy's sheer astonishment and delight.

Approaching Pittsburgh, Dennis gave Kathleen the heads up on his ruse. Catching Larry unawares as he rode in the passenger seat, Kathleen drove from our home down Orr Road to find Dennis disguised as a hitchhiker. Kathleen prevailed in picking him up as Larry flinched in adamant protest. Gotcha!

Later, Kathleen drove our mother to the South Hills Village mall where they found Santa front and center, a rather large "child" on his lap, the likes of her full-grown son Dennis. Floating mists of teary-eyed joy, the emotional embrace epitomized what endeared us to our brother.

In the fall of 1973, Dennis enrolled in Georgetown University's law school in Washington, D.C. Upon earning a Juris Doctor degree, he practiced law with Hohn, Loeser, Freedhaim, Dean & Wellman in Cleveland, from 1976 to 1981, before going in-house with Firestone

Tire & Rubber Company. Shortly before making the switch, Firestone recalled 14.5 million defective "Firestone 500" Steel Belted Radial tires in response to a National Highway Traffic Safety Administration (NHTSA) investigation. Up to that time, the tire recall was the largest in history and the largest civil penalty assessed on any U.S. corporation under the Safety Act. Firestone agree to pay a $500,000 fine ($1.6 million in 2024 dollars) before Dennis came on board. For five years, he served Firestone as assistant general counsel.

In the year he joined Firestone in 1981, Dennis married **Marian Elizabeth née Kinney** (b. 1954) in her hometown of Ann Arbor, Michigan. In 1987, he joined Cincinnati-based Macy's, Inc., which was then known as Federated Department Stores, Inc. Federated had become America's retail powerhouse, owning some of the biggest names in the business including Bloomingdale's in New York, Bullock's in Los Angeles, Rich's in Atlanta, and Filene's and Filene's Basement in Boston. Dennis onboarded as vice president and deputy general counsel. He quickly advanced to senior vice president and general counsel, and then secretary of the board of directors. In 2009, Macy's elevated him to executive vice president.

Circumstances brought a dramatic turn for the company in 1988 when a Canadian real estate developer set his sights on Federated and a takeover ensued. Little more than a year later, the retail giant—weighed down by the massive debt incurred by Robert Campeau to finance the acquisition—stared down the barrel of what would soon become the largest retail bankruptcy in United States history.

In 1989, Dennis called on a professional associate with the international law firm Jones Day. From their days working together at Hahn Loeser in Cleveland, Dennis knew David G. Heiman, partner and chairman of Jones Day's global business practice group and head of the group's business restructuring and reorganization practice. "I hadn't seen him in almost 10 years, but I knew he was head of Jones Day's bankruptcy practice." As Dennis recalled, "Our operations were fine, but we had substantial interest payments on the takeover debt. So, I asked Dave to meet with our senior management team, explain the Chapter 11 bankruptcy process, and help us determine the best way to reorganize."

So began a mutually beneficial relationship that would see Federated file for bankruptcy reorganization in 1990, confounding the experts by exiting bankruptcy protection in only two years without any major divestments. The company quickly set off on one of the great comeback stories in American retailing. As general counsel, Dennis [and Jones Day] also played a pivotal role in the acquisition of archrival R. H. Macy & Co. in 1994 after it too, had filed bankruptcy.

At age 50 in 1998, Dennis and Marian adopted **Grace Kinney** (b. 1998) from Kunming, China. Though the couple eventually divorced, together they nurtured the Asian beauty throughout her formative years in Chicago where Marian established residence and Dennis commuted from Cincinnati on weekends. Now as then, Dennis and Marian remain every bit as committed to each other and their family of three.

Meanwhile, Dennis managed all legal aspects that accompanied Macy's phenomenal growth during his tenure (the company changed its name from Federated Department Stores, Inc. in 2007). The 400-plus department stores generated annual revenue of more than $15 billion in 2004, nearly doubling in 2015 to $27 billion from 870 stores in 45 states and online sales from the macys.com, bloomingdales.com and bluemercury.com websites. Dennis retired from Macy's, Inc. after nearly 30 years of service in 2016.

The 4th of Dan and Yo's nine children, Dennis remains an avid Notre Dame fan. The basement of his Cincinnati home memorializes his coveted alma mater in museum-like fashion. For several decades running, Dennis hosts an annual "game weekend" at his alma mater during every football season with a large group of family and friends. Steeped in tradition, the weekend includes a regular stop to the graveside of legendary coach Knute Rockne (1888-1931) where the group gathers to pay their respects. The boom box (or Bluetooth speaker) blasts the Notre Dame Alma Mater, the Notre Dame Victory March, and Rockne's famous pep talk to his players. A consummate showman, Rockne recreated the pep talk for the newsreels around the late 1920s, not for any particular game but to show his motivational technique with the players. An excerpt from Knute Rockne's legendary speech follows:

"We're going inside of 'em, we're going outside of 'em – inside of 'em! outside of 'em! – and when we get them on the run once, we're going to keep 'em on the run. And we're not going to pass unless their secondary comes up too close. But don't forget, men – we're gonna get 'em on the run, we're gonna go, go, go, go! – and we aren't going to stop until we go over that goal line! And don't forget, men – today is the day we're gonna win. They can't lick us – and that's how it goes . . . The first platoon men – go in there and fight, fight, fight, fight, fight! What do you say, men!"

The brief ritual at Highland Cemetery in South Bend orchestrated by Dennis each year includes a student and alumnus who take turns sharing prepared remarks with the group on what Knute Rockne means to them personally. The informal program concludes with a round of Jameson's Irish Whiskey, shot glasses raised in honor of the Norwegian-born American gridiron coach who built the University of Notre Dame into a major power in college football, becoming the intercollegiate sport's first true celebrity coach:

> Rockne's death in a plane crash in a Bazaar, Kansas, wheat field on March 31, 1931 at age 43 shocked the nation and prompted tributes from President Herbert Hoover and King Haakon VII of Norway. An outpouring of popular biographies and testimonials to Rockne's genius culminated in the 1940 film, *Knute Rockne—All-American* with Ronald Reagan playing his most famous player, George Gipp. "Win one for the Gipper" guaranteed Knute's immortality as arguably the most revered of American college football coaches.
>
> The national outcry over the disaster that killed Rockne and seven others triggered sweeping changes to aircraft design, manufacturing, operation, inspection, maintenance, regulation, and crash investigation, igniting a safety revolution that ultimately transformed airline travel worldwide from one of the most dangerous forms of travel to one of the safest.

Not long before his death in 2008 at age 82, the youngest and last survivor of Knute's four children, South Bend resident John "Jack" Vincent Rockne (1926–2008), got wind of the tribute paid to his father each year by the intimate group led by Dennis. Jack was just five-years old when his father perished in the plane crash. Jack met a friend of Dennis's at a bar in South Bend and the conversation led to the decades-long ritual of meeting at Knute Rockne's graveside each year to pay homage. Jack suffered an ailment late in life that precluded his ability to speak. In response to learning about the custom from Dennis's friend, he wrote on a slip of paper, "Can I come?" Can I come?!? We witnessed Jack's visceral response at our next gathering to pay his father our deep respect.

Overcome with emotion, tears streamed down Jack Rockne's cheeks as we honored his beloved father some 75 years after his passing. Jack's presence touched us deeply, and the memorial Dennis leads honoring the legendary coach each year lives on.

In retirement, Dennis spends time at his home in Cincinnati, with Marian in Chicago, and in Madison at our family's summer home which he jointly owns with Larry and Tim. He also stays at the adjacent lake house Dennis and Tim bought two doors from our grandparents' and Larry's former summer home. Yard work, golf, horseback riding, long-haul motorcycle trips with his buddies, enchanting family vacations, and Notre Dame football occupy much of his time otherwise.

WE COME TO THE MIDDLE CHILD and first "lefty" among us— **Nancy Ann Broderick Boru** (b. 1950). In 1964, Alfred Adler developed a theory on the importance of birth order on personality development, claiming that although children may be born into the same household, their birth order greatly influences their psychological development. True enough.

Sandwiched between the rest, Nancy competed with both the older and younger siblings to find her place. In the process, she developed rebellious behavior and the stereotypical middle-child "black sheep" label. Instead of watching from the sidelines, she risked ostracism by breaking a taboo. She had the audacity to step into the fray and participate in the activities the boys engaged in, whether "king of the mountain," horseback riding, softball, wrestling, skateboarding, or any other variety of sport the boys considered their domain. I suppose they didn't much like her butting in as a tomboy. She was a *girl*, after all, albeit possessing a belligerent personality trait that sharply contrasted with Kathleen's well-mannered, compliant nature.

Because our parents genuinely favored the boys, the girls naturally fell out as worth something less. As our mother maintained a closeness to Kathleen as the oldest daughter, Nancy suffered neglect as the second girl, causing her to challenge the status quo at seemingly every turn. Passionate and fiercely independent, strong-willed and determined, she stood her ground with rigor, but the derision only escalated. Taunted incessantly, Nancy played defense but invariably lost the battles in the homemade Broderick war.

By her own admission, Nancy developed into an ill-tempered child with anger issues. Aggravated by the arrows thrown her way, in defiance, she found in Patty—as the next youngest—an outlet to channel her pent-up frustration.

The established pattern of punishment Nancy meted out when Patty so much as looked at her the wrong way evolved in their teenage years—as it did when I came along after Patty, and Terry after me, triggering a combustible chain reaction. The animosity among and between us proved palpable. More than the others, however, Nancy's defiance—coupled with her disregard for the consequences of her actions beginning at an early age—caused some in the family to spurn her as a persona non grata. Our father's intolerance set the course—ultimately leading to her estrangement from our parents and at least one in the lot among the rest of us. In trademark fashion, Nancy fought back and ultimately persevered in the absence of the nurturing that she—and many of the others of us—so desperately needed and deserved.

Nancy began to spread her wings in the summer of 1966. As our father's business hummed along, he conceded to her request to study with her Fontbonne Academy classmates in Vichy, France. [Naturally, all four Broderick girls studied French in high school.] Our dad stipulated that Kathleen would need to accompany Nancy even though—two academic years ahead of her—Kathleen had just completed her freshman year at St. Mary's College. Chaperoned by Fontbonne's diminutive and most delightful French teacher Sister Patrice, they entered the five-week program at the Lycée Presles in central France with stops in London, Paris, and Switzerland. The international experience opened Nancy's imagination to a life outside Pittsburgh and Madison.

The following summer, Nancy and Kathleen worked the 3–11 p.m. shift as nurses' aides at the Broadfield Manor nursing home in Madison. It was Nancy's first full-time paying job if you don't count her $20 take to Dennis's $50 for the joint project that had them paint the perimeter fencing around our parents' Orr Road property in Pittsburgh the prior summer. At our parents' insistence, the girls worked at the nursing home where they made an hourly wage of $1.05 to deliver dinners and feed and clean the bereft residents under highly disturbing conditions. With trepidation, they returned to Broadfield Manor each day assaulted by a litany of heartbreaking and shocking encounters.

The experience weighed heavily on Nancy, evidently leaving quite an impression. Fifty years later, her vivid memory brings to mind the looks, sounds, and smells of many of those colorful characters, even recalling many of their names. Among them, Glenn B. stands out as the 30-year-old Down Syndrome resident whose mother and sole caretaker resided in a separate room at Broadfield Manor. One day Nancy found Glenn nearly inconsolable because a young worker broke his promise to take him outside to play catch.

Nancy gathered up Glenn's gear, and out they went to play ball. Her mouth nearly dropped when she witnessed his pitching arm in action. Glenn threw the ball so hard and fast and far that it sailed beyond her. Her stunned reaction delighted Glenn and he beamed with pure joy. With that, Nancy took Glenn home one day to play an actual game of softball with all the neighborhood kids gathered in our backyard. She described him as a baseball savant who probably had the best day of his life. It made Nancy's day to see that broad smile painted across Glenn's sweet face. He quickly became a superstar among the Brodericks and the passel of neighborhood kids gathered for the game. With that, the girls returned to Broadfield Manor the following summer.

Although the nurses' aide position proved jarring, the tangential experience of lifting spirits at the nursing home—Glenn's and the other disheartened residents—rewarded Nancy and Kathleen with a developing sense of compassion and empathy. With her characteristic levity, Nancy jokes that she also learned to store up mass quantities of sleeping pills so she never finds herself having to live in a place like Broadfield Manor!

At summer's end in 1967, Nancy enrolled at St. Francis College in Loretto, Pennsylvania. Larry's advice as he dropped her off as an incoming freshman—study business and don't get a boyfriend right away. Nancy, of course, knows best the resistant path that steers her away from conventional wisdom. She started on the advised track by declaring business as a major, sticking with it for only one semester, however.

Nancy switched her major to French and with questionable judgment began dating someone who proved to be a bad influence. The boyfriend introduced her to sex, drugs, and rock and roll at an impressionable age. When St. Francis College expelled him, Nancy gravitated to his off-campus "hippie" lifestyle to her detriment. Though an eager student, she went to her classes doing the minimum amount of schoolwork to maintain a "C" average when Catholic guilt set in.

Supporting all nine children in private schools, our father had begun to feel the effects of both the Fed's fiscal tightening to close the budget deficits stemming from the Vietnam War and monetary tightening to raise interest rates. The threat of a major recession loomed on the horizon. Acknowledging the financial outlay spent principally to maintain her social lifestyle, Nancy dropped out of school after her sophomore year at age 19. She spent that summer—the summer of Woodstock in 1969—in Ocean Grove, New Jersey, where she got her first waitressing job.

With her boyfriend, Nancy set off for the epic three-day pop and rock music festival on a 600-acre dairy farm in Bethel, New York, where the organizers expected a crowd of 50,000 people. Arriving ahead of the throng of more than 400,000, the couple established their base. As highways and roadways came to a standstill stacked nine miles long, the carefree concert goers simply abandoned their cars and trekked the rest of the way on foot. The barrage gave way to an incredible scene never before experienced:

> The jam-packed "peace and love" revelers surrendered to an outpouring of rain, muck, long lines for too few portable toilets—600 in total—scarce food and water, and the most fantastic lineup of music ever gathered in one spot. Richie Havens kicked things off as the first of 32 acts. Among the other headliners "rocking the night away"—Joan Baez; Janis Joplin; The Who; Jefferson Airplane; Joe Cocker; Crosby, Stills, Nash & Young; and Jimi Hendrix. The sweet aroma of marijuana wafted

The ubiquitous "Peace" symbol

across the fields of the festival all weekend long. Into the wee hours as the assembled crowd danced and caroused, many of the "stoners" also tripped on acid, smoked opium, snorted cocaine, and ingested magic mushrooms and every other form of psychedelic they could get their hands on. Suffice it to say, the drug war took a discernible hit at Woodstock!

The legendary festival gained fame as a symbol of the counterculture movement and retains its allure as the most momentous music event in American history. Woodstock defined a generation of music and a cultural phenomenon. It represented a culmination of musical genius with the earliest seeds of rock 'n roll germinating a decade earlier with the likes of Buddy Holly, Ritchie Valens, and J.P. "The Big Bopper" Richardson. The sudden death of the trio in a plane crash in 1959—"The Day the Music Died"—marked a new chapter for the youth of the 1960s, notably young musicians who found inspiration in rock 'n roll in this decade of political protests.

Staging a new wave of folk, gospel, and pure R&B revivals, the Woodstock music resonated in the soundtracks we played over and over again on vinyl. The emerging artists of the day blended unique musical styles with melodies and complex rhythms that captivated our generation. Few if any of us could forget the day in 1964 when the Beatles made their debut in the U.S. with their first live American television appearance on *The Ed Sullivan Show*. A hysterical mob followed them and countless other bands that quickly became household names—too many to mention here. Collectively, they rewarded us with the best musical entertainment of all time, in the process sparking a youth rebellion in teenagers like Nancy.

Although Nancy lived through the Woodstock experience and like the others, probably reached a state of nirvana crowded in with the devoted fans, she and her friend exited early. An ill-timed ailment causing unrelenting runs left her with no choice but to cut out well before Jimi Hendrix closed the festival with a glowing performance. Her boyfriend was none too happy to miss the finale, which may have contributed to the ultimate split that brought her back to Pittsburgh.

Back home, while employed for three short weeks with an outfit that sold encyclopedia sets door-to-door, Nancy met her trainer and future husband **Howard "Glenn" Aston** (b. 1948). As she moved from job to job in quick succession, Glenn convinced her to go back to college. A year after pulling out of St. Francis College, Nancy enrolled at Duquesne University in Pittsburgh as a commuter, first as a French major before switching to history. Nancy and Glenn married during her senior year. On the heels of a horrifying ordeal stemming from a benign tumor on her uterus—made worse by a most unfortunate misdiagnosis—Nancy graduated on the Dean's list with a B.A. in history in the spring of 1972. Up to this point she had bought the family line that she was far from bright. By staying focused and applying herself, she came to learn that she actually has some smarts and in fact is very bright.

At Glenn's urging, Nancy applied to Notre Dame's law school but none other. Although she garnered an impressive score in the law school admission test, Notre Dame denied her admission. Instead, she and Glenn spent a summer in Hyannis, Massachusetts, on Cape Cod, where she became pregnant with **Aimée Phillips** (b. 1973).

Nancy and Glenn moved to Rutland, Vermont, where Aimée was born. The family of three then ventured west to Colorado. After a short spell in Montrose, in 1974-75 they settled in Telluride until cracks in the marriage broke them apart. Back in Pittsburgh, Nancy met **Alfred "Al" Leonard Kinzler** (b. 1951) with whom she suffered a volatile 12-year marriage that ended immediately following Danny and Linda's murders in late 1989.

With Al, Nancy gave birth to **Nicole Westcott** (b. 1980)—the one and only "GEN 13" Westcott descendant to carry the family name—and **Ian Allen** (b. 1981). When she reached age 12, Aimée left the nest to live with her father and his second wife in Maryland. They offered her the promise of a stable home that was fleeting in Pittsburgh. Though heartbreaking, Nancy knew the move was in her eldest child's best interest.

Throughout most of her marriage to Al, Nancy worked as a waitress at Wright's Seafood in the neighboring borough of Heidelberg and Al as a motorcycle mechanic. Meanwhile, she found herself questioning everything, not the least her Catholic faith. Lamenting her lack of spirituality, she met two Jehovah's Witnesses when they came knocking on her door. She read the Bible with them and soon found herself attending services at the Kingdom Hall. Once baptized into Jehovah's Witnesses, she did not celebrate birthdays or holidays with her family. She obliged the order with door-to-door preaching about "our last days" before becoming disillusioned and abandoning the denomination altogether. To be expected, her conversion did not sit well with our parents and grandparents—all devout Catholics. By this time, my father in particular had just about enough. Nancy's widening estrangement from our family became painfully obvious.

I'm reminded of "GEN 4" Simon Sackett, son of my G7 grandparents Joseph Sackett and Elizabeth Betts Sackett. Our many-times great-uncle Simon married a comely young Irish girl. His parents did not approve of his marriage. His cultured sisters treated Simon's bride with great coolness, if not actual rudeness, when, after his return to his native land, he took his bride to the Sackett home. Resenting the treatment, Simon left with his wife and never returned. Nancy never left altogether but kept an obligatory distance with unwelcome reminders that she does not fully belong.

In time, as Nancy grew further apart from our family, Al became more verbally abusive toward her. Their fractious relationship spiraled, ultimately leading to the threat of physical harm and Nancy's decision to leave him.

While Al took off on a hunting trip—just five weeks after we lost Dan and Linda to murder—Nancy rented a truck, loaded essentials, pulled Nicole (age 10) and Ian (age 7) from school, and fled into obscurity. Spending 30 days at a women's shelter, she formulated a plan, scraped together $1,500, changed her name, and with the children traveled cross-country in a beat-up car that broke down twice before they landed in Colorado. She concealed her identity by taking the name "Nancy Boru" and settled the family in Norwood, Colorado. Here, they lived 30 miles northwest of Telluride for the next twelve years, or in the case of Nicole and Ian, until they graduated from high school and enrolled in college outside the state.

During her history studies at Duquesne, as she learned about Brian Boru, Nancy recalled that our father once told of the Brodericks' descent from the 10th century high king of Ireland. Though in all likelihood a fabricated tale, Nancy chose to conjure the blending of our aristocratic Westcott pedigree with the fabled Brian Boru whom she credited with ending the Viking domination of Ireland as one of the most successful and unifying monarchs in medieval times. In her quest for a new identify, she recalled this history and the connection she felt to the unrivaled war leader. She liked the sound of "Boru," what she learned Brian Boru stood for, and the fact that she had never come across anyone with that name before. So, in hiding, my sister adopted "Nancy Boru" as the name she proudly carries to this day.

Living surreptitiously in Norwood, Nancy Boru remained determined to give Nicole and Ian the best possible chance at life. It did not come easily, but she adapted to her highly challenging circumstances with resourcefulness and lucky breaks. While living in county-sponsored "Section 8" housing for low-income residents, Nancy enrolled the kids in school and scraped pennies first as a census taker, and then as a shuttle bus driver for the town of Telluride. She also became an office manager and reservations manager for Olympic Sports in Telluride. Lasting three years, her employment with Olympic Sports afforded the family free ski passes and discounts on ski equipment and clothes. Nancy then endeavored to make a living inside her home in Norwood, first by baking and selling fresh sweets to local businesses. An accomplished baker, Nancy perfected our paternal grandmother's chocolate cake-like cookies with creamy white frosting—"Ooh Ooh" cookies—and a variety of other scrumptious baked goods before someone ratted on her for cooking commercially out of her home against food safety code.

Having inherited our mother's artistic gene, Nancy relentlessly pursued crafts as another way to make money. Early on, she designed three dimensional macrame wall hangings, lamp shapes, and plant hangers. With a sparkling imagination, she made picture frames out of fabric. She also learned how to decorate cakes and how to sew. With a friend, my industrious sister started "Sew Fine," sewing for interior designers in the area while making duvet covers, curtains, and pillows for the newly refurbished Norwood Inn. She also worked as a "handy" woman, as a fast order cook, at the local hardware store, in the office of a custom wooden door maker, and then for a manufactured home builder. It seemed that she could do it all. Nancy's kids never went hungry, and she never had her lights turned off.

Nancy's most successful and enduring trade came in the form of toffee. Inspired by Lone Cone Peak, the westernmost peak of Colorado's San Juan Mountain range facing Norwood, in 1996, she launched "Lone Cone Toffee." She dedicated herself to making, packaging, and shipping the delectable treat as a seasonal business during the months leading up to Christmas. The business tag line, *"Where do you hide yours?"* brings back memories of our mother's sweet tooth and her reputation for hiding candy from the kids. The laborious toffee-making work was not especially lucrative, but Nancy stuck with it and achieved great renown during Lone Cone Toffee's 17-year run.

When not working to sustain her family, Nancy engaged in her community with a passionate heart for children and animals. Committed to making some lasting contributions, she ran and was elected by the townspeople to the Norwood School Board and the "All Around" board that ran the fairgrounds. She also served on the town board; the board of the San Miguel Resources that combats domestic violence; and a recreational committee she spearheaded with the county. Among her most significant contributions, Nancy fought for the bond issue the community passed to build a new school. Her son Ian joined others in the new school's first graduating class.

A cowgirl at heart, Nancy truly loved the beauty of the Colorado mountains along with the thrill of horseback riding. Her favorite pastime came when given the opportunity to saddle up. Otherwise, she made memories in her exploits with many interesting and curious characters in Norwood, Colorado. Making lifelong journal entries, many of her colorful tales lead you to question the veracity of the stories only because of their fantastical nature. I suggested she publish her collection of short stories under the pen name "Grancy Boru". It has a good ring for a black sheep writer; *Black Sheep Tales* strikes me as a fitting title.

During Nancy's years in Norwood, her oldest daughter completed college, married, and gave her two granddaughters. By this time, Al had learned of Nancy's whereabouts from his stepdaughter, Aimée. No longer in hiding, Nancy did not hear from Al as feared. Nicole and Ian became reacquainted with their father not long before they went off to college.

Three years before leaving her beloved state and heading east, in the year of the new millennium when Nancy turned 50, the "GEN 12"

Broderick girls gathered at Larry and Lynda's magnificent vacation home in Grand Lake, Colorado. It stands as the one and only time the four girls traveled together, without any others—just we sisters. I customized long-sleeved t-shirts for the occasion featuring a photo of a younger version of each of us on the front side. The back side distinguished the recipients as "The Pretty One" (Kathleen), "The Passionate One" (Nancy), "The Funny One" (Patty), and "The Sentimental One" (yours truly).

Days before the birth of Aimée's third and youngest child at the start of 2003, "Grancy"—as Nancy is lovingly known by her grandchildren—packed her bags and moved to Charlotte, North Carolina, to lend support.

As a newcomer to Charlotte, Nancy lived on the same block as her family and soon began freelance work as a bookkeeper and as a photographer's assistant and food stylist. From Thanksgiving to Christmas, she backed off bookkeeping to concentrate on Lone Cone Toffee. In 2011, she opened Dolce Paradiso Bakery with a partner. Along with freshly baked goods, the storefront provided the outlet she needed to sell toffee year-round. Two years passed when issues surfaced with her partner, however. At that point, Nancy threw in the towel on the bakery and folded Lone Cone Toffee.

At age 63, Nancy decided she'd had enough of the food business, partners, and self-employment. She then entered the mortgage loan business as a processor, first in Charlotte and subsequently in Knoxville, Tennessee, where she now resides. The relocation coincided with her son Ian's move for a job opportunity when expecting his second child. Nancy uprooted in order to do what she does best: lend support as an integral part of her grandchildren's lives in their formative years. She is a doting "Grancy," an entertaining storyteller and writer, an avid reader and canasta player, a talented karaoke singer and water colorist, a fabulous baker, and a compassionate soul. She officially retired in 2023.

On Nancy's 72nd birthday, her daughter Aimée entered this post on Facebook:

> *She taught me about strength and courage and resilience. She's the reason I'm crafty, scrappy, and have a sweet tooth. She gifted me a love of reading, and games, and an appreciation for carefully crafted words. She taught me right*

from wrong and the importance of protecting the vulnerable and standing up to the bully. From Landon's birth until the [three] girls were teens, she lived next door, sharing those same things with them, and now with my brother's kids. None of us would be who we are without you, Mom.

Defying the odds stacked against her, I am so proud of the legacy our "black sheep" created for her family—my family by extension. I admire "Grancy Boru" for the love she has engendered in her eight "GEN 13" and "GEN 14" children and grandchildren.

ON THE BACK SIDE of our "GEN 12" pack of nine, **Patricia "Patty" Broderick** (b. 1951) tied the sibling score with her birth as the 6th Broderick—three boys, three girls, still counting.

Patty is the sibling who missed out on a middle name. How is it possible that our parents failed to come up with something? If nothing else, surely my mother's given middle name "Westcott" would have sufficed. Did it not occur to them that it might be challenging for a child to stand alone among six—eventually nine—without a middle name? It would have given me a complex, and I know it troubled Patty as a youngster.

As a gift for Patty as she prepared to graduate from high school in 1969, our father planned to monogram luggage for her. He asked "Yolande" to remind him of Patty's middle name. When she replied that Patty didn't have one, he quipped, "What do you mean she doesn't have one?" He made up his mind that she should have a middle name so he conjured the name "Ann" which belonged to both Nancy and me. Settling the matter, the luggage came monogrammed with the initials "PAB."

As mentioned, scant sisterly love bonded Nancy and Patty in our formative years. By extension, the same held for Patty and me. We always shared a bedroom, but Patty had little regard for me as far back as I can remember. Prompted by nothing more than eye contact, with contempt she would form her facial expression like putty, curling her lip and turning up her nose. With every fateful glance, the return sneer toward me came naturally. When quibbles escalated to full-fledged cat-fights, an amused sibling might step in to break up our bruising, hair-pulling brawls.

I could do little to earn Patty's favor, and I had little incentive besides. But that did not stop me from trying. I was six or seven and Patty two years older when, coincidentally, we both developed a speech impediment at the same time. Patty could not pronounce the "sss" or "shh" sounds while I stumbled with "sss" and "chh." Mrs. Marjory Scanlan came to our house twice weekly for hour-long, after-school speech therapy sessions. For two years, we slurred our speech and performed mouth exercises guided by our therapist's encouragement, all the while facing our brothers' mockery. Then one day, with no apparent explanation, Patty blurted out the proper "sss" and "shh" sounds. Miraculously, I followed her lead nearly simultaneously.

I suppose it is possible that I mimicked Patty's slurred speech as a convoluted way to gain her acceptance. She demanded distance, however, and may have subconsciously believed that regaining proper speech would set her free from me. It was wishful thinking.

Patty managed to shield herself from the skirmishes that presented themselves in our family with humor. She is perhaps the funniest person I know, loving nothing more than to laugh and make others laugh with her. Quick witted, she regales in amusing others, whether with practical jokes or recounting embarrassing stories about people in her large circle of family and friends.

The one thing in which she finds no humor is mice. As a youngster, Patty developed "musophobia," a condition she formed in reaction to the scene that played out as Terry gripped a dead mouse when he was 18-months old. The hysterical Irish au pair in our family's employ ordered Patty—four years older—to remove the dead mouse from Terry's clutch. Screaming "GET IT OUT OF HIS HAND," the terrified Noreen McDonough traumatized Patty thus seeding her lifelong rodent phobia.

Ten years passed when our family moved to 241 Orr Road in Upper St. Claire's Trotwood Acres, in 1964. Here, periodic mouse sightings were made, imagined, and feared—notably in the barn and the bedroom that Patty and I shared in the attic. My own fear of scampering mice when entering the attic was palpable, but Patty nearly went into convulsions when spotting one herself. One time, on approach to the house from the barn, she visualized a scurrying mouse chasing her as she frantically ran up the hill to escape what turned out to be one of our oversized dogs. I don't recall if it was our 120-pound Newfoundland, "Thor," but know she never lived that one down.

Not infrequently, Patty got into trouble in high school for her humorous pranks. The most notable to my recollection came during a Glee Club performance at the "all girls" Fontbonne Academy. The Christmas program had the high school seniors enter the gymnasium single file from the rear, taking their place up front on the bleacher steps for maximum visibility. To engender the holiday spirit, the music conductor, Sister Florence, directed the girls to come dressed for the season wearing hats, scarves, and mittens. Patty and her friends obliged. With her stiffening back to the audience of families and fellow students, Sister Florence noticed the garb worn by Patty and one or two of her closest friends— knitted ski caps pulled over their faces with holes revealing nothing more than their eyes and mouths. Tension filled the air as the carolers joyously belted out *Jingle Bells, Deck the Halls,* and *O Holy Night* among other holiday favorites. Predictably, Sister Florence kicked Patty and her friends out of Glee Club the instant the performance ended. Thereafter, Sister Florence kept a keen eye on me as a sophomore Glee Club member to be sure Patty's tainted sister wouldn't give her any more trouble!

When Patty wasn't endeavoring to make people laugh, she revealed a determination that bode her well in her many pursuits. Among the earliest, she took up sewing and succeeded in cranking out many articles of clothing during her late high school years. Occasionally, she let down her guard to make items for me. I delighted in picking out patterns but had no talent for stitching fabrics as Patty did.

Like Kathleen and Nancy, Patty participated in a study abroad program that brought her to Tours, France, under the tutelage of Fontbonne's Sister Georgine. The Fontbonne students pooled with a group made up of 200 high schoolers from all over the East Coast, among them her lifelong friend Floyd Bradley from Short Hills, New Jersey, and the future broadcast journalist and television personality Meredith Viera from Providence, Rhode Island. The 1968 summer program also brought Patty to Paris, London, and Spain.

Endowed with luxuriant, thick brown hair that flowed well past her shoulders, Patty stood out in a crowd. Ever popular, she had a steady boyfriend and many close friendships among Fontbonne girls and South Hills Catholic boys throughout much of high school and well beyond—to the present. At the Thanksgiving dance her senior year, her classmates nominated her "Turkey Queen!" With her date, Rob Coombes, she naturally fit in as the life of the party.

Once Patty took off for the University of Dayton in Ohio, she softened toward me with frequent letter exchanges but managed to jab me with insults from afar. In an early letter, she shared her reaction to my getting my driver's license. "I almost died when I found out you got your license. I find that unbelievable. God. Have you crashed either car yet?" In another, "You should see the pictures Larry took at the lake. They were great. Yours, of course, were blurry." In yet another she wrote, "Thanks for sending those pictures but no thanks. I put them in the attic in hopes of never seeing them again." In yet another letter she wrote, "I sent Timmy a letter. Of course, all through the letter I insulted him even worse than I do in person. On the bottom I wrote this as you see it. 'You ~~don't~~ make me sick. I hate ~~love~~ you, etc.'" She signed that letter to me, "Hate, Patty." You get the idea. I'm not sure that I did.

With her recurring insults written from afar, Patty shared her escapades, often admonishing me to keep what she shared to myself—"Don't tell!" And it seemed she always wanted something from me. "Do [this] . . . Get me [that]," whether it be money Nancy owed her or something as mundane as contact information. "If the opportunity comes up, mention that I'm low on $ and that I could really use some extra." "And very important—tell Nancy to send the $! If I knew I'd be having trouble with her I wouldn't have made this deal." "Please do what I've asked you right away." "Look for this . . . Call so and so . . . Tell her—send those things immediately." If I didn't oblige in kind to Patty's incessant appeals, she badgered me until I followed through. Her persistence worked in getting results—an attribute that bodes one well in life, I suppose.

As an incoming college junior, Patty bought a Honda 100 motorcycle similar to the one Danny once owned. "I take everyone for rides; maybe I'll give you one this summer if you pay me enough." Now into her 70s, Patty still rides although I can't honestly recall ever riding with her. Perhaps I wasn't willing to pay her price!

In Dayton, Patty worked at the Cork 'N Cleaver restaurant to earn spending money which allowed the social butterfly to visit college friends in the Northeast and reunite in New York with her steady boyfriend Rob at Fordham University during breaks. Upon graduating from the University of Dayton with a Bachelor of Science in elementary education in 1973, she relocated to the Boulder, Colorado, location of the Cork 'N Cleaver chain; Rob worked for Larry at Lothlorien Lumber & Logging Company in Montrose. ["Boulder Cork" celebrated 50 years in business in 2019.] Following a romance that lasted several years, Patty and Rob split up soon after he left Colorado.

In 1975, once she and her high school sweetheart broke up for good, Patty returned to Pittsburgh, for a short time living at the homestead when Timmy reached high school. Nine years younger than Patty, Timmy was then the only sibling who had not yet left the nest. "Spending time with Timmy is really an advantage to being home. I've gotten so close to him and I just love it. He can really be so much fun. We've had some great talks. Tonight's was on how to attract girls. I went into how important it is to at least look clean—he's so cute. It's a bonus being here [in Pittsburgh] with him around." Patty and Tim have remained exceptionally close throughout the decades to the present.

Complementing her quick-witted humor, Patty has a strong work ethic and often held more than one job to make ends meet in her early adulthood. While employed by the Family Planning Council of Western Pennsylvania in Pittsburgh, she completed a paralegal course and at the same time waitressed at The Saloon of Mt. Lebanon. She had an absolute ball working at the Saloon, especially when given the opportunity to contribute to *The Saloon's Spittoon* as the newsletter's editor and ghost writer "Vicky." The regularly featured "Dear Miss Vicky" column underscores Patty's funny side.

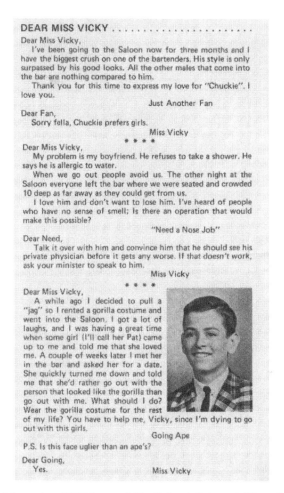

DEAR MISS VICKY . . . .

Dear Miss Vicky,
I've been going to the Saloon now for three months and I have the biggest crush on one of the bartenders. His style is only surpassed by his good looks. All the other males that come into the bar are nothing compared to him.
Thank you for this time to express my love for "Chuckie". I love you.

Just Another Fan

Dear Fan,
Sorry fella, Chuckie prefers girls.

Miss Vicky

* * * *

Dear Miss Vicky,
My problem is my boyfriend. He refuses to take a shower. He says he is allergic to water.
When we go out people avoid us. The other night at the Saloon everyone left the bar where we were seated and crowded 10 deep as far away as they could get from us.
I love him and don't want to lose him. I've heard of people who have no sense of smell; Is there an operation that would make this possible?

"Need a Nose Job"

Dear Need,
Talk it over with him and convince him that he should see his private physician before it gets any worse. If that doesn't work, ask your minister to speak to him.

Miss Vicky

* * * *

Dear Miss Vicky,
A while ago I decided to pull a "jag" so I rented a gorilla costume and went into the Saloon. I got a lot of laughs, and I was having a great time when some girl (I'll call her Pat) came up to me and told me that she loved me. A couple of weeks later I met her in the bar and asked her for a date. She quickly turned me down and told me that she'd rather go out with the person that looked like the gorilla than go out with me. What should I do? Wear the gorilla costume for the rest of my life? You have to help me, Vicky, since I'm dying to go out with this girls.

Going Ape

P.S. Is this face uglier than an ape's?

Dear Going,
Yes.

Miss Vicky

The November 1977 issue of *The Saloon's Spittoon's* "Dear Miss Vicky" column featured our brother Dennis as "Going Ape"

Patty did not spare our brother Dennis insults when she featured him in the newsletter as "Going Ape." Her inspiration came from his sporting an ape costume in front of those attending the King Kong feature film when released to theatres in 1976. In fact, he *did* make an appearance at the Saloon—in costume—immediately following the showing. He made a spectacle of himself to the sheer delight of the bar's patrons.

While editing *The Saloon's Spittoon* newsletter and playing in a girls' softball league, Patty fell in love again though the romance was short-lived.

Meanwhile, the Family Planning Council promoted her to buy supplies and medications as purchasing agent for 44 clinics.

Around 1977, Patty enrolled part-time in a graduate program at the University of Pittsburgh, justifying her quest as follows: "I've always been a social butterfly type anyway so why not get paid for it." She earned 21 credits toward a Master's degree in rhetoric and communications.

By definition, "rhetoric" develops the art of persuasion. The study is an excellent first rung for those interested in politics or lawyering, but Patty had no interest in those fields. Instead, the coursework prepared her for the role she assumed as public relations agent to the musician who swept her off her feet at a rock 'n roll bar in Pittsburgh's hip East End. While enrolled at the University of Pittsburgh in Oakland, Patty frequented nearby Shadyside's Razzberry Rhinoceros where the local vocalist and guitarist **"Frank" Emilio Cappelli** (b. 1952) often performed.

Before I had even met Frank, Patty shared that she was engaged to be married and that she and her fiancé had started up a singing telegram business—the first to make the scene in Pittsburgh. "Horsefeathers" proved a resounding success thanks to Frank's impressive vocals and Patty's relentless pursuit of bookings and promotional opportunities as business manager.

Two or more years before Patty met Frank in 1978, she began to toy with writing lyrics such as this one she sent to me on the occasion of my 23rd birthday:

> *Now that you are twenty-three,*
>
> *It's time to act seriously;*
>
> *Move back home as Daddy requested,*
>
> *Away from Boston and being molested.*
>
> *There's the lake and the softball to tempt your return,*
>
> *And tennis from me you can surely learn;*
>
> *So celebrate your birthday right,*
>
> *Hop on a plane and return tonight.*

The pleasures of Pittsburgh may seem but few,

I guess it depends on what excites you;

Have a great day, have lots of fun,

We'll celebrate on the 4th in Madison.

The pastime ditties may have inspired Patty when she persuaded Frank to change direction from his routine night club gigs. Shortly after meeting her future husband, Patty cajoled him into delivering his first singing telegram. As a going away surprise for a media buyer from Pittsburgh's WFFM radio station where Patty worked in sales, the jingle she wrote and the telegram Frank delivered in song wearing formal attire became the hit of the party. The couple immediately knew they were on to something. With Frank on the musical end and Patty tending to the business and writing, the married couple ran Horsefeathers for five years until 1983. Patty liked to refer to herself as Horsefeathers' president and Frank as "messenger boy." She handled all of the finances, bookings, copyrighting, public relations, and marketing for the enterprise.

Among many other creative avenues to promote bookings, Patty and Frank entered into an exclusive cross-sell agreement with the area's largest florist. Producing thousands of melodic messages during its tenure, Horsefeathers directed its most notable telegram to a very animated Ronald Wilson Reagan (1911–2004) three days before the former actor's election as the 40th U.S. president in 1980. Sung to the tune of "California Here I Come," Frank delivered the ditty during Reagan's "whistle stop" at the Freight Shops at Station Square—formerly the site of the old Pittsburgh & Lake Erie Railroad Station—because Reagan had a longtime affinity for trains.

When in 1983 the competition set in and singing telegrams began to lose their novelty, Patty and Frank sold Horsefeathers and with their children **Giuseppi "Beppi" Emilio** (b. 1981) and **Caroline Broderick** (b. 1982) moved to Castle Rock, Colorado. At the wholesale lumber company Rivendell Forest Products in Denver, our brother Larry employed Patty as office manager and eventually Frank worked in sales. By that time, our youngest sibling Tim had graduated from the University of Notre Dame and worked in the business as well.

In 1987, homesickness brought Patty and her growing family back to Pittsburgh with Giuseppi, Caroline, and our brother's namesake, young **Timothy Patrick** (b. 1985), in tow. Patty is the only one of the nine of us who settled in our hometown of Pittsburgh.

Returning to their roots, Patty and Frank immersed themselves in a new musically-oriented business venture, all the while developing a knack for finding unique and exciting ways to put Frank's musical talent to work. Intent on making music that parents could enjoy with their youngsters, they endeavored to tap into the children's market (aged 3-7) with a new "musical productions for children" business they called "Animal Crackers" (later changed to "Peanut Heaven"). According to Patty in a feature article showcasing their business, "Frank was always wonderful with children. And we wondered if his musical and entertainment talents could be put to use working with children, entertaining them while teaching them constructive ideas and values in line with school and parental teachings and values." To her credit, Patty's tenacity and talent for messaging, targeted marketing, and public relations captivated widespread interest from producers, distributors, and news outlets alike.

Upon pitching the idea of a "fun but educational tape with a 'big people' sound" to a production company, two audiocassettes soon appeared in the local market. When a distributor of children's tapes picked up *Look Both Ways* and *You Wanna Be a Duck* under Frank and Patty's "Peanut Heaven" label, they were off to the races. Aided by his natural ease and trademark walrus mustache, Frank's vocals, guitar accompaniment, and original music stole the show. Mostly featuring Frank's originals composed by the couple, the tapes contained 10 songs each. "Do You Want to Make a Pizza," "Washing My Face," "Giuseppi's My Boy," and the others—all upbeat—conveyed messages about safety, good behavior, and sound relationships.

The Peanut Heaven collection was adapted to a simple musical format enabling small children to quickly memorize words and sing along. Bolstered by Patty's unceasing publicity push, Frank gave live performances as part of Peanut Heaven's entertainment business and as a way to promote the tapes. Our extended family, our friends, their children, and a national market wholly embraced the tunes. "Giuseppi "became the family favorite as it captured the sweet essence of Frank and Patty's oldest child who was born with Down syndrome. The sounds still resonate with "Beppi"—now 43 years old—who enjoys nothing more than listening to his father's entertaining songs.

Frank's musical talent and the creative outlets Patty pursued to promote his work yielded performances that advanced arts education programming. Frank appeared at elementary schools, sang the National Anthem at Pittsburgh Steelers and Pirates games, performed fundraising gigs benefitting Children's Hospital, and became the Pittsburgh Symphony's Tiny Tots attraction at Heinz Hall. By 1988—in the year Patty gave birth to the couple's 4th and youngest child **Frank Emilio**, Jr. (b. 1988)—the couple released two more audiocassettes, *On Vacation* and *Good*.

Aided by the "Roberto" soundtrack co-written by Frank and Patty's close high school friend, Fred Thieman, the Peanut Heaven record label grew in popularity. A tribute to the Pittsburgh Pirates' icon Roberto Clemente who died in a 1972 plane crash while on his way to aid earthquake victims in Nicaragua, "Roberto" became an instant hit. The local top-rated KDKA-AM station picked up the track, the NBC-TV affiliate in Pittsburgh used the track on a sports show, and various local publications ran stories on the song. Patty and Frank's Peanut Heaven entered the big league with the breakout "Roberto" on the *Good* album and national distribution of all four tapes.

The collection of songs succeeded in making education fun through music with messages about growing up, love, feelings, independence, and imagination. Students, parents, teachers, and principals delighted in singing, learning, and laughing with the talented musician and composer.

Peanut Heaven gave way to *Cappelli & Company*, a weekly children's television variety show hosted by Frank and co-produced by the ABC affiliate WTAE-TV in Pittsburgh. Premiering in 1989—20+ years after *Mr. Rogers' Neighborhood* made its network debut on the same local station—*Cappelli & Company* included taped segments with a studio audience comprised of children ages 3 to 7; videos using Frank's original songs; special guests; and "how to" illustrations showing how such things as pasta, soda pop, crayons, silly putty, and mattresses are made. Frank mixed his live sing-and-dance-along segments with music videos; interviews with the likes of a magician; and a film on making Slinkys among other products to fascinate young children. As business manager, Patty booked the live audiences for each of the 63 episodes that aired.

In 1989, a watershed career break came when A&M Records agreed to release all four audiocassettes, along with those that followed, *Pass the Coconut* and *Take a Seat*. The tapes and A&M's video recordings of *Cappelli & Company* brought nationwide coverage in numerous publications including *People Magazine, Billboard, USA Today, Entertainment Weekly*, and *TV Guide*. The worldwide promotion and distribution contract with A&M Records led to a promotional tour in nine cities and performances with the Louisville Symphony and the Buffalo Philharmonic drawing on Frank's original songs from the Peanut Heaven series of children's tapes. Frank credited Patty who engineered much of their success. "She is one of the main reasons I was signed by A&M."

Patty and Frank's show reached a significant milestone in 1992 when ABC-affiliated network stations syndicated *Cappelli & Company* in the Boston, Baltimore, Kansas City, Milwaukee, and Dayton markets. Within six months, the show began airing on the children's cable network, *Nickelodeon*, which at that time broadcast programming into 57 million homes. The *Cappelli & Company* series received two Emmys for outstanding programming for children and led to Frank's live performance to a captive youthful audience at Disney World. With my nephew, Rhett, I had the good fortune to see Frank dazzle the large crowd in Orlando. Patty and Frank's hard work, perseverance, creativity, and talent brought them to the pinnacle of their success in children's musical productions with A&M's full backing.

Believing Frank's musical career to be in good hands with A&M's muscle, Patty redirected her business focus by becoming a real estate sales associate to augment the family's income. As a realtor with Howard Hanna Real Estate Services beginning in 1991, Patty saw gradual success in her new occupation and emerged as the primary breadwinner when she devoted all her energies to residential real estate. By 1997, Frank struggled to gain traction with the pilot episode of a new *Frank's Garage* television concept he had developed. Unable to secure financing to launch the series and as royalties for the audiotapes and bookings of the *Cappelli & Company* episodes started to taper off, Frank pulled back and somehow lost his way.

After 31 years of marriage, the couple separated in 2009. Though she vacated their home during the separation, Patty returned to the residence once the divorce became final in 2012. They remained co-custodial parents to Giuseppi until Frank passed away from a heart attack at age 65 in 2018. Beppi lost his best friend and now lives permanently with his mom. He still loves listening to his father's Peanut Heaven recordings.

Patty is now into 34+ years with Howard Hanna in Pittsburgh. As a top performer, she regularly qualifies for annual company-sponsored trips to highly desirable destinations with a guest. In 2017, I accompanied her to Cabo, Mexico, where Howard Hanna pulled out all the stops for their star agents. It proved to be one of the more relaxing trips hosted by the firm, which was providential so far as Patty was concerned. Only weeks before, a neighbor's towering tree fell on her house while she was inside, causing well over $150,000 in damages. Grateful to have survived it, she nonetheless needed to calm her nerves from the episode. Cabo provided the respite she required. Returning from the trip to face a daunting renovation project, she accomplished it with refined taste in upgrading her lovely home and furnishings.

Patty has benefitted from a relentless work ethic and connections with our extended Pittsburgh relatives and local Broderick friends over the years. Always in the know, she has her finger on the pulse and does a great job keeping the siblings posted on news from the home front. Maintaining close relationships with many childhood and college friends, Patty retains a wicked sense of humor, still loving nothing more than to have fun and still making her circle laugh.

THE 7th OF DAN AND YO's nine children, **Christine "Christy" Ann Broderick Emmanuel** (b. 1953) came along to break the gender tie in the girls' column for the first and only time. It's too bad I don't have a memory of that brief period when we daughters reigned as the majority over the Broderick sons during those fleeting 23 months before Terry came along, but the notion of it feels good and just. I wonder if

Kathleen—just six years ahead of me with Dennis, Nancy, and Patty sandwiched in between—wasn't old enough to taste the sweetness.

My Westcott Lineage

GEN 1	Richard Westcott m. Joanna Adams
GEN 2	Daniel Westcott m. Abigail Gaylord
GEN 3	Ebenezer Westcott m. Barbara Foster
GEN 4	David Westcott m. Rachel Dare
GEN 5	John Westcott m. Sarah Diament
GEN 6	James Diament Westcott m. Ame Harris Hampton
GEN 7	Hampton Westcott m. Elizabeth Grant
GEN 8	Thomas Grant Westcott m. Joanna "Josie" Gould
GEN 9	Susan "Susie" Gould Westcott m. Walter Scott Hoke
GEN 10	Joanna "Yolande" Gould Hoke, m. Laurance Sterne Gordon
GEN 11	Yolande 'Yo' Westcott Gordon, m. Daniel Thomas Broderick, Jr.
GEN 12	Christine "Christy" Ann Broderick, m. Patrick Gibney Emmanuel, Jr.

As I reflect on my place in my maternal bloodline, I am awestruck by the women and the burdens they carried—my mother and grandmothers rippling across generations. Life's random circumstances and unwelcome curveballs saddled these girls who grew into women with exceptionally heavy loads:

GEN 1 – At age 20, Isabel Pearce Sackett crosses the Atlantic Ocean on a brutal mid-winter voyage from England—her homeland—accompanying her husband and infant child for the rugged shores of Boston in 1630. Left a widow within a year, my G9 grandmother takes a leap and with her two young children joins a band of pioneers to reach Hartford by foot. Among America's earliest European settlers, Isabel faces grave peril with her family. Leaving her past behind, she prevails in making a better life for herself and her sons Simon Sackett II and John in this foreign land.

GEN 2 – Escaping unspeakable religious persecution in France, French Huguenots Marie de la Warenbuer and her young family flee to Germany for their very survival. Losing the Ferree family home, in exile Marie is left to fend for herself with six children upon her husband's death. She musters remarkable courage to lead her family from their French homeland to England where she seeks out William Penn and successfully gains entry to America for herself and her family in 1708, with permission granted by Anne the Sovereign Queen of England.

GEN 7 – At age 17, Elizabeth Ingleton Grant marries Hampton Westcott, a man ten years her senior. Three years pass when her husband dies at sea in service to his country. My G3 grandmother is left a widow and the single mother of a three-year-old son. The child is shunned by the five sons she bears with the man her father insisted she marry—William Grant Cook. The whole lot of Cooks are unscrupulous, overbearing bullies. Young Thomas spends at least a part of his formative years apart from Elizabeth and the Cooks, safely distant while living in the home of Elizabeth's parents. The unrelenting stress may well have triggered the stroke that killed her at age 43 in 1859.

GEN 8 – At age 6, Joanna "Josie" Sackett Gould loses two siblings while living through the cataclysmic Hickory Run Flood of 1849. Later suffering a strained marriage, she outlives her husband Thomas Grant Westcott by 21 years. A widow at age 32 with three children of her own and three stepchildren, Josie defends herself in a lawsuit filed by a spurned lover when she reneges on his proposal of marriage. In a letter to her daughter preparing her for the imminent trials and sorrows that lay ahead for Susie as a newlywed, my G2 grandmother Josie shares this sentiment: "I shall pray that you may not be left alone with limited income and others dependent upon you to battle with a cold uncharitable world as has been my sad fate." Josie Gould Westcott dies single, lonely, and financially vulnerable at age 53.

GEN 9 – At age 21, Susan "Susie" Gould Westcott takes a bullet at point-blank range from a spurned lover who fires his 32-caliber Colt revolver when she refuses his marriage proposal. Failing to penetrate her steel-ribbed corset, Doctor George H. Curry takes his life by placing the muzzle against his own temple. Susie holds off for three years before conceding to Walter Hoke's persistent appeals to marry him. My great-grandmother joins him in Bordeaux in 1888 but endures many unhappy years apart from her family before permanently separating and returning stateside following a 30-year run.

Susie Westcott Hoke dies single and financially insecure at age 69. Forty years will pass before she is honored with a tombstone at her graveside.

GEN 10 – On the cusp of becoming a young adult, at age 17, Joanna "Yolande" Gould Hoke witnesses the unfolding World War I as a lifelong resident of Bordeaux, France. A volunteer in the Red Cross, she nurses soldiers who suffer from chemical and trench warfare and the deadly H1N1 influenza. Upon marrying and giving birth to a child, my grandmother leaves behind her father and childhood memories for Duluth, Minnesota, in 1920. Distant from her father in France and her mother and three siblings in New York, Yolande endures the isolation, frigid Duluth winters, and the protracted Great Depression while raising my mother and her two siblings. Likely suffering from the harrowing experience of war and the Depression on its heels, Yolande's marriage collapses as her mental state declines. She becomes institutionalized at a mental hospital in a neighboring state removed from every member of her family. Mentally ill, Yolande Hoke Gordon dies alone at age 59.

GEN 11 – A product of the Great Depression, 18-year-old Yolande Westcott Gordon arrives with her sister in France for long-anticipated studies at La Sorbonne but misses out when escalating military moves threaten world order. She bids her fiancé a sad farewell as he enters World War II with the U.S. Navy four years later. In time, my mother endures the unforeseen failure of her husband's once lucrative lumber business and later, she suffers the cold-blooded murder of her firstborn and his new bride by his first wife in 1989. In domino fashion, Yolande is stricken with Parkinson's disease; my parents lose their magnificent home to financial constraints; and she spends the last 2-1/2 years of her life rapidly deteriorating in a small-town nursing home trapped in her body with immobility yet a fully-functioning mind. Residing a few short miles from my father, at age 74, Yolande Gordon Broderick—mother of nine—nonetheless dies alone while still grieving the horrific loss of her beloved son.

GEN 12 – Although the ending is yet to play out, my trials heretofore seem miniscule compared to what these brave women experienced— many painful, heart-wrenching, life-altering chapters that left many of them terribly isolated and alone. Although I struggled through some pretty rough patches, the worst a traumatic sexual assault by a stranger at age 12 in 1965, I have worked my way out of them for the most part and enjoy a caring, loving relationship with my life partner of 40+ years. But for the sacrifices endured by Isabel, Marie, Elizabeth, Josie, Susie, Yolande, Yolande "Yo," and all the other courageous women and men in our lineage, I would not be here today sharing our stories. Despite the hardships they and all others in my bloodline suffered, I remain keenly aware of the rich inheritance and tremendous privileges our forebears made possible for me and for us, their descendants and our nation. On that note, my personal story follows.

I was born in the year the United States first inaugurated two-term Dwight David "Ike" Eisenhower as our 34th president (1953–1961) and Richard Milhous Nixon his vice president. Having led the victorious forces in Europe as Supreme Commander of the Allied Expeditionary Forces during World War II, five-star General Eisenhower was imminently qualified to lead our nation's course forward.

> In the same momentous year of my birth—1953—North Korea with the United States and China signed an armistice ending the three-year Korean War; Britain crowned Queen Elizabeth II (1926–2023) of England; Dr. Jonas Salk announced success in testing the polio vaccine; dictator of the Union of Soviet Socialist Republics (USSR) Joseph Stalin (1929–1953) died of a stroke at age 74; the Shah of Iran, Mohammad Reza Shah Pahlavi, was restored to power; and Sir Edmund Hillary and Tenzing Norgay performed the first ascent to the summit of Mount Everest.

My notable achievement came from entering the world as the first Broderick blonde. Evidently overwhelmed by the family scene with so many brothers and sisters, I struggled to develop my own identity, feeling stifled and somewhat powerless to make my mark. Hard to read or please my father while internalizing my mother's seeming inattention—she did birth nine children after all—I navigated my way with a certain diffidence that I did not break before graduating from college.

I was a timid child, observant, somewhat fearful, and terribly mistrusting. I could not help but wonder who was lurking to scare me, what grenade would be thrown next, how unfairly punishment was leveled in reaction to chaos. Yes—I was complicit in the game of dominoes. The looks Patty gave me insinuated pure disgust. Lashing out, I treated Terry terribly. He gave me my only outlet to play offense until his overwhelming strength brought me to my knees. With my screeches drawing calls from our mother to "STOP IT, Christy!" the double whammy arrows thrown by the inflictor and judge brought me down time and again. I quickly assumed and have retained an unhealthy defensive posture in response to our family dynamic.

Our parents did not read to us as I recall. No one read to me. Consequently, I didn't read. I did not like to read. I am a slow reader. I trudged along, enjoying numbers much more than words in my youth. Numbers were safe. Words brought humiliation. I felt stupid—a "moron" as reinforced by some in the family. It became a self-fulfilling prophecy. I self-actualized that false identity to my ultimate demise before the tide turned as a young adult. St. Bernard's reinforced my guarded belief in myself as no better than average when the grade school pegged me in the "C" class behind "A" and "B" though gratefully ahead of "D." Perhaps it explained my reluctance to speak up, speak out, and stand tall.

As an exceptionally shy child, I reveled in the attention my Grandpa Broderick directed toward me when he nicknamed me "Sparkie"—short for *Sparkle Plenty* in the so-named comic strip published during my childhood. To be singled out that way made me feel special and loved.

But what a dummy. Words took on a literal meaning. When I was old enough to know better, I actually thought the "Hunchback of Notre Dame" played a position on the so-named university's football team. A nature lover old enough to know better, I considered my father's wholesale lumber enterprise a wholly noble profession by every measure without making the connection to felled trees cut down from virgin forests for logging. Older still, as a waitress I once asked the kitchen staff if anyone had a screwdriver in response to a restaurant patron's request without identifying it as a drink order. A literal thinker, I become the butt of everyone's jokes and didn't like it one bit. Justifiable perhaps, but humiliating.

Since the time I could walk myself to my bedroom alone, I have feared solitude in dark places. The scare tactics perfectly executed by my brothers likely had something to do with it. I risked heart failure each time I climbed the stairs alone and walked the hallway to my bedroom in the dark at our house on Vernon Drive. The fear did not subside when I turned 11 and we moved to Orr Road. From the second floor, a set of wooden stairs led to Patty's and my bedroom in the long, narrow attic where mice often scampered. At the homestead on Orr Road, I also had to muster courage in negotiating two sets of basement steps and a whole new series of dark spaces, one doorway leading to the next without the benefit of knowing who would lurch out at me or when. The scariest room of all was the dark, dank incinerator room where I was often relegated to burn the day's paper trash . . . alone, vulnerable, defenseless. Now aged 71, at no time in all these years have I lived alone.

That feeling of insecurity was magnified by a life-altering experience that came shortly after my 12th birthday on June 12th in 1965 as a 12th generation (American) Westcott descendant. Yes—I still like numbers. We spent that summer in Pittsburgh rather than Madison, as our family had moved from Vernon Drive to Orr Road the year prior and needed the time to acclimate to our new suburban surroundings. Following the family dinner on that fateful August evening while daylight still lingered, I took off alone on my bicycle. As I rode solo destined for a friend's home a mile or so away, a young white adult male stepped out of his car, grabbed me from my bike, and sexually assaulted me. Retreating in horror, nothing audible would come from my mouth where he forced his privates. He fled in an instant, but the wretched moment lodged deep in my psyche leaving a permanent invisible scar. Mortified, I relayed to the police and my parents the few details you might expect of a meek 12-year-old. My older brothers took off in search of the highly distinguishable getaway car, canvassing our neighborhood and scouring every aisle of the parking lot surrounding the just completed South Hills Village shopping mall nearby, but to no avail. The predator got away without detection. Absent counseling or an opening by anyone in my family to discuss it further, the forbidden subject never surfaced again, leaving me a victim of my secret affliction.

Two later experiences with the law came in high school one right after the other, which I will get to below. Admittedly, I tested the limits with my parents as they seemed to become more lenient with each new addition to the family. As I prepared to enter the sixth grade in 1964, our move to Upper St. Clair necessitated a change in schools. Finishing up my elementary education at St. Thomas Moore, I enrolled at short-lived Fontbonne Academy. The all-girls' high school drew students from three or more neighboring townships in the "South Hills" of Pittsburgh with just 64 in my graduating class. At Fontbonne, I quickly adjusted to the blending of classmates who had been my friends at both St. Bernard's and St. Thomas Moore. Lucky me! With a ready-made network of high school friends at Fontbonne and the all-boys South Hills Catholic High School, we frequently gathered at my family's expansive quarters for "unsanctioned" parties. If my parents were home, my friends and I gathered undetected in the three-story barn at the bottom of the hill a safe distance from the house. When my parents went out or left town, we often partied in our basement. If I was especially daring, we caroused in the sunken first-floor formal living room which I knew to be off-limits except during special "family" occasions including Christmas.

To this day, my friends who were complicit in the "chandelier" episode recall the shenanigans of one particular evening when we had the house to ourselves. Fully aware of the restrictions placed on use of the living room, we dared to crank up the music from the stereo console, something I never attempted previously. Making play, a couple of the guys left the room for a few minutes before returning in dramatic fashion. Each with his hair slicked back and a cigarette pack rolled into his rolled-up shirt sleeve, the pair descended the steps in dramatic fashion as a Sha Na Na tune blared from the living room stereo. In perfect unison, they synchronized lifting an arm to the beat of the music—"Na Na Na." As they hit the last note with arms raised high, one of them knocked the chandelier. Pieces of the broken crystal cup fell to the ground, triggering my dreaded panic. I could not imagine absolving myself of this fiasco. In a display of genius, however, the guys stepped up to resolve my dilemma. They removed the identical crystal cup from the matching chandelier in hopes that no one would notice the change. No one ever did.

My parents did not consider me a troublemaker because I never got caught for the parties I hosted behind their backs. Fortunately, our mischief never drew the attention of the police—except for one time. It happened not on our property but when I borrowed my dad's Cadillac, destined for somewhere other than where I told my folks I was headed.

With a carload of friends, we ventured south ten miles from home before "drinking under the influence" carried today's strict legal limits and the enforcement of harsh penalties. A policeman spotted us in the vicinity north of Canonsburg when my friend, Ellen, threw an empty beer can out the car window onto the paved lot of a strip center just about the time I was expected back home. Instead of making my 11:00 p.m. curfew, I found myself headed to the home of the township's squire who with his wife awakened to deal with the late-night infraction. Instead of my parents coming to get me, several of my older siblings—home from college for the Christmas break—picked me up. The squire glowered as my cheerful siblings entered his home single file and Nancy blurted out "Merry Christmas, everyone!" Still awake when we arrived back at the homestead, my father was highly amused by the incident while my mother seethed at his reaction. She revoked my driving privileges for a solid six months except to run errands at her beck and call during the last semester of my senior year in high school.

I found myself on the right side of the law the next time I had occasion to deal with law enforcement. In this case—as a second semester high school senior—I learned thirdhand at school the identity of the "public school" culprits who had reportedly vandalized my parents' pristine property two days prior. I thought it only right to inform my father who exerted great effort and took tremendous pride in maintaining his immaculate grounds. Except for three of my closest friends in whom the vandals had reportedly confided, we had no proof of the allegation. My dad and I appeared at small claims court expecting my three friends—the purported "hearsay" witnesses—to give testimony. One after the other, they declined to acknowledge their acquaintances' complicity or to discuss the topic with me personally. What I perceived as betrayal undermined my faith in some of my closest friends, further degrading what little self-esteem I had and my capacity to trust others.

On a brighter note, I did manage to cement several lifelong friendships from those crazy childhood days in Pittsburgh—the oldest, my fellow four-year-old playmate on Vernon Drive, Anne Macdonald Peniston. The stories we still tell!

Long before setting off for college, I became a regular letter writer. It started with handwritten letters I wrote and received when I was 14. I regularly corresponded with older siblings upon their leaving the nest or graduating from college and with my friends in Pittsburgh while my family summered in Madison. The exchange of $.05 postage-stamped letters occasioned a brisk letter writing and collection practice that now spans nearly 60 years. I relied upon these family letters for several of the "Broderick" stories that appear in this "GEN 12" segment. Much like the Westcott ancestral records now in my possession, I value the vast letter collection as a timeless treasure worth safeguarding.

In 1971, I continued a family tradition by enrolling at St. Mary's College, albeit on a probationary basis given average grades and an abysmal Scholastic Aptitude Test (SAT) score. Our incoming class faced unique impacts stemming from plans made by the Sisters of the Holy Cross and the Congregation of Holy Cross to align St. Mary's and the adjoining University of Notre Dame.

Going back to the fall of 1965 when Kathleen entered St. Mary's as a freshman, the administrations introduced a new co-exchange program through which students could take courses at either institution. [I took five Notre Dame courses during my tenure at St. Mary's.] By the time Kathleen graduated in 1969, the co-exchange program had expanded with a modified freshmen liberal arts curriculum across campuses; integrated dining options; joint-seating at athletic events; and synchronized academic calendars. While these measures hinted at a potential merger, Notre Dame's president Father Theodore Hesburgh (1952 to 1987) had previously denied rumors of any such talk.

Just one year following Notre Dame's activation of St. Mary's students as members of the Notre Dame cheerleading squad, talks between the two institutions ratcheted up to the next level. In May of 1971, the boards of trustees at both schools formally approved plans to seek unification of Notre Dame's 6,300 undergraduates and St. Mary's

1,600 students with a targeted completion date in the 1974–1975 academic year—my senior year. The envisioned Catholic university for both men and women under the Holy Cross order would combine the student body, academic programs, faculty, administrations, and boards of trustees.

The imminent merger influenced the decision many of my classmates made to enter St. Mary's in the fall of 1971. Had the plan materialized, our 1975 graduating class would have been the first with co-educational Notre Dame degrees. Six months into the negotiations, however, the merger talks fell apart due to insurmountable financial and administrative hurdles purportedly stemming from the Sisters' reticence. As a consequence, 15% of my class of roughly 400 women left St. Mary's following our freshman year. Meanwhile, Notre Dame became co-educational when the university accepted 200 women as sophomores in the fall of 1972, one-half transferees from St. Mary's. Currently, nearly half of Notre Dame's 8,875 undergraduate students are women (48%):

> Founded just two years after Notre Dame's 1842 launch, St. Mary's, with a current enrollment of 1,400 students, proudly celebrates its rich history and liberal arts curriculum as one of roughly 30 women's colleges in the U.S. (down from 230 in the mid-1960s). Led by dynamo Dr. Katie Conboy as president 50 years since the merger talks fell apart, the momentum under the sponsorship of the Sisters of the Holy Cross assures St. Mary's a sustainable future independent of Notre Dame. [The dwindling Sisters of the Holy Cross congregation is no longer directly involved in the college's governance.]

I never returned to Pittsburgh for more than brief visits once I left home for college at age 18. For several years once out of the nest, I don't think I made a trip back without a crying episode. Something always set me off course with sufficient reason to feel weak, stupid, dull, and insignificant. With heightened sensitivity and ultra-thin skin, I did not take kindly to the derision, offensive humor, and what came across as emotional neglect and detachment. Invariably, as the time came to bid a sad farewell, I would develop an uncontrollable lump in my throat. Perhaps longing for things to be different, I knew in my heart that in fact they would always be the same.

Occasioned by Danny's internship with a Los Angeles law firm in 1972, I jumped on the opportunity to spend the first summer break from college living with Danny and Betty in Westwood, California, and as needed, looking after their two oldest children, Kim and Lee, who were then little tykes. I also worked at a women's clothing boutique in Westwood Village. At different times, I marveled at my good fortune to assist actresses Dyan Cannon and Goldie Hawn with their purchases at "Women's Rings and Other Things," a sister store to "Splendiferous" in the very hip village of Westwood. With Danny and his family, I enjoyed a fun and adventuresome summer in sunny Southern California.

As a second-semester sophomore, I fulfilled my grandmother Yolande's dream for her daughters—my mother and Aunt Jinks—by studying in Paris. [I knew nothing of their missed opportunity to study at La Sorbonne before researching the "GEN 11" details for this book.] Having missed the window to join St. Mary's and Notre Dame's joint year-long program in Angers, France, I entered a program sponsored by Michigan-based Alma College at L'Alliance Française. Unaffiliated with St. Mary's, Alma College made an exception allowing me to join the group of Americans for the French-speaking coursework mid-term in January of 1973. On arrival, I found virtually all of my classmates with an impressive command of the language, notably my roommate Jane Kuntz who in later years earned a doctorate and became a francophone scholar.

We resided at a pension on Rue du Four in the 6th arrondissement in the heart of the Left Bank. The quintessential Parisian neighborhood is home to Saint-Germain-des-Prés, the Latin Quarter, and the exquisite Luxembourg Gardens through which we walked to classes each day. Jane—one year ahead of me and the only other St. Mary's student among us—had become fluent in French by the time I arrived, which I found highly intimidating. That detail aside, nothing could compare to the eye-opening Parisian experience and extensive travels that followed that summer with my high school friend, Ellen Durocher, from Pittsburgh. Although French did not come easily, I developed a keen appreciation for art history, especially Impressionism, and covered tremendous cultural ground with my backpack and two-month "Eurail" pass. I returned to the States a changed woman. I now wonder how the immersive experience as an impressionable teenager growing into adulthood might have similarly changed my mother's course.

Living on campus when I returned to St. Mary's as a junior proved confining and highly challenging for me. Once my parents conceded to my pleas to live off-campus, I settled into a comfortable routine during my remaining 1-1/2 years as a college student. I quickly befriended peers who had simultaneously studied abroad, in their case through St. Mary's and Notre Dame's year-long joint programs in Rome, Italy; Angers, France; and Innsbruck, Austria. The friendships that many of us seeded in college continue as precious treasures to this day.

Upon returning to St. Mary's from Europe, I developed an interest in photography by taking two related courses, one in the dark room. Camera-ready, this art form has sustained me all these years since. Meanwhile, I pursued the study of sociology before settling on social work. In the summer of 1974, I earned 12 credit hours interning at a children's group home in South Bend and later, with the juvenile probation department in Elkhart, Indiana. Entering a prolonged "moonlighting" period, I spent most of those summer evenings waitressing at the Ice House in Elkhart.

In the spring of 1975, broadcast journalist Walter Cronkite reported on the official end of the Vietnam War with his signature "And that's the way it is" sign-off. Weeks later, I graduated with a B.A. in social work but could not find employment in my chosen field. The year marked the start of the nation's economic recovery from a prolonged recession with the unemployment rate peaking at 9.2% and the prime interest rate hovering around 7%. As I prepared to enter the workforce, inflation had only just begun to ease from double-digit figures. Meanwhile, President Gerald R. Ford continued tax cuts with eyes on the upcoming election and Congress passed legislation maintaining oil price controls. With this backdrop, I slapped a $.10 postage stamp on 300+ letters in pursuit of any opportunity in social work anywhere in the Midwest or Northeast before graduation day. Rejection letters came one after the other if I got a response at all.

Disheartened, I accepted Larry's generous offer of employment at Lothlorien Lumber & Logging Company in Montrose, Colorado, on the western slope of the Rocky Mountains. With the wings my parents gifted me upon graduation in the form of a stripped-down yellow Toyota Corolla with a four-speed manual transmission, "Sunshine" and I took off for the western frontier. [I still drive a Japanese car with a manual-transmission—a highly-dependable 2004 five-speed Honda Accord.]

I arrived for work in southwest Colorado one week after earning my degree. Drawing an annualized salary of $6,000, I didn't last six months as an office clerk. Surrounded by lumber mills in a town whose best entertainment was the "Dew Drop Inn," somehow this Pittsburgh-bred, blue-eyed, long-haired dirty blonde didn't fit in with the area's cowboys and other locals. I waited long enough for my sister-in-law to give birth to Casey—Larry and Kathy's oldest of three—before pulling out one day later.

Next stop—provincial New England. I decided to take my chances at finding work once I got wherever I was destined to land. Boston became home for the next four years. Of course, I knew nothing of my ancestors having landed on the banks of Boston Harbor from Devon(shire), Kent, and Yarmouth, England, in the 1630s, only that a few college friends had preceded me as residents in the "Cradle of Liberty."

While looking for a job in social work, I set up my own dark room, signed up for temporary assignments in office jobs, and waitressed in the private dining room at Boston's Museum of Science. Competing with as many as 150 applicants for social work openings proved highly challenging and very frustrating. I actively searched for nearly a year when the museum approached me about the assistant volunteer coordinator position that was about to become vacant. Why not? Three challenging years followed as I honed administrative skills to manually support 650 volunteers rotating through our doors each year, placing them in roles to accommodate the museum's annual draw of 1 million visitors—just the director and me—at a starting annual salary of $8,000. Throughout those three years, I continued to moonlight as a waitress in the museum's private dining room every Friday evening.

Although the personal computer was introduced to the public in 1977, my first exposure to the electronic device came seven years later. Consequently, I processed the scores of people, records, training materials, and the like with a typewriter and a rudimentary filing system. I credit the Museum of Science experience for instigating my affinity to compile, organize, and document information and artifacts with attention to the requisite details.

In Boston in 1979, I met my future husband, **Patrick "Rick" Gibney Emmanuel, Jr.** (b. 1950), then a mental health counselor in the rehabilitation field. A resident of Tallahassee, Florida, Rick happened to be in town visiting his sister, Mary Jo Emmanuel Hanover (1952–2012). Originally from Pensacola, Florida, my joyful friend graduated with me from St. Mary's. She and her husband, Dennis "Hans" Hanover, a Notre Dame graduate, by chance lived briefly in Boston while I was there. Rick and I seeded a long-distance romance from their introduction. Rick fell for a girl he perceived as sensitive, tenacious, and independent—but not insecure. Except for my siblings, few detect that sunken feeling that on occasion still holds a tight grip on me.

As much as I love Boston—my favorite city in the U.S.—I knew of no viable advancement opportunities at the museum and had little confidence in finding social work locally given my prior search experience. I decided to pull up stakes, but not before developing a talent for parallel parking on the congested streets of Boston. The knack has served me well since giving "Beantown" a fond farewell all those decades ago.

With little reason other than the climate and intrigue, Virginia and North Carolina appealed to me as "new," so I quit my job in 1979 and Sunshine and I hit the road again, this time with coordinates pointing south-west. On route to Charlottesville, Virginia, as the first planned stop to begin my job search in earnest, I first visited my closest Pittsburgh friend, Mimi Donnellon Kimball, in La Plata, Maryland. The Museum's volunteer director knew only of my planned stopover to visit Mimi on approach to Virigina. She tracked me down at Mimi's house to gauge my interest in an opportunity with a travel agency in Chicago. Hmmm—why not?

I boarded a plane for Chicago from Richmond and immediately following the interview, I accepted the job offer on the spot. While still "dating" Rick from afar, I coordinated and hosted snow ski and beach trips for college students, bringing me to Spirit Mountain, Minnesota; Winter Park, Colorado; and Daytona Beach, Florida, where Rick paid me weekend visits from Tallahassee during my three-week stay. Later, on the payroll of another travel agency, I hosted a European tour in Paris and Brussels for high school students and their chaperones. All the while, throughout the course of my one-year stint in the "Windy City," I waitressed 3-4 nights each week at long-standing Ranalli's Lincoln Park, clocking out as late as 2:00 a.m.

Having made the joint decision with Rick to take our relationship to the next level, I loaded my possessions and Sunshine and I drove from Chicago straight through to Tallahassee in 1980.

With a B.A. in psychology from the University of Florida in Gainesville and two master's degrees in community psychology and rehabilitative counseling earned at The Florida State University (FSU) and Florida A&M University in Tallahassee, Rick enjoyed stability working as a counselor at Apalachee Community Mental Health Center. I quickly found work with United Cerebral Palsy in conjunction with a federally-funded block grant in benefit to disabled students in Florida's community college system.

Within months of arriving in Tallahassee where Sunshine took her last breath without the creature comforts of air conditioning, Rick decided to change careers, and I followed suit. Rick enrolled in the law school while I pursued a Master of Business Administration at FSU. I knew nothing of my family's tie to James Diament Westcott III in whose honor the administration building is named, nor of his father James, Jr. and his uncle John—brothers of my G3 grandfather Hampton Westcott. Both James, Jr. and Dr. John Westcott had been residents of Tallahassee and renowned figures at the state capital; James, Jr. and James III are buried there. I wish I had known then what I now know about my family's Tallahassee and extended Florida roots.

Having never taken a business course in college, I completed nine foundation classes before advancing to an area of concentration toward earning an MBA. Late into the first year, I made up my mind to pursue finance for the technical knowledge it promised. It seemed a daring move as I seriously questioned whether I had the chops to make it through business school. At the same time, I applied and was accepted as the sole legislative intern with the Health & Rehabilitative Services Committee in the Florida House of Representatives. Being selected to fill the coveted slot proved a much-needed confidence booster. I chipped away at my studies while working at the state capitol 24 hours each week researching and writing for the committed year. It floored me to earn an annual stipend of $12,000—more than I had ever made before working full-time.

With the legislative internship completed, I finished out the coursework while employed as a research assistant to tenured market research professor Dr. Armen Tashchian in FSU's College of Business. The dual experiences helped me get over my insecurity with words while developing skills as a decent writer.

Rick and I graduated from FSU on the same day in December 1983. His parents attended his law school ceremony and with us celebrated the news that earlier that day, I accepted Rick's proposal of marriage. It was a proud day as I reflected on the fact that, with no savings to lean on, I financed my degree on my own by working and borrowing student loans. Moreover, I earned a cumulative 3.9 grade point average. As Nancy found out when she graduated with honors from Duquesne University, I began to think that perhaps I wasn't such a dummy after all.

Rick and I settled on Tampa, Florida, as our planned post-graduate destination. In synch, we lined up jobs before that momentous graduation day and then stepped into and from our 33-year careers at precisely the same time. I paid no regard to my father's suggestion that I pursue secretarial work which he evidently thought was the best I had to offer.

We launched our chosen careers in Tampa as I planned our May 1984 Pittsburgh wedding, accomplishing virtually every detail in a week's time on a trip back home before starting work one month following graduation. But for my mother's slipping on our wedding day as the Brodericks continued the post-reception party at our homestead, Rick's and my plans came together without a hitch. Sadly, we learned of Yo's accident and broken hip the morning after the ceremony. In the hospital, I shed a bucket full of tears seeing the groggy patient in a terribly painful state before bidding her another sad farewell to begin my next chapter as a 30-year-old newly married woman.

In Tampa, Rick became a commercial real estate transactional attorney in private practice, initially as the ninth attorney with Taub &

Williams. My foray into the business world led me to establish a 14-year commercial banking career, first at headquarters in Tampa with the state's then largest independent bank, First Florida Bank. Entering as a commercial credit analyst in 1984, I learned to operate a computer while creating financial spreadsheets using Lotus 1-2-3 software—the predecessor to Microsoft Excel. The Credit Department's Wang personal computers were the first to make their way into the bank over the objection of then bank president Anders L. "Dursie" Ekman who feared we would waste our time playing games.

In the span of eight years at First Florida, I advanced from my role as an analyst to credit department manager, commercial lender, and finally, commercial banking administrator at the corporate level when the bank went through a major reorganization. The Commercial division executive to whom I reported assumed oversight of commercial lending, commercial real estate lending, indirect lending, cash management, and international banking. Beginning with this latter position, I accepted newly created, one-of-a-kind corporate roles working directly with executive and senior level managers throughout the balance of my professional career.

While working corporately at First Florida and subsequently at Barnett Bank, I assumed numerous leadership positions with Robert Morris Associates—now known as Risk Management Association (RMA)—the national association of commercial loan and credit officers based in Philadelphia. I made my mark in business research and writing as a member of the professional association, first winning the Florida chapter's statewide paper writing competition on the subject of credit risks associated with corporate trusts. Later, my submission on the "Statement of Cash Flows" associated with the newly released Statement of Financial Accounting Standards (FASB) No. 95 placed second in RMA's national journalistic excellence competition; the article appeared in RMA's journal with a subscriber base of 15,000 members. Speaking engagements and leadership opportunities followed, culminating in a one-year term as president of the 500-member Florida Chapter in 1991-92.

Witnessing First Florida's spiral when the United States entered a recessionary downturn spurred by the meltdown of the savings and loan industry, in 1991, I fortuitously moved to the bank's largest local competitor 11 months *before* Barnett Bank acquired First Florida. At Florida's largest bank, I led Barnett's renowned six-month management associate program for the central region of the state within the commercial banking unit. With a corporate reorganization, I then became one of three regional sales managers of the newly formed Small Business Banking division. While in this role, Rick and I relocated to Jacksonville, Florida, so that I could advance my career at Barnett's corporate headquarters. As a consequence, Rick gave up his two-year Tampa-based solo law practice and spent the next eight years working in-house as a commercial real estate attorney at Winn-Dixie Grocery Stores' corporate headquarters with 1,100+ locations.

In 1998, NationsBank Corp. acquired Barnett Banks, Inc. in the then largest banking deal in U.S. history, making NationsBank the third-largest banking company in the nation (now the second largest as Bank of America behind JPMorgan Chase). Disgruntled with the *Pac-Man* "anything that consumes indiscriminately" mentality of the industry, I chose to abandon banking in pursuit of a Jacksonville-based financial services-oriented nonbank. I landed with ALLTEL, a publicly-traded mortgage information technology company and division of the former telephone conglomerate. As the standard in the mortgage industry, ALLTEL's Mortgage Servicing Platform (MSP) remains in use by residential mortgage loan servicers to process payments, escrow, and defaults on more than 30 million active loans.

As a technology company with a robust mainframe and innumerable software applications wrapped around it, ALLTEL contended with the all-consuming "Y2K" year-2000 computer programming glitch that threatened world order. Across the globe, businesses scrambled to solve the daunting 21st century problem. Up to that point, the coding of most computer programs allowed for only two digits to record and store data defined as "year." The systems accommodated "99" as connoting the year "1999" but could not distinguish "1900" from "2000." Seemingly every employee on staff played a role to circumvent the worst-case scenario everyone feared. Like a hawk, all eyes watched the clock at the stroke of midnight on December 31, 1999. We—ALLTEL employees and the world over—felt a palpable sense of relief as the new millennium entered like a lamb. All computers and networks operated without disruption to our customers and society at large. The "Y2K apocalypse" went down in history as a non-event at which point productive efforts pivoted to the revenue-producing business at hand.

Working for a stable mortgage information technology company reliant on the mainframe rather than the Internet, I found job security outside of commercial banking. My efforts primarily supported the industry's business partners aligned with U.S. mortgage originators and servicers at ALLTEL. I performed various business administration, communications, and project management functions over an 18-year span before retiring at the outset of 2017. The "Pac-Man" followed me from the banking world, however, as my nonbank employer, too, went through many acquisitions, divestitures, spin-offs, and outright sales—twice to Fidelity National Financial (FNF). In my sunset years, I worked with the Fortune 500 company FNF, which provides synergistic title and settlement services to the real estate and mortgage industries.

In 2005, Rick and I relocated to his hometown of Pensacola, Florida, where he had an opportunity to work in his father's law firm, Emmanuel, Sheppard & Condon, with 20+ other attorneys. [The firm celebrated its 100-year anniversary in 2013.] Remotely, I continued to work for FNF (then known as Fidelity National Information Services) for 12 years before retiring.

As a "semi-native" resident, I am awestruck by the rich history of my adopted town and the newfound knowledge of my Westcott family's ties to legendary Pensacola:

> Shortly before his promotion to Navy Lieutenant, in 1827, my "GEN 7" grandfather Hampton Westcott deboarded the sloop *Erie* in Pensacola where he took a leave of absence awaiting orders for his next deployment; his brother James Diament II is known to have traveled here from Tallahassee during his tenure as territorial secretary and acting territorial governor beginning in 1830; their brother (youngest of 15 siblings) Bayse married Eliza V. L. Roberts (3rd of four wives) at the Pensacola Navy Yard chapel in 1867. One hundred and thirty-eight (138) years passed between Bayse's marriage and my arrival as a resident and fellow Westcott descendant in 2005.

Presently, nearly two centuries distance me from my G3 grandfather Hampton's days walking the grounds I now call "home."

As to her notable history, Pensacola is distinguished as drawing the first band of European settlers—1,500 in total—to the geographical area that would later become the continental U.S. If not for the hurricane of 1559 that doomed Spaniard Tristán de Luna y Arellano's "first settlement" within a month of arriving here—just 71 years before the landing in Boston of nine of our English lineal ascendants in 1630—my adopted city would have emerged as our nation's oldest European colony. The sinking of de Luna's 12-vessel fleet left those who remained without ships to make their escape. Without enough food for sustenance, the surviving colonists disbursed within two to three years' time after establishing their "Panzacola" settlement. In Volume I of this Westcott chronicle, I traced 18 lineal ascendants who emigrated from Old England to New England before the Spanish returned to Pensacola 137 years later, in 1698. Spain held on to Florida for the next 123 years except for the 21 years when France (three years) and England (18 years) occupied the territory.

During the lifetime of my G3 grandfather Hampton and his brothers James and John Westcott, U.S. General Andrew Jackson invaded West Florida three times between 1814 and 1821, when Spain lost its major colonies of Florida, Mexico, and Peru. With the stroke of a pen in 1821, a dramatic shift occurred in the way of life, political organization, religion, the miliary, and economy of the Territory of Florida as then part of the United States. [This was 24 years before Florida united as the 27th state in 1845.] In 2021, the bicentennial celebration of the new U.S. territory of Florida here in Pensacola marked the advent of a transitional period in our nation's history from colonial rule to U.S. democracy. For me, the 200-year mark likewise memorialized the linkage of the Westcotts to Florida's rich heritage.

From the comfort of home in historic Pensacola, the last assignment of my professional career had me working across multiple time-zones with employees in Bangalore, India, to whom FNF offshored its defaulted mortgage field services and title processing as a "captive" operating entity. Shortly before calling it quits, I traveled to Bangalore to spend time with my colleagues, some of the most gracious, hard-working, and dependable people with whom I have worked. It would not surprise me to learn that my Westcott relatives Hampton, James, Jr., and Bayse felt the same about the hospitable Pensacolians they met in my adopted hometown all those years ago.

While employed remotely, I made every effort to engage in the Pensacola community I have come to cherish. Over the course of ten years, I volunteered with MANNA Food Pantries to provide emergency food assistance—roughly 40,000 bags of nonperishables each year—serving six years on the board including one term as board president. Collaborating with United Way and community leaders, I also participated in the grassroots development of poverty solutions. Since 2007, I have contributed to the all-volunteer women's philanthropic "IMPACT 100" which annually pools a $1,000 donation from each member. Collectively, we review applications and award $100,000+ grants to nonprofits. Currently supported by 1,200+ local members, I am immensely proud knowing that, since inception in 2003, the all-volunteer *IMPACT 100 Pensacola Bay Area* organization has awarded 165 grants for a combined total of $17,492,000 toward nurturing our community's families, education, health, environment, and arts and culture. I am not aware of a town more philanthropic than Pensacola, "the western gate to the Sunshine State, where thousands live the way millions wish they could" as aptly coined by former Mayor Vince Whibbs.

In 2017, we sold our primary residence and relocated to Innerarity Point, the sanctuary we purchased outside Pensacola in 1999 contiguous to the Intracoastal Waterway frontage that Rick's paternal grandfather bought in 1938 and 1939. Before building a new home in the heart of Pensacola's historic district in 2023, we found peace living one with nature while gardening and maintaining our beautiful grounds neighboring the property where five generations of Emmanuels have found respite. All the while, we enjoyed a close relationship with Rick's parents, Patrick and Olivia. The quintessential Southerners, both centenarians, fostered a rich local history of their own making. [The Emmanuels died peacefully in their home of 60 years—Olivia at age 101 in 2022 and Patrick at age 104 in 2024.] Although "Mrs. E" lost a child at birth, I find it remarkable that both my mother and mother-in-law bore eight children in 11 years. Further as to the parallels, all of Rick's and my brothers graduated from Notre Dame. Each of us has a sister who attended St. Mary's and two sisters who did not. Excepting Rick who attended a public university, 15 of the combined 16 children born to Dan and Yo and Patrick and Olivia graduated from Catholic colleges. Rick and I have each lost a sibling—Danny and Mary Jo—both with a November 22nd birthday.

The notion of working harder and more passionately in retirement than while employed holds true from my personal experience. Walking aside, yoga builds my strength while two book clubs keep me reading—at long last. Months after retiring, I accepted a part-time, year-long position as an independent contractor with The Florida Bar Foundation. Coming full-circle to my early days in social work, I project-managed a community experiment aimed at integrating legal services into the continuum of direct service care for Pensacola's vulnerable population.

Not one to sit idle, I then leisurely entered a writing contest sponsored annually by the Perdido Key Area Chamber of Commerce and watched time flurry by as a retiree. My first-place 300-word entry led to publication in the Chamber's annual directory; a newfound interest in oral history writing; and the fortuitous introduction to local businessman H. Britt Landrum, Jr. by a mutual friend. As the world preoccupied itself with the COVID-19 pandemic, over the course of 17 months, as Mr. Landrum wrote, I edited his memoir *Working a Better Way: A Fifty Year History of LandrumHR*. An exemplary businessman, the author describes a remarkable journey leading his human resources company to enduring success by valuing relationships and following the Golden Rule. In the very month Britt Landrum self-published his compelling story in August 2020, I received a call from Susie Newcomb setting in motion my own book and this publication of *The Westcott Story*. Without the modern convenience of the Internet in this digital age, notably my loyal friend "Google," this story of my maternal lineage may not have come to fruition.

A parting note follows about "family" in this, my memoir as a "GEN 12" Broderick. To this day, reunions keep the batteries charged among Brodericks. In 1999, from Jacksonville, I organized our first family reunion in Madison, Ohio. Except for a hiccup caused by the global spread of the COVID-19 virus, our family has gathered for this coveted occasion every three years since. Kathleen and kin took the lead in organizing our ever-expanding family in 2002; Terry in 2005; Tim in 2008; Larry's son Larry II "Brodie" in 2011; Larry and Brodie in 2014 (a departure from custom as we gathered in picturesque Grand Lake, Colorado); Patty in 2017; Nancy in 2021; and Danny's family in 2024. Next up—Dennis faces the daunting task of assembling 77+ in 2027 for our 10th "all-hands-on-deck" get-together . . . God willing. All sibling bases will then be covered before the official handoff to "GEN 13!"

In 2021, the Brodericks' epic gathering brought a record 68 of us together. The *2021 Broderick Cup* hosted by Nancy and her family featured every competition imaginable. We savored four uninterrupted days of tennis, cornhole, kickball, volleyball, canasta, flip cup, ultimate frisbee, a scavenger hunt, a talent show, music trivia, obstacle course runs—and no shortage of fabulous home-cooked meals and alcohol consumption. The frequent downpours did not diminish spirits as four multi-generational teams competed for "winner" recognition at the informal awards ceremony on our final night. I am not aware of another family with our mass as committed, nor with the organizational skills, to pull off reunions as fun and memorable as ours. The Brodericks are resolute in keeping this most cherished tradition alive.

Although our differences can sometimes set me off-balance, I appreciate my family's influence in the purposeful decisions I have made and the relationships I have developed in my lifetime. I am grateful to my parents for the advantages they afforded us in our formative years—not the least a private education. I also credit my forebears and siblings for the work ethic and resiliency they instilled in me and each of us across generations. But for the inheritance of privilege and willpower and the gift of providence, I would not have come nearly as far along in my journey on a personal and professional level.

Reaching 40 years, Rick's and my marriage outpaces all of my siblings' as the longest-surviving union. One year after tying the knot in 1984—six years after Rick and I began dating—my mother inquired in a letter: *Any little bambinos in the offing?* She continued, *Come on kids—let's go. My parents had 19 grandchildren and only 3 kids. I should certainly be able to beat them—5 to go. I'm counting on you for 2 or 3 of them.* I suppose her offspring were not the only competitive ones in the whole lot.

Mom wanted to beat her parents' score and did so by a hair without Rick's and my contribution. Who better to carry the day than Tim? While Patty and Frank subsequently had their 4th child, Tim and Ann cranked out all four of their sons to give our mother an even 20 grandchildren before her death in 1995. Another three came thereafter—Dennis and Marian's Grace; and Terry and Jennifer's two—Hailey and Dillon. As of this writing, our parents' progeny includes 23 grandchildren and 26 great-grandchildren. I wonder how many more Brodericks will grace this earth before my time, too, comes to pass.

FOLLOWING THREE GIRLS IN A ROW, I can only imagine our father's relief when **Terrence "Terry" Michael Broderick** (b. 1955) came along as ostensibly the last of our parents' eight children. Whew—lucky for him—another BOY! Tied score. I suspect my mother was relieved too.

The tyke quickly emerged as a feisty youngster. From his earliest years, Terry liked nothing more than annoying me as his closest sibling. He excelled at it. A Christmas family photo in my possession says it all. Just as Mom was about to snap the shot of the eight of us, two-year old Terry grabbed an icicle-shaped ornament from the Christmas tree and jabbed it at me for fun. He seemed quite determined to make me cry. Success! As the years passed, he made a concerted effort and succeeded at every turn to get some cheap laughs at my expense no matter how insensitive or inappropriate. Actually, insulting humor appears to be a Broderick knack that spares no one.

The domino effect that advanced from the older boys to Nancy to Patty to me did not leave Terry unscathed. Because of Terry's physical strength and Dad's loyal backing, however, the release that came from trouncing the next youngest sibling did not greet me to the extent it had Nancy and Patty in particular.

From my perspective, our mother clearly favored the older boys and Kathleen as the oldest girl. She absolutely adored Timmy, her unscheduled gift who brought her more joy than a mother could dream possible.

But the manner in which I (we) saw Dad favor Terry was beyond the pale. I intensely resented Terry for his favored status, and unfortunately for him, so did the rest of the family—our mom included.

Dad was a firm, no-nonsense disciplinarian throughout his parenting years with all of us, less so when Terry came along. Without an inkling that Timmy would follow, he likely justified his blatant preference for his then youngest by virtue of his good fortune in finally bearing another son. That's how I perceived it, anyway. There is no other way to rationalize the extreme to which he exhibited favoritism toward his golden boy.

Our father showered Terry with affection and with the most extravagant of material things. Made worse, Dad flaunted his giving spirit to the rest of us with a "rub-it-in" warped sense of humor. Whether toys, a bicycle, a horse, a moped, a trampoline, a car—Terry became accustomed to getting what he wanted. While Terry was a student at Notre Dame, Dad even bought him a house! The deed appalled me, as I was forbidden from even living off campus when I first returned to St. Mary's following my studies abroad. Whether or not the purchase was a prudent financial decision didn't matter to my way of thinking—it simply wasn't fair.

One day in Madison when he was eight years old, Terry brought home a stray dog that was vicious to anyone who came near our brother. "Rover" was a lawsuit waiting to happen. However, Terry wanted to keep the German Sheppard mix and so we did. Rover calmed down as the years passed but never left her master's side. She proved her might as Terry's dutiful bodyguard for 12 years before her passing.

One year after Terry claimed her as his own, Rover went missing in Madison. A couple of weeks later, Rover returned pregnant, evidently sired by a beagle. Determined NOT to keep any of the pups from the litter, back in Pittsburgh, our dad snuck over to his friends' homes and dropped off a pup at each of their houses for the fun of it. Besides the puppy the Wohlebers opted to keep, I don't know what became of the others. In 1975, when Terry came home as a sophomore in college, he found Rover in a sorry state due to old age and neglect. At our mother's pleading, Terry took her to the vet to be euthanized. He still feels guilty about dropping her off that day to be put down.

I can recall only one other occasion when I thought, "Poor Terry!" In Madison, Terry endured a terrifying experience at age 14 when a bug crawled deep into his eardrum. As the squirming beetle vibrated in his ear, jolts of pain sent him into an inconsolable rage. As the kids' injuries and ailments invariably fell to our mother to nurse, she located a Waterpik and attempted to drown the pest by placing a heavy-dose of water pressure inside Terry's ear. As I remember, after several hours of trying, she succeeded in stilling the bug to Terry's immense relief before taking him to a doctor the next day. The doctor removed the beetle's dead body from Terry's inner ear using long surgical tweezers. Although fleeting, an overwhelming feeling of empathy came over me as witness to that horrifying episode.

Often, our father would get an enormous charge from witnessing the kids' hostile reaction to the preferential treatment bestowed on Terry. You'd hear him bellow out uncontrolled laughter which motivated us to resent Terry all the more. It was infuriating enough to witness the flagrant injustice. What made the sting worse was the reality that our father rarely expressed an ounce of emotion to any of the rest of the kids. I suspect he didn't do my younger brother any favors. For a long time, it seemed that Dad's reinforcements motivated Terry to just get by.

Terry had just received his driver's license in September 1971 when Kathleen wrote and told me about his most recent escapade:

> *I don't know if you heard yet about Terry! He put donkey ["Dickie"] in the corral with the horses, started out the driveway in the Vega, got as far as the gate, heard donkey hee-hawing, saw that the horses were chasing donkey, put the car in park, jumped out to save donkey from certain destruction, and turned around to watch the car drift backwards down the driveway and smash into the last elm tree before the house! Isn't that cute? You can be sure that when Dad comes home, he'll rationalize the whole thing out to being anyone's fault but Terry's.*

Terry, Terry, Terry. To each of us, it became a foregone conclusion that he would get away with his many errant ways, although he did have a soft spot for poor Dickie, Rover, and the other animals that shared a home with us. And, of course, he felt great satisfaction when pleasing our father.

Nancy recalled a particular incident—one of many over the years—that attests to how Terry could unnerve his sisters:

> *One day, while I was moving one of the horses and holding onto the rope, the horse started running. I held onto the rope and ran with her while pulling on the rope to get her to stop. The end of the rope got wrapped three times around my bare thigh and I fell and got dragged through the field for some distance. The horse finally stopped. I had a triple stripped coil of bleeding rope-burn on my thigh and off in the distance I heard hysterical laughter. I looked up and saw Terry, leaning on his crutches from a recent injury, doubled over in laughter. I tied the horse up to a stake, climbed up the hill to where Terry was still in paroxysms of hysteria, and I kicked his crutches out from him.*

In time, Nancy and Terry—the two left-handed members of the family—put aside their differences and actually became quite close. The great leveler happened to be marijuana. I, too, enjoyed my fair share of cannabis, and I came to bond with Nancy and Terry as a result.

As a scrappy teen, Terry followed Larry's lead by joining the wrestling team at South Hills Catholic High School. Not infrequently, he practiced using me as his punching bag and then had the nerve to want to hang out with me and my circle. He did not heed my advice when I insisted that he find his own bloody friends. The problem—my buddies seemed perfectly fine having Terry mix with our crowd. Consequently, he become something of a fixture.

Before heading off for college, Terry recalls earning money by doing chores around the house, notably raking leaves—lots of them—and cleaning up after the horses in the barn stalls. Tough duty. Two years behind me, he set off for Holy Cross College in the unincorporated census-designated area of "Notre Dame" in the fall of 1973:

> "Notre Dame, Indiana" encompasses the tri-campuses of the University of Notre Dame, Saint Mary's College, and Holy Cross College. A private, Catholic, co-educational, residential institution founded by the Brothers of the Holy Cross in 1966, Holy Cross College enrolls roughly 500 students. After 36 years as a junior college, the school converted to a four-year college in 2003.

Little did Terry know when he enrolled at Holy Cross that our father would reside on the same campus in one of Holy Cross Village's independent living residences a little over a quarter century later and die there 11 years hence . . . a stone's throw from "God's country" at Notre Dame.

With his gaze fixed on our father and brothers' alma mater, Terry lived in St. Joseph Hall on the campus of Notre Dame with a handful of Holy Cross classmates who were intent on transferring to the University. They lived in the residence hall alongside seminarians who were discerning the Lord's call to the Roman Catholic priesthood. With gratitude, Terry fulfilled his dream when he transferred as a second-semester sophomore.

Also establishing roots at Holy Cross College before transferring, Notre Dame football legend Daniel Ruettiger (nicknamed "Rudy") lived at St. Joseph Hall while Terry was a resident there. Many know his story from the iconic movie "Rudy":

> The inspiration behind the 1993 sports film "Rudy," Daniel Ruettiger overcame poverty, dyslexia, a diminutive stature, and three rejections from Notre Dame before fulfilling his lofty dream of taking the field for the Fighting Irish. Joe Montana called the signals as quarterback when Rudy finally got into his first varsity game as a 5'6" defensive end.
>
> As it played out, Montana sustained an injury earlier in the 1975 season when Notre Dame hosted Georgia Tech on November 8th. He witnessed the iconic moment from the sidelines when Coach Dan Devine gave the walk-on senior the opportunity to dress for the final home game. Ruettiger activated for three plays—a kickoff, an incomplete pass, and in the final play a sack of Georgia Tech's quarterback Rudy Allen. Following the sack recorded to "Rudy" on the final play of the home finale, his teammates carried him off the field, thus bolstering his morale and rallying the cheering fans in the thrilling victory.
>
> The movie "Rudy" celebrates the spirit and determination of this underdog whose hopes were all but dashed before the end of his unlikely college football career. Though he struggled to overcome financial and physical hurdles in pursuit of his goal, he never gave up. In the end, this poor boy from the outskirts of Chicago became a Notre Dame legend and compelling inspirational speaker. One can

only imagine him praying for the intercession of St. Joseph while a resident of the hall named after the beloved saint—that Notre Dame might accept him and that he might play for the Fighting Irish. St. Joseph delivered for "Rudy" and for Terry too.

Terry did not attend the Notre Dame-Georgia Tech game and therefore did not see in person the play that made "Rudy" a household name. But he was naturally thrilled when the University accepted him into its architecture program as a second-semester sophomore earlier in 1975. His experience in academia brings to mind that of our father who could not hack engineering and instead transferred to journalism. Sadly, Terry did not make the cut in architecture on account of his struggles with math. With hair grown past his shoulders, he pleaded his case to the administration and convinced them to allow him to transfer into the fine arts program. Although he was able to transfer credits, he lost a year in the process of changing majors, thus graduating from college in five years. Meanwhile, he developed a talent in dimensional art.

Terry evidently found inspiration in Larry as a role model. As mentioned, Larry preceded Terry in wrestling at South Hills Catholic, although Terry got only as far as intramurals and did not earn a title. He also followed Larry's lead in his exploration of art. Both became quite adept in high school although Larry regrettably opted not to pursue his natural artistic ability. I suspect they both would profess repute for snow skiing in their prime—Terry considered himself a "fantastic" skier while Larry, too, took naturally to the slopes. Taking it a step further, at Notre Dame, Terry followed Larry's footsteps as a Bengal Bouts boxer and lightweight champion under the tutelage of Coach Dominic "Nappy" Napitalano (1908–1986).

The legendary "Rudy" Ruettiger boxed with the Bengal Bouts in 1974, 1975, and 1976, finally winning the title in the 175-weight-class in his final tournament. Terry won in his 125-weight-class in 1975 and the 135-weight-class in 1977. Although he was slated with Rudy as a contender in the 45th year of the program in 1976, Terry pulled out a week or so before the tournament due to an injury. The perpetrator of a knife attack outside the Bridget McGuire's bar in South Bend sliced his thumb, dashing Terry's hopes for another win in his column with the storied Bengal Bouts program:

Legendary football coach Knute Rockne first organized boxing at Notre Dame around 1923 as a way to keep his football players in shape off season. Yet its purpose of raising funds for the Holy Cross Missions in Bangladesh gave the Bengal Bouts its identity in 1931. As a student, Coach "Nappy" assisted then went on to become director and coach of the Bengal Bouts for over 50 years. His words "Strong bodies fight, that weak bodies may be nourished" became the motto of the Bouts.

In 1955, *Sports Illustrated* columnist Bud Schulberg remarked that the Bengal Bouts under the direction of Nappy "established the ideal atmosphere of sportsmanship, safety, and lack of any commercial taint." Schulberg noted that if you attend the Bengal Bouts, "you'll see boys battling harder for the University championships than some heavyweights have fought for the championship of the world. You will see contestants beautifully conditioned and boxing under rules of safety precaution that have precluded any serious injury . . . Here are boys who will fight their hearts out in the five-day tournament for pride and the pure sport of it."

Each year, some three months before the Bengal Bouts, 15 to 200 boys, many of whom never before wore a glove, put themselves in Nappy's hands to prepare for the tournament. Nappy trained Terry as well as Larry nine years before him and Tim two years afterward. He oversaw their two-mile roadwork each day, calisthenics, and daily workouts with each other. By the time they were ready to enter the ring in the second week of March, they had trained as carefully, as intensely, and as long as Rocky Marciano prepared for a defense of his title as a professional boxer. (Rocky Marciano held the world heavyweight title from 1952–1956.)

As a senior at St. Mary's with camera in hand in 1975, I approached the ring to photograph Terry in action during his first tournament. It was difficult to watch let alone get the desired shots with a steady hand. I cringed witnessing Terry and his opponent punch, jab, hook, then strike each other's face and head through the viewfinder. As difficult as it was to watch, Terry won the championship in his weight class that year and again in 1977.

Terry spent his college years and more than one summer in the house our father purchased for him in South Bend, hanging out with the "townies" more often than not. He graduated from Notre Dame with his two boxing championships and a Bachelor of Fine Arts in 1978. Although he did not make a living as an artist, he never lost his passion for artistic expression as he continues to develop a remarkable talent to this day.

Returning to Pittsburgh, Terry obtained his real estate license and took the lead on our parents' behalf to subdivide their acreage for partial development. He got as far as developing a site plan when Danny and Larry offered to purchase the property outright. In so doing, as owners our brothers preserved the vacant land while enabling our parents to stay put in their home until 1990.

Over the course of five years—1982 to 1987—Terry lived in Denver working for Larry in sales at Rivendell Forest Products, at one point becoming the top salesman. He excelled in this role and considers it a highlight of his working years, but regrettably, he did not live up to Larry's high standards and Larry let him go.

Around the time Patty and Frank returned from Denver to Pittsburgh, Terry relocated to Chicago. He worked for the Chicago Mercantile Exchange on the trading floor as a pit reporter in the "live cattle" pit. As a pit reporter, Terry reported the brokers' prices by walkie-talkie to the computer input operator who then posted the numbers to reflect the latest recorded price. He was on the floor of the Exchange when the stock market crashed in 1987. At the time, the exchanges did not have circuit breakers in place to slow the market down in a free fall. Terry witnessed the chaotic scene when the Standard & Poor's (S&P) stock index pit stopped trading as the market collapsed:

> The first contemporary global financial crisis unfolded on October 19, 1987, a day known as "Black Monday" when the Dow Jones Industrial Average dropped 508 points, losing 22.6 percent of its value in a single day. A chain reaction of market distress sent global stock exchanges plummeting in a matter of hours. At the time, the setback marked the sharpest market downturn in the United States since the Great Depression. The Black Monday events served to underscore the concept of "globalization"—relatively new at the time—by demonstrating the unprecedented extent to which financial markets worldwide had become intertwined and techno-logically interconnected.

The market crash was significant not just because of the swiftness and severity with which the market tanked. It also exposed the weaknesses of the trading systems themselves and how they could be strained and come close to breaking in extreme conditions. As revealed when the S&P pit stopped trading, these problems interacted with the price declines to exacerbate the crisis.

After a year as a pit reporter, Terry leased a seat that allowed him to trade on his own account. He began trading at the Exchange in the Eurodollars pit and then the future options pit.

When Terry switched from working for the Chicago Mercantile Exchange to working on his own account as an inside trader, he drew suspicion by virtue of the "USA" badge symbol he had chosen. During this time, in early 1989, the Federal Bureau of Investigation authorized a sting operation with an undercover agent posing as a commodities trader. The FBI staged the agent to buy a seat worth several hundred thousand dollars on the Chicago Board of Trade in an attempt to document allegations of widespread fraud at the world's largest futures exchange. The disclosure came as federal agents delivered subpoenas to the Board of Trade and the Chicago Mercantile Exchange, the world's second largest exchange, demanding all documents describing commodities trades dating back to 1983. Thinking Terry with his "USA" badge symbol might be one of the agents, fellow dealers began to treat him with distrust.

During his last foray at trading, Terry acquired a home computer and from his apartment bought and sold futures contracts, in the process applying Microsoft Excel logic to program optimal timing of customized trades. Although he enjoyed the real-time transaction trade, he acknowledged that it wasn't a good fit. He gave Chicago his best for three years before pulling out in 1990 and returning to Denver for another go at Rivendell Forest Products. The move was short-lived, however, as the high-volume, low-margin business began its downward spiral fueled by emerging recessionary pressures at that time.

The first of two murder trials in the deaths of Danny and Linda drew Terry to San Diego in 1990. Deciding to make it his home, he transitioned from trading futures and options to working in the securities industry with Dean Witter. With the requisite security licenses in his pocket, the brokerage and securities firm sent him to their headquarters in the South Tower of the iconic World Trade Center in New York City for three weeks of training. A little more than a decade later, on September 11, 2001, trainees were among the 2,696 "Morgan Stanley/Dean Witter" employees on site when Islamic terrorists flew into the World Trade Center's North and South towers. All but nine made it out alive:

—The second airplane flew into the South Tower—

Retired Army Reserve Col. Cyril Richard "Rick" Rescorla, vice president of Security for Morgan-Stanley/Dean-Witter, then the largest tenant in the World Trade Center, lost his life with eight colleagues and 2,987 others from 93 nations on that fateful day. Miraculously, he saved nearly all of his coworkers by directing them to exit the building with haste before pointing upwards toward the chaos he heard in the stairwell above in the South Tower. "I have to help get them out!" With extraordinary foresight and preparation stemming from the 1993 terrorist attack when a truck bomb detonated below the North Tower of the complex, the Vietnam veteran put his heroics on display. Rick Rescorla is credited with saving the lives of 2,700 people before losing his own.

Terry contemplated the "what if" scenario and his good fortune in escaping the incomprehensible reign of terror that took the lives of fellow Morgan Stanley/Dean-Witter colleagues a decade following his training at the World Trade Center. The four coordinated attacks carried out by Afghanistan-based al-Qaeda on "9/11" killed 2,753 people in New York, 184 at the Pentagon, and 43 aboard United Airlines Flight 93 flying over Pennsylvania. As many as 6,000 sustained injuries. Larry's brokerage partner and friend Jim Paul is among the unfortunate souls who perished at the Twin Towers on that infamous day. "September 11, 2001" is indelibly etched in the memories of people the world over as a visceral reminder of our vulnerability to terrorist attacks on American soil.

Determining on his own that he did not have a passion for securities, Terry migrated to commercial real estate instead. He put 24 years into brokering commercial real estate deals in the greater San Diego area. While raising a family, he developed a niche in apartment investment properties, notably with NAI San Diego; Caldwell Banker Commercial

| Almar Real Estate Group; and Pacific Investment Properties | Pacific First Mortgage. However, in the background and throughout his adult life, you could always find Terry tinkering with and chasing some new entrepreneurial venture fueled by his fascination with computers, programming, spreadsheets, graphic arts, and fine arts.

Early in his real estate career after moving to San Diego, Terry met his future bride **Jennifer Gardner Ellis** (b. 1967) through a mutual friend. Some time passed before they reconnected at a Halloween party dressed in costume. Coincidentally, one dressed as a bird, the other as a bee. Evidently perfectly suited, they married in 1996 as Terry's real estate career got underway. In quick succession, the "bird-and-bee" couple bought the house in which they still reside and had the first of their two children, **Hailey Katharine** (b. 1998), when Terry was 43 years of age. The youngest of Dan and Yo Broderick's 23 grandchildren, **Dillon Terrence** (b. 2002), came three years later.

As with many of my sibling relationships over the decades, Terry's and mine ebbed and flowed before he came to nurture a family of his own. Fatherhood softened him, and I'm grateful for the closeness we developed that now keeps us in regular contact despite the 2,000 miles between us.

First acquired while employed with Rivendell in Denver and further developed in Chicago as a trader, Terry gained proficiency working with computer software, particularly Microsoft Office Excel spreadsheets. He claims he can make Excel sing! He exploited Excel to develop a buy/ sell strategy with hopes of commercializing his custom software. Later, he developed and built out an Internet platform, "Go-Local.Biz," intended for businesses to scale from a local to national marketing presence using an online drill-down custom tool. In more recent years, he applied technology for his own pleasure and as a possible commercial venture. "ImageArtStudios" employs software to artistically render visual effects using a variety of styles. Terry uses a digital process to transform photographic images, giving them the semblance of an impressionist painting before printing them on canvas. Inquisitive and extremely creative, he continues to plug away, exercising a relentless passion for artistic expression.

Since high school, the constant in Terry's life has been his art, no doubt inherited from our great-grandmother Susie Westcott Hoke and by extension, our grandmother Yolande Westcott Hoke and mother Yolande Gordon Broderick. He first mastered drawing and then oils as a medium, and more recently, mosaic tile art. Influenced by his brief studies in architecture at Notre Dame, Terry initially gravitated toward interiors and then buildings as subjects, often married with reflective bodies of water. He perceives the distance between the background and foreground of his compositions as a way to manipulate depth of perception and space using light. The following was written in a 2019 review of his mosaic tiles by artist Joe Moorman: "If we gave an award for best use of iridescent tile to create a sense of lighting in a scene, artist Terry Broderick's mosaic 'Pittsburgh Cityscape' wins."

Although he is not as forthcoming with it, Terry also has musical talent that escaped the rest of us so far as I know. He has casually played guitar for the last 50 years. While at Notre Dame in 2019, Terry and I walked into the Hammes Bookstore where a grand piano sits in the open foyer. His rendition stunned me as I had no idea he could play this instrument too. He and Jennifer bought a piano some 15 years ago wanting the kids to learn to play, but they didn't have the interest. After Dillon learned to play Beethoven's Für Elise in first grade, he decided it wasn't for him. Decades later, Terry picked it up by downloading from the Internet a collection of song sheets capturing the chords and lyrics to a variety of songs he likes. Learning by ear without reading notes, he can play just about anything on the piano—jazz, blues, fusion, pop. Playing chords only, from the song sheets he has learned many of his favorite tunes as yet another creative outlet.

Now retired, Terry is playing more music and creating more art than ever, all the while inspiring his daughter Hailey's artistic bent.

Twelve years his junior, Jennifer directs her passion toward education as an elementary school teacher and activist for the hard-earned rights of teachers in the Alpine Union School District where she has worked since 1993. A San Diego native, Jennifer earned a Bachelor's in sociology and psychology from the University of California, Santa Barbara, before completing a two-year postgraduate teacher education program at the University of California, San Diego, and later, earning a multiple-subject teaching credential. Jennifer then obtained a Master's degree in curriculum and instruction from San Diego State University and a cross-cultural, language and academic development (CLAD) credential from the University of San Diego. News of the 2022 massacre of nineteen 3rd and 4th graders and two teachers at Robb Elementary School in Uvalde, Texas, struck Jennifer especially hard as she relates to children as a 4th grade teacher herself at Mountain View Learning Academy.

Terry is exceptionally proud of his marriage and children, and grateful for the relationships he has sustained with all of his siblings despite the conflicts that materialized in our formative years when he stood alone in our father's favor. Although we had our differences early on, he emerged as a tenderhearted soul and an absolute godsend in our dad's final years and days—able to step in as comforter when none of the rest of us could.

OUR FAMILY LEAPED WITH JOY when **Timothy "Timmy" Patrick Broderick** (b. 1960) came along on February 29, 1960. *All* of us considered our blued-eyed, curly-haired baby brother a gift sealed with a kiss. The only other blonde and seven years younger than me, Timmy endeared each of us with his adorable looks and personality. In no time, he became every bit the gift to our mom as Terry had been to our dad. Timmy is the last in the line of Laurance Sterne and Yolande Hoke Gordon's 19 "GEN 12" grandchildren.

Clearly an accident, Timmy followed Terry by five years when our mom was 40. As if something was in the water, a lot of her friends had accidents around the same time. I believe Donny Wohleber, Eddie Frankenberry, and Brian Cannon all came as surprises too, to their mothers' way of thinking especially. As the new decade yielded to the receding baby boom, I suppose the mothers wanted to extract from the era all the life they possibly could. The boom years *were* the best of times, after all.

Flanking the Broderick siblings at each end, it seemed that Danny and Timmy had the most endearing personalities amongst the nine of us. As such, they earned the siblings' greatest affection. The consensus on that point is somewhat ironic only because they were, well—ahem—boys. Moreover, when Timmy came into this world, the scale tipped forever in favor of Broderick males. Hands down, Timmy became everyone's favorite.

I suppose their birth order had something—maybe a lot—to do with Danny's and Timmy's enviable qualities. Typical of the first and last born, they both received a heavy dose of parental nurturing and unconditional love that somehow had diminished strength for those of us sandwiched between them. We credit our mother who showered them both with deserved, unyielding adoration.

As Patty's recalls, "Timmy was an old soul who loved everything his siblings loved—TV shows, movies, music. I remember his brothers and sisters messing with him relentlessly and he always came back for more."

Shortly before our family moved from Mt. Lebanon to Upper St. Clair in 1964, Timmy found himself in the wrong place at the wrong time. A terrible accident nearly caused him to lose his sight in one eye. As I remember it, just after supper, some of the brood darted to the street corner to hang out with the neighborhood kids before dark. At age four, Timmy joined the pack when urgent cries for help soon echoed indoors. Innocently enough though foolhardy, Quentin Cannon had thrown a spear of some kind, possibly a ski pole, aiming at the telephone pole as his target but missed. The tip of the spiked object pierced Timmy's eye on impact. A bloody mess gushed over our mother as she held her beloved in her arms before someone took them to the emergency room. The excruciating hours before receiving news of Timmy's prognosis held the rest of us in a prolonged and uncharacteristic trance. Our baby brother made it through and recovered fully.

I recall just one time when Timmy got himself in real trouble. It wasn't long after the accident. We had just moved into our spacious new home on Orr Road. Considering the house a relic worthy of preservation, we didn't want to touch anything we might damage or break. Timmy did more than touch. He took a black magic marker when no one was looking and marked the wall the entire length of the imposing staircase. Oh my God—an egregious abuse of his privilege to live on such stately grounds! Yet our mother treated him with kid gloves in reaction. It *was* Timmy, after all. And he was no older than five.

As mentioned earlier, Patty and Tim have remained very close despite the nine-year age difference between them. The two have laughed over the years about Patty's referring to everything related to him as "little" when Timmy was young. If he wanted to go somewhere or get something which required money, Patty would tell him to run upstairs and grab his "little" nickels. Not just a knucklehead, he was a "little" knucklehead. Among other games, he loved to play Battleship with Patty. Although he suspected why he never won, he always circled back asking her to play another round knowing he would inevitably come out the loser. That's what we call a good sport.

When Patty moved back home after college, she was making some money and Timmy—then around 12 years old—wanted a job. She hired him to be her personal assistant in the fashion of Louise to Iris Carrington in *Another World*, the soap opera to which she and I were pretty much addicted along with prime-time *Peyton Place*. As Patty relayed, "Timmy had to screen my phone calls, fold my laundry, and pretty much take care of whatever I needed him to do. I bought a pink 'While You Were Out' pad which he was required to use for my phone messages. The part that really ticked him off was that he had to sign each pink slip 'Louise.' That really frosted his buttons but the straw that broke the camel's back was folding my underwear. His employment with me did not last more than a couple/few weeks. It also got under his skin that Mom thought it was funny."

Our mother stood firmly as Timmy's best friend throughout his formative years. They became inseparable as Timmy shadowed her everywhere. One might well have thought of him as an only child. They confided in each other, laughed, traveled back and forth to and from Madison countless times together, and thoroughly enjoyed each other's company. The duo had a ball visiting family members once they landed in San Diego, Denver, Cleveland, and elsewhere across the country. Mom absolutely delighted in her devoted travel companion.

From his earliest years, Timmy had the sweetest disposition. He never fussed when the girls cuddled him as a baby, dressed him up as if a doll, or had fun with him in ways that would test the patience of most children. And he never got caught in the fray of his older siblings' rivalries—to his good fortune and credit I might add. As Tim reached toward adulthood, I could not help but notice his openness, honesty, and integrity—all of which appealed to me as highly admirable traits.

I don't know how he related personally with his brothers, but with a big heart worn on his sleeve, Timmy would tell his sisters everything. No matter how personal, he spoke candidly about what he was thinking and what was happening in his life, even the romances. What girl doesn't love that honesty in a guy?

I recall an incident that shed light on Timmy's integrity when he was 14 years old. As eighth graders at St. Thomas Moore, the students had their own lockers. Tim walked into class one day to hear the teacher's ultimatum: If the person(s) who had started the fire in one of the lockers didn't come forward as the culprit, there would be consequences. No one stepped forward. But Tim knew who was behind the misdeed. The teacher presented the same ultimatum a day later but upped the ante. Everyone would pay if no one stepped forward to confess what they knew about the incident. By the third day when the guarded secret still remained under wraps, Timmy came forward with his information. It pained him to do so, but he reasoned it altogether unfair that one person should make the entire group pay for his transgression.

Some would consider his action ill-advised. In fact, he paid dearly for it the following year. When Tim left St. Thomas Moore for Upper St. Clair High School, he joined peers from his elementary school who didn't forget what he had done by stepping forward as a "rat." Their condescension affected Tim deeply, interfering with his ability to freely make new friends early on. But he overcame and became a better person for the experience of standing on principle.

Personally, I admired Timmy's fortitude to stand up for what he thought was right and just. Looking back at the Westcotts' story, I'm reminded of our many-times great-uncle James Diament Westcott, Jr., the Florida statesman who ardently stood behind his action and word affirming his position on the Mexican-American War. Tim's avowed stance did not carry James's bravado, but he made his point clear, unfortunately drawing adverse judgment by several of his classmates.

In high school, while routinely playing golf, Timmy joined the drama and tennis clubs. The cast director selected our youthful "little" brother, the thespian, to play the shy, self-conscious, and adorable ten-year-old Winthrop Paroo in *The Music Man*, a role made famous by actor Ron

Howard (who later became a renowned director/ producer / screenwriter) in the 1962 film. I returned home from Boston for Tim's inaugural performance. With his scripted lisp, Timmy's rendition of the song *Gary, Indiana* brought down the house. He did justice to Winthrop and made those of us in the audience immensely proud. The following year—in 1977—Timmy secured the lead role of *Oliver* in the musical by the same name. However, as luck would have it, a series of climatic and macroeconomic factors foiled his planned grand performance:

> Following the peak in domestic natural gas production that supplied one-third of the nation's energy in 1973, a gradual decline depleted reserves to a dangerously low level. Exacerbating the nationwide natural gas crisis in late January of 1977, the effects of a bitter, persistent cold spell closed schools and forced the shutdown of stores, restaurants, entertainment centers, and factories in Pennsylvania and elsewhere. The first freezing of the Ohio River in 30 years stalled dozens of barges loaded with fuel oil, road salt, and other products then in short supply.

> With 50,000 people already out of work in Pennsylvania and many thousands of additional layoffs predicted, the loss of supply could mean weeks rather than days of joblessness given the time required to restart kilns and blast furnaces to produce steel. The crisis demanded severe measures to avert a catastrophic situation as stockpiles fell perilously close to minimum protection levels.

> Into 1977, as new layoffs impacted hundreds of thousands of people in a dozen states, governing bodies warned of possible further hardships with an edict to cease all "nonessential" usage of natural gas. As cold weather, supply shortages, and high energy bills continued unabated, every sector stepped up to minimize the impact of the disruption, including affected institutions of learning.

To conserve energy, Upper St. Clair High School ceased all "nonessential" after-school activities for six to eight weeks. When the time came to ramp back up, Timmy had to choose between acting in the musical and playing tennis, as the latter was about to pick back up with the warmer weather. He opted for tennis as he couldn't do both. Around that same time, the little guy reached a milestone shortly after turning

17. Mom measured him and shared with me that he finally reached the five-foot threshold! Like the others among the boys, he grew by inches in college.

Once, when Timmy was a senior in high school, our parents planned to go out of town and asked Patty to spend the weekend with him. Out of college, she then worked at The Saloon and had an apartment of her own. When Patty arrived at the homestead one night that weekend after work, she quickly discovered that she had locked herself out of the house. Desperate to get to a bathroom, she rang and rang the doorbell and pounded the front door, certain that Timmy was upstairs sleeping. She finally broke off the trim outside the back door leading to the kitchen, removed the chain lock, and ran to the bathroom as fast as she could. Enraged, she then ran upstairs to wake up Timmy and scream at him for ignoring her urgent calls for help. As he rolled over, she realized he was completely smashed. Our innocent "little" brother had gone to a high school graduation party where he drank spiked punch. The first taste of alcohol in his life, Timmy loved it and got wasted. With Tim fearing a reputation as the biggest dork in his class because he so hated people who drank or smoked marijuana, Patty of course thought it was hysterical.

In 1978, Tim followed Terry's lead by attending Holy Cross College before transferring to Notre Dame and joining the Bengal Bouts in the lightweight division. Mom absolutely dreaded his leaving the nest. As she said in a letter to me, "I'm glad we have the trip to Ireland coming up. . . otherwise I don't know how I'd get through the shock of his being gone." Indeed, she hated the solitude with all nine of her children out of the nest, although Nancy and Patty lived in Pittsburgh at the time, and both Kathleen and Dennis lived in Cleveland, in close proximity to Madison.

At Holy Cross, Timmy focused on his grades and got a job washing dishes for the Christian Brothers. He earned $2.00 an hour plus his meals. Brother Leo recommended his transfer to Notre Dame after his freshman year. Even before his acceptance became official, Larry—in a celebratory mood and with typical generosity—bought him a used yellow Subaru.

Timmy competed with the famed Bengal Bouts in the Spring of his sophomore and junior years. He did not prevail victorious in either tournament, but he managed to build up his physique during the rigorous training.

Shortly after his Notre Dame graduation with a Bachelor of Business Administration in marketing in 1982, Tim spent six months in Minneapolis working in Rivendell's reload facility then joined Larry at his business in Denver. He progressed to senior account executive at Rivendell Forest Products where he worked from 1983 to 1991 before the company closed. At Rivendell, Tim met Denver native **Ann Marie Pfannenstiel** (b. 1961) who then worked in the company's accounting department with a Bachelor's in accounting from Denver-based Metropolitan State College. They married in 1988 and in quick succession gave birth to four sons, each two years apart: **Sean Patrick** (b. 1988); **Conor Michael** (b. 1990); **Timothy Daniel** (b. 1992); and **Shane Christian** (b. 1994). Ann later worked in public accounting as a certified public accountant and tax advisor and retired from Wipfli, LLP in 2023.

Once Larry liquidated the assets of Rivendell, Tim worked for a year at Denney Transportation. In 1992, he followed Larry at SteelWorks (now known as Acme Manufacturing). Exhibiting the same tenacity and work ethic that appear ingrained in the "GEN 12" Brodericks, Larry rewarded Tim with advancement opportunities throughout their 30-year ride together at Acme.

Beginning in 2016 until his retirement in 2023, Tim led Acme's 200+ employees as president and chief operating officer while Larry served as chief executive officer. With locations in Denver as well as Cullman, Alabama, and Lancaster, Pennsylvania, the business continues to set sales records while growing organically and through acquisitions.

A traditionalist to the core, Tim embraces his heritage. A love of Notre Dame and our family's childhood retreat in Madison will stay with him and with Dennis all the days of their lives. Predictably, Tim endeavored to establish new traditions with Ann and their four sons early on. Notably, they revolve around the Christmas holiday, presumably in homage to our mother. Both inside and out, he labors to make a splash. The multi-week project kicks into gear as he decorates and lights up every tree that grows on his sizeable property. Regardless of weather conditions—whether rain, sleet, or snow—you'll find him outside untangling strings of lights and equipped with a light strapped to his head as he hikes up each tree. All the while, you will hear him cussing when he invariably blows a fuse or trips a breaker in his quest to light up the night sky. Without a theme or color scheme in mind, his objective is simply to make a statement with a stupendous display. A family affair for years on end, Tim puts the boys to work as helpers to create a showpiece. On-lookers ooh and aah in acknowledgement of his engineering feat. The proverbial apple does not fall far from any one tree considering our mother's obsession with this revered holiday.

Tim's family has also made an annual tradition of going into the mountains in nearby Winter Park to cut down a choice Christmas tree. Trudging through snow, they would pick a favorite, fasten down the tree to the top of their car, and file out among other similarly-minded tree choppers. One year, not paying attention, Tim pulled out of a spot and rear-ended the tree strapped on top and fronting the car situated next to his. He managed to snap a couple of feet off the crown of the tree that extended past the car's fender—somehow without drawing the driver's attention. To tell or not to tell, that was the question Tim and Ann debated the entire ride home. The boys never forgot it and hopefully learned a lesson from the Christmas tree drama that played out before them as mere innocents.

Christmas aside, Tim picked up our father's dedication to keeping his yard in pristine condition. His kids might go so far as to call his habitual attentiveness an obsession. When not tinkering with stringed lights, they often find him working to adjust the sprinklers. When the kids were youngsters, Tim and Ann brought home a pup. A golden retriever, Trusty one day dug deep into the ground, reached one of the buried sprinkler lines and ran with it, pulling out the line several feet across the yard. A calm and even-keeled guy typically, Tim came home from work to discover the disturbance to his manicured lawn. He went ballistic at the sight of it. Seething, in his work clothes Tim sprinted into a fast run, chasing the feisty pup at a high speed before someone intervened in the nick of time. Many dogs enlivened the Broderick home over the years— Seamus the Norwegian terrier; Maddie the Labrador retriever; Cody the golden retriever; and Penny the beagle among them. Yet Trusty somehow emerged as the family's absolute favorite.

With Larry and Dennis, Tim co-owns the Madison home our parents built in 1951. In a move to gain water access, in 2005, Tim, Ann, and

Dennis jointly purchased a lakeside house in Madison two doors from our grandparents and Larry's former home and a block from our childhood Norton Drive property. While the latter still plays host to the famed neighborhood "Norton Drive Softball League," the two parcels together accommodate large numbers among us during family gatherings. Tim and his growing Denver family enjoy spending time in Madison as often as possible and at the Breckenridge, Colorado, "log cabin" the couple purchased in more recent years. Traveling and playing golf also rank high as forms of family entertainment.

Guys (1945–present)

MY AUNT AND UNCLE Virginia "Jinks" Stone Gordon and Douglas Bennett Guy raised six children in Palo Alto, California. With its iconic sunshine, sand, surf, and glamor, California asserts the beauty of the Pacific coast and the fitness of its people. Before moving to the "Golden State" for a summer in 1972, my imagination ran wild thinking about what it would be like growing up there. In photos, my cousins reinforced my idealized image of America's "best-looking people."

The way Jinks spoke of her family made me envy their lifestyle and the high regard she held for each of them. She sang their praises when she spoke of her children—Dianne Gordon (b. 1945), David James (b. 1947), Laurance "Larry" Bennett (b. 1948), Joanna "Jo" Hoke (b. 1951), and fraternal twins Denise "Dennie" Sterne (b. 1958) and Theresa "Terrie" Ann (b. 1958). Noteworthy are the Gordon, Bennett, Hoke, and Sterne families whom Jinks and Doug honored when naming their children. But not a Westcott? Surely David or Terrie would have been pleased to carry the Westcott family name.

Thirteen years separated the oldest from the youngest among the Guys. Like my brother Tim who arrived five years after Terry, Denise and Terrie likely came as a surprise to their parents. They trailed their closest sibling Jo by seven years—and as twins no less! Doug was a tough but loving father to the children while Jinks came across to them as happy, mellow, carefree, fun, and adventurous—she was up for anything and everything. As members of the renowned Santa Clara Swim Club that has produced many World and Olympic champions, Doug spurred the kids' early interest in swimming. The family also enjoyed a long history—perhaps 15 years running—traveling every Christmas to ski in the Sierras, notably Echo Summit on the south shore of Lake Tahoe where my nephew Rhett Broderick later bought and occupied a home.

In 1960, when Dianne as the eldest approached 16, Doug and Jinks acquired the family's weekend home in Aptos in the vicinity of Santa Cruz, California. It became a haven for water sports year-round, notably swimming, surfing, and water polo. They were the best of times for the budding Guy family who gravitated toward cats rather than dogs as their pet of choice. The Siamese "Lulu" and dark-haired tabby "Poncho" became two of their favorites.

All but David—the most eligible bachelor among "GEN 12" Westcotts—married and raised children of their own. All but Dianne have called California "home" since birth with one exception when Jo lived briefly in Mexico.

ONCE WORLD WAR II ENDED and within a year of Danny's birth, cousin **Dianne Gordon Guy Hoge** (b. 1945) was born in the town where her parents married, in Walla Walla, Washington. Soon thereafter, the trio relocated to Menlo Park, California, before planting seeds in nearby Palo Alto. Here, Doug established his own advertising and marketing agency in close proximity to his alma mater, Stanford University.

Dianne led the pack of Guy children at St. Albert's elementary school. Her three siblings closest in age followed her at Palo Alto High School. Jinks believed the children would be better off with a public education for their secondary studies.

My eldest first cousin took up swimming and taught synchronized swimming after placing first in competitions. Influenced by her brothers' example, Dianne got into surfing once the family established a weekend base in Aptos. Evidently surfers are territorial when it comes to the waves. The surfing dudes gave David and Larry some leeway in cutting off to take the waves with their sister who happened to be one of the few girls with a board among them in the day. Ever popular, Dianne became a cheerleader at Palo Alto High School. David describes his sister as a character and the focal point of the family. He shared that Dianne was "Miss Everything—smart, beautiful, and funny." She had an active social life and dated often.

A fun-loving party girl, Dianne had perhaps too much fun in Boulder where she attended the University of Colorado. She had to pull back briefly but returned to earn a Bachelor's degree in remedial education. While teaching at an elementary school in the inner city of Oakland, California, Dianne met her future husband, **Ronald "Ron" Norris Hoge** (b. 1945)—originally from Darby, Pennsylvania—who then studied at Stanford University.

With a Bachelor's degree in mathematics from Amherst College in Massachusetts, Ron received a Master's degree in public affairs from the Kennedy Public Affairs School at the University of California, Berkeley. He went on to earn a Master of Business Administration in marketing from Stanford University's Graduate School of Business in 1970. In that same year, Ron and Dianne married. Within a couple of years, they caught the travel bug. They made the plunge by quitting their jobs and taking a full year to explore the world. Among many notable adventures, they climbed the 19,341-foot Mount Kilimanjaro. Located in the country of Tanzania a distance of 205 miles from the equator, Kilimanjaro is the tallest mountain in Africa and the world's tallest free-standing mountain. The varied experiences prepared Ron and Dianne for the international work opportunities that followed.

Ron launched a highly successful 40-year career with executive leadership roles in eight different companies before landing with Pinnacle Engines as chairman and CEO in 2011. Like my brother Larry early in his business career, Ron developed global connections as a member of the esteemed Young Presidents' Organization. From Fortune 500 firms to venture-backed startups, Ron has led businesses on three continents through their startup, growth, reorganization, and disposition phases.

Early on, Ron and Dianne established residency in Portola Valley, California, before Ron's business took them out of state. In Columbus, Indiana, they started a family with **Stephen Guy** (b. 1976). Diane gave birth to **Ian Guy** (b. 1978) in Leamington Spa, England, and **Kristina Guy** (b. 1982) in San Páulo, Brazil, where Ron picked up Portuguese as a second language. Returning to the U.S., Ron and Dianne first moved to Minnetonka, Minnesota, where they reconnected with our Gordon relatives. They then moved closer to Dianne's roots, settling for a time in Rancho Palos Verdes in Southern California before business relocated them yet again—to Nashville, Tennessee. Their final move brought them to the "Golden City" of San Francisco. For a brief time, they kept a second residence in Manhattan Beach near Los Angeles.

Sometime after the kids established roots outside the home, Ron joined Silicon Valley-based Pinnacle Engines where he became Chairman and CEO. Advancing the development of internal combustion engine efficiency, the company received the second largest award ever granted by the U.S. Department of Energy in 2018. The Department of Energy recognized Pinnacle for its cutting-edge research and development to push thermal efficiencies to the limit, and it lauded the firm for the potential of its technology to "radically improve U.S. economic prosperity, national security, and environmental wellbeing."

The Hoges reside in San Francisco's Nob Hill neighborhood and established secondary quarters in close proximity to Dianne's alma mater in Boulder. "Di" has developed a talent as an artist with a bent toward abstract art. With a strong interest in the performing arts, she became a trustee of the American Conservatory Theatre while Ron has remained active as a venture advisor and consultant to several clean tech startups in the San Francisco Bay area.

THE MOST "ELIGIBLE BACHELOR" in the extended family, **David James Guy** (b. 1947) followed his sister Dianne by 15 months. The two felt animosity toward each other growing up and fought often. This was during an early period when David had a bit of a temper and frequently chased the kids around. Into his teenage years, he incurred Dianne's wrath when he befriended the cheerleaders and gained the affection of her friends. The siblings have long since made up; Dianne now likes nothing more than to talk on the phone with David about the family. They favor remembrances of their mother with whom David was exceptionally close. Beset with a difficult pregnancy before his birth, Jinks was advised to abort the fetus. She adamantly refused and after several weeks, the hemorrhaging stopped and she gave birth to a healthy boy, her first son. She would tell anyone who would listen including David's siblings, "Isn't he wonderful?" David saw himself in his mother, notably her easy-going demeanor, and he would do anything she asked of him.

Physically fit, David took to the Pacific early as a swimmer, surfer, and windsurfer. Following his tenure at Palo Alto High School, he enrolled at Foothill College in Los Altos Hills.

> The founding board launched the school as a junior college for 3,500 full-time students, the first of many junior colleges built in California after World War II. Originally named Foothill Junior College, founding president Calvin C. Flint insisted that his new college would not be junior to anyone. The board dropped "Junior" from the name in 1958. Widely recognized as a pioneer in new campus design, the school's architect Ernest Kump and landscape architects Hideo Sasaki and Peter Walker created the 122-acre space to resemble a neo-Japanese garden.

Transferring after two years at Foothill College where he pursued an interest in psychology, David enrolled at the University of California, Santa Barbara (UCSB). He changed his focus area and graduated with a Bachelor's degree in social science with an emphasis in history. David then relocated to the county seat of Santa Cruz where he spent some time working as a bartender at the panoramic Crow's Nest, a popular harborside restaurant that celebrated its 50-year anniversary in 2019.

Soon after his younger brother Larry launched Guy's Gutters in Redwood City, California, in 1973, David joined him in business. The distance between Redwood City and David's residence led to a parting of ways, however. While Larry developed his company as Guy's Roofing and Rain Gutters, in 1981, David independently established a sheet metal specialty with similarly-named Guy's Gutters in Watsonville. In the vicinity of their parents' vacation home in Aptos, David served the greater Santa Cruz area as owner of the business, later pulling back from some of the day-to-day operational duties and now fully retired.

Previous to 1985, David rented his parents' Aptos vacation home as their tenant. In 1985, at fair market value, Doug and Jinks sold the home to David. He has lived there ever since. Equipped with a gym, he regularly works out from the comfort of his home. Having once worked at a nursery owned by the parents of a friend, he also retains a passion for gardening.

Located on Monterey Bay, Aptos gives David access to rich marine life to feed his soul. Up until the devasting floods that battered the shoreline in early 2023, David developed a close friendship with a coastal creature whom he affectionately named "Peggy Sue"—presumably in homage to rock 'n' roll trailblazer Buddy Holly who released the so-named single in 1957. The one-legged seagull spotted David a mile away from its regular perch at the Seacliff State Beach fishing pier, in bird's-eye view of the sunken S.S. *Palo Alto*. An Aptos landmark, the cement ship once stood as a 435-foot long, 7,500-ton oil tanker built for use during World War 1. Until the recent flood decimated the popular pier, David routinely met up with Peggy Sue at the fish breeding grounds, feeding his feathered friend a handful of cashews as a reward for her loyal following.

David the avid surfer has put aside his board—at least for a while. On the heels of his brother's heart attack while riding the waves, David suffered a similar fate under nearly identical circumstances in 2015. The episode took place in front of his Aptos home when the water was especially cold. The shock of immersion in cold water against the skin triggers the adrenal glands to react by pumping out stress hormones, in turn causing blood vessels supplying the skin to narrow. The stress response conserves heat but also shifts even more blood to the chest, thus taxing the heart as in David's case—and possibly Larry's as well. With a recent history of clogged arteries, David is naturally reluctant to take another chance, but he clamors for the adrenaline that comes from pulling into the barrel of the ominous Pacific Ocean waves.

Why didn't David marry? He never met the right girl. One time, he did, and he thought, "This is the one." However, she wasn't that interested in him. Somewhat shy, he waited for someone to come around and make the moves on him. The stars have not yet aligned, but among his loved ones, hope runs eternal. Meanwhile, his many loyal friends continue to look after him with affection and tender loving care.

STATISTICS SHOW that as much as 12.5% of DNA is shared among first cousins. My brother Danny and cousin **Laurance "Larry" Bennett Guy** (b. 1948) in particular share a striking resemblance and both proved to be highly driven. Unlike Danny, however, cousin Larry Guy excelled as a competitive athlete in his early years—notably in aquatic sports. David considers his brother one of the best athletes he has ever known. Although never boastful, with confidence Larry wills himself in the belief that he can beat his opponent. He has prevailed time and again.

With great eye-hand coordination, Larry and Denise spent countless hours together playing ping pong while he developed as a competitive swimmer. Then tiring of swimming laps, Larry's father suggested he try water polo. In junior high school, Larry tried out and found that he loved the sport. It came easily to him, and he quickly broke the water polo league record. In his senior year, Larry broke the all-time high school scoring record held by a player who went on to compete in the Olympics. The Olympic committee courted him. One insurmountable problem surfaced, however. Larry was not personally affiliated with a "club team." The playoffs pitted club teams against each other without regard to the talent of individual players in the sport. The UCLA coach of the water polo club contending for qualification in the Olympics said to Larry, "I've got to put my team in front of you." Larry accepted the decision and then found himself ready to move on.

Like many of the Brodericks, Larry possesses an independent streak and a strong sense of humor. His siblings regard him as a very funny guy, always quick with a joke or pranks, and especially daring during his high school and college years.

From Palo Alto High, Larry attended Foothill College for one year. At Foothill, Larry's team won the national championship and he became an All-American for his outstanding athletic ability in water polo. Stanford University courted him for his off-the-charts talent. Although his father encouraged him to sign on with his alma mater, Larry felt the pull to develop his independence. He was ready to move out of the area when the University of California, Santa Barbara, recruited him to play on their water polo team. At UCSB, he again earned "All-American" status and pursued his love of surfing at the same time.

While Larry was enrolled at UCSB, on a visit his parents got caught in the crosshairs of one of the many riots that erupted across the nation in defiance against President Richard Nixon's prolonged Vietnam War:

The most notorious of the riots led to bloodshed on the Kent State University campus in May of 1970 when Ohio National Guardsmen gunned down unarmed activists, killing four students and injuring nine others. Renowned journalist Bob Woodward later described the bloodshed as "a moment that shook the conscience of everyone." Neil Young's legendary "Four Dead in Ohio" still rings as one of the many popular songs rendered by folk-rock band Crosby, Stills, Nash & Young in the 1970s:

> *Tin soldiers and Nixon's comin'*
> *We're finally on our own*
> *This summer I hear the drummin'*
> *Four dead in Ohio . . .*

In California, Jinks and Doug caught a first-hand glimpse of growing opposition as the sustained anti-war movement gained momentum. On approach to see Larry in Santa Barbara in 1970, they encountered a massive gathering of hostile demonstrators:

A crowd of young protestors stormed the Bank of America building in the UCSB-adjacent community of Isla Vista and set it on fire. Fueled by student protests against the Vietnam War, a fiery speech led UCSB students from campus to a park adjacent to the Bank of America which they condemned as a symbol of capitalism and "the establishment."

Creating pure bedlam, the rioters turned a police car on its hood and set it on fire. As the police could not control the anarchy in the streets, the firemen could not safely tend to the bank building fire. Following the incident, then Governor Ronald Reagan took action. He ordered the National Guard into Isla Vista and instituted a curfew. People were afraid. The police shot off tear gas and beat students down. It took a student's death to quell the violence.

Facing the curfew that Governor Reagan instituted at Isla Vista, Doug and Jinks witnessed the flashing lights of helicopters signaling those on the streets to go home. The situation became so disruptive to the university that the professors purportedly gave all students passing grades—not that Larry wouldn't have earned passing grades otherwise. During that time, some professors were known to inflate grades in order to keep students from being drafted. All across America, college students and some faculty united in protest against the Vietnam war.

From UCSB with a Bachelor of Arts in history, Larry worked briefly for his father before starting his own business in Redmond City in 1973. Initially, he installed rain gutters and then expanded the service once receiving a Master of Business Administration from the University of Santa Clara. Ever the astute risk-taker, Larry developed Guy's Roofing and Rain Gutters which had a solid track record in the Bay area before he sold the business and retired in 2005.

At UCSB, Larry met his future bride, **Peggy Ptak** (b. 1950). During their studies, Peggy spent a semester on the high seas with World Campus Afloat, affiliated with Chapman University in Irvine, California. In 1977, the couple married in Rancho Santa Fe where Peggy's parents had moved the Ptak family from Lincoln, Nebraska, when she was a child. Peggy's father Ray Joseph Ptak gained fame for coaching his friend Warren Buffet, chairman and CEO of Berkshire Hathaway, in the game of golf. A prom queen at San Dieguito High School Academy in Encinitas and very popular, Peggy took up tennis before picking up golf as her sport of choice. From college, she practiced as an X-ray technician at Redwood Medical Clinic. Larry and Peggy established themselves close to his business in Menlo Park where they raised **Cory James** (b. 1977) and **Kimberly Rae** (b. 1979). Here, Larry and his young family developed their athleticism as avid tennis players before establishing residence in Portola Valley.

Once the kids left the nest and began to have children of their own, Larry and Peggy relocated to Santa Barbara on California's central coast to be closer to their growing family. In 2004, on a stormy winter day when surf conditions were optimal, Larry suffered chest pains as he came to shore after riding the waves in his wetsuit. Requiring assistance to walk to his car, he found his way home. With Larry's wetsuit stripped to his waste, Peggy took a look and drove him straight to the hospital. Thinking she had dropped him off at the emergency entrance so she could park the car, she later learned of the emergency room's actual location on the opposite end of the hospital grounds. Larry managed to walk the distance.

Upon entering, the staff mistook him for a bum without recognizing his dire state. Larry was within an hour of expiring when a doctor inserted a stent that saved his life. As Larry came to, he heard Peggy explaining to the doctor that her husband had a golf tournament planned at week's end. "Can he make it?" The answer came back as a resounding "No!" Larry later learned that his father's dad had died of a heart attack at age 46; his mother's dad, Laurance Gordon, suffered heart issues when he died at age 62. The wake-up call may well have contributed to Larry's decision to retire the year following his own heart attack. As mentioned, Larry's brother David has also battled the effects of "myocardial infarction."

In Santa Barbara, Larry and Peggy established residency in toney Montecito Birnam Wood, a premier gated golf course community situated between the Santa Ynez Mountains and the Pacific Ocean. With oversight of some 18 committees, Larry served as president of the Birnam Wood Golf Club when catastrophic flooding of the San Ysidro Creek took out the Guy home in 2018. The disaster brings to mind the tragic story Josie Gould Westcott relayed about her family's experience during Pennsylvania's Hickory Run flood in 1849—nearly 170 years before her G2 grandson's misfortune. The *Montecito Journal* covered the story of the Montecito mudslides on January 18, 2018:

> "In the early morning hours on January 9, as pelting rain fell at the rate of half an inch in just 5 minutes, a giant mudslide formed on denuded mountain slopes just below the Los Padres National Forest. Fire-baked foothills stripped of vegetation and recently ravaged by the Thomas Fire—the largest in California's recorded history—covered a firestorm area nearly twice the size of the state of Rhode Island. Now, with concentrated rainfall, the mountain began to move.

> "The rolling sea of mud and ooze, interspersed with giant boulders and uprooted trees that turned into river ramrods had an immediate and devastating effect. Before they had a chance to escape, residents witnessed snapped off power poles, destroyed homes, and structures ripped in half."

Two days later, the *Los Angeles Times* reported on the many people still trapped as the death toll continued to rise:

> "Teams of rescuers waded through hillsides blanketed by mud and debris looking for victims of mudflows that killed at least 17 people. As firefighters dug through battered homes, helicopters searched from the sky for survivors who might be trapped behind roads made impassable by downed power lines and waist-high muck."

Putting his own affairs on hold, Larry joined the rescuers in the evacuation of his Birnam Wood neighbors. Overall, the deluge that flowed down through the upscale hillside community and onto the 101 Freeway cost 23 lives and destroyed 63 residences. Some families lost multiple relatives as the raging waters swept their homes away.

Mother nature dealt Montecito a horrific one-two punch with fire and rain. The unfathomable destruction led to Larry's and Peggy's decision to relocate once again, this time to San Diego where they could get even closer to their children and grandchildren. Coming full circle, they currently reside where they married, at Rancho Santa Fe in the northern outskirts of San Diego.

THE FOURTH IN LINE and second girl among "GEN 12" Guys, **Joanna "Jo" Hoke Guy McNamara** (b. 1951) is known by her siblings and cousins as "Joanne" or "Jo" for short. Her birth name presumably derives from our G2 grandmother Joanna "Josie" Sackett Gould Westcott.

Like her siblings, Jo took up swimming early but she also explored her creative side, thanks largely to the influence of her father—my Uncle Doug—whom she adored. How fun to have a father with an advertising / branding bent who engaged the whole family to produce trifold promotional pieces he dropped in the mail to drum up business for his advertising agency. Not only did he engage his children in the laborious task of folding the pieces for mail delivery, he sometimes incorporated their creative work in the collateral he mailed. He clearly challenged and thereby shaped Jo's penchant as a talented and passionate artist.

Following her brothers' path, Joanna attended Foothills College though only briefly. She completed junior college at Cabrillo Junior College in Aptos. As Denise and Terrie were about to enter their second semester at Jordan Junior High as 8th graders, Jinks and Doug gave the greenlight for the girls to enroll in school in Aptos and for their sister to chaperon the twins. The "experiment" was fun but short-lived, however, as Jo gave the twins perhaps a little too much free rein for Jinks and Doug's taste. Jo had a Vespa scooter at the time. When not driving the twins in the car their parents had left for them, Jo loaded the three on the two-wheeler to get around. They often cruised up and down the shore and took in the sunsets. One time, a farmhand caught them red-handed when they snuck into a strawberry patch to fill a bag with the succulent fruit. As fast as their short legs could run, they darted for the scooter and piled on. Jo kicked the clutch and sped ahead of the high pursuit. They laughed to their hearts' content once they safely distanced themselves in the getaway Vespa.

The realities of life soon followed the carefree exploits of that period. Jo learned of the tragic death of her boyfriend, a surfer from Aptos who perished following a horrible car crash in Mexico. As a way to heal, Jo's mother suggested she enroll at the Universidad de las Américas Puebla located in Cholula. Although the awakening experience in the oldest city in Latin America had a profound impact validating her artistic talent and generally expanding her horizons, Jo stayed just shy of a year. Shortly thereafter, Jinks pulled the twins out of their elementary school classes in Los Altos and with David, the four drove the Ford Country Squire with Jo's dog, Aragon, to pick her up and bring her back home. On route, they enjoyed a respite at a villa in Puerto Vallarta owned by friends of Jinks and Doug. Doug, Jo's sister Dianne, and Dianne's husband Ron met the family there. The twins' month-long absence from school was excused— they simply had to write a paper about their "learning experience."

Returning to Los Altos temporarily, Joanna enrolled in the art program at Humboldt University in Arcata, California, a town colonized in 1850 and a distance of 315+ miles north of Los Altos. It wasn't long before Joanna realized that she could not make a living in art. Her dad had contacts at the Veterans Hospital in Palo Alto who seeded her pursuit of a career in occupational therapy. Jo enrolled at San José State University to satisfy the science prerequisites for an occupational therapy degree before completing an internship closer to home at Stanford Hospital. During a ski trip with friends, Jo met **Robert S. Welti** (b. 1951); they married in 1977.

Rob graduated from Stanford's School of Medicine in 1978. While completing his residency at Stanford, the couple lived in Portola Valley. Rob then accepted a position as an anesthesiologist in Santa Barbara. Here, Jo and Rob raised sons **Tyler Guy** (b. 1980) and **David Guy** (b. 1983). Until Jo and Rob's divorce in 1996, they spent several holidays with Jo's sister Terrie and her husband, Phil, who likewise reared their two children in Santa Barbara. Except when parenting the boys as children, Jo maintained her certification as a practicing part-time occupational therapist until her recent retirement from Providence Santa Rosa Memorial Hospital in Sonoma County.

At her 25th Palo Alto High School reunion, Jo became reacquainted with a high school classmate, **William "Bill" McNamara** (b. 1950), a botanist and poet. Quickly sparking a romance, the couple soon married and "JoJo" blossomed. She became a stepmother to Bill's children— Alaina in Sonoma, Kaily in South America, and Liam in East Bay.

Until his retirement, Bill and his wife, Jo, lived on the grounds of Quarryhill Botanical Garden located in Glen Ellen in Sonoma Valley. Bill's tenure with the exquisite botanical garden began when he was hired as a landscaper. Recognized for his field knowledge, he advanced to become president and executive director (now "Emeritus"). In the company of other distinguished peers, he botanized extensively in the wilds of Asia, venturing in the mountains of China, Japan, India, Nepal, Vietnam, or Myanmar each fall for three decades in search of plants to further his interest in conservation. Bill's muse is clearly nature, especially trees.

Today, the 25-acre Quarryhill Botanical Garden features over 25,000 wild-sourced and seeded plants—many trees—that Bill collected throughout his celebrated 32-year career before his retirement in 2019. He has received numerous prestigious awards, both nationally and internationally as one in an exclusive group of esteemed horticulturalists. Bill now serves as a field associate of the Department of Botany with the California Academy of Sciences while writing poetry that reflects his intimacy with nature. In 2022, he published a collection titled *Collected Poems: The Later Years*.

Joanna has made a hobby of photographing nature, the indigenous people, and wild animals during her extensive Asiatic travels with Bill. The photos now serve as subjects for her striking paintings on canvas.

She has dabbled in oils and, more recently, in pastel portrait painting. Jo collaborated with Bill on his book of *Collected Poems* with illustrations by "Joanna McNamara." Traveling, gardening, and grandchildren consume much of their time otherwise.

The couple entered a new chapter post-retirement as they settled into a house they previously acquired in Truckee, California, a small mountain town north of Lake Tahoe in the High Sierras. Living distant from their Sonoma friends and in a climate most conducive to snow skiing, the move proved a bit of an adjustment as they navigated their way with travel always on their mind. Clamoring to return "home," they made the move back to Sonoma in 2024.

LIKE HER SISTER YO, Jinks gave birth to three girls in a row. Fraternal twins **Denise Sterne Guy Incerpi** and **Theresa "Terrie" Ann Guy Bugay** (b. 1958) came five minutes apart at Stanford Hospital in Palo Alto. With great affection, Dianne, David, Larry, and Joanna looked after the adorable twins with a protective guard.

Denise and Terrie followed the lead of their older brothers and sisters by attending St. Albert's Elementary School, but they transferred to Crescent Park Elementary as 4th graders before progressing to Jordan Junior High School (grades 6-8). At St. Albert's, Terrie evidently lived in Denise's shadow. Jinks and Doug initiated the transfer to Crescent Park in hopes that splitting the girls into separate classrooms at the public school would bring Terrie out as her own person. It proved to be the right decision as Terrie began to branch out and develop her own interests and set of friends.

Evidently linked to genetics, **Denise** along with her brother David developed dyslexia in childhood. Challenged to keep up her grades, Denise prevailed with the benefit of speech therapy in elementary school. The condition subsequently passed to two of Denise's three children and one other among the "GEN 13" Guys.

Around the time Jinks became a real estate broker, under Jo's supervision, Denise and Terrie relocated to Aptos where they transferred from Jordan Junior High to Aptos Junior High School in their second semester of 8th grade. Their stay was short-lived, however. On their 14th birthday in 1972, Doug and Jinks moved from Palo Alto into their new home in Los Altos. The girls enrolled as freshmen at Los Altos High School where they remained through their senior year.

Spending the summer before high school in Aptos where their parents joined the teenagers on weekends, Denise learned to apply to tennis the eye-hand coordination she had developed with Larry in ping pong. She was the first in the family to became adept at the sport. Following Larry's example with his mental toughness and aptitude for winning, Denise progressed as a competitive swimmer and badminton player.

Denise's future husband **Eugene Rodney "Rod" Incerpi** (b. 1956) graduated two years ahead of the twins at Los Altos High School. While Rod played football as a star athlete, Denise competed on the tennis team. Rod continued to play football on a scholarship with the University of Oregon in Eugene until an injury sidelined him from the sport. He stayed on with the university to earn a Bachelor's degree in business.

For roughly a two-year period in the early 1970s at the height of the nation's stagflation-fueled recession, Doug and Jinks moved out of their Palo Alto home to make it available as a rental. Coincidentally, while they lived briefly in Menlo Park, Rod became a tenant in the Guy home, residing in Denise's bedroom of all places.

Denise attended Chico College for a quarter session before coming home and attending Foothill College. She completed a summer term at Santa Barbara City College where she became friends with and briefly shared a rental with her former beau's friend—her twin Terrie's future husband Phil Bugay. Denise moved on to receive a degree from Foothill College in respiratory therapy.

Halfway through their studies, Denise and Terrie took an extended vacation in Europe. During this time, they had the opportunity to meet up with Dianne, Ron, and their young family in Covington, England.

In 1984, our devoted Uncle Larry drove cross-country in order to attend both Rick's and my wedding in Pittsburgh and Denise and Rod's wedding a week later in Los Altos. Going to great lengths, Uncle Larry rarely missed out on any of the extended family celebrations.

Denise and Rod settled close to their childhood homes in Los Altos where they raised **Alicia Gordon** (b. 1986), **Ryan Guy** (b. 1989), and

Kacey Madison (b. 1996). All three attended Denise and Rod's alma mater at Los Altos High School. Meanwhile, Denise practiced as a respiratory therapist at Stanford Hospital for five or more years before migraines and debilitating arthritic pain to her back and neck forced her to abandon her profession.

As a dutiful assistant to his father who developed polio when Rod was just five years old, Denise's husband learned about home repairs at an early age while effectively functioning as Ronald Incerpi's arms and legs. In 1966, on land Rod's grandparents had previously owned and operated as a 16-acre orchard in Los Altos Hills, friends of Rod's father built the Incerpi family home. Rod and his mother, Carel, insulated the house when he reached age ten.

The early experience doing home improvements and repairs prepared Rod for success as a general contractor in the residential building sector with all manner of construction, electrical, and plumbing skills. Rod has worked for himself as long as he and Denise have been together.

In 1980, the couple bought vacant land from a client of Rod's on the west shore of Lake Tahoe where they built a second home on Rubicon Bay. At the time, landowners in the vicinity could not build without winning the privilege in a lottery. Rod negotiated a deal that would pay the seller a premium if he should strike gold with a winning lottery pick. He did!

Taking possession of the Incerpi family home in Los Altos Hills upon his father's passing in 2008, Rod completed major renovations and sold a portion of the land to satisfy his dad's prior obligations. For a couple of years until recently, Rod and Denise opted to lease their Los Altos Hills home in favor of living full-time on Lake Tahoe. While enjoying the serenity of their picturesque surroundings, they filled their days boating, fishing, walking, and hiking. They also fit in as much time as possible with their geographically-distant children and grandchildren until the separation became too much. While retaining their Lake Tahoe property as a second home, they sold the Incerpi home in Los Altos in 2024 and relocated to Bend, Oregon, where their oldest daughter, Alicia, and her family reside.

MUCH AS MY BROTHER Danny and cousin Larry Guy shared a strong resemblance, I heard the same observation about **Terrie** and me in our formative years. I recall one of my closest high school friends mistaking us when Terrie briefly stepped out during the wedding ceremony and Mass for my brother Larry and Kathy in Pittsburgh. Five years younger than me, at age 16, Terrie with her long blonde hair and then slouched posture dropped her head low, still feeling the effects of an underage hangover brought on from far too much drinking the night before the wedding. Terrie stood out as the only blonde among the Guys, just like me among Brodericks before my brother Tim came along.

While Denise focused her energies on tennis in high school, Terrie developed athleticism in gymnastics and diving. Although naturally close, the twins pursued different paths following their secondary education. Upon graduating, Terrie enrolled at the University of California, Santa Barbara. Gymnastics tugged at her though, so she took something of a sabbatical after a term at UCSB to pursue circus training with the Wenatchee Youth Circus in Wenatchee, Washington, as an extracurricular educational experience:

> In 1952, a Wenatchee junior high school principal asked English teacher and circus aficionado Paul K. Pugh to put together a tumbling team that could entertain crowds during school sporting events. Pugh assembled a troupe that started practicing flips, somersaults, and other tumbling routines. The troupe soon expanded its repertoire to include tightrope walking and trampoline feats. The one-ring show became known as the Wenatchee Youth Circus.

> Within a decade, the Wenatchee Youth Circus was getting coverage in national magazines such as *Life* and the *Saturday Evening Post*, and in 1962, the troupe performed for a week at the Seattle World's Fair. Some of the alumni went on to professional circus careers, performing with Cirque du Soleil, Ringling Bros. and Barnum & Bailey Circus, and the Flying Wallendas.

> Although most of the performers lived in Central Washington, others like Terrie Guy came from neighboring states and even as far away as Australia. The out-of-towners were asked to attend trainings during the school year and then commit to touring with the circus

for several weeks in the summer. They trained after school in the winter and spent the summer months on the road entertaining communities large and small.

Following her summer in Wenatchee, Terrie briefly returned to UCSB before breaking for three months in order to tour Europe with Denise and spend time with the Hoges at their quarters in England. Again, Terrie came back to UCSB for a quarter term before transferring to the University of California, Santa Cruz, while still training with the circus and living in Aptos. She came back to UCSB to finish her senior year where she met her future husband, **Philip "Phil" Jewett Bugay** (b. 1956). Both Terrie and Phil graduated from UCSB with a Bachelor's degree in business economics.

The youngest of three children born in Santa Barbara, Phil was six years old when his parents, Jack and Patty Jewett Bugay, divorced. His mother elected to move the children to England and then Scotland where Phil attended St. Andrews and the historic Edinburgh Academy with roots dating to 1824. While his siblings returned to Santa Barbara for their secondary education, Phil did not make the move until half way through high school. He quickly acclimated, gaining success in rugby, soccer, and football. He then became student body president at Santa Barbara High School in his senior year.

Following her 1980 college graduation, Terrie took a summer job with UCSB's (alumni) Family Vacation Center and then briefly returned home and worked as a waitress. For two months, she traveled in Southeast Asia with her brother David and his friend before returning to Santa Barbara, this time for good.

In 1983, Terrie and Phil married. They raised **Bridgette Gordon** (b. 1987) and **Braden Guy** (b. 1989) in Santa Barbara while Terrie developed her game in tennis. Ten years after her summer stint with UCSB's Family Vacation Center, she returned as program director. Eventually stepping away, she worked with a couple of nonprofits, and she became president of the Parent Teacher Association. Later, she took up bookkeeping, staging houses for sale, and interior decorating. During the most recent four or more years, Terrie has worked as a residential realtor with Keller Williams.

Phil pursued a career in financial services as a portfolio manager with Morgan Stanley Smith Barney beginning in 1981. He earned a Certified Investment Management Analyst credential at the University of Pennsylvania's Wharton School in 2002. After many years, he left Morgan Stanley as a senior vice president to venture out on his own as a financial advisor. As founder of the Bugay Group, Phil dedicated himself to providing investment consulting and management services to institutions and families with a high net worth.

Phil has remained active with the alumni association of his alma mater. When appointed to the University of California Board of Regents as an alumni representative in 2006, UCSB Chancellor Henry T. Yang recognized Phil's financial expertise and spirit for public service. In 1995 and 1996, Phil served as an appointed member of the Santa Barbara City Council and assisted the city government in navigating a fiscal crisis associated with the bankruptcy of Orange County. He then served as a board member and treasurer of the Santa Barbara County Public Finance Corporation. Appointed by Governor Pete Wilson in 1992 and 1996, Phil also served as a board member and president of the State of California's 19th District Agricultural Association. Locally, he became a founding board member and now past president of the Santa Barbara Public Education Foundation.

Much like her auntie Yo and cousin Nancy, Terrie has become a prolific craftswoman. Among her many talents, she is especially adept at shibori, a style of fabric dying derived from Japan. In addition to creating objects from driftwood, bamboo, and seashells, she refurbishes furniture and makes jewelry from their home in Santa Barbara. In retirement, Phil's creative outlet comes in the form of writing stories and poetry when he is not gardening. With a heart for service, he also enjoys preparing and delivering meals each week to a local nonprofit that feeds the vulnerable population.

Gordons (1948–present)

WHILE YO RAISED HER KIDS IN PITTSBURGH and her sister Jinks established her family in sunny Northern California, their brother Larry opted to anchor his crew where the siblings were raised in Duluth. "The North Star State" or "Land of 10,000 Lakes" has earned a reputation for its friendly people, relaxed pace, affordability, and abundant freshwater. Without having set foot in the state before my work took me to Spirit Mountain to lead a ski trip for college students in 1980, I visualized the Gordon homestead as remote and unbearably "cold" with temperatures often dipping below zero Fahrenheit. It had not occurred to me that this upper Midwestern state could be graced with such beauty.

I drove alone to reach my destination from Chicago at night, getting as far as Duluth before parking "Sunshine" on the side of the road for some much-needed rest. Awakened by sunrise an hour or two later, I ventured into the town of my mother's birth with little time and virtually no knowledge of her family's local history.

Absent reference points other than the town itself, I wandered aimlessly observing the topography that distinguishes Duluth—the birthplace of legendary singer-songwriter Bob Dylan. The port city is dominated by a steep hillside that climbs from Lake Superior to high inland elevations reminiscent of San Francisco. Before long, I set off for the ski resort, hugging the shoreline of the greatest of the Great Lakes to reach Spirit Mountain. The glorious scenery took my breath away. The cloudless sky matched the brilliant blue cast from Lake Superior, an imposing body of freshwater noted as the world's largest lake by surface area. Equally dazzling, the fresh-fallen snow mirrored the stark white bark of the spectacular birch trees lining the shore as I inched my way up the gradual incline. The stunning natural beauty rivaled any scene I had taken in ever before. This is "Gordon" country—the territory where, following World War I in 1920, Yolande Hoke and Laurance Gordon staked their future from Bordeaux as a married couple with baby Jinks in tow.

Following family tradition, Larry and Pat raised the Gordon children in the Catholic faith. Living in the far reaches of the upper Midwest a distance of 155 miles from the Canadian border, "GEN 12" siblings Patricia Kirby (1948–2013), Laurance Sterne III (b. 1950), Jeanne Starr

(b. 1952), and Elizabeth Armella (b. 1955) spent many carefree days in their childhood playing on the majestic lakes and in the fluffy snow. Like the Brodericks at Lake Erie and the Guys in Aptos, California, the Gordons found respite at their vacation home in Twig, located 15 miles northwest of their Duluth roots. The respective homes remain in the Broderick, Guy, and Gordon families as of this writing.

Uncle Larry completed the first phase of the complex he built on Twig's Grand Lake when his daughter Pat reached middle school age around 1955. Shortly thereafter, the family moved 160 miles south to Minnetonka in the outskirts of Minneapolis and in close proximity to St. Paul, the Twin City and state capital.

Through the children's high school years, the Gordons spent every summer in Twig from Memorial Day to Labor Day. With the Bell family, close neighbors with seven or eight kids lock-stepped in age with Pat, Larry, Jeanne, and Elizabeth, my cousins created vivid childhood memories. The "GEN 12" Gordons spent every waking hour from sun-up to dinnertime developing independence in the great outdoors while biking, horseback riding, fishing, boating, and playing volleyball and tennis. Their dad organized a large gathering of friends drawn mostly from Duluth every 4th of July, which featured softball and a celebratory fireworks display. Once she was old enough to hold down a summer job in Minneapolis, Jeanne recalls the nearly three-hour drive to Twig with her dad to meet up with the family on weekends. They cemented an especially close bond during that period.

The Gordons, too, favored pets at their homestead. Among the canines, they raised Irish setters, a dalmatian, and a beagle. Elizabeth remembers at least one summer when the family kept three sheep that roamed about the cabin grounds. One of the sheep evidently fell while sleeping on a rock at the lake's edge and drowned. Later, as the season wrapped up and before returning to Minnetonka, the onus fell on my Uncle Larry to get rid of the remaining sheep since he did not consider bringing them back home an option. When one of the children inquired after them, their witty dad informed them that the family had eaten the mutton for supper. No one ever learned if what he actually fed them was a fictitious tale.

TO MY KNOWLEDGE, cousin **Patricia "Pat" Kirby Gordon League** (1948–2013) distinguished herself as the only one of Yolande Hoke Gordon's 19 grandchildren who carried a memory of her. Yolande had met her two oldest grandchildren—Danny Broderick and Dianne Guy—as infants, but Pat alone carried memories given their close proximity in Duluth before Yolande was institutionalized in Council Bluffs, Iowa.

Setting the course for her three siblings, Pat as the oldest of Larry and Pat's children was born in Duluth and attended elementary school in Minnetonka at Immaculate Heart of Mary. She then entered St. Margaret's Academy which the Sisters of St. Joseph of Carondelet founded in Minneapolis in 1907. Pat was bused across town to the all-girls high school she came to love. She continued her studies at Colorado College in Colorado Springs where she began dating her future husband, **Michael "Mike" D. Mallinger** (1950–2010), a St. Paul native and noted hockey player. As a devoted hockey fan herself, my Aunt Pat first made contact with Mike while selling tickets for the summer hockey league in which he played. Cousin Pat and Mike then met while both studied at Colorado College.

Pat earned a Bachelor of Business Administration from Colorado College in 1971, the same year my brother Dennis graduated from Notre Dame. Following Pat and Mike's marriage, they relocated to Milwaukee, Wisconsin, where Mike played hockey professionally with the American Hockey League (AAA) and the East Coast Hockey League (AA). Four years later, the couple returned west to make a permanent home in Colorado Springs. Here, Pat gave birth to **Amanda Therese** (b. 1981). Once Mike retired from hockey, he worked for a local commercial developer finishing out building interiors, principally as a carpet layer. After several years in marriage, Pat and Mike divorced in 1994.

Later, when Pat married **Daniel Noel League** (b. 1936) in 1985, she became a stepmother to his four adult children—Mike, Burt, Brian, and Suzy. An entrepreneur, Dan became successful turning start-ups into profitable businesses. All the while, Pat remained especially close to her father. She worked for many years in public and private accounting, but after she and Dan married, they traveled frequently, and Pat became a community volunteer. She assumed leadership roles with the Colorado

Springs Symphony, the Colorado Springs Fine Arts Center Performing Arts Committee, and her first love, the Cheyenne Mountain Zoo.

Pat became an avid reader, golfer, and dog aficionado. She doted on her Irish setter "Fletcher," golden retriever "Chauncey," and her beloved chocolate brown Newfoundland "Gus." Pat also took to playing classical music on her baby grand piano, and she went out of her way to stay in touch with her Broderick and Guy cousins with whom she maintained a strong bond. Although she fought valiantly, Larry and Pat's firstborn lost a courageous battle to ovarian cancer at age 64. Before my cousin's passing, her daughter Amanda gave birth to two of Pat's three grandchildren in Denver—Davis and Emmett. Those boys sparked priceless joy in their grandmother before Patricia Gordon League finally succumbed to the dreadful disease in 2013.

AMONG MY GUY AND GORDON COUSINS, I know the least about my grandfather and uncle's namesake, **Laurance "Larry" Sterne Gordon III** (b. 1950). Like me on the Broderick side and David among the Guys, Larry III is the only "GEN 12" Gordon without children, and he is the last in our line to carry the Gordon surname.

From his siblings, I learned that Larry III "glowed in the dark" in the sense that he stood out as the one who invariably got caught for the trouble he made. Personally, I could relate to the epic parties he hosted in Minnetonka during his later teenage years while his father spent the summer weekends in Twig. Larry III and his friends did some crazy things in an inebriated state like taking turns spinning in the industrial-sized washing machine. Given his bad luck, the steel tank probably broke with one of them whirling inside it.

Larry III played hockey while attending Hopkins High School in Minnetonka before entering junior college. He quickly determined that college was not for him and somehow managed to avert military service during the Vietnam War without a college deferment. Instead, for a brief period, he worked as a salesman in his father's food brokerage business. My Uncle Larry set a high bar for his only son, but Larry III managed to fall short of those expectations. Within a short period, my cousin separated from his dad's company.

With a friend, Larry III operated a muffler business for two or three years before deciding to create some distance from his parents. He met his first wife, **Judy Oberdorff** (b. 1950), a nurse who practiced in Milwaukee, shortly after going to work for his dad. The couple exchanged wedding vows at the Gordons' summer home in Twig and made a home in Milwaukee within the vicinity of his sister Pat and her husband Mike who then played hockey for the Milwaukee Admirals. Larry III lived under the radar for roughly ten years during which time he had little contact with his parents.

After his marriage fell apart, Larry III relocated to Colorado Springs where Pat's first husband introduced him to some of his business associates in the construction trade. Here, Larry III developed a niche in concrete pumping and married his second wife, **Cindi Prisdorf** (b. 1950). Raised on a farm in Nebraska, Cindi with her husband Larry III established permanent roots in Colorado Springs.

Riddled with rheumatoid arthritis, Larry III retired prematurely due to his disability and now lives with non-Hodgkin's lymphoma. A race car afficionado, he closely follows the excitement of speedway racing, notably NASCAR.

WHAT ARE THE ODDS of siblings Yo and Larry both having leap year babies? There is a 1 in 1,461 chance of having a baby on "Leap Day" given the 1,461 days that pass every four years. Less than .1 percent of the world's population claims a February 29th birthday.

Born on February 29th—eight years before my brother Tim—"leaper" **Jeanne Starr Gordon Dietz** (b. 1952) split her high school years between St. Margaret's Academy and Hopkins High School. Following Larry III's path, she found her niche and graduated from the public school in 1970.

Afterward, Jeanne attended Regis College in Denver, the only Jesuit university in the Rocky Mountains. Majoring in French, as a junior she immersed herself in the language as an exchange student in Dijon, the capital city of the Burgundy region in eastern France. Jeanne lived with a family during her first semester abroad and then moved into an international dorm for the second half of the school year. Following local tradition in which French students were expected to take a second language beginning in first grade, Jeanne found herself sitting in a beginning German class with middle school-aged children while immersing herself in French. It was during this same time that I studied in Paris although our paths did not cross in Europe.

Originally from Waukegan, Illinois, Jeanne's future husband **Timothy "Tim" Victor Dietz** (b. 1952) transferred to Regis College from Quincy College in Illinois at the start of his junior year while Jeanne studied in France. Upon returning from her year-long studies abroad, Jeanne met Tim, who by then had established mutual relationships with Jeanne's friends. During their senior year, Tim interned with KUSA's 9NEWS Team in Denver and then accepted a position with KUSA's farm station in Phoenix, Arizona, upon graduating in 1974. Jeanne joined him there a month later.

As Jeanne pushed to move back to Denver, Tim received the reassignment he requested after spending 3-1/2 years in Phoenix. In Denver, Jeanne worked briefly with a real estate management company and obtained a real estate license to handle real estate closings. With her credential, Coors Brewing Company recruited her to work in the company's real estate department. Eventually transitioning to human resources, Jeanne advanced at Coors to become the director of Human Resources in the sales division. She remained with the company for 25 years.

Jeanne and Tim married in 1978 and raised three children in Golden, Colorado—**Heather Starr** (b. 1985), **Tyler Justin** (b. 1987), and **Bridget Chelsea** (b. 1991).

While Jeanne oversaw the brewery's sales personnel, her husband Tim developed fame in the broadcasting industry where he spent his entire working career. Before retiring early in 2021, he had become something of a legend with Denver's 9NEWS Team (KUSA Channel 9). Tim worked at the station for 48 years, first as a college intern, and then as a news photographer. His tenure ended with oversight of the television station's interactive services. From film to video tape; analog to digital; broadcast to online; desktop to mobile, Tim held a front row seat in witness to the technological revolution in news, entertainment, and sports programming.

The National Academy of Television Arts & Sciences acknowledged Tim's extraordinary contributions to the industry as a 2016 inductee:

> "Tim [Dietz] has done it all. He has met five U.S. Presidents and countless star athletes and celebrities. He met Pope John Paul II during World Youth Day in Colorado in 1993. KUSA's coverage of that historic event garnered national attention. He has been to four Super Bowls and is the Denver Broncos's programming guru. Beginning with the Summer Olympics in Atlanta in 1996, Tim has covered nine Olympic Games by organizing coverage for 9NEWS and Gannett (now TEGNA) in Sydney (2000), Salt Lake City (2002), Athens (2004), Torino (2006), Beijing (2008), Vancouver (2010), London (2012), and Sochi (2014). [He also covered Rio de Janeiro in 2016.] Tim's commitment . . . is largely responsible for the extraordinary level of coverage viewers in Colorado have come to expect."

Tim found himself at the forefront of the technological advances that propelled broadcast media to modern standards. The National Academy lauded him as a champion for launching 9NEWS.com in the mid-1990s. Twenty years later the state's local news and information platform delivered as many as 50 million monthly online impressions. Tim also helped to pioneer high-definition television in the early 2000s by placing the first Helicopter Director (HD) in the air to accelerate coverage of breaking news stories.

Jeanne is a breast cancer survivor and lives her life to the fullest. With Tim's retirement, she scaled back her work with A Small Business Solution, Inc., a full-service accounting and tax preparation firm with whom she worked part-time from her home. With Tim, Jeanne still lives in Golden. She enjoys reading, leisurely travel, and family time with four grandchildren, all of whom live in the greater Denver area.

THE YOUNGEST OF LARRY AND PAT'S FOUR children, **Elizabeth Armella Gordon Ramstad** (b. 1955) miraculously survived infancy as a preemie weighing just 1-1/2 pounds at birth. With understandable worry, my aunt and uncle doted over their little girl and gave her an extra dose of support that carried her along the way. My siblings and I knew of our cousin as "Little Bits."

Elizabeth followed her siblings at Immaculate Heart of Mary School before transferring to Glen Lake Elementary in 4th grade. She then entered West Junior High for 7th and 8th grades, and after, St. Margaret's Academy. Upon graduating, Elizabeth worked briefly with her father doing secretarial work at his company. She enrolled at the University of Minnesota in Minneapolis but after two or three years, she opted to pull out without graduating. Attempting to find her place, Elizabeth hopped between jobs in data entry and computer programming before establishing herself as a front desk elementary school clerk with Minnetonka's Hopkins school district where she worked for 26 years before retiring in 2020.

In 1980, at a bar following a Gopher Hockey game, Elizabeth met her future husband, **Robbin "Robb" Charles Ramstad** (b. 1950). Robb had completed cabinet-making coursework at a junior college and was then operating his own business as a "jack of all trades" handyman. Sometime after the couple married and completed their family with the births of **Kirby Lee** (b. 1986) and **Kelli Cristin** (b. 1988), Robb took an eight-year leave from his own business to work for his brother Clifford John "CJ" Ramstad who gained fame as a snowmobiling legend:

> CJ Ramstad launched his career in snowmobiling in 1969 while writing snowmobile advertisements for an ad agency. He began taking pictures and writing articles before founding his own magazine, publishing books, and becoming editor of *Snowmobiling Magazine* and then co-publisher of *Supertrax*. In 1991, while trail riding with fellow snowmobile enthusiasts, CJ and his friends founded the Saint Germain, Wisconsin-based nonprofit, Snowmobile Hall of Fame and Museum. Later, he became involved in sponsoring races and established trails that doubled for snowmobiles and all-terrain vehicles (ATVs) with the change of the seasons.

Up until 2007, Robb worked for his brother selling advertising, packaging group travel deals, following snowmobile and ATV races, leading trail rides, and writing stories. In that year, CJ and his 17-year-old son, John Jacob "JJ" Ramstad, died in a tragic car accident. As a memorial to Robb's brother, the Minnesota Department of Natural Resources manages the C.J. Ramstad/North Shore State Trail, a 146-mile-long multi-purpose, natural surface trail from Duluth to Grand Marais in northeastern Minnesota. The trail winds its way through the forests on the ridgeline overlooking Lake Superior, providing access to what many consider some of the most rugged and beautiful scenery in the state. In winter, the trail connects with hundreds of miles of snowmobile club trails linking many communities in the area.

Upon leaving the employ of C.J., Robb resumed his handyman and painting contracting business and retired in 2010. Referred to as "Bitz" by her husband and friends, Elizabeth and Robb did a lot of camping while raising their girls. They enjoy the outdoors, gardening, and watching sports although as Minnesotans, they are naturally partial to hockey.

Having raised their two children on the top floor of Larry and Pat's homestead in Minnetonka, Elizabeth and Robb assumed ownership of the home and the "Red Cabin Inn" in Twig upon the passing of the Gordons' mother, Pat, in 2018.

I WONDER WHAT THE FUTURE HOLDS for us "GEN 12" Westcott descendants as we approach our sunset years in official "senior" territory. The period that places us into our 80s is fast-approaching. Yes—time is running its course. But we have decades of hopes and dreams and joy-filled days still ahead of us.

Now looking back at the notable histories among my siblings, first cousins, and me, an inflection point is revealed in the waning influence of God's presence in our daily lives. Tracing 400+ years since the birth of the immigrant Richard Westcott in 1566, I detect in "GEN 12" descendants a perceptible crack in our acceptance of God's full armor. Regardless of denomination, an abiding faith guided Westcott forebears in every generation before ours. Placing their trust in God, our ancestors in America put their fears aside to worship as an assembly of believers. Truth, righteousness, faith, salvation, the Word of God, and prayer gave meaning to life across centuries of Americans. In our lifetimes though, it appears that we have loosened our grip on Christian doctrine coinciding with the erosion of our trust in authority at large. Challenges to organized religion, generally tied to moral beliefs, power, money, politics, exclusivity, and emerging clergy sexual abuse scandals, unfortunately keep increasing numbers at bay.

If I could make it happen for the generations that follow "GEN 12," I would reignite the flame of faith that yields abundant hope and gratitude. I would also ensure that Westcott descendants heed the words of our Grandpa Gordon who implored his three children Jinks, Yo, and Larry to do the right thing: "Come hell or high water, knit your families closer and closer together and if ever one needs help, the Gordon clan sticks together."

The endearing sentiment evokes images of my nieces and nephews whom my brothers and sisters raised to value a strong family connection. My trust lies in the "GEN 13" trailblazers among us who have every opportunity to set the same standard with their own children by example.

GENERATION 13 – 1970–2024

*Technology Fuels a Paradigm Shift in Lifestyles
Among Emerging Dual-Income Families*

———————————

The Children of My Siblings and First Cousins

Brodericks
Guys
Gordons

BY THE NUMBERS, my "GEN 10" maternal grandparents Laurance Sterne and Yolande Hoke Gordon had three children ("GEN 11") who produced for them 19 grandchildren ("GEN 12"), 41 great-grandchildren ("GEN 13"), and 49 great-great-grandchildren ("GEN 14")—as of this writing. The combined 41 children of my siblings and first cousins are identified below:

"GEN 13" Westcott Descendants

BRODERICKS

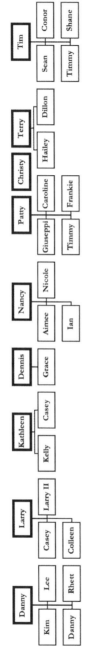

GUYS

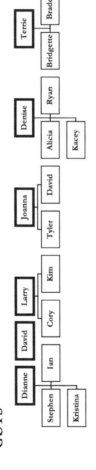

GORDONS

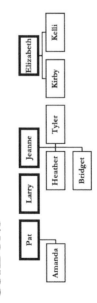

"GEN 13" Westcott descendants emerged during a contentious period in American history. As referenced earlier, into the 1970s, a fragile nation struggled with high inflation and unemployment and a crippling energy crisis. With this backdrop, as the nation began the transition from manufacturing to a service-based economy, a liberal movement fueled by the parents of "GEN 13" questioned the societal costs of America's affluence.

Launched by President Lyndon B. Johnson, reforms of the 1960s meant to alleviate poverty and promote economic vitality stalled as a national discussion continued on how best to institutionalize and extend the gains of the Civil Rights movement led by Martin Luther King, Jr. At the same time, Americans started to question attitudes about sexuality, marriage, and the traditional family unit as they debated policy initiatives on abortion, gender equality, gay rights, and the reach of government into our personal lives. While a contingent pushed for greater individual freedoms, others warned of declining moral standards. All the while, the lasting impacts of the protracted Vietnam War and the Watergate scandal saddled a dispirited and increasingly distrustful nation.

Present day socio-political strife might lead one to think that little has changed. But fifty years ago, the counterculture movement emerged in sharp contrast to mainstream society. Today, the lines appear relatively blurred. As well, we see in "GEN 13" a convergence on the equity scale as young girls gained advances to catch up with boys in educational activities including sports.

On the heels of Title VII of the Civil Rights Act of 1964 that offered protections for women in the workplace, the enactment of Title IX in 1972 granted equal opportunity in education: "No person in the United States shall, on the basis of sex, be excluded from participation in, be denied the benefits of, or be subjected to discrimination under any education program or activity receiving Federal financial assistance." Although the federal legislation did not explicitly address athletics, the females among our "GEN 13" relatives clearly benefited from the equal opportunities afforded them in sports. On the playing field, many of Jinks and Doug's granddaughters in particular took full advantage of the equal rights conferred by the act of Congress one half-century ago.

Along with the political upheaval and profound changes in societal norms, the era into which this next generation was born introduced disco dance music, quirky fads, and new fashion choices. Bell bottom pants, flowing ankle-length dresses, plaid fabrics, ponchos, frayed jeans, and long hair dominated 1970s fads—a far cry from the vogue of the stylish "Roaring 1920s." As the decade progressed, handicrafts like tie-dye, decoupage, and macramé became popular, yoga and meditation gained traction, and young people used their hard-fought freedom to simply do as they pleased: to wear what they wanted, to grow their hair long, to have premarital sex, and to do drugs. The children of my siblings and first cousins came into this intensely liberated world with observant eyes wide open.

My nieces, nephews, and first cousins once removed grew up with dual-income parents who struggled to balance work and home life as the norm. Recalling their own formative years in the presence of stay-at-home mothers, many "GEN 12" parents managed their guilt by overcompensating for the time cut short with their children. A level of anxiety naturally seeped into many families as a result.

"GEN 13" Americans witnessed the breakup of marriages at an unprecedented rate, partly reflecting the change in expectations as their mothers entered the workforce. Divorce in the U.S. more than doubled in the 1960–1980 period before reversing course—50% of first marriages ended in divorce at the peak in 1980 versus 40% today. A dramatic shift, roughly half of the children born to married parents in the 1970s saw their parents part ways compared to just 11% of those born in the 1950s. Among the Brodericks, 74% of my nieces and nephews—17 of 23—experienced the dissonance that comes from navigating as children in families of divorce.

As they transitioned into the workplace themselves, "GEN 13" Westcott descendants were the first among all generations heretofore to gain comfort with technology early in their careers. Their young offspring are the beneficiaries of the gains they made with increasing proficiency in machine learning and data processing. The ensuing proliferation of tech-oriented companies has presented job opportunities of a kind we could not begin to imagine a generation ago.

Presumably motivated by a desire to find fulfillment and a better work-life balance, young workers—notably the so-called "Millennials" and "Gen Y"—are prone to switch jobs and careers frequently as reflected in the anecdotes that follow. This trend clearly escaped their working grandparents, many of whom benefitted from lucrative pensions as a reward for longevity, and to a lesser extent their "GEN 12" parents who enjoyed relative job stability.

While nurturing families of their own, this generation seems committed to giving their children every conceivable advantage. Although inadvertent, the trend toward shielding their sons and daughters with a cautious, protective veil strips the youngest among us of the freedom at play that dominated "GEN 12" in our formative years. Yet those who fall into this next generation prevail as impassioned people with steadfast purpose and determination to make their mark, which is emblematic of the Westcott pedigree throughout the ages. I am immensely proud of them for their successes as devoted parents, as diligent students with a quest for learning, and as contributors to the greater good of our extended family and the communities they serve in their work and free time.

In providing context for my nieces, nephews, and first cousins once removed, I have opted to group them with their siblings, as applicable, ordered sequentially in tandem with the birth order of their "GEN 12" parents—first the Brodericks, followed by the Guys, and lastly the Gordons.

Brodericks (1970–present)

THE TWENTY-THREE "GEN 13" Brodericks span more than three decades in age—32 years separate Danny's daughter Kim from Terry's son Dillon. Kim's two daughters and two of Nancy's "GEN 14" granddaughters came before Dillon's birth in 2002.

Like her father who led the "GEN 12" Westcott pack, **Kimberly "Kim" Curtin Broderick Piggins** (b. 1970) came first among the 41 "GEN 13" Westcott descendants. She is the oldest of Dan and Betty's four children, all of whom were born and raised in La Jolla, California, and attended Francis Parker School. Kim studied at the University of Arizona in Tucson when her father and stepmother were slain. Pulling out of school to deal with unimaginable anguish, she quickly stepped into the role of matriarch. In part, this meant buffering her family while fending off the unscrupulous press and "entertainment" moguls with their insatiable appetite for "the story." The detrimental intrusion into her family's private life—protected as the "freedom of the press" by the First Amendment to the U.S. Constitution—has continued unabated for more than thirty years.

Kim prevailed in spite of the challenging circumstances she and her siblings faced. Amidst the unwelcome distractions, she attended the University of Colorado in Boulder before graduating from the University of Southern California with a Bachelor's degree in psychology and education studies.

At Merryvale Vineyards in Napa Valley in 1997, Kim married **Jonathan "Jon" David Piggins** (b. 1970) of Racine, Wisconsin. As family and the wedding party gathered for the rehearsal dinner, news broke of the imminent death of the beloved Diana Spencer (1961–1997), Princess of Wales, who suffered fatal injuries in a car accident in Paris, France:

> Traveling at a high speed with her partner, Egyptian billionaire Emad "Dodi" Fayed, and her bodyguard, Trevor Rees-Jones, to evade a paparazzi pursuit, their driver crashed into a wall in the Pont de l'Alma tunnel, killing him and Fayed instantly. At age 36, Diana succumbed to her injuries within hours, leaving behind sons Prince William and Prince Harry at ages 15 and 12, respectively.

Kim and Jon hosted an unforgettable weekend in spite of the heart-wrenching broadcast of Princess Diana's untimely death which gripped the wedding guests and the world over.

Kim went on to pursue a career in early childhood education. She assumed roles as a pre-K and kindergarten teacher and administrator at the Baldwin Academy and Francis Parker School in San Diego, the latter where she and her siblings had once been enrolled as students.

Kendall Curtin (b. 1998) and **Madison "Maddie" Ireland** (b. 2001) were born and raised for a time in San Diego before Jon and Kim's divorce. When the cost of living in San Diego became unsustainable, in 2009, Kim, Kendall, and Maddie relocated to Hailey, Idaho. The terrain was familiar, since Kim and her siblings as youngsters had joined their parents to ski and snowboard at nearby Sun Valley.

Within two years of the move, Kim accepted the position of Director of Big Wood School, a preschool located at the Presbyterian Church of the Big Wood in nearby Ketchum. The matriarch shares unbridled enthusiasm in devotion to her family, her colleagues, and the children she feels privileged to serve. Never one to sit still, Kim remains passionate about travel and having fun with her extended family and her wide circle of loyal friends. She stays physically fit walking and running, and spiritually uplifted during her regular hikes trailing the wildflower-filled meadows with panoramic mountain views.

Early in life, Kim's spunky sister **Lee Gordon Broderick** (b. 1971) showed great athleticism in gymnastics with her cartwheels, forward and backward rolls, handstands, and back bends. She demonstrated balance, flexibility, and agility like none other. Like many teenagers, she outgrew the sport and some of her mettle during her adolescence. Struggling to forge ahead, Lee instead spent every opportunity hanging out at the magnificent La Jolla beach.

Known by some as "Kathy," Lee took somewhat of a rebellious stance as she challenged the status quo and gravitated toward similarly vulnerable peers into adulthood. Following a restive period, Lee earned a dental hygiene certificate from the Concord Career College before joining a pediatric dental practice in San Diego. In time, she opted to leave the field and then worked at a deli in La Jolla. The high cost of living forced Lee, too, from her hometown. In recent years, she moved and worked for a similar establishment in Hailey, Idaho, before an injury sidelined her. Lee now lives in relative seclusion in the heart of the Wood River Valley amidst the majestic Central Idaho Rockies and a stone's throw from her siblings Kim and Rhett.

Following the sudden death of their father and stepmother, Kim and Lee's brothers Danny and Rhett lived briefly in Denver with their aunt Kathy and cousins Casey, Larry II, and Colleen around the time my brother Larry and Kathy separated. Clamoring to return "home," when he turned 16, **Daniel "Danny" Thomas Broderick IV** (b. 1976) finished out high school in San Diego while living with Kim. A model of hope and perseverance overcoming personal tragedy, Danny graduated from La Jolla High School as a Presidential Academic Scholar in the class of 1994.

DTB IV carries many of his father's enviable traits that endear him to Kim especially but also to his extended family, colleagues, and a passel of life-long friends. Danny entered Stanford University in Palo Alto, earning a Bachelor's degree in economics and psychology. A La Jolla commercial real estate professional since graduating, he worked in office leasing and sales as a senior associate with Burnham Real Estate Services and served as senior vice president in the equity sales division of Eastdil Secured. He also became president and CEO of Cassidy Turley BRE Commercial before assuming progressive leadership roles with Cushman & Wakefield. From president of Cushman & Wakefield's Americas West region covering the Western U.S., Canada, and Latin America, he now serves as president of the firm's Americas Advisory. In this capacity, he oversees the delivery of brokerage and transaction services for all product types across markets in North and South America. Following my brother Larry's lead, several years ago Danny became a member of the prestigious Young Presidents' Organization (YPO).

In an email post to our family in 2009, Danny announced his engagement to San Diego native **Megan Emily Cooper** (b. 1979) with this introduction:

> *She is smart, sweet, athletic, fun, beautiful, cultured, and she has a wonderful family . . . She is an incredible singer, she's run 10 marathons (we ran her 10th together), she lived in Paris, she's traveled the world, she gives back to society, she lived in NYC for 4 years working for NBC and Ellen DeGeneres (her current employer). She now lives in LA. We see each other every weekend, and have done more together than you would believe in a relatively short time—skydiving, skiing, races, weddings galore, multiple east coast trips, Napa, Vegas. What recession?!?!?*

Danny proposed at the Stein Eriksen Lodge in Deer Valley, Utah, on New Year's Eve. He popped the question on a one-horse open sleigh while overlooking a valley of Christmas lights. Megan's family surprised her at dinner that evening, and Kim, Kendall, and Maddie were present too. Danny went so far as to arrange for fireworks outside the lodge at midnight—the very definition of a thoughtful guy and a romantic!

Danny and Megan crossed paths long before they reconnected via Facebook when she still lived in Los Angeles. Their fathers, both with medical degrees, had known each other professionally; their mothers participated in a finance club together; and Kim babysat Megan and her brother, Tyler, as children. Danny lured Megan back to San Diego where they married in 2009 and now have three daughters—**Molly Cooper** (b. 2011), **Brynn Morgan** (b. 2012), and **Sawyer Kimberly** (b. 2015). Megan earned a Bachelor's degree in communications from Wake Forest University and after the couple married, she received a Master's in marital and family therapy from the University of San Diego. She works as a licensed marriage and family therapist and the director of counseling at The Bishop's School—grades 6 through 12—where she went to school herself. Fitness enthusiasts, Danny and Megan maintain their wellbeing with an exercise regimen that for many years placed long-distance running, including marathons, front and center.

A sweetheart born on Valentine's Day, **Rhett Terrence Broderick** (b. 1979) became an orphan at age ten. Unlike Danny, his older brother by three years, Rhett moved often once uprooted from San Diego. When after two years Danny returned to their birthplace from Denver, Rhett proceeded to live with his maternal uncle and his family in St. Louis, Missouri, and then Phoenix, Arizona. Having survived extreme therapeutic wilderness and boarding school experiences, Rhett spent his last 1-1/2 high school years as a boarding student at the esteemed Wilbraham Monson Academy in the outskirts of Springfield, Massachusetts. Energetic and highly spirited, Rhett was honored to represent his classmates as their designated senior class speaker at the commencement ceremony.

Attending the University of California, Berkeley, Rhett graduated with a Bachelor's degree in economic geography and a passion to both travel and teach. In 2000, he bought a home at Echo Summit on the southern shore of Lake Tahoe, living there for three years then maintaining the property as a rental before selling it in 2018.

Before venturing into the workforce in earnest, Rhett took off on an around-the-world excursion with his future wife **Veronica Ashleigh**

Noffke (b. 1981) of Ann Arbor, Michigan, whom he met at a bar in Oakland shortly before his departure. In 2007, Rhett began his high school teaching career at Dunn School in Los Olivos outside Santa Barbara, California, where he taught world history. The couple married at Ambergris Caye in Belize in 2011 before making a move to Bend, Oregon, two years later. Here, they bought a home and Rhett earned a Master's in education at Oregon State University with high hopes of securing a teaching position locally.

Stiff competition forced the couple out of their beloved Bend, however, leading them to the greater Los Angeles area where Rhett taught Humanities and Advanced Placement (AP) Human Geography at Vistamar School in El Segundo. At the same time, while living in Manhattan Beach south of Los Angeles, Veronica earned a Master's degree in literacy and language arts from Loyola Marymount; her Bachelor's in apparel and merchandising came from Indiana University in Bloomington.

The exorbitant housing costs in Los Angeles prompted yet another move, but not before the birth of Rhett and Veronica's daughter **Naomi Valentine** (b. 2014), nicknamed "Mimi." The young family followed Kim and her girls when they relocated to Hailey, Idaho, where **Harper Rose** was born (b. 2017). Rhett is secure teaching English and Social Studies at Wood River High School in Hailey while Veronica teaches kindergarteners at Ernest Hemingway Steam School in nearby Ketchum. Like Kim and Danny, Rhett is extremely active, invariably entertaining, and always up for an adventure. He loves the great outdoors and the opportunity to ski, snowboard, and hike in his own backyard.

With their combined seven daughters spread 18 years apart and bonded like sisters, Kim, Danny, and Rhett spend a great deal of time together as one big happy family. Lee has opted to stay somewhat reclusive, but the proximity in Hailey enables her to engage with the lively brood.

LARRY AND KATHY RAISED three children in Denver, Colorado, before and after their divorce around 1990. The three, as well as Danny and Rhett during the two years they lived with the family, attended Kent Denver School in Cherry Hills Village. Tracing its founding to 1922, in 1974, the middle and high schools combined Kent School for Girls and the all-boys high school, Denver Country Day School. Casey, Brodie, and Colleen entered as 6th graders and graduated as high school seniors from the non-sectarian private school. Larry and Kathy sold their lakeside home in Madison, Ohio, when Colleen was two or three years old. Until then, the family spent many summers at Lake Erie, which occasioned the close bond my mother "Grinny" developed with the Denver-based family.

Casey O'Meara Broderick Prate (b. 1975) arrived in Montrose the day before I pulled stakes and headed to the East coast following a brief stint as office clerk in Larry's business. As I recall, Kathy was in labor only briefly. The hospital staff scrambled to make preparations for the rapid delivery. In later years, Casey and her brother Brodie attended St. Mary's Academy in Englewood through 5th grade. As a youngster, Casey became adept at snow skiing. By age 12, she took to the black slopes with ease. Thanks in part to her father's customary delegation of tasks, Casey also learned to solve problems and gained independence at a very early age.

Larry so wanted Casey to attend Notre Dame. During a home football game attended by many in the extended family, he arranged for a private plane to fly over the stadium with a banner that read: "Casey, Notre Dame wants YOU!" I knew nothing about his scheme when I observed the flyover firsthand, but I rightfully suspected Larry was behind it.

Although she was accepted at Notre Dame, Casey did not cave to the pressure. She graduated with a Bachelor of Science in mechanical engineering from Stanford University—in the same class as her cousin Danny. She then bought a condominium unit and lived in Washington, D.C., before transferring to Paris, France, as a consultant with Booz Allen Hamilton. In the "City of Lights," Casey became fluent in French and around 2005, she met her future husband, **Thierry Michel Yves Prate** (b. 1973). A native of Lausanne, Switzerland, Thierry developed a consultancy that came from earning a Bachelor's in economics and statistics and a Master's in economics and finance from the Université de Montpellier in southern France. Originally from Clermont-Ferrand, France, his father and his family moved to the capital city of Algeria in Al-giers when World War II broke out; they then relocated to Paris.

Casey and Thierry both worked at Booz Allen Hamilton at the time of their epic dual-wedding celebrations in Provence, France, in 2009.

Enthralled by the impressionistic imagery that once drew Vincent Van Gogh, Paul Cézanne, and Pablo Picasso to the region, the bride and groom prepared a week-long itinerary to the sheer delight of Casey's large extended family—notably the "GEN 12" Brodericks and Schmitts with nine kids each who grew up together in Pittsburgh.

Within a year of their nuptials, Thierry and Casey gave birth to **Tristan Wescott** (b. 2010) in Paris. The young family then relocated to Casey's hometown of Denver where Tristan's brother **Remi Archard** (b. 2012) was born. Tristan and Remi's older half-brother **Thomas Anthony Daniel Prate** (b. 2003) made regular visits to Denver from Southwick in southeast England where he grew up following his parents' divorce. Born in Bedford, England, Thomas charms his extended American family with humor, a sweet disposition, and a proper British accent. Thomas attended Shoreham College, an independent day school founded in 1852 for boys and girls aged 3 to 16. A current student at the University of South Wales in Cardiff, he changed his major from wildlife biology to environmental consulting and expects to graduate in 2025.

For a time, Casey worked in her father's company at Acme Manufacturing as vice president of strategy and analytics and president of the All American Threaded Products division that manufactures and distributes steel threaded rods, studs, anchor and u bolts, fasteners, and custom bent products. She then acquired a business and now owns and operates Denver-based Armani Fine Woodworking, maker of custom wood countertops. Thierry has developed a career advising clients from the public and private sectors on strategic issues related to infrastructure and transportation. In his role as managing director of KPMG's Infrastructure Deal Advisory Practice and Global Head of Rail, Thierry led a team advising the California High-Speed Rail Authority. Among his notable achievements, he was instrumental in developing strategic delivery options for the initial high-speed rail line segment connecting Silicon Valley and the Central Valley. The ongoing construction now spans more than 115 miles across five counties.

In the middle among Larry and Kathy's three children, **Laurance Gordon "Brodie" Broderick II** (b. 1978) falls closest in age to Dan's son Rhett among his Broderick cousins. While he worked toward receiving a

Bachelor of Business Administration from the University of San Diego, Brodie spent a brief period of time living with his uncle Terry and his family.

Perhaps inspired by his mother, Kathy, who remains a fabulous cook, Brodie set his sights on restaurant operations. He worked from the ground up, initially with eateries in Chicago and then as a deckhand on private yachts in South Florida with one route extending into northern Alabama. Returning to Colorado, Brodie pursued his lifelong dream. In 2015, he established a classic French brasserie-style restaurant in picturesque Vail, in every way reminiscent of a traditional Parisian café. With stiff competition, Brodie initially differentiated "Vintage" by offering brunch. He has since created a vibrant indoor / outdoor scene featuring a "champagne brunch + cocktails + dinner + wine lounge." The restaurant is lauded for its sweet and savory menu and ambient European charm.

In 2018, Brodie married **Jose Pablo "JP" Alvarez Franco** (b. 1991) in Las Vegas. A native of Mexico, JP was born in Torreon, Coahuila. His family first moved to Juarez and a couple of years later, to Saltillo, Mexico, where he spent most of his life before coming to America. JP studied hospitality and is now similarly occupied in the restaurant operations trade.

As the youngest child, **Colleen Dillon Broderick** (b. 1986) became the apple of her father's eye. Diverging from her siblings, she attended the public Cottonwood Creek Elementary School before joining Casey and Brodie at Kent Denver School as a 6th grader. Perhaps in part owing to her parents' separation when Colleen was two-years-old, she gravitated to her teachers more than her peers to cultivate relationships. The greatest influence, though, came from her beloved "Nanna," a first-generation Irish American who moved into the house where Kathy and the children lived when Colleen turned age 7. Nanna ran the car pool, cooked dinners, did the laundry, and hung out with "Col-d-dol" a great deal of time during Colleen's formative years. Nanna remained in the home until after Colleen headed off to college. The two maintained especially close ties before Nanna's passing at age 93.

At Kent Denver School, Colleen got into diving, lacrosse, and volleyball, and she engaged in clubs oriented around social issues like human rights, gay rights, and racial justice. Academically, Colleen thrived in literary studies, especially writing. Between her junior and senior high school years, she completed a service project in the Dominican Republic where she became smitten with a young "local." The love interest forced her out of the program before its conclusion. The draw pulled Colleen back to the Caribbean nation on more than one occasion to visit the Dominicans with whom she became especially close.

Colleen's choice of Kenyon College in Gambier, Ohio, was motivated by the reputation of the school's English Language and Literature program. Known as "The Writers' College," the small, liberal arts school dates to 1824. [Notable graduates of Kenyon College include poet Robert Lowell and novelists E.L. Doctorow and William Glass, as well as actor Paul Newman and Rutherford B. Hayes, the 19th President of the United States.] Regrettably for Colleen, she had a bad experience in her first English class and opted to change majors. Instead, she earned a Bachelor of Arts in Spanish literature. Colleen continued to leap and spring into the pool as a diver through her second year in college. Perhaps owing to the fact that she did not drink or party, she developed relatively few friends, and she felt that she didn't fit it. She made plans to pull out as a second semester sophomore, but she had an epiphany shortly before enrolling in a summer program in Barcelona. No longer resisting upon her return, Colleen gave into what she came to love about Kenyon and made a last-minute decision to stay put for the duration.

Following graduation, Colleen spent two months traveling in Southeast Asia with her closest friend Sarah whom she met in Barcelona. Returning stateside, she moved to Chicago where Brodie then lived. For nearly three years, she bartended, waitressed, and worked briefly with a telecommunications company, but the mountains called her back home. Living a happier and healthier lifestyle back in Denver, Colleen completed a Power Teacher Training Program in 2011 and loved all she learned about yoga. A year later, she became the studio manager of One Yoga, launched with the financial backing of Denver Nuggets basketball coach George Karl to support both cancer patients with yoga therapy and the general populace with yoga workouts.

In 2015, Colleen took off once again, initially in her recreational vehicle to visit family and friends across the country over the span of eight months, then to Malalane, South Africa, where she courted a romance. Into her five-year residency in the farming community, Colleen taught yoga and worked part-time in the office of the farm where the yoga classes were held. Returning solo to her happy place in Denver where the wide-open spaces and nature feed her soul, Colleen now works for her father at Acme Manufacturing. She is quite content to be home, within reach of the majestic mountains and amongst family members—this time likely for good, although the travel bug will never leave her. With her boy-friend, Christopher Warren Jackson, Colleen purchased her first home in the foothills of Denver in 2024. She has developed an especially close bond with Tim and Ann's four sons, and with Christopher she enjoys skiing, hiking, and keeping up with Moose and Pickle, the dachshunds she acquired while a resident in South Africa.

KATHLEEN AND HER FIRST HUSBAND DENNIS raised their daughter and son in both Cleveland and Seattle. The children were four and two years old when the family made their first move from Cleveland to Seattle. Four years later, in 1991, they returned to Cleveland. Then, when the kids reached ages 11 and 9, the family made a permanent move back to Seattle. Here, Kelly and Casey attended Belleview High School. Sometime after Kelly and Casey's parents separated ways, their father returned to Cleveland where he was born and raised and where he passed away in 2023. Their mother and stepfather live a short distance from Seattle in Tacoma, Washington.

The Irish lass and social butterfly **Kelly Broderick McCormack** (b. 1983) came two days shy of St. Patrick's Day. She gave soccer a whirl as a youngster and joined the swimming team at Belleview High School, but like her mother and her aunts Patty and Christy, she didn't find her calling in competitive sports. When she came of age, Kelly spent every opportunity working at Starbucks as a barista during school breaks. Currently boasting 33,000+ coffeehouses worldwide, in 1991, Starbucks got its start a stone's throw away from the McCormacks' home at the Pike Place Market in downtown Seattle, when Kelly was eight years old.

Concentrating in marketing and management, Kelly earned a Bachelor of Business Administration from the University of Montana in Missoula. Following graduation, she returned to Starbucks in Seattle, this time finding employment at corporate headquarters. She served as a customer account analyst when Starbucks and Nestlé signed a global licensing deal that granted Nestlé perpetual rights to market Starbucks packaged coffee and food service products globally in 2018. As a result of the alliance, Nestlé absorbed the division in which Kelly had worked. As a Nestlé employee, Kelly found herself maneuvering the supply chain tangle precipitated by labor and transportation shortages. Shipping bottlenecks stymied the delivery of product inventory to retailers' shelves at the onset and throughout the protracted COVID-19 pandemic beginning in 2020.

To alleviate the stress and to adjust to remote working conditions occasioned by the coronavirus outbreak, Kelly set up a Peloton in the workroom of her Madison Park apartment. With two half-marathons under her belt, she also competes in group fitness challenges and a micro-diet regimen to stay fit. In mid-2023, having worked remotely for roughly three years, Kelly was called back into the office to work onsite three days each week.

Before returning to the office, Kelly took the plunge and acquired a two-year-old terrier mix rescue pup born in Mexico whom she named "Finn" in homage to her Irish heritage. As she dotes on her bosom buddy, Kelly is also fiercely loyal to her family and friends. She seeded many of her closest friendships in Montana and stays in regular contact with them. Although she is not typically front and center as the revelry plays out at Broderick family reunions, Kelly can be found with the others in the thick of the partying. She enjoys the camaraderie with her cousins perhaps more than the others due to the physical distance that enables only periodic get-togethers.

Trailing Kelly by two years, **Casey Gordon McCormack** (b. 1985) weighed just 3 pounds–15 ounces at birth. Outgrowing "preemie" status, he gained strength playing hockey as a child and football as a high school freshman before latching onto lacrosse. He continued playing lacrosse at the University of Montana in Missoula where he studied for two years.

Casey turned 16 when his parents divorced. Following his high school graduation, Casey's mother remarried and then moved to Pullman, and afterward to Olympia, Washington. With his dad then living out-of-state, Casey became something of a rootless wanderer. Kathleen's husband,

Dave, somehow learned about and put him onto a possible opening at a boys' camp in the Berkshires that materialized into a position Casey filled. He spent the next five summers at Camp Mah-Kee-Nac in Lenox, Massachusetts, where he coached the youth in lacrosse.

Casey met his future bride **Elisha Paige Smith** (b. 1987) during his fifth and final summer at the camp. With a friend, Elisha arrived from her hometown of Perth, Australia, and worked as an office clerk at the camp that summer. Elisha had secured a visa to work in Canada and planned to move there for a year when the two met. Casey decided to go along for the ride.

The couple lived for a year in Whistler, a municipality in British Columbia. Casey worked at a restaurant bar, and Elisha as a hotel receptionist before they pulled stakes yet again. They spent a year holding similar positions in Elisha's hometown of Perth, and another year in Wellington and Queenstown, New Zealand, before settling stateside in Seattle. After a stint bartending at the popular Palisades, Casey found his stride as a craft brewer at Freemont Brewery while Elisha managed the office of a Seattle-based architectural firm. The couple together ran a marathon in Seattle, and independently, Casey ran his second in Portland, Oregon; Elisha ran her second in San Diego.

In 2016, Casey and Elisha married at Geographe Bay in Dunsborough, Australia, 150 miles south of Elisha's hometown of Perth. Casey's mother and sister, Kathleen and Kelly, flew the arduous 9,000+ mile distance from Seattle to attend their nuptials. During Elisha's pregnancy in 2021, the newlyweds opted to permanently relocate to Perth before the birth of **Brooks Patrick** (b. 1921). Here, Casey pursued his passion in the brewery business while Elisha cared for their child full-time. In mid-2022, Kathleen again made the transcontinental trek to meet her grandson. She returned 1-1/2 years later to meet Brooks's brother, **Bailey Cooper** (b. 2023). In 2024, the couple opted to return to the great Northwest U.S. as now a family of four. They reside in close proximity to Katheen and Dave in Tacoma where Casey has his sights on obtaining brewer certification.

DENNIS AND MARIAN ADOPTED a beautiful girl under age one in Kunming, China, in 1998. **Grace Kinney Broderick** (b. 1998) is special in multiple ways—she is lovely, brilliant, and stunning for what she has accomplished in her short 26 years. I only wish I knew her better.

Grace was raised in Chicago where she attended the University of Chicago Laboratory Schools, a nursery-to-grade 12 co-educational day school where Barack and Michelle Obama's daughters, Malia and Sasha, also studied. Nearly half of the school's students have a parent who is on the faculty or staff of the university. At an early age, Grace joined the varsity tennis team and became fascinated with dinosaurs and the study of paleontology, a passion that has stayed with her all these years to the present. She pursued a rigorous course of study in the field of paleontology while developing proficiency in Chinese and French languages and studio arts. She also honed impressive leadership, research, and documentary skills with award recognition before leaving home for college. For a week one summer, her high school chose Grace as one of 12 students to study marine biology at the Woods Hole Marine Biology Laboratory in Falmouth, Massachusetts. Later, as part of her senior year project, Grace spent two weeks shadowing various staff at the Walt Disney Animation Studios in Burbank, California.

While earning a Bachelor's degree in environmental geoscience with a minor in film studies from Boston College, Grace gained valuable research experience at nearby Harvard University's Comparative Zoology Laboratory where she prepared fossil specimens and conducted research for her thesis on the sphendontian fossil. At every opportunity since the age of 14, Grace has found her calling at the fossil laboratory of Dr. Paul Sereno at the University of Chicago, first as a volunteer then as a research assistant up until 2021. For several summers before the coronavirus disrupted her plans in 2020, Grace accompanied Dr. Sereno as a field assistant on an excavation of a dinosaur graveyard in Wyoming's Bighorn Mountains. In her spare time as a college student, Grace trained in Zumba; volunteered as a film editor; held a seat as an executive board member of the "EcoPledge" student-led organization; and became president of the Boston College Irish Society.

In 2021, the excitement of scientific discovery and exploration led Grace to England where she completed a one-year paleobiology Master's program at the University of Bristol. As she wrapped up her thesis, Grace followed through on her long-held goal to participate in a paleontological dig in Africa. Into the next chapter, she volunteered as a research assistant in the Field Lab at the University of Cambridge, England. A self-proclaimed bird enthusiast, Grace segmented the bones of birds both extant and extinct. With a focus on paleontology, she entered the university's earth sciences doctoral program in the fall of 2023. Meanwhile, she immerses herself in travel and extraordinary wildlife photography documenting the movements of exotic birds. Grace's innate curiosity will continue to take her to faraway places to gain further insights into the history of life on earth and our place within the natural world we see around us.

NANCY RAISED THREE CHILDREN—Aimée with Glenn Aston; and Nicole and Ian with Al Kinzler. As adults, Aimée, Nicole, and Ian settled in the Southeast U.S., drawing Nancy from her beloved San Miguel Basin as a former resident of Norwood, Colorado, in 2003.

Born in Rutland, Vermont, **Aimée Phillips Aston Dodson** (b. 1973) found her way to Pittsburgh via Telluride, Colorado, before Nancy and Glenn divorced. Nancy's firstborn lived under the roof of her second husband, Al, once she remarried and resettled in Pittsburgh, until Aimée turned 12. By then, Aimée's half-siblings, Nicole and Ian, had come along, but Nancy and Al struggled to make ends meet. Mature beyond her years, Aimée understood that her prospects were better suited living with Glenn, his second wife Patti, and two half-brothers, Ryan and Sean, in Silver Springs, Maryland. Off she went, graduating from Springbrook High School while maintaining a close bond with her Pittsburgh family and visiting as often as she could.

Following her high school graduation in Maryland, Aimée enrolled at the University of Colorado in Boulder. Here, she met her future husband, Dallas native **Kenneth Earl "Trace" Dodson** (b. 1972). Soon after earning a Bachelor's degree in theatre and communications, Aimée married Trace on the mountaintop at scenic Keystone, Colorado, in 1996. As an accomplished cook and manager of restaurant operations, Trace accepted a position in Minneapolis, Minnesota, where the couple had their first of three daughters, **Sydney Morgan** (b. 1998). With another restaurant management opportunity in the wings, the family soon relocated to Charlotte, North Carolina.

While raising Sydney and her sisters **Riley Loren** (b. 2000) and **Landon Jade** (b. 2003) in Charlotte, Aimée launched a solo freelance bookkeeping business which included a mortgage company among other clients. In the same line of freelance work, her mother Nancy did the books for Casey Crawford. An aspiring businessman and former National Football League player and Super Bowl champion with the Tampa Bay Buccaneers, Casey then set out to open his own mortgage company. Coincidentally, Nancy's former client hired Aimée as the fifth or sixth team member of Movement Mortgage, a private mortgage company he co-founded in 2008. Against the backdrop of one of the biggest financial meltdowns in American history, Movement Mortgage worked through the 2007–2009 crisis and economic contraction that followed a decade-long expansion in U.S. housing activity. Launched with a winning formula, the company now employs 4,500 people in 775 locations across all 50 states.

Aimée has assumed progressive leadership roles, presently serving as National Director of Affiliate Relationships and arguably the company's most enthusiastic cheerleader. For a time, Aimée's mother, mother-in-law, sister, and daughters all gained employment with Movement Mortgage; her daughter, Riley, has launched her post-college career with the "movement of change" loan originator. Trace changed direction mid-career and is now an independent contractor making his mark in residential real estate construction. Trace's completed projects include a number of major improvements to his and Aimée Charlotte-based home and construction of a Maggie Valley, North Carolina, house that he built from the ground up alongside and for his parents.

Aimée inherited her maternal ancestors' creative gene. Among her other talents, she took Creative Memories™ scrapbooking by storm when she photo-documented more than one Broderick reunion into impressive hardbound books as cherished keepsakes. As a couple, Trace and Aimée share a love of games and cards to while away what little free time they can muster. They also have developed a passion for children in need. They took **Zyana Yepes** (b. 2001) under their wing as their adopted child as a teenager. Zyana excelled under their stewardship and graduated from East Carolina University, Greenville, with aspirations of becoming a physician assistant. As well, with compassionate hearts they subsequently fostered another teen. Meanwhile, Trace still demonstrates his culinary skills as he and Aimée regularly host blowout parties as social beings and hosts extraordinaire.

Upon establishing roots in Colorado from Pittsburgh, Nancy's youngest two, Nicole and Ian, enrolled in Norwood Public School (K-12) where they remained through high school. **Nicole Westcott Kinzler** (b. 1980) became a cheerleader of all sports—football, basketball, wrestling—and like many girls her age, she found herself enamored by boys, boys, boys. Pretty and, according to her mother, flirtatious, Nicole did not have much to do with the girls except for a couple of close friends. Meanwhile, the school was small, with roughly 20 students in each graduating class. Nicole enjoyed skiing the slopes and, at one point during high school, she worked as a maid at Franz Klammer Lodge in Telluride. The lodge carries the name of the Austrian Alpine skier and 1976 Olympics gold medalist with whom my brother Larry and his wife Lynda have since developed a close friendship.

Aimée and Trace's brief residency in Minneapolis influenced Nicole's college choice. She attended the University of St. Thomas in nearby St. Paul and studied economics in Sydney and Melbourne, Australia, for a month during her junior year. She graduated with a Bachelor's degree in marketing management. When the Dodsons pulled stakes and relocated to Charlotte, North Carolina, Nicole soon followed. She worked in the hospitality industry as a waitress and then joined Movement Mortgage where she advanced in human resources. Nicole became a senior compensation analyst before calling it quits after some ten years with the company. Returning to waitressing, she finds herself making more money while working fewer hours. The providential move led to her meeting **Michael "Scott" Snead** (b. 1989), whom she married in Jamaica in 2024. Together, they continue to work in restaurant operations.

At the peak of COVID-19, Nicole developed a knack for solving complex 1,000-piece jigsaw puzzles in her down time. The life of the party, when she comes out, Nicole brings out the fun in everyone!

Nancy's youngest and only son, **Ian Allen Kinzler** (b. 1981) was prone to hanging out with the many friends he made upon arriving in Norwood. He segued from skiing into snowboarding as his favorite sport during high school. Upon graduating, he enrolled at the Art Institute of Fort Lauderdale. My husband, Rick, and I drove from Jacksonville, Florida, to greet him as he arrived solo. Likely influenced by his father's career as a motorcycle mechanic, Ian obtained a Bachelor's degree in industrial design and then cut his teeth at Eddie Trotta Thunder Cycle Designs. Ian developed expertise as a computer-numerically controlled (CNC) programmer and operator, custom chopper builder, and skilled leatherman. For several years running, Ian "rambled on," carrying a fleet of Eddie Trotta motorcycles to Sturgis, South Dakota, for the annual Sturgis Motorcycle Rally. Founded in 1938, the event attracts as many as one-half million people for the ten-day "ride-roar-rally" celebration.

In 2015, Ian met and married Fort Lauderdale native **Leah Lew Jacobson** (b. 1981). Leah is the mother of **Jacoby "Coby" Henry Summers** (b. 2004) and a long-standing bartendress. In Fort Lauderdale, Ian and Leah gave birth to **Ellie Paige** (b. 2012) and **Wyatt Allen** (b. 2017) before pulling roots from the Sunshine State.

Ian accepted a position similar to his role at Eddie Trotta when Oxnard, California-based Scott's Hotrods 'N Customs elected to relocate its entire operation to Knoxville, Tennessee, in 2018. With meticulous attention to detail, Ian and the team of industrial craftsmen manufacture a complete line of chassis, independent front suspension, and rear suspension kits for any make and model of street rod, hot rod, and pro touring ride built between 1925 to 1987. They also handcraft the building of complete custom vehicles. Soon after the Kinzlers moved to Knoxville— once Aimée's youngest daughter turned 16—"Grancy" followed from Charlotte so as to be present in the lives of her youngest grandchildren.

PATTY AND FRANK CAPPELLI RAISED FOUR children in Pittsburgh while developing their niche in children's musical productions. Among countless others, they had a loyal following with their own children, Giuseppi, Caroline, Timmy, and Frankie, which continued after Patty departed from the business once A&M Records picked up the Peanut Heaven record label and Cappelli & Company video recordings to pursue a career of her own as a realtor.

Giuseppi "Beppi" Emilio Cappelli (b. 1981) gave his parents quite the scare when they learned 24 hours after birth of his genetic disorder. Caused by an abnormal cell division resulting in extra genetic material from chromosome 21, Down syndrome manifests in developmental and intellectual delays. Throughout his life, Beppi has greatly benefited from the care bestowed upon him by his three siblings, all of whom nurture him with sweet tenderness. Although he lives at home with dependence for his basic needs, Beppi manages to work part-time. He attained an associate degree in food services from the Allegheny Community College to prepare him for job placement. He worked in the kitchen of a nearby senior living facility and later took a job in fulfillment services.

Beppi's verbal skills make it challenging to communicate with him, but his youngest sibling, Frankie, is convinced he knows far more than he lets on. When Patty's fifth grandson Jack came along, Beppi's sister Caroline found him wearing headphones while holding her baby. It took no time for Beppi to solve the disturbing sound of the baby's cries. He was evidently bound and determined to quash the irritant because he loves nothing more than holding babies. Growing up in the extended Broderick family has provided him ample opportunity!

With his sweet disposition, Beppi is happy and succeeds mightily in entertaining himself by listening to music—notably his father's Peanut Heaven recordings—watching his favorite television shows, and playing with car toys. For many years, Beppi was fixated on lining up hundreds of the miniature cars as his favorite form of play. Since Frank's passing, Patty has succeeded in weening Beppi off his addiction to junk food and Coca Cola (to a degree). He lost a lot of weight as a result and now maneuvers better than ever as a regular on the softball field with the Miracle League in Pittsburgh.

Patty and Frank's only daughter, **Caroline Broderick Cappelli** (b. 1982) arrived within a year of Beppi's birth as an "Irish twin." In their formative years, she set a wonderful example for her younger brothers in looking after Beppi.

Following her graduation from Mt. Lebanon High School, a stone's throw from the Broderick homestead before our move to Upper St. Clair, Caroline enrolled at West Virginia University in Morgantown. She later earned a Bachelor's degree in psychology from La Roche College before her short-lived marriage to Pittsburgh native **Scott Crimone** (b. 1977) at St. Bernard's Church in 2008. Along with two others, Caroline chose as wedding party attendants her seven Broderick cousins—Kim, Lee, Casey, Colleen, Kelly, Aimée, and Nicole.

Caroline spent several years as a bartender and server, first at The Saloon where her mother had worked in Mt. Lebanon and then in downtown Pittsburgh at Il Pizzaiolo. At the same time, she got her footing in real estate at Howard Hanna where Patty has spent her career as a real estate agent. Here, Caroline met her future husband, Pittsburgh native **Michael "Mike" Wayne Cowden** (b. 1980). Directing sales at a top performing Howard Hanna office, in 2016, Mike qualified to attend the all-expenses-paid trip the company hosts for top performers each year, this time in Italy. In typical fashion, Patty attended as a top performer, this time with her son Timmy as her guest; meanwhile, Mike brought Caroline as his guest. Immediately following the retreat, Mike and the Cappelli clan proceeded to the Amalfi Coast where Mike and Caroline wed. Within two years of their marriage, Caroline gave birth to **Jack Broderick** (b. 2018), and she completed a Master's program in professional counseling at Carlow University. Following her divorce from Mike, Caroline worked in insurance sales for Liberty Mutual in Pittsburgh and since then has secured a position in counseling services. All the while, she takes after her mother with a sense of humor and an affinity for teasing and making fun.

Named after his mother's closest sibling, **Timothy "Timmy" Patrick Cappelli** (b. 1985) was born in Colorado when his parents lived briefly in Castle Rock while working for my brother Larry. Back in Pittsburgh, as an exceptionally young teenaged entrepreneur, Timmy succeeded in his launch of a "handy boy" business to earn money and please his clientele with exemplary service. A Mt. Lebanon High School graduate, Timmy attended Lynn University in Boca Raton, Florida, where he earned a Bachelor of Arts in advertising and communications and developed an interest in event planning and supervision. He spent a summer as a marketing intern at the five-star hotel, The Little Nell in Aspen, Colorado, and he assumed various roles in food services and at special events—with Panera Bread, Mario Lemieux Golf Tournament, The Club at Nevillewood in Pittsburgh, the Palm Beach International Film Festival, and Au Bon Pain in Baltimore, Maryland.

Tim traveled extensively while working as an independent contractor with video and television production companies—notably producers of reality TV. Working various assignments, he landed a production manager position while living in Los Angeles before returning to his roots in 2018. In Pittsburgh, Tim continues to freelance as a production manager for various entertainment companies. Meanwhile, he works out regularly and travels at every opportunity while enjoying the outdoors with his partner, Mike Balistreri. In 2021, EdgeMediaNetwork reported that Tim tied as a recipient of the Gay Travel Award presented by GayTravel.com in the category of "Gay Travel Influencer." The category consists of creators who inspire travel with their inclusive spirit, a drive for diversity, and a desire to change the world for the better.

As a youngster, **Frank "Frankie" Emilio Cappelli, Jr.** (b. 1988) loved to fool around and have fun while developing his love of baseball. Upon entering the high school where Caroline and Timmy had gone, he came to his senses and decided it was time to get serious about his studies. Initiating the request granted by his parents, Frankie enrolled as a sophomore at The Kiski School, founded in 1888 and one of the oldest all-boys private preparatory boarding schools in the United States. Located 30 miles east of Pittsburgh on 350 acres in Saltsburg, Kiski challenged Frankie with its rigorous curriculum. He gained leadership skills, and with the glee club, he fostered the musical talent he inherited from his father with impressive vocals and the guitar.

Frank attended Virginia Polytechnic Institute and State University in Blacksburg. Months before enrolling in 2007, he questioned his choice when a Virginia Tech student went on a rampage, gunning down 32 people and injuring 23 others on campus before taking his own life. At that time, the massacre was recorded as the deadliest mass shooting in modern U.S. history.

Ultimately committing to Virginia Tech, Frank went "all in." While working toward a Bachelor of Science in accounting and information systems, he received scholarships for academic achievement and award recognition for his leadership in numerous campus activities. During and briefly following graduation, Frank consulted in cybersecurity with Booz Allen Hamilton in Washington, D.C.

During a brief stint with Otis Elevator as an account manager in Tampa and Pensacola, Frank courted his future bride **Emily Sylvia**

Templeton (b. 1987), a Tufts University graduate with a Bachelor's degree in economics who then worked for the Partners Capital Investment Group in Boston. As an usher at a friend's wedding in Pittsburgh, Frank escorted the bride's first cousin (Emily) to her seat and a love-at-first-sight romance followed.

Returning to the Tampa Bay area following a short stint in Pensacola with Emily, Frank developed his niche as a solutions consultant and systems engineer in the human resources information technology space, initially with Ceridian. As a native of Bangor, Maine, Emily soon tired of Florida's stifling heat. She delivered the first of their four sons, **Emilio "Leo" Frank** (b. 2014), in Pittsburgh. In 2016, Frank and Emily married in Bradenton, Florida. The family of three relocated to Black Mountain, North Carolina, outside Asheville, where Frank continued to work for Ceridian remotely before onboarding with Oracle, and now with Workday.

In Black Mountain, the couple purchased and for several years operated the bed and breakfast "My Place Inn" as live-in proprietors. Before the birth of **Daniel Paul** (b. 2017) in nearby Asheville, Emily worked remotely as a product manager for Primary Intelligence out of Draper, Utah, and now works part-time in a similar capacity for Boston-based Dynamo Software. After **Charles "Charlie" Templeton** (b. 2019) came along and shortly before the arrival of **Theodore "Teddy" John** (b. 2020), Frank and Emily opted to cease bed and breakfast operations in order to accommodate their growing family with needed space. Frank serves on the Black Mountain Recreation Commission addressing policies and programs related to the town's Recreation and Parks Department. As often as possible, he likes to take the boys to baseball games rooting for the minor league Asheville Tourists. The family of six also enjoys Emily's favorite pastime—swimming—and many outdoor activities at their lakeside cabin in Taylorsville near Hickory, North Carolina.

Into the foreseeable future, the Cappelli's will set aside those leisurely pursuits as they grapple with the remnants of Hurricane Helene which took more than 225 lives across six states upon making landfall in the "Big Bend" of Florida on September 26, 2024. The disastrous storm exacted an unprecedented, agonizing toll on western North Carolina a day later. Felled trees, breached dams, downed power lines and telephone poles; demolished bridges; destroyed water lines; raging muddy floodwaters that devoured homes and vehicles—the search continued for dozens of people who remained unaccounted for one month after Helene powered through pristine Asheville and neighboring communities including Black Mountain. In the wake of the ferocious storm, shell-shocked residents absorbed their new reality with nearly 100 lives lost in North Carolina alone. A month into the nightmare, Emily recounted details of the visceral experience with this reflection:

> I spend a lot of time thinking about humans as animals these days. The way our human structures were crumpled like cardboard by water and wind. I've been thinking about the way we came together as scared mammals after the storm. I've not heard of one person who was not deeply touched, deeply changed, by the feeling of communing with our neighbors, opening our doors, sharing our resources, hugging strangers, speaking with deep curiosity and vulnerability . . . we are meant for a deeper level of connection. We are meant to take care of each other. We are such clever animals . . . but the structures we've built to keep us comfortable have also been keeping us apart. I aim to not lose sight of this truth so brutally revealed to me.

Adversity builds strength. People engender hope. Forever changed, the Cappelli's will work through the trauma and will become better people for the experience of taking care of their own and appreciating the value of human connection.

WHEN IN 2016 TERRY MARRIED Jennifer, 12 years his junior, he was aged 43 years. Consequently, their children came relatively late in life for my younger brother.

Born and raised in San Diego, Hailey and Dillon carry particular pride in their Ukrainian heritage on the side of their maternal grandmother, Kathy neé Burbella Ellis, whose four grandparents migrated from the East Slavic nation to the United States in 1911–1912. Ukrainians' long history of dislocation stemmed from their quest to avoid danger and secure fundamental resources denied them in their ancestral homeland. These innocent refugees are Jennifer, Hailey, and Dillon's people. Terry's family waves the blue and yellow Ukrainian flag as a show of support for President Volodymyr Zelenskyy and a symbol of unity with these valiant loyalists who have been battered time and again. The Ukrainian people have demonstrated remarkable resilience in fighting off the unprovoked yet unrelenting enemy attack by Russia's President Vladimir Putin that has raged since February 2022.

I am not familiar with the physical traits of Ukrainians to discern a resemblance in Hailey or Dillon. However, I do know that in both looks and personality, I felt an especially strong connection to **Hailey Katharine Broderick** (b. 1998) in her early years. As a youngster, the blue-eyed blonde came across as exceptionally shy, kind, thoughtful, and empathetic. Did I mention her talent with a hula hoop? Or that she is a perfectionist? Hailey worked harder than most to keep up her grades while following a rigorous curriculum. While running on the advanced track team as an eighth grader, in 2013, Hailey surfaced as one of four among 400 classmates to receive the Harvey Gold Standard Award for academic excellence, citizen behavior, and physical education.

With the same resolve Hailey exhibited at Patrick Henry High School to keep up her grades, she pursued a Bachelor of Science in financial management and statistics at the University of California, Santa Barbara. In the spring of 2022, she graduated among the top 5% in her class—half of them graduate students—and she completed 50% more units than the amount required to complete her upper-level courses. Hailey clearly has an affinity for numbers and problem solving, skills she put to use as a junior trading analyst with San Diego-based Plaza Home Mortgage, a wholesale trader of mortgages in the secondary market. She has since found her niche in New York City as a client associate with RBC Wealth Management.

While working her right brain with logical, analytical thinking, Hailey is similarly endowed on her creative left side. Her father shared that she is a naturally gifted artist with a talent for composition, including colors. She is also introspective and passionate about the health of the environment. As Hailey has observed, more frequent and intense drought, storms, heat waves, rising sea levels, melting glaciers, and warming oceans threaten the world with direct harm to animals, destruction of their habitats, and disruption to people's livelihoods and communities. Deeply concerned about the future of her own generation let alone those to follow, Hailey embraces coordinated solutions to tackle the climate crisis as it affects human and natural ecosystems across the globe.

According to Terry, **Dillon Terrence Broderick** (b. 2002) favors his mother who is prone to stay focused and results-oriented. While he and his sister are highly driven, Dillon's persistence yields results as if on cue. Goal-directed, self-disciplined, and judicious with his time, he loves school and stays on task academically. Always up for a challenge, once Dillon takes on a hobby and learns as much as he can, he is ready to tackle something new. As a youngster he excelled at striking and blocking in martial arts, earning a blue belt before retiring at age 8. He then gravitated to the computer as if a toy to be manipulated and soon learned to compete in remote gaming with his friends. Racing against time, he also proved his might in solving the puzzle of Rubik's cube.

Dillon jumped right in as a student at Patrick Henry High School, holding the school record in solving the Rubik's cube in 10.37 seconds. He ascended to president of the Rubik's Cubes Club, the Math Club, and the Mock Trial program. He earned distinction as "pre-trial attorney" of the year in a countywide competition with contestants from 50 high schools in his senior year. Dillon also became a member of the Robotics Club and rookie of the year in badminton.

Early recognition came to Dillon as recipient of the Math Council Award for his "highly sustained interest in Math"; the Yale Book Award for academic achievement; and the President's Excellence Award for placing among the top 10 of his senior class in academics.

More impressive yet, Dillon graduated as senior class Valedictorian with a 4.88 grade point average, ranking #1 academically among 680 classmates. The commencement program captured this description of the Westcotts' youngest "GEN 13" descendant: "Exceptionally creative, hardworking, kind, considerate, inquisitive, self-confident; active participant; asked for feedback; deep understanding; rarest of students." Perhaps most striking, Dillon came in on top while learning remotely throughout the entirety of his senior year. To minimize the spread of COVID-19 infections, the San Diego school district mandated distance learning for all K-12 students during the 2020–2021 school year.

As if COVID-triggered involuntary distance education was not taxing enough for the seniors, as incoming college freshmen, the high school class of 2021 faced particularly challenging admissions hurdles.

Many colleges and universities granted a "gap year" to students registered as freshmen in the class ahead of Dillon's. This meant that they held a spot for these students if they opted to pull out and re-enroll as freshmen in the subsequent year. The concession ultimately increased demand for 2021 college enrollment and thereby placed more restrictive admissions standards on Dillon and his peers.

As much as Dillon aspired to study computer science at an Ivy League school on the East coast, in 2021, he chose to enroll at the University of California, Los Angeles. Although he was accepted at the University of Notre Dame, his father's alma mater, the tipping point came with UCLA's superior ranking in computer sciences. It should come as no surprise that Dillon finished his freshman year with a perfect 4.0 grade point average. Aided by AP coursework, he entered his sophomore year as an officer and webmaster of the Tau Beta Pi Association, the oldest engineering honors society and the second oldest collegiate honor society in the United States. By all indications, Dillon has a bright and inventive future ahead of him as an aspiring computer scientist. In the summer of 2024, shortly after completing an internship in Manhattan with "Meta" Platforms, Inc., he accepted a full-time position that will commence following his studies in the spring of 2025. Although a long distance from San Diego, Hailey and Dillon expect to thrive in their professional pursuits will living in close proximity to each other.

BORN AND RAISED IN DENVER, Tim and Ann's four tightly-knit sons—Sean, Conor, Timmy, and Shane—grew up with good manners, engaging personalities, a sense of humor, and a high regard for one another.

Active in competitive sports, as youngsters they played hockey foremost, and baseball, and some soccer, lacrosse, and basketball. Of course, they share their father's enthusiasm for golf, football, and all things Notre Dame. Tradition runs deep in this family. Two years apart down the line, the boys attended Regis Jesuit High School in Aurora, which shares much of its 145+ year history with nearby Regis University in Denver. Later, the boys headed single file to the University of Miami in Oxford, Ohio:

Founded in 1809, the public research university is the tenth oldest in the U.S. and the alma mater of Notre Dame football coach Ara Parseghian (1923–2017) who led the Irish to two national championships in 1966 and 1973; author, conservative satirist, and political commentator P.J. O'Rourke (1947–2022); and Pittsburgh Steelers' 18-season starting quarterback Ben Roethlisberger (b. 1982).

All four Broderick boys pursued degrees in the Farmer School of Business and studied abroad for a semester in their junior year—Sean in Luxembourg, and Conor, Timmy, and Shane in Barcelona. Except for Shane who returned to Denver from Oxford, Ohio, directly, the others followed circuitous routes back home where they have planted roots with families of their own. The thread that binds the brothers is tightly woven. As if by design, Sean, then Conor, and then Timmy married in quick succession. Respectful of age order, each of the three delivered a grandchild to Tim and Ann, all within a span of under six months. Following suit, Shane as the youngest has the opportunity to play catch-up given his mid-2023 marriage.

Tim and Ann's firstborn **Sean Patrick Broderick** (b. 1988) set a sterling example for his brothers as he is strong in character, loving, respectful, and studious. He majored in finance and accounting and became active in Alpha Beta Psi, Delta Upsilon, and Habitat for Humanity. Immediately upon graduating, he followed his mother's lead by earning credentials as a certified public accountant.

Sean joined the audit practice of KPMG USA in Chicago where he met his future bride, **Marcia Elizabeth McDonnell** (b. 1986). A native of Ottawa, Illinois, and a graduate of St. Mary's College at Notre Dame with a Bachelor of Business Administration in finance, Marcia started her career as a senior associate in business risk advisory services with Ernst & Young in Chicago. She met Sean while working as the finance manager of a human and financial resources nonprofit. Before tying the knot and relocating to Denver, Marcia worked with a for-profit company in financial operations and as a senior manager of strategic initiatives.

Not unlike Marcia's experience at Ernst & Young, the notorious grind at the then "big 5" accounting firms led Sean to make a change.

He gained valuable business experience as an associate in management and turnaround advisory services with Silverman Consulting in Skokie, Illinois, before returning to Denver. He then worked with his father and uncle Larry for five years at Acme Manufacturing. Here, he became a sales and marketing analyst before leading business development as director in the Coyote Landscape Products division. In June 2019, Sean married Marcia at Le Mans Hall on the campus of St. Mary's College with an outdoor reception alongside picturesque Lake Marian. Soon after, the newlyweds bought a historical Denver home and started a family with the birth of **Quinn Marie** (b. 2021). While Marcia established herself as a leadership delivery consultant with Denver-based Slalom, Sean broke from Acme to start a new business venture. With his parents and brothers as stakeholders, he launched a limited liability company to buy, improve, then sell residential real estate properties for gain.

With Marcia's encouragement, in the fall of 2023, Sean entered the Master's level three-year landscape architecture program in the Architecture School at the University of Colorado. Within two months of Sean's enrollment and in the throes of a major home renovation project that includes adding a second story, Marcia delivered the couple's second child, **Oliver Westcott** (b. 2023).

Acme Manufacturing became an early training ground for **Conor Michael Broderick** (b. 1990). He interned as a statistical analyst before setting off for Miami University. Later, he interned as a financial analyst at Owen Corning out of Toledo, Ohio, the world's largest manufacturer of fiberglass composites. With a finance degree, Conor entered a comprehensive rotation with a financial leadership development program to hone his financial planning and analytical skills. He then spent four years in Atlanta, Georgia, with SunTrust Robinson Humphrey delving into complex financial transactions in the healthcare and energy and power infrastructure sectors as a credit underwriter and research analyst. At SunTrust Robinson, Conor met his future bride **Mary Catherine "MC" Wilkison** (b. 1991), a graduate of the University of North Carolina in Chapel Hill where she earned a Bachelor of Science in business administration concentrated in finance. At SunTrust Robinson, MC became similarly adept in capital market research and analysis as an investment banking analyst in the consumer and retail sectors before joining a broadcasting company as a financial analyst and manager in corporate development and strategy in New York City. Conor took his training to Chicago where he joined Monroe Capital, LLC as a senior associate. With a transfer and advancement to assistant vice president, he reunited with Mary Catherine in New York City, albeit briefly as he fully expected to live in the "Big Apple" only on a temporary basis.

Taking a bite out of the big apple, "CM" and "MC" followed through on their plans to relocate to Conor's hometown, marry, and start a family. They set a wedding date for June 2020 and made plans for their nuptials in MC's hometown of Pinehurst, North Carolina. However, COVID-19 forced an agonizing last-minute decision to delay.

This graphic pretty much tells the "stand down" story of the pandemic that undermined virtually every plan in every household and sector across the globe in 2020. Unlike most couples who with fits and starts postponed marriage plans into 2021 and later—or cancelled them altogether— Conor and MC proceeded to wed in front of their families but reset their "official" wedding date five months out. They exchanged vows in front of fewer guests than planned, but still had a significant gathering at Pinehurst Resort of golf fame in November 2020.

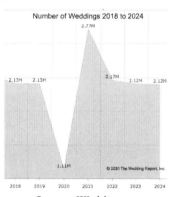

Source: Wedding Market Research

Even before Sean and Marcia delivered Quinn, the newlyweds came to expect **Daniel Wilkison "Wilkes"** (b. 2021) who followed his cousin Quinn Marie by five months. Meanwhile, in Denver, Conor served one year with Silicon Valley Bank as a vice president before switching to ArrowMark Partners shortly before Wilkes's birth. Conor is now an investment analyst with the local employee-owned asset management company founded in 2007. Mary Catherine took maternity leave before returning to her position as manager of strategic finance with Ibotta. She took another leave from the digital marketing firm with the birth of **John "Johnny" Mathers** (b. 2024), which coincided with Ibotta going public on the New York Stock Exchange. Sharing a nanny who alternates each week between the homes of Sean and Marcia and Conor and MC, Wilkes, Quinn, Oliver, and Johnny enjoy child's play while developing a special bond much like siblings.

Named after his father and paternal grandfather, **Timothy "Timmy" Daniel Broderick** (b. 1992) grew up with a distinctly stylish flair. Ever the smart dresser, Tim concentrated his studies in business management. In Oxford, Ohio, the business school nominated him to showcase speech communication and delivery on their behalf in a university-wide competition. Shortly thereafter, the Golden Key International Honor Society accepted him for academic achievement. During his tenure at Miami University, Timmy volunteered with the American Red Cross as a representative of Sigma Alpha Epsilon.

Young Tim spent three years in Cincinnati following his graduation where he enjoyed quality time with his uncle Dennis. He first worked as a transaction manager in industrial services with DTZ—later acquired by Cushman & Wakefield—and as an associate commercial real estate development manager with AI. Neyer, founded in 1894. Never one to sit idle, Tim was called home in 2018.

In Denver, while working as a territory development manager then account executive for software company Ping Identity, Timmy revived a romance with his high school sweetheart **Taylor Olivia Engel** (b. 1993). As posted on a website where the couple shared their story and wedding plans, Tim wrote:

> *A tale as old as time—boy meets girl and immediately falls madly in love with her. As a multiple-sport, varsity athlete and future Prom King, it isn't long before girl falls head over heels for boy. They date for 8 years before eventually getting engaged.*
>
> *Well, our love story really wasn't like that at all, except for falling madly in love with each other from an early age. It all began in 2011, when we were first introduced by a mutual friend in the courtyard at Regis Jesuit High School. We were just 14 and 15 years old. Since Taylor was not allowed to go on an actual date until she was 16 years old, we spent the first year of our relationship . . . with each other's families. However, after . . . our first*

official date, we proceeded to date each other for another two and half years before heading off to college. I went to Miami University in Oxford, OH and spent a few years in Cincinnati, and Taylor attended Loyola Chicago and spent a year in the city before heading back to Denver.

Never did we think that our paths would lead us back to one another, but it has been a dream come true, a classic love story. After getting back together after more than seven years apart, it is as if nothing has changed. The love that originally brought us together is still there. We have both grown up and have become each other's best friend. I proceeded to propose to Taylor in Paris, France on the Alexander III bridge on a night that will be the most memorable of our lives.

Taylor received a Bachelor's degree in marketing from the Quinlan School of Business at Loyola University Chicago. She minored in Spanish at Universidad Rey Juan Carlos in Madrid, Spain. Shortly after graduating, Taylor returned to Denver and worked as a carrier sales executive with a supply chain and freight shipping company when she and Tim reconnected. The couple's plans to marry in Aurora, Colorado, in September 2020, rested squarely on the state of the volatile COVID-19 virus. However, unlike Conor and MC, they managed to pull it off as originally scheduled.

Shortly before their wedding, Tim changed jobs to develop new business in the marketing technology sector with Bombora. He now serves as an account executive with Performio, a software developer of incentive compensation plans, processes, and strategies. Taylor also changed jobs after their wedding and now manages logistics as the manager of business execution at Flock Freight. Meanwhile, Tim and Taylor's daughter **Kennedy Layne** (b. 2021) arrived just ten days after the birth of her cousin Wilkes and six months after cousin Quinn.

Shane Christian Broderick (b. 1994) is the youngest of my five Broderick godchildren behind Aimée, Rhett, Caroline, and Casey (McCormack). He is entrepreneurial and most deliberate in both his plans and his actions. One might think of him as a follower of his siblings, but he has emerged as a thoughtful leader as well. At Miami University, Shane majored in finance and minored in entrepreneurship. He then gained five years of business experience before enrolling at the University of Notre

Dame as an MBA candidate in the Mendoza College of Business, graduating in 2023. Tim and Ann's youngest is the only one of Dan and Yo Broderick's 23 grandchildren to earn a degree from Notre Dame.

Following summer internships at Acme Manufacturing as an operations analyst and at Open Road Snacks through Colorado Startups in Denver, Shane got his official start in business at Regal Brands, a portfolio of companies in the door hardware industry that Acme acquired in 2001. Here, Shane honed his skills as an account manager in e-commerce. He developed first party (1P) and third party (3P) marketplace platforms supporting sales from wholesale supplier to retailer and from retailer directly to end users. Ready to strike out on his own, in 2019, Shane launched a new business, Bye Bye Bogie. He developed the e-commerce platform selling an array of golf products online, some of which reached the buyer from the supplier directly and others that Shane warehoused himself. He stayed with it for 3-1/2 years before entering Notre Dame's MBA program.

Seeing his three older brothers marry in quick succession, Shane determined that it was time to cement the foundation for a lucrative career that will support a family. Shane is an observer. He learned much from his parents and brothers, mostly what to do right—pinpoint the goal and make it a reality. Like Timmy and Taylor, Shane's courtship of **Kendel Ann Lloyd** (b. 1994) dates to high school (class of 2012)—long before Sean and Conor met their wives. Shane and Kendel's protracted relationship began in 2009 when they were high school sophomores. They broke off during college but came back together when Shane returned to Denver. However, he did not feel sufficiently secure to support a family—until now.

While pursuing an MBA focused on corporate finance and investments, Shane completed a summer internship in middle market mergers and acquisitions with Harris Williams in Richmond, Virginia, and he studied for seven-weeks in Santiago, Chili. He proposed to Kendel while enrolled at Notre Dame, and the couple married in Adare, Ireland, immediately following his graduation in mid-2023.

A graduate of Colorado State University in Ft. Collins with a Bachelor of Arts in communication studies and a minor in sociology,

Kendel worked as a marketing advisor in Denver with the Compass real estate firm before tying the knot.

The prospects appear bright for the newlyweds who on the heels of their nuptials relocated to Richmond. Shane accepted an offer of employment from Harris Williams and worked for one year in the firm's mergers and acquisitions space as an investment banking associate. In mid-2024, the newlyweds relocated to Fort Worth, Texas, where Shane now works in the finance division of American Airlines.

Guys (1976–present)

ALL FOUR "GEN 12" GUY GALS chose their birth surname for their progeny. Seven of Doug and Jinks's 12 grandchildren proudly carry "Guy" as a middle name, including all three of Dianne's children and both of Joanna's sons.

The eldest of the "GEN 13" Guy offspring, **Stephen Guy Hoge** (b. 1976) came one week to the day before my parents' fifth grandchild and first grandson, Daniel T. Broderick IV. Stephen was born during his parents' brief stint as residents of Columbus, Indiana. A scientist and physician, Stephen and his siblings gained international experiences at a very young age thanks to their father Ron's career as a successful business executive. At the age of two, Stephen and his family lived in Covington, England, and four years later, in San Páulo, Brazil. Returning stateside, Ron and Dianne and their three children relocated many times before Stephen broke off to study neuroscience at his father's alma mater. Upon graduating from Amherst College in Western Massachusetts in 1998, he enrolled at the University of California, San Francisco, earning a Doctor of Medicine in 2003.

Following a brief rotation as an emergency medical physician and then two years as a partner with McKinsey & Company in New York City, in 2012, Stephen joined Moderna Therapeutics in Cambridge, Massachusetts. Here, he found his true passion. The biotech startup developed a novel approach to making vaccines and medicines harnessing messenger RNA (mRNA) to help the body create proteins at the cellular level. Stephen quickly advanced to president and head of scientific research and clinical development.

Before January 2020, industry observers regarded mRNA technology as promising but unproven. COVID-19 then brought Moderna into frontrunner status with Pfizer when the U.S. government opted to fund large-scale vaccine development at a critical juncture in the fight to save lives. Although Moderna had made strides showing that nine mRNA-derived vaccines yielded protective immune responses in cancer, cardiac disease, and as an antiviral remedy in pre-clinic and clinical trials, the pharmaceutical and biotechnology company had not brought a single product to market before 2020. It took the global pandemic for Moderna to prove its mettle as an effective, innovative, and nimble combatant benefitting the vulnerable among 8 billion people worldwide. Imagine Stephen's exhilaration upon learning in mid-November 2020 that the National Institutes of Health quantified a 94 or 95 percent efficacy of the mRNA vaccine in Moderna's data.

At Moderna, Stephen found his purpose and reason for optimism. Dianne and Ron's eldest child is steadfast in his resolve to tackle life-saving mRNA therapies for a broad spectrum of cancer, cardiac, infectious, metabolic, and autoimmune diseases through scientific discovery. The mission-critical work of Stephen and his peers is nothing short of awe-inspiring.

In a 2021 presentation he made to students at the nation's oldest school in continuous existence—Roxbury Latin School founded in Boston in 1645—Stephen offered this perspective about the study of science:

I came to love what I thought was science in high school, but I didn't understand it . . . I thought science was this really cool set of facts about the universe - biology, physics, chemistry, how things worked. I thought science was a collection of information, that it was knowledge. I was totally wrong. Science is a way of asking questions about something you don't yet understand, which helps you generate new information, and adding that information to the world. As I began to truly practice science, that's what I came to love the most about it: It's an approach to the unknown.

When Stephen figured out that he needed something focused more on the scientific unknown than the practice of medicine, he went in search of companies that were tackling the unknown "in a big and bold way, and where conventional wisdom said they have maybe a 5 percent chance of success." That's when he found Moderna, where exploration of the big unknown is the name of the game. Thanks to the curiosity, persistence, and optimism of Dr. Hoge and his fellow scientists, doctors, researchers, and entrepreneurs, Moderna's scientific approach and bio-technology offer tremendous promise in the realm of global public health like nothing we have seen heretofore. Further to Moderna's credit, during an intensely chaotic period for businesses in the three-year period ending in late 2022, the vaccine-maker placed second among Standard & Poor 500 contenders in performance rankings compiled by *The Economist.*

An innovative pioneer, Stephen received an honorary Doctor of Science from his and his father Ron's alma mater in 2023. In the presence of his wife, children and parents, Stephen delivered inspirational remarks at Amherst College's commencement titled "No False Hope," which captured these three themes—purpose, curiosity, and optimism. Stephen finds purpose in failure—if a failed experiment teaches us something, then it becomes knowledge which carries value as it passes to successive generations. He approaches science as a study of the unknown that comes from asking questions to explain and contextualize data. And in the belief that tomorrow could be better, he embraces optimism to move things forward in a positive direction. The combination of these three forces fuels the promise of Moderna's mRNA science to create transformative medicines for patients into the future.

Stephen and his siblings moved often during their formative years and attended several different schools as a result. **Ian Guy Hoge** (b. 1978) was born in Covington, England. The frequent relocations came to weigh on him as a teenager, leading Ian to embark on a spiritual journey while learning the ancient practices of meditation, mindfulness, yoga, energy healing, and the modern practice of psychology. Ten years after receiving a Bachelor of Arts in sociology from Trinity College-Hartford, Ian entered Antioch University, Los Angeles, where he completed a Master's program in clinical psychology in 2013.

A resident of Santa Monica, Ian is a licensed marriage and family therapist, parent coach, and child mindfulness expert. In addition to his role as the primary therapist at Visions Adolescent Treatment Centers, he maintains a private practice while directing mindfulness, meditation, and yoga as a teacher to both adults and adolescents in the Los Angeles area. In his capacity as a psychotherapist, Ian offers trauma-informed yoga therapy and "brainspotting" trauma therapy. In 2003, Dr. David Grand discovered the therapeutic benefit of brainspotting as locating points in the client's visual field that help to access unprocessed trauma in the sub-cortical brain. The point of the associated therapy for Ian is to help his clients cultivate inner resilience and self-agency.

In 2010, with co-author Bernadette Luckett, Ian published *21 Days of Enlightenments: A Guided Journey of Service*. The interactive workbook channels daily opportunities for fun and exploration allowing readers to discover more about themselves and their relationship with others and all living things. Multi-talented, Ian is also a voice-over actor and a singer / songwriter. With two albums to his credit, which he wrote and recorded about personal and spiritual growth, Ian also writes songs for network television and has recorded voice-overs for numerous companies and television networks.

The youngest of Dianne and Ron's three children, **Kristina Guy Hoge** (b. 1982) was born in San Páulo, Brazil. With a love of singing and performing, she received a Bachelor of Fine Arts in musical theatre from the Boston Conservatory at Berklee. Early in her career, Kristina began working in development, special events, and corporate relations at The Public Theatre, the Film Society of Lincoln Center, and the Manhattan Theatre Club in New York City. As a fundraiser in her production consultancy role, Kristina had the opportunity to produce the StoryCorps's 2013 gala hosted by Stephen Colbert. She also consulted The Public Theatre on its 2013–2015 "Shakespeare in the Park" spring gala which led to a full-time position. As Senior Director of Development, Kristina now oversees all fundraising initiatives for The Public Theatre.

In 2010, Kristina married the eclectic prankster **Jake Bronstein** (b. 1978) of Philadelphia. Jake is an entrepreneur, Internet personality, blogger, and former editor of the U.S. edition of the men's magazine, *FHM*. A self-proclaimed "fun evangelist," Jake gained name recognition on MTV's *Road Rules* and as co-creator of the desktop toy Buckyballs consisting of tiny magnetic balls that link to form geometric shapes.

Jake also gained fame for his publicity stunts, such as bathing in the Bryant Park Fountain; taking advantage of a loophole to get into the NBA draft; auctioning on eBay the lead singer position in his band; offering himself for marriage; launching a "50 Dates in 50 States" quest by soliciting invites from women on the Internet; and offering 1,000 strangers a hand-written love letter. ABCNews.com picked up the story of Jake's love letters which reached the far corners of the globe. He posted an offer on the Internet: If posters sent him their addresses, he would send them a handwritten love letter, not believing he would get more than a handful of responses. While Jake dated Kristina, a fellow scribe, the pair wrote stacks of random love letters at a time—occasionally slipping one to each other. They wrote the letters to make people smile and feel good about themselves. It worked. [Jake's letter campaign brings to mind the love letters that Kristina's "GEN 10" distant cousin Henry "Reed" Hoke wrote "for guys who were too lazy to write their ones-and-only." Reed's letter writing "on how to project warmth, friendliness, sincerity" led to his innovative career in direct mail as a sales medium.]

In 2009, CBS's *The Early Show* picked up the story of Jake's whisper chain at a New York bar that actually did set a new world record. Catching Kristina unawares, he sent around the message, "Kristina, will you marry me?" to a roomful of bar patrons—both friends and strangers. After the proposal passed through 59 people, a random stranger whispered the message in Kristina's ear. As conveyed by Kristina, "I was completely shocked. Some strange man asked me to marry him. I turned around to ask Jake to beat his guy up and Jake was on his knees." Stunned, she joyfully accepted Jake's proposal in front of a sentimental, enthusiastic crowd of revelers.

Following a stint leading partner innovation with the digital media company "BuzzFeed," Jake now takes his brand marketing and content consultancy to publishers at large. Jake and Kristina have succeeded mightily with their unique ability to entertain. Just imagine the fun brewing in their Brooklyn home with sons **Hudson Hoge** (b. 2014) and **Charlie Hoge** (b. 2018).

THE ELDEST OF LARRY AND PEGGY'S two children, **Cory James Guy** (b. 1977) made his mark early in life as a standout tennis player. To occupy their kids while they played tennis socially at the local country club, Larry and Peggy handed them rackets and balls to bat around for the designated hour. Cory and Kimmie played singles together and developed impressive skill on the court, soon beating their parents long before they reached their teenage years.

Cory emerged as a star player at St. Francis High School in Mountain View, California, which the Brothers of Holy Cross founded in 1955. His uncle David shared that, as a junior in high school and about to compete in a tennis tournament, Cory was paired against a player who was favored to win. His coach said, "Cory, you've got to beat this guy. You know you're better than him." David said, "He turned it on and waxed the guy." When a local reporter for the *Santa Cruz Sentinel* praised him in an interview, Cory reportedly said, "I think everybody makes way too big a deal about all this stuff." But he continued to play and later became an inductee in the St. Francis High School Hall of Fame.

Cory was one of the top-ranked players in the country with multiple scholarship offers and ultimately chose to play at the University of California, Santa Barbara. Years later, a renowned tennis coach who knew about his talent claimed that if Cory had played under him, he would have gone to Wimbledon. He was that good. Cory graduated with a Bachelor's in geography in 1999 but not before striking up a romance with a fellow student, his future wife **Kristin Armstrong** (b. 1976) of Villa Park in Orange County. World-ranked, Cory competed as a professional player on the Association of Tennis Professionals (ATP) Tour prior to launching a career in real estate in 2001, notably commercial real estate and the syndication of real estate securities offerings. Cory and Kristin married in 2002.

In association with a variety of firms, Cory progressed from broker associate to account executive to regional vice president, the latter with Grubb & Ellis Capital Corporation in Orange County as a wholesaler of various real estate security products. At Capital Square Holdings based in Newport Beach, California, Cory raised capital through the broker-dealer channel for real estate investment trust programs (REITs) and 1031

Delaware Statutory Trusts (DSTs). He brought his credentials as senior vice president of sales to Four Springs Capital Trust and more recently, Versity Investments, where he raises capital for REITs, 1031 DSTs, and limited liability companies across the Southwest region of the country.

Since graduating from UCSB, Cory's wife Kristin has spent her career in early childhood education as an elementary school teacher. The couple lives in Newport Beach with their three children, **Riggs Douglas** (b. 2005), **Gavin Daniel** (b. 2007), and **Cate Cory-Mae "CC"** (b. 2011). The eldest, Riggs—at 6'3" tall—won a national title with his volley-ball team at Newport Harbor High School where in 2021 he started as a sophomore.

Affectionately called "Kimmie" by her family, Cory's sister **Kimberly "Kim" Rae Guy Hoggatt** (b. 1979) held her own as a rising tennis star while at St. Francis High School. As she considered the options for her higher education, Kim targeted Notre Dame because the university then ranked as one of the top Division 1 tennis colleges in the U.S. Kim proved herself while starting in the lineup with the Division 1 women's team during her freshman year. As a strong competitor and tough nego-tiator, she prevailed in securing a scholarship into the second half of her sophomore year and then for the duration. Kim earned the rare distinc-tion of becoming a four-time Monogram winner with honors from Notre Dame in recognition of her prowess on the court.

Upon graduating with a Bachelor of Business Administration in mar-keting and computer applications in 2001, Kim put competitive tennis to rest. She signed an employment contract with Arthur Anderson and made plans to move to Chicago. Fortuitously, Arthur Anderson severed the contract before she started and paid her to move on without objection due to impending legal woes. Kim took this opportunity to get back to the West Coast where she reunited with family and friends and followed a divergent career path.

Kim moved to San Diego and worked with a public relations firm briefly before entering the field of health care as a pharmaceutical sales rep-resentative for Eli Lilly in 2003. She then made her mark at Ethicon, Inc. as a senior sales representative and field sales trainer where she sold medical devices and earned numerous performance awards. During her tenure at

Ethicon, Kim earned a Master of Business Administration at San Diego State University (SDSU) in 2009. Following a brief stint at Bristol-Myers Squibb, she landed at GE Healthcare Systems as an account manager and sales specialist in the field of diagnostic imaging agents and radiopharmaceuticals. With her team, Kim's efforts focus on a nuclear brain scan for Parkinson's, the disease that took the life of my mother in 1995.

Kim's first conversation with her husband **Cory Hoggatt** (b. 1977) was sparked by the fact that he shares her brother's first name. Perhaps the stronger draw came from learning that he competed on the water polo team for California State University, Long Beach, much as her father Larry had done at UCSB. Cory then transferred to SDSU where he earned a Bachelor of Science in business and information systems. He completed a Master of Business Administration and Management at the University of Redlands near San Bernardino immediately before Kim entered the MBA program at SDSU.

Having spent several years as a senior sourcing specialist in supply chain management at Qualcomm, Cory moved to a similar role with ViaSat in 2015. He is now senior manager of the global communication company's supply chain for high-speed satellite broadband services and secure networking systems covering military and commercial markets. Cory's extensive international business and travel experience supporting strategic supply chain initiatives, business development, and partner relationships has brought him to China, Thailand, Indonesia, Singapore, Europe, Brazil, and Mexico.

In Cardiff Beach, Kim and Cory are raising three children: twins **Graham Laurance** and **Gracie Rae** (b. 2011), and **Griffin Guy** (b. 2016). As Kim was especially close to her grandpa Doug "DoDo" Guy, she marvels at how closely her son Graham favors his great-grandfather. She claims that Graham looks, talks, walks, and acts exactly like him.

In place of tennis, Kim has found her game in pickleball, presently the fastest-growing sport in America. She also enjoys trips back to Notre Dame where a year or so ago she reunited with six roommates, their children, and spouses—27 in total. In her "kim *half* kept" blog for moms, Kim writes, "We live in a small beach town in northern San Diego, called Cardiff by the Sea. I believe in God, family, good friends [including her second cousin and his wife—Danny and Megan Broderick], LOTS of humor and a nice tall glass of vodka soda. With lime." As a working mom with three young children, Kim acknowledges that her life is "NUTS." As a result, she "loves finding things that make running my household easier or notably more enjoyable." She also aspires to make her readers laugh as she shares product, service, and household tips.

THE ELDEST SON of Joanna and her first husband Rob, **Tyler Guy Welti** (b. 1980) was born in Palo Alto, California, shortly before the family moved south. In Santa Barbara, Tyler started high school at Laguna Beach then transferred to Santa Barbara High School. He received a Bachelor of Arts in English from his father's alma mater at Yale University in New Haven, Connecticut. Three years after graduating, Tyler entered law school at the University of Virginia in Charlottesville where he earned a Juris Doctorate.

Certified to practice law in the state of California and Washington, D.C., Tyler began his legal career in D.C. as a trial attorney with the Environment and Natural Resources division of the U.S. Department of Justice. During his tenure, he litigated the Deepwater Horizon criminal case that resulted from an explosion of the offshore drilling rig 41 miles off the coast of Louisiana on April 20, 2010. Compounded by the sinking of the BP-leased rig two days later, the toxic marine oil spill from drilling operations became the largest in American history, leaking as much as 60,000 barrels per day at its peak according to government officials. By early June, oil and tar balls had made landfall on the sugar-white beaches of my adopted home of Pensacola and then further east. In all, an estimated 1,100+ miles of shoreline became polluted from the crude oil slick extending to more than 57,500 square miles of the Gulf of Mexico:

> The hundreds of lawsuits resulted in the largest criminal penalty with a single entity in U.S. history. BP pled guilty in 2012 to 14 felony charges, among them 11 counts of felony manslaughter and violations of the Clean Water and Migratory Bird Treaty acts. To settle all legal actions brought by the U.S. Justice Department and the states of Louisiana, Mississippi, Alabama, Texas, and Florida, BP agreed to a staggering environmental fine of $18.7 billion payable over 18 years.

Triumph Gulf Coast, Inc. formed to oversee the expenditure of 75% of all funds recovered by the Florida attorney general for economic damages to the state that resulted from the 2010 Deepwater Horizon oil spill. Distributed funds—$1.8 billion in total to be awarded over 18 years—support the recovery, diversification, and enhancement of the economy in eight disproportionately-affected Northwest Florida counties with benefits still accruing to Pensacola and neighboring communities.

Tyler's tireless efforts litigating the Deepwater Horizon case on behalf of the American people earned him an award of special distinction from the Department of Justice. Moving into private practice in D.C., he then litigated all manner of environmental and natural resources cases in state and federal courts while advising clients on regulatory processes and compliance with renewable fuel standards. From private practice, Tyler clerked for the Honorable Consuelo M. Callahan in the U.S. Court of Appeals for the Ninth Circuit in Sacramento, California. He returned to private practice in the San Francisco Bay Area, currently as a partner with Venerable LLP in Oakland. He assists clients with complex energy, natural resources, land use, commercial space, transportation, and regulatory and litigation matters.

A Washington, D.C. native whose father worked for the CIA, Tyler's wife **Kate Perper** (b. 1980) works in the areas of teen pregnancy/reproductive health research and early childhood development. A graduate of the University of Pennsylvania with a Bachelor of Science in economics, Kate continued her studies at Georgetown University where she earned a Master of Public Policy in education, family, and social policy. She works as a research scientist with the nonprofit, Child Trends, where she conducts social science research based on quantitative methods and data analysis. Kate's interests include the effects of poverty and family structure on family wellbeing and the role of social policy in improving outcomes for children and families.

Today, Tyler and Kate reside in Oakland where they are raising **Lila Grace** (b. 2011) and **Dylan Perper** (b. 2014).

Tyler's brother **David Guy Welti** (b. 1983) is known as a free-spirit, a "diamond in the ruff" as his mother describes him. At Santa Barbara

High School, he picked up painting, and he went on to earn a double major at the University of Colorado in Boulder. He studied economics with a finance emphasis and minored in philosophy. For a number of years, David lived in San Diego brewing beer and rekindling his love of surfing. Later, he found his passion on the slopes as an accomplished snowboarder and skier.

David resides in Mammoth Lakes in California's Sierra Nevada mountains. Known for its majestic scale and the expanse of the valleys, the name Mammoth Lakes derives from the area's "mammoth" mountains and the numerous crystal-clear mountain lakes that dot the dramatic landscape. The only incorporated community in the county of Mono, Mammoth Lakes seems perfectly suited for David's adventurous spirit in the great outdoors. He regularly explores the stunning scenery of the eastern Sierras by foot, bike, board, and skis.

THE THREE CHILDREN of Denise and Rod Incerpi shared impressive athletic ability during their upbringing in Los Altos. All three siblings became swimmers and competed on swim teams at a very young age. At Los Altos High School and in the Los Altos Athletic League, **Alicia Gordon Incerpi Brewer** (b. 1986) excelled while playing varsity tennis, soccer, and swimming. She was recognized as a Varsity Blanket recipient for her participation in the three sports during 9+ varsity seasons. In 2004, the De Anza Force NorCal State Cup crowned Alicia and her soccer teammates as regional champions.

Alicia continued her education and athletic interest at the University of Oregon, Eugene, where she earned a Bachelor of Science in sports marketing and economics in the College of Business. During her four years of study, she became an active member of the Oregon Ducks' Warsaw Sports Business Club with an eye toward changing the world through the power of sport. Alicia also participated in sports at the university. Among many roles, she became a football intern in the Athletic Department, Director of the World Cup, an intern with Kidsports, and a Kidsports soccer coach for girls.

The Eugene stars aligned when Alicia met her future husband **Christopher Brewer** (b. 1987. Chris, too, was engaged in the Oregon

Ducks' exclusive Warsaw Sports Business Club. They graduated together in 2009 with Chris earning a Bachelor of Science in business administration.

Upon pulling up stakes from Eugene, Alicia and Chris relocated to Baltimore, Maryland. While Chris honed his marketing and communications skills, Alicia worked with a full-service ad agency and then a brand development agency. The couple relocated to Chris's hometown of Bend, Oregon, in 2014. Chris joined his father's "The Brewer Team" as a financial advisor with Morgan Stanley. In Bend, Alicia has developed leadership skills in project management, notably while onboarding and managing digital marketing projects with G5, SmartRent, and currently, San Francisco-based Clearbit with whom she is employed remotely.

When not working, the Brewers cheer on the Oregon Ducks as avid fans, and they find plenty of ways to play in and around beautiful Bend with their two children, **Weston "Wes" Douglas** (b. 2016) and **Madeline "Maddie" Gordon** (b. 2018).

The second of Denise and Rod's three children and only son, **Ryan Guy Incerpi** (b. 1989) inherited the Guy eye-hand coordination gene. In addition to becoming an All-American swimmer, he advanced to captain and MVP of the water polo team during his time at Los Altos High School.

Ryan set off from Los Altos for scenic Lake Tahoe after high school. He worked as a food server at one of T S Restaurants' renowned establishments when opportunity struck in Hawaii. In 1977, a pair of best friends and young entrepreneurs founded a collection of eateries in locations where they wanted to live, work, and play. Destiny brought Ryan and two other employees to Maui to set up a new location for the owners. Ryan spent ten years as a lead server then assistant manager at one of T S Restaurants' brands—Duke's—before returning to Tahoe.

The allure of island living brought Ryan back to Maui one or two years later. Settling in as a resident of Lahaina, he launched a gardening maintenance business while in his free time playing guitar and singing vocals in a band that aired "blues and rock 'n' roll with a dash of alternative."

An enthusiastic sports fisherman, Ryan and his father, Rod, enjoy deep sea fishing. The pair angled their way to Alaska for an excursion in

May 2022. The *Lahaina News* reported on Ryan's exhilarating catch—a 395.5-pound marlin—while fishing with a captain and his deckhand deep in the Pacific Ocean. Months later in Lahaina where "the livin' is easy," Ryan played host to some 40 relatives among the Incerpis and extended Guy clan over the Thanksgiving holiday.

"Easy livin'" does not come close to describing Lahaina since a wave of horrific blazes burned the historic Maui town for several days beginning on August 8, 2023. Living history, Ryan survived the deadliest natural disaster since Hawaii became a U.S. state in 1959, which also registered as the deadliest U.S. wildfire in more than a century:

> One week after the first spark lit, the death toll had risen to 99 with as many as 1,000 people still missing. One month following the firestorm, Maui County and the police department confirmed the death toll at 115 with roughly 66 persons missing. Once home to 13,000 people, surviving residents described their harrowing escape as the devastating blaze reduced the Hawaiian town of Lahaina to ash.
>
> A rare combination of factors reportedly fueled the disastrous brush fires in this present "climate change" era—notably drought conditions; the high-pressure system wrought by category 4 Hurricane Dora; and invasive, highly inflammable nonnative grasses spread over the island's abandoned farms and ranchland. Lahaina's geographical orientation, in the direct line of downslope winds moving from the northeast to the southwest—known in Southern California as Santa Ana winds—contributed to a perfect storm once the fire ignited, possibly from power lines downed by wind gusts. The hot, dry, downslope winds aimed flames and embers from the mountains to the shoreline, leaving some people nowhere to flee except to the harbor.

Residing north of the town's center, Ryan's quarters survived the wildfires. Moving into high gear, he put everything aside to help the thousands left homeless and traumatized in the wake of the incomprehensible disaster. With a heavy heart, Ryan will surely face a prolonged period of healing along with all the "Aloha-spirited" people of Maui. Leaving the island life behind, Ryan is on the move, writing his next chapter as he actively pursues music with his trusted guitar and vocals.

Her mother describes **Kacey Madison Incerpi** (b. 1996) as a dynamo. "When Kacey walks into a room, she makes her presence known." Teasingly, Denise said that if Kacey had come first, she would have been the last of her children. In fact, Kacey came last among Jinks and Doug's twelve grandchildren.

At an early age, Kacey developed athleticism in tennis as a foray into private coaching. She also played soccer, but when she turned ten, Kacey's folks asked her to choose between the two sports. Following four years on the women's varsity tennis team at Lewis & Clark College in Portland, Oregon, where she earned a Bachelor of Arts in rhetoric and media studies, Kacey resolved to stay involved with the team. She returned to the college the next season as a volunteer assistant tennis coach, committing over 10 hours each week to team practices, recruiting, and creating a lifting and conditioning program for the student athletes.

Kacey still lives in Portland. Her unbridled enthusiasm and love of people promises her a bright future, whether in coaching, sales, or relationship management—all areas in which she has dabbled since graduating from Lewis & Clark. In her spare time, Kacey takes every opportunity to enjoy nature, art, live music, and snowboarding.

TERRIE AND PHIL'S ELDEST CHILD **Bridgette Gordon Bugay** (b. 1987) graduated from Santa Barbara High School with a solid record in water polo. Affiliated with the California Interscholastic Federation as a league championship team for four years, Bridgette contributed to her water polo team's first-place national ranking during the 2003–2004 season. She also competed in swimming.

Upon graduating, Bridgette attended the University of California, San Diego. During her studies, she played on the NCAA Division women's water polo team and was honored all four years as both a student-athlete in the Academic-All-America program and member of the Western Water Polo Association All-Academic team. Her social conscience developed as co-founder and vice president of marketing for the campus's environmental program, Greeks Gone Green. She also served as chair of philanthropy for her sorority. Bridgette spent a semester abroad as a public relations and marketing intern at London-based Matthew Williamson, a retailer of apparel and fashion. She then graduated from UCSD with a Bachelor of Arts in political science and a minor in (studio) visual arts focused on music.

From San Diego, Bridgette returned to England to study at the London School of Economics (LSE) and Political Science. She concentrated her Master's degree in global media and communications with an emphasis in development, human rights, digital activism, and media representations. The London School recognized her dissertation on "Hospitality in the Modern Mediapolis: Global Mediation of Child Soldiers in central and east Africa" as one of the best authored by students from the LSE program. Brigette completed her master's in San Diego where she became an elected student representative in the LSE / University of San Diego (USC) degree program.

In San Diego, Bridgette developed public relations and communications training with Invisible Children, Inc. The opportunity led to her meeting her future husband **Sean Christopher Poole** (b. 1988), originally from Pasadena, California. Launched in 2004, Invisible Children sought to end two decades of mass violence and child abductions by Joseph Kony and his Lord's Resistance Army (LRA). The nongovernment organization (NGO) was instrumental in helping to end Joseph Kony's reign of terror in partnership with peacebuilders across central Africa committed to stemming the tide of violent conflict.

Sean acted on altruistic instincts similar to Bridgette's when he joined the NGO. His training came from earning a Bachelor of Arts in international studies from Point Loma Nazarene University in San Diego and a Master of Science in international development economics from the SOAS University of London. He also completed coursework through Michigan State University in Istanbul, Turkey. Through their work with NGOs, Sean and Bridgette developed a passion for helping people across the globe.

Upon completing a global fellowship with USC's Annenberg Center on Communication Leadership and Policy in Los Angeles, Bridgette joined Sean in Kampala, Uganda, where they worked with Invisible Children for one year. With frequent travels to the conflict-affected areas in the Democratic Republic of Congo, the Central African Republic, and South Sudan, Bridgette developed messaging content using film, photography, and writing, along with strategic communication tactics to encourage the surrender and reintegration of rebel combatants. At this same time, Sean identified gaps in humanitarian assistance and provided program management and technical support that revolved around protection and defection programming.

Returning stateside, Sean continued on with Invisible Children for another four years as director of international programs and USAID-funded projects in New York City. In Brooklyn, Bridgette signed on with the nonprofit, Witness, to produce videos and multimedia content aimed at protecting and defending human rights. She then worked in communications and program management with Open Road Alliance which endeavors to accelerate social impact initiatives by removing funding roadblocks.

Shortly before the onslaught of the COVID-19 pandemic, in 2019, Bridgette took the leap to build a consulting practice with the formation of bgb consulting. She targets nonprofits, businesses, United Nations agencies, and funders to deliver services that revolve around social impact. Her first consulting engagement came by way of introduction from Sean who now manages programs for "charity: water," a New York-based nonprofit that funds clean and safe drinking water for people in developing nations. Sean and Bridgette's humanitarian work continues toward the wellbeing of the coping public in austere environments.

Once the couple settled in New York and shortly before Bridgette launched her consulting business, Sean and a couple of his childhood friends co-founded Sunday Beer Company. They distribute the "craft light lager" in New York and Pennsylvania as the perfect accompaniment to a healthy and active lifestyle. Evidently a light beer connoisseur dating to a wildly successful homebrewing stint in college, Sean manages brewery sales on the side while conducting his sustainable water programming work. With what little free time he has, Sean could be spotted on a run in New York City wearing Lycra on the Palisades Parkway, or going on an adventure with Bridgette and their Regal Cavalier King Charles Spaniel, Lulu. Their adventures include cross-country travels in their Airstream. Like her cousin, Ryan, Bridgette also sings and plays guitar, which should delight her son **Leighton Taylor Bugay-Poole** (b. 2023) who ranks 16th among Jinks's and Doug's great-grandchildren. Leighton was born in Santa Maria, California, in close proximity to Arroyo Grande in the central coast region where the couple now resides.

Trailing Bridgette by two years, **Braden Guy Bugay** (b. 1989) exceled in math as a youngster. Progressing past what he could learn from his teachers in an accelerated math program as a sixth grader, Braden took an algebra class at Santa Barbara City College. He satisfied his high school math requirements by his sophomore year at Santa Barbara High School. Here, he developed a physical workout regimen by playing soccer and basketball. His sister, Bridgette, describes Braden as the smartest person she knows.

In 2012, Braden earned a Bachelor of Science in sociology at the University of California, Davis. You will recall that his grandmother Jinks's first cousin, Bill Newcomb, taught at UC Davis during his sunset years before his death in 1999. Braden also discovered his artistic side in college. He picked up drums and played in a couple of bands for a period of time.

As a post-graduate living in San Francisco, Braden entered the apparel industry with managerial responsibilities on the floor of both American Apparel and Alternative Apparel. He then simultaneously worked at Hellbent Booking and Getaround. At Hellbent, Braden coordinated the booking of live bands locally and on tour. Peer-to-peer car rental service Getaround engaged him four years after its launch in the Bay Area. The car sharing platform includes a smart phone application enabling users to find and book a car and proprietary hardware to unlock and secure the car without personal contact.

Braden remained with Getaround for nearly five years, performing a variety of customer service and troubleshooting assignments, initially in San Francisco and then as part of a market expansion team when the company established a presence in Los Angeles. Following stints as a field specialist and onboarding hub coordinator, he moved into a service role with Mothership, an online freight marketplace pairing shipments with vetted carriers. In Los Angeles, Braden now works in operations for Simcor LLC, a multi-faceted art service company centered around one of the largest private modern art collections in the world.

Gordons (1981–present)

AMANDA THERESE MALLINGER JOZSA (b. 1981) holds distinction as the eldest of Larry and Pat's six grandchildren. Born and raised as an only child in Colorado Springs by my cousin Pat Gordon League and her first husband Mike Mallinger, Amanda and I share a fascination with her great-grandmother Yolande Hoke Gordon. Inspired by her grandpa Larry Gordon's genealogical research, Amanda at age 16 wrote a six-page essay about his mother—my grandmother—in 1997. Although Amanda did not call it out in her writing, the year she authored the paper just so happened to coincide with the centennial anniversary of Yolande's birth in 1897. Coincidence? Amanda was intrigued by *Joanna Gould Hoke* who, as mentioned earlier, embraced the name *"Yolande Westcott" Gordon* upon arriving in America from Bordeaux at the start of 1920.

Amanda submitted the essay "The Perilous Journey" as a school assignment just one year before her grandpa Larry's sudden passing. She had the benefit, if not the foresight, of asking questions while he lived. Among several other sources, I drew from Amanda's paper in relaying my grandmother's chronicle for *The Westcott Story*.

Amanda grew up riding horses and spent every waking moment outdoors when not in school. Upon graduating from Cheyenne Mountain High School, she entered Colorado College in her hometown where she met her future husband **Jason Michael Jozsa** (b. 1981) of Calgary in the Canadian province of Alberta. While Jason played ice hockey at Colorado College, the couple earned their degrees. They graduated in the same year, both with a Bachelor of Arts in economics.

For the next seven years, Jason played professional hockey for several minor league teams—Toledo Storm; Greenville (South Carolina) Grrrowl Hockey Club; Las Vegas Wranglers; Grand Rapids Griffins; Milwaukee Admirals; and Cincinnati Cyclones. Working briefly in software consulting, Amanda decided to change course. Three years out of college, she enrolled in dental school at the University of Colorado, Denver. In 2010, upon earning a Doctor of Dental Surgery (DDS), Amanda launched a dentistry practice in Denver, and Jason hung up his hockey skates to pursue a career in business.

While raising **Davis Michael** (b. 2011), **Emmett Gordon** (b. 2013), and **Aiden Grace** (b. 2017), Dr. Amanda Jozsa practiced dentistry for 12 years. She purchased a 48% interest in Edgewater Modern Dentistry and Highland Dentists and partnered as a franchisee with Pacific Dental Services. With a compassionate heart to give back to the community, Amanda donated more than $65,000 in dental treatment to 16 patients at Donated Dental Services. Sadly, a tremor-related disability forced Amanda to retire from the profession. She sold her interest in the practice in 2022. Not one to sit idle, she has since become an executive coach for healthcare practitioners working with Fortune Management.

Beginning as a recruiter and advancing in an executive business development role with Aerotek, Jason has worked for the nationwide staffing and talent solutions provider for more than a decade. With the firm's decision to break its specialized business units into three separate operating companies, he continues in the same capacity now with Aston Carter under the Allegis Group umbrella.

Amanda's mother Pat referred to her daughter as "Manda." Pat passed away before Manda and Jason's daughter, Aiden, came along. Pat would have spoiled Aiden rotten. Amanda still loves being around horses, still clamors for the outdoors, and has made a habit of getting into the gym and working out on the Peloton when not enjoying time with her family. They make regular jaunts to Colorado Springs to see the children's loving grandfather—Amanda's stepfather Dan League.

IN GOLDEN, COLORADO, Jeanne and Tim Dietz raised three children, all of whom opted to settle in the Denver vicinity upon completing their schooling. The eldest, **Heather Starr Dietz LoSasso** (b. 1985) received both a Bachelor of Arts in psychology and a Master of Arts in clinical counseling at the University of Northern Colorado in Greeley. She put her credentials to work with special needs youth in the setting of childhood education. Heather then transitioned from play therapy to working with autistic children and their parents and teachers at Edgewater Elementary School. Following a brief period as a therapist with the Mental Health Center of Denver, Heather now works as a social emotional learning specialist in the Jefferson Country school district. Along with a passion for working with young children and their families, she specializes in modalities that allow children and adolescents to communicate in their native language.

Heather's husband, Denver-native **Anthony "Tony" Daniel LoSasso** (b. 1983), received a Bachelor of Science in accounting from Metropolitan State College of Denver before earning a Master of Business Administration from Carson-Newman University. A corporate finance and mergers & acquisitions advisor, Tony serves as managing partner of Mile High Business Consulting which offers an array of solutions for clients interested in leveraging technology to optimize business outcomes. In addition, he renders property acquisition and management services as the principal and a licensed Colorado real estate broker with LoSasso Properties.

Heather and Tony are raising their two children, **Nickolas "Nicko" Kaden** (b. 2015) and **Ella Starr** (b. 2017), in Arvada, Colorado.

Jeanne and Tim's middle child and only son, **Tyler Justin Dietz** (b. 1987), graduated from Colorado State University in Fort Collins with a Bachelor of Science is sociology concentrated in criminal justice. For seven years during high school and college, he worked part-time as a banquet server and organizer for Golden-based Rollings Hills Country Club. Since graduating, Tyler has worked mostly with Sierra Nevada Corporation, a privately-held aerospace and national security contractor specialized in aircraft modification and technology integrations in the aerospace and defense sectors. In his current role as a materials planner, Tyler relies on his experience in project management and training in supply chain logistics and quality control to plan and schedule the movement of raw materials and finished goods in coordination with both internal and external stakeholders.

Tyler and his significant other, Tiffany Stedman of Wisconsin, are proud parents of **Avery Brooklyn** (b. 2018). They reside in Broomfield, Colorado.

Bringing up the rear among Jeanne and Tim's children, **Bridget Chelsea Dietz** (b. 1991) attended the Pima Medical Institute in Denver where she gained training in general dentistry to become a dental assistant. She applies her skills as an oral surgery dental assistant in support of Dr. Eric Jahde Endodontics in Denver.

Bridget is the mother of **Chelsea Jeanne Palmer** (b. 2017), both residents of Wheat Ridge, Colorado.

ELIZABETH AND ROBB RAMSTAD are the parents of two daughters whom they raised in Elizabeth's family home in Minnetonka, Minnesota. Larry and Pat Gordon shared their home with the Ramstads who lived in their own quarters on the top floor of the two-story home. The family remained especially close to Pat before her passing in 2018.

Kirby Lee Ramstad (b. 1986) and her sister Kelli graduated from Hopkins High School a generation behind their uncle Larry and aunt Jeanne. Kirby earned a Bachelor of Arts in philosophy from Grinnell College, a small liberal arts college in Grinnell, Iowa.

Currently located in Oakland, California, Kirby conducts legal research for a forensic attorney.

Kirby's sister **Kelli Cristin Ramstad Haddad** (b. 1988) received a bachelor's degree in child psychology from the University of Minnesota, a public land-grant research university in the Twin Cities of Minneapolis and Saint Paul. She has been employed at Alphabet, Inc.'s Google for more than a decade. Kelli progressed from a staffing channels specialist role to become a site program manager. In this capacity, she plans project requirements in coordination with the many internal stakeholders and oversees initiatives through the entire lifecycle of the projects to which she is assigned.

Kelli's husband, Columbus, Ohio-native **John Haddad**, earned a Bachelor of Science in construction management from Ohio University in Athens. He started his career as an electrical field superintendent at Peter Kiewit & Sons in San Francisco before signing on with Shimmick Construction in Belleview, Washington. Progressing in project management roles, John now works as the Washington and Northern California regional manager in Shimmick's mechanical, electrical, and plumbing division.

Kelli and John have two daughters, **Avery Elizabeth Haddad** (b. 2020) and **Etta Lee Haddad** (b. 2023)—the latter the youngest of Uncle Larry and Aunt Pat's eight great-grandchildren. They live in the town of Woodinville in the greater Seattle area.

THIS WRAPS UP the narrative on all 41 "GEN 13" Westcott descendants. On the whole, we find a collection of talented, highly-educated, accomplished, and passionate individuals who illuminate the enviable traits of their forebears. With tenacity, one after the other has proven an uncanny ability to forge ahead with dogged determination no matter the obstacles. Whether in sports, academia, business, or in the interest of humankind, these emerging "GEN 13" leaders have set high standards with a promising future ahead of them all but assured.

Yo, Jinks, and Larry's grandchildren came of age in the new millennium with computer literacy. Early into the 21st century, they embraced technology, many building careers on the advances made possible by the omnipresent microchip. At the same time, they have found a work-life balance that eluded the generations before them. For the most part, among "GEN 13" married couples, we find both partners working, the majority in professional careers. Those with children share equally in parental duties. They appear highly engaged and committed to building the confidence of their offspring with unwavering social and emotional support.

Before leaving this segment on "GEN 13" Westcott descendants, it seems only right that I mention a prominent physical trait that manifests in many of them, in many of us. Their parents—my siblings, first cousins, and I—call it the "Gordon nose." There has been much ribbing about it over the years. Our parents—Jinks, Yolande (Yo), and Larry—did not escape this distinctive facial feature. Nor did many of their children and grandchildren. From which line did that characteristic long, pointed nose derive, you ask? I have often wondered. The revelation came from delving into my maternal ancestors' story, leading me to the family into which Susie Westcott Hoke married. "GEN 9" Walter Scott Hoke and at least two of his six brothers sported the distinguished nose. I found an uncanny resemblance among this cast of characters spanning several generations.

But wait! What about the Westcotts? Susie Westcott Hoke certainly sported "the nose." So, too, did those all the way up the ancestral line at least to "GEN 7" Hampton Westcott—and back down to some of the youngest among "GEN 13" Westcott-Hoke descendants.

Those among us so endowed should lift up that trademark Westcott-Hoke nose and carry it as a badge of honor. "The nose" runs deep as a standing joke in the Guy family between Larry and Terrie. The Brodericks and Gordons certainly did not escape unscathed. The jury is still out on "GEN 14" Westcott descendants, many of whom have not grown past the infancy or toddler stage as of this writing.

The extent to which they inherit the physical traits stemming from Yolande Westcott Hoke Gordon matters not. Rather, the instrumental qualities derived from Yolande and her pedigree carry great promise into the future for the youngest among us—tenacity, courage, integrity, intellectual curiosity, creativity, imagination, independence, ambition, and responsibility. My hope is that, sooner rather than later, each of them comes to recognize the privileges afforded them by virtue of their extraordinarily rich inheritance.

GENERATION 14 – 1998–2024

Hope Springs Eternal

THE YOUTHFUL "GEN 14" Westcott descendants among us have ample reason to leap in acknowledgement of our family's legacy. Their heritage is nothing if not remarkable—on so many levels. We are an educated people with a strong genetic makeup. With the benefit of knowledge, proven skills, and deep connections, we stand united in our boundless potential to make a lasting contribution to our families and the greater good, much as our ancestors did before us.

While our documented history speaks to life's challenges, it also points to the promise of what lies ahead. Our ancestors in every generation had crosses to bear, many enduring unimaginable circumstances and heartache. Yet, while the Westcotts sacrificed much, they prevailed with grit and resolve in benefit to their kinsfolk. We need look no further than the comparative lifestyle each of us enjoys to appreciate how far we have come on America's arduous 400-year course to the present time.

In this last act of the Westcott chronicle, we come to "GEN 14" where the exposed familial strands manifest as strong genetic traits. I point out for the record that two among "GEN 14" Westcotts carry the family name: **Tristan Wescott Prate** (b. 2010), son of Casey Broderick and grandson of my brother Larry, with a derivative spelling; and **Oliver Westcott Broderick** (b. 2023), son of Sean Broderick and grandson of my brother Tim. How fitting that the second youngest among us featured in *The Westcott Story* preserves the coveted family name!

I fully expect this generation will come to recognize the fortune they share as an illustrious family and proud nation with extraordinary foundational roots. With their constitution, the youngest among us can withstand the personal and societal hurdles that will surely present themselves in their lifetimes.

"GEN 14" Westcott descendants

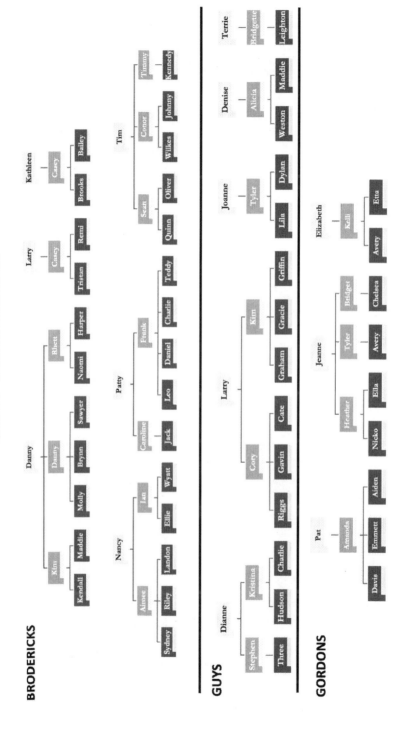

Hope is the heartbeat of the soul. The fifth and—as of this writing—the youngest generation descended from "surnamed Westcotts" stands on tall shoulders. Surely each of these 49 privileged souls is capable of making something of themselves. It is now up to my "GEN 14" great-nieces, great-nephews, and first cousins twice removed to tap the tremendous potential within them.

How best can we honor our forebears who gave life to our very being and to the enduring spirit that emanates within us? Perhaps by emulating the reasoned choices most of them made to do the right thing and pay the upfront price as a way to carry our gifts forward.

"GEN 14" descendants arrived during a period of seismic change on virtually every measure.

The millennial year 2000 does not seem that long ago. But consider the transformative changes brought to the fore since the world prepared for "Y2K," during the time when the oldest in the Westcotts' "GEN 14" camp—Sydney (b. 1998), Kendall (b. 1998), and Riley (b. 2000)—transitioned from toddlers to young adults now holding college degrees.

At warp speed, the Internet, smartphones, and social media developed as universal means of communication, entertainment, commerce, and community building. The rate and magnitude of societal change spurred by these technological innovations is unprecedented in human history:

> Nearly everyone has a cell phone of necessity, some tethered to their hand-held device more than others. Virtual learning increasingly substitutes more traditional face-to-face forms. Employees perform jobs in versatile work environments, many of them remotely. Robots complete repetitive tasks once handled by humans. Drones make deliveries more accessible, property inspections more efficient, and both surveillance and reconnaissance more effective. People are poised to get around in self-driving cars. Artificial intelligence recognizes our preferred buying habits and problem-solving capabilities. Augmented reality brings us in touch with an imaginary world.

The English lexicon now includes this partial list of words and phrases that did not exist twenty or so years ago: Google—as both a noun and a verb; the "Internet of Things"; auto-suggest; selfie; vlog; unfriend; podcast; truther; sexting; YouTuber; crowdfunding; hashtag; tweet; retweet; photobomb; anti-vaxxer; Instagram; emoji; Wi-Fi; and cryptocurrency. In 2022, my living "GEN 11" centenarian parents-in-law, Patrick and Olivia Emmanuel, could not begin to conceptualize the meaning of terms recognized by Merriam-Webster since the turn of the 21st century.

This digital age has revolutionized how we connect and communicate but with unintended consequences. Cyberbullies tend to dominate social media platforms in a quest to humiliate the least among us. We also see cybersecurity ramping up to minimize potentially catastrophic damage as cybercrime lurks in seemingly every corner. To the vast number of Internet users, "cyber" consumes our daily lives with inescapable social, cultural, and economic impact. Much of it is beneficial, but negative consequences permeate into the crevices as well.

As a culture, we have become brazen in our use of social media and increasingly intolerant of views that differ from our own. The explosion of information, misinformation, and falsehoods compels us to choose sides thus widening discord. Divisiveness both in the political realm and within the confines of our sacred homes has never been more apparent.

At a time when geopolitical tensions threaten world order, this cyber age presents a plethora of both vulnerabilities and opportunities that "GEN 14" Westcott descendants will maneuver as a way of life. They are not alone considering the unique challenges faced by our ancestors across generations who similarly established dynamic new frontiers in uncharted waters as pioneers.

The fledglings among us will sooner or later formulate positions on contentious issues morphing from the Black Lives Matter and #Metoo movements; the Supreme Court's decision overturning Roe v. Wade; gender identity and pronoun preferences; gun control; political grandstanding; and so much more. I trust that Yolande and Laurance Gordon's G2 grandchildren will comport themselves with humility in an informed, dignified, and respectful manner. Modeling their American forebears spanning 13 generations, with integrity and purpose, this next generation stands to achieve greatness amidst the obstacles and distractions.

Perhaps the overarching question to wrap up *The Westcott Story* is this: How will the grandchildren of my siblings and first cousins choose to be remembered? What impact will they make on history? How will these 49 specks among now more than 8 billion lives stand out? That is the question Terry and Jennifer's "GEN 13" son Dillon asked of himself as a sophomore at Patrick Henry High School in San Diego in 2019. In a report he submitted as a class assignment titled "Tiny Little Specks," Dillon Broderick wrote:

> *I believe in little specks of dust: the 7,346,235,000 little specks of dust that live on this earth; the seven billion little specks of dust that wake up every morning, go to their day jobs, and then come home and eat dinner." He continues, "Think about yourself. You are one out of the other seven billion specks on this earth. The earth is orbiting the sun that is 109 times bigger than itself. The sun is hurtling through the milky way galaxy that is six and a half billion times the size of the sun. We are all miniscule specks of dust that are zooming at 500,000 miles per hour through our ever-expanding universe.*

When writing his essay, Dillon contemplated his own meaning in life as but a tiny little speck: "I always want my existence to mean something. If our time on earth is temporary and in the end our existence is meaningless, why not make the best of it? Without others remembering our presence and our impact on the world, then did we even live?" The philosophical query remained stuck in Dillon's mind as a puzzle to solve—a personal challenge to conquer. It resonates deeply as I dare to probe the same profound question myself.

I interpret what Dillon is saying this way: Be deliberate in making something of yourself that matters—something that matters to you and the people who define your circle and sphere of influence. Capitalize on the opportunities to engage as our ancestors most assuredly did before us. Make something bigger of yourself and others in tandem. Then maybe that speck will spark—the ultimate celebration of living productive lives as Americans whose interest is as much the collective as each of us individually.

As time marches on, I wonder who will take the lead to revive the inspiring untold stories yet to play out among "GEN 14" Westcott descendants and theirs—each a tiny little speck with ample reason and every opportunity to be remembered.

"While we have time, let us do good."

—St. Francis Assisi

AFTERWORD

This concludes the magical mystery ride I steered in pursuit of uncovering details about my maternal lineage. From page one, I wrote *The Westcott Story* from a clean slate without a roadmap or outline aside from wanting to weave my bloodline into the fabric of our nation generationally. From page one, beginning to end, I sought to unravel a tangled thread in order to narrate anecdotes of these fascinating characters in the context of America's unfolding history. The revelations came one after the other, many as epiphanies to my sheer delight.

I uncovered deep insights not only about my extraordinary pedigree but also about human nature, and history, and the circle of life. And yes, genetics. I am profoundly grateful for the opportunity, the experience, and the knowledge gained in the process of researching and writing *our* story.

America—the land of the free because of the brave. What we accrue as a nation comes largely from the sacrifices carried on the backs of our ancestors. *The Westcott Story* brings life to our nation's past and potential: *Faith. Hope. Love. Courage. Sacrifice. Compassion. Perseverance. Resilience.* To my way of thinking, this chronicle speaks as much to our place as Americans as to mine as a Westcott descendant. The pioneers among all generations exhibited these same foundational traits. Our Founding Fathers did so with a strong dose of conviction. Their brilliant crafting led to America's coveted Declaration of Independence and the United States Constitution which, taken together, enshrine our values as a free people and united nation.

I have never felt more strongly about America's need to preserve and protect her enviable liberties that continue to propel us forward as innovators and problem solvers, now with 400 years invested. In deference to our precious forebears, may we ever strive to bridge divisiveness and reverse growing opportunity gaps in concert with Americans' unalienable rights—among them life, liberty, and the pursuit of happiness for one and all. Our sacrifices relied on preservation of those rights. Succeeding generations will depend on them.

"May the child not yet born one day find respite in the shade of our ancestors." My greatest hope is that our family and our nation's value as depicted in *The Westcott Story* is treasured by generations past, present, and to come. This is us—collectively—the heart, soul, history, and potential of America in living color.

If you enjoyed reading *The Westcott Story*,
kindly post an online review.

INFORMATION SOURCES

Below find the primary sources the author referenced to develop *The Westcott Story:*

Bullock, Hon. J. Russell (1886), *Incidents in the Life and Times of Stukely Westcott (of Rhode Island) With Some of this Descendants.* Private printing.

Glick, Juneanne Wescoat (1991), *Westcott: The Name Renewed.* Clayton, New Jersey, private printing.

Gordon, William A. and Gordon, Lewis H. (1973), *Gordon Gordon: Ancestry, Family, and Life.* Private printing.

Neergaard, Richard Hampton (n.d.), Westcott pedigree chart and extended family archival collection.

Newcomb, Susan Hester (n.d.), vast Westcott archival collection.

Weygant, Charles H. (1907), *The Sacketts of America: Their Ancestors and Descendants, 1630-1907.* Higginson Book Company.

Whitman, Roscoe L. (1932), *History and Genealogy of the Ancestors and Some Descendants of Stukely Westcott--One of the Thirteen Original Proprietors of Providence Plantation and the Colony of Rhode Island.* Otsego Publishing Company.

Citations of all 300+ information sources can be found on the author's website at https://www.ChristineBEmmanuel.com.

PEOPLE INDEX

The author "memorializes" 1,535 people in *The Westcott Story*. Among them, she claims 175 as her lineal ascendants. In total, 342 of those referenced in the chronicle share her family's lineage; another 655 distant relatives share ancestry as extended family members.

The listing can be found on the author's website at https://www. ChristineBEmmanuel.com. Sequenced by generation, she captures each name, their relationship to the author, and a description of how each person fits in as a family member, distant relative, or noted non-relative.

ABOUT THE AUTHOR

BEN M. WORD

"GEN 12" CHRISTINE "Christy" BRODERICK EMMANUEL is a resident of historic Pensacola, Florida, with roots planted in Pittsburgh, Pennsylvania; Madison, Ohio; and Notre Dame, Indiana.

Raised as one of nine children and married to Patrick "Rick" G. Emmanuel, Jr., the author counts 75 Brodericks and 45 Emmanuels as family members among the living. She earned a Bachelor of Arts in social work from St. Mary's College, Notre Dame, Indiana, and a Master of Business Administration in finance from The Florida State University in Tallahassee, Florida.

Inquisitive by nature, Emmanuel actively engaged in research and business writing throughout her 33-year corporate career in the commercial banking and mortgage information technology sectors. Recognized for technical writing and journalistic excellence, she placed first or second in statewide and national competitions as a commercial banker. Since retiring in 2017, she placed first in a local chamber of commerce writing contest and edited *Working a Better Way: A 50 Year History of LandrumHR* © 2020 by prominent Pensacola businessman H. Britt Landrum, Jr. Her credits also include *Wine and Words: A Book About a Book Club* © 2013 as co-author; and *The Impact of IMPACT 100 Pensacola Bay Area* © 2014 and © 2019 as co-editor and co-author, respectively.

Like a Westcott—strong-willed and tenacious—Emmanuel tackled the project of writing her family's story with focused attention and profound respect as she loosened the soil of knowledge and dug deep.

Made in the USA
Columbia, SC
08 February 2025

53533311R00224